Personality and the Prediction of Behavior

The Michigan State University
Henry A. Murray Lectures in Personality

ROBERT A. ZUCKER, JOEL ARONOFF, AND A. I. RABIN (Eds.):
Personality and the Prediction of Behavior

Personality and the Prediction of Behavior

Edited by
Robert A. Zucker
Joel Aronoff
A. I. Rabin

Department of Psychology
Michigan State University
East Lansing, Michigan

1984

ACADEMIC PRESS, INC.
(Harcourt Brace Jovanovich, Publishers)
Orlando   San Diego   San Francisco   New York   London
Toronto   Montreal   Sydney   Tokyo   São Paulo

ACADEMIC PRESS, INC.
Orlando, Florida 32887

United Kingdom Edition published by
ACADEMIC PRESS, INC. (LONDON) LTD.
24/28 Oval Road, London NW1 7DX

Library of Congress Cataloging in Publication Data

Main entry under title:

Personality and the prediction of behavior.

Bibliography: p.
Includes index.
1. Personality assessment. 2. Prediction (Psychology)
I. Zucker, Robert A. II. Aronoff, Joel. III. Rabin,
Albert I. [DNLM: 1. Personality. 2. Behavior. BF 698
P4655]
BF698.4.P47 1983   155.2'8   83-10030
ISBN 0-12-781901-0

PRINTED IN THE UNITED STATES OF AMERICA

84 85 86 87   9 8 7 6 5 4 3 2 1

Contents

6. The Stability of Behavior across Time and Situations
Seymour Epstein

7. On the Predictability of Behavior and the Structure of Personality
Walter Mischel

Contributors

Numbers in parentheses indicate the pages on which the authors' contributions begin.

Lorna Smith Benjamin (121), Department of Psychiatry, University of Wisconsin—Madison, Madison, Wisconsin 53706

Seymour Epstein (209), Department of Psychology, University of Massachusetts—Amherst, Amherst, Massachusetts 01003

Robert R. Holt (179), Department of Psychology and Research Center for Mental Health, New York University, New York, New York 10003

Jane Loevinger (43), Department of Psychology, Washington University, St. Louis, Missouri 63130

Salvatore R. Maddi (7), Department of Behavioral Sciences, The University of Chicago, Chicago, Illinois 60637

William J. McGuire (73), Department of Psychology, Yale University, New Haven, Connecticut 06520

Walter Mischel (269), Department of Psychology, Columbia University, New York, New York 10027

Introduction to the Series

The Henry A. Murray Lectures in Personality, presented by Michigan State University, are designed to advance our understanding of personality in depth, across situations, and over the range of the human life span. The lectures offer a spacious forum in which leading psychologists can explore the most difficult questions in personality theory and research from the perspective of their own work. It is hoped that this series will encourage the conceptual risk-taking that will lead to the imaginative, strong, and theoretically organized work that is needed to advance the science of personology.

These lectures are named in honor of Henry A. Murray in order to draw upon a spirit of inquiry that has directed much of the best contemporary work on personality. Throughout his distinguished career, Murray dealt with the most difficult theoretical and methodological questions with all the skills available to the scientist and the humanist. His wide-ranging mind took him across the gulfs that separate alternative approaches to the study of human beings. Murray argued for a science of personology that would include the physiological and the phenomenological, that would rely on the specialties of test construction as well as of literary scholarship, that saw the need for the taxonomist of personality as well as the psychotherapist of persons, that studied the isolated incident as well as entire lives, and that could encompass subjects as diverse as the study of mythology and the study of personnel selection. It is hoped that the series of Murray lectures may continue to draw upon all these sources in order to advance the science of personology and to contribute to human welfare.

Preface

In the first presentation of the Murray lecture series, delivered at Michigan State University in 1978 in commemoration of the fortieth anniversary of the appearance of *Explorations in Personality*, our intent was to review major developments that had occurred between the personality psychology of 1938 and the personology of the late 1970s. By all reports, that mission succeeded well. While acknowledging the great contribution of Murray's work, in both the spoken and the extended and revised version that became *Further Explorations in Personality*, the lecturers were also concerned to note the ways that their theoretical work and research had moved beyond Murray's era. Although all contributors utilized middle-ground theory rather than the grand schemes more common to the 1930s and 1940s, they were equally ambitious to come to empirical terms with the larger measure of man-in-the-world, as Murray had in his own earlier explorations.

As was true for the earlier volume, the present contributions represent the extended and revised versions of lectures originally given in East Lansing. The second set of meetings was held in May of 1982. In selecting the theme for this volume, the editors were stimulated by a different concern that had also been of significance to Murray. We were interested in two questions that had practical as well as theoretical significance and that had preoccupied Murray and his colleagues during World War II. As part of the contribution of psychology to national needs, Murray's group had been asked to select personnel for Office of Strategic Services activity behind enemy lines, as well as for positions involving a dispassionate analysis of wartime information. The major questions of this work, reported in *Assessment of Men*, seemed equally germane to current personality theorizing and research, and thus became the basis for the lectureship commission and the theme of the present volume. We asked most of the contributors to deal with the questions

(1) How well can personologists now predict behavior? and (2) What factors facilitate or constrain our ability to do this? We hoped that participants would, from the special vantage point of their own work, consider the theoretical, methodological, and empirical issues that these apparently simple questions pose. We also allowed for a challenge to the framework within which such questions are asked.

Chapters are organized into three parts. The first includes chapters by Maddi and Loevinger and is concerned with the constraints on predictability engendered by the intellectual framework—both substantive and conceptual—that guides research. The authors comment on some of the major frameworks guiding research today and suggest shifts in attention and conceptualization needed for continuing progress in the field.

Part II focuses on phenomenological and social aspects of behavior and deals with the extent to which interpersonal behavior is both caused by and a source of the person's phenomenological sense of self. Both McGuire and Benjamin do this in the context of their own well-developed and articulated research programs. McGuire concentrates on how children develop a number of the most important attributes of their concept of self; Benjamin elaborates the scaffolding for a three-level, two-axis model of interpersonal space and illustrates its utility.

Part III treats the limitations on predictions that can be anticipated by the nature of personality. The three contributors to this part consider the question in several quite different ways. Holt deals with the epistemological question of world view as it impinges on the question of predictability itself, whereas Epstein and Mischel deal both conceptually and empirically with the question of how we can predict the occurrence of events when behavior is itself transient and variable. The category systems they apply to these phenomena and the directions they suggest make their answers interesting and different from one another in important ways.

A number of people gave their time, energy, and resources to make the conference and the present book a reality. The support of Marc Van Wormer, in earlier stages of planning, and of Edith Wright, in the later stages and implementation of the meetings, was crucial in making the lectures the success that they were. Robert B. Noll, Gary E. Stollak, and Dozier W. Thornton also helped in important ways in the implementation of the meetings. Provost C. L. Winder and Dean Gwen Andrew continued to support this enterprise, as they had in the past. Phillip Marcus, Director of the Michigan State University Social Science Research Bureau, helped in the early stages of fund raising. Gordon Wood, Chairperson of MSU's Department of Psychology, continued his sponsorship of and personal participation in the running of the lectures; we are also grateful for the department's more concrete support that was available when we needed it.

We are especially grateful for the advice, shepherding, and support of John E. Cantlon, Vice President for Research and Graduate Studies, Michigan State University. In addition, the editors wish to express their special appreciation to the Michigan State University Foundation and to Joseph E. Dickinson, President, Ron D. Laughter, Executive Director, and Thomas Tenbrunsel of the foundation staff, for their aid and commitment to our work. The lectures and the current volume were, in large part, made possible by the generous support of the foundation.

PART I

Metatheoretical Issues in Personology

In the day-to-day business of doing psychology, it is easy to get lulled into a belief that the science has truly advanced simply because adequate prediction has been achieved. We instruct our students (and ourselves) to take manageable problems, apply a middle-level theory for the portion of human behavior related to that smaller realm, collect data on easily available (college student) respondents, use the results to fine tune the theory, and then move on to the next middle-level problem. The contributors to this first part clearly do not offer this advice. Both are preoccupied, to paraphrase White (1981), with the study of personality the large way.

Maddi, who is perhaps the most important commentator on personality theories of the second generation after Murray, steps back from ongoing research to describe present work in the field and asks where it should be going in the next decade. He sets a broader framework within which to comprehend the work of two of our most vigorous present-day personality researchers and debaters, namely Mischel and Epstein. He reminds us that the debate about personality stability is really not a new one, but has been dealt with repeatedly ever since Allport (1937) published the first personality text. Maddi enjoins us to expect behavioral coherence of organization and of goal rather than repetition of specific behaviors. His position is that the major problem of the situationalists is a theoretical one: the trait psychology they embrace leads them into the embarrassing position of believing that personality *should* be overtly consistent across situations. Maddi also notes that this constraint is easily handled if, like Murray, one builds a concept of motivation into one's personality schema. Such a concept, involving the notion of underlying purposiveness or direction, is useful in that it implies personality processes that render dissimilar behaviors into functionally equivalent alternatives solely on the basis that they satisfy the same end or goal. The phenotypic catalog of such behaviors may, in fact, be quite dissimilar at different times or in different situations, but the similarity of goal is the unifying underlying element.

Maddi is concerned that theoretical and substantive changes of focus parallel changes in method. From a theoretical standpoint he argues for an isomorphism between types of constructs and types of measurement techniques. This is a deceptively simple point—simple because of its apparently obvious nature. As it is difficult to follow, it is honored more in the breach than by way of implementation. This is not a wholly new observation, but perhaps it takes one who is cognizant of theory to make it and to remind the rest of us about it.

When discussing where research attention should be directed in the next decade, Maddi underscores two important points that are counter to current trends. First, he encourages researchers to spread their nets more broadly, to understand situations not strictly from a phenomenological perspective, but also by developing a methodology that will catalog the nature of the situation/environment. Such multiple perspectives might include social consensus measures of the environment, or the judgment of experts. He suggests that perhaps new construals and methods need to be evolved to portray adequately this aspect of the stimulus situation (see Garbarino & Sherman, 1980; Moos, Finney, & Chan, 1981).

Second, Maddi advocates an explicit shift away from a value-free science. Rather than pursuing the simple accumulation of facts, he reminds us of Murray's humanism and argues that personology, as a scientific enterprise, should attempt to discover more and more about more and more important human problems. The study of what Maddi calls *possibility* and *potential,* rather than just actuality, is part of this focus as well.

Loevinger's chapter uses a summary of the major theory that she has developed over the course of the past two decades as a touchstone and a springboard for her subsequent review and commentary on important issues in current personality research. There is much that she and Maddi agree on. Both note, without surprise, that atheoretical, mindless prediction leads to poor prediction and no understanding. They are concerned that good personality research can only be done with complex, theoretically sophisticated models. Both also reject a trait theory approach that generates simplistic predictions, which are then taken as criticisms of the coherence of personality.

Beyond these agreements, Loevinger's piece is a major theoretical statement that addresses both the prediction issue and the metatheoretical issue concerning that which is personality. In dealing with this volume's theme concerning prediction, she articulates a probabilistic view of behavior that builds upon the work of her teacher, Egon Brunswik. From this perspective, the behavior of the moment is only partially fixed, hence only partially predictable. Originality, creativity, even negativism and surprise may enter in to alter the anticipated sequence of events. There is a parallel here with Kenny's (1979) notion that free will lies in the error term of predictive equations, not because the behavior is intrinsically capricious, but because the individual's capacity to break the set always leads to imprecision in the equation.

Loevinger argues that it is not simply the poor choice of content variables that leads to poor predictive precision; she sees the problem as a more basic conceptual one, related to the structural model of personality being used to formulate the predictions to be made. Using Brunswik's (1952) lens model, Loevinger convincingly maintains that the nature of the relationship being examined is critical to the success of the prediction effort. The stream of behavior is organized into three areas: *receptor aspects* (concerning stimulus characteristics and the perceptual apparatus), *central layer variables* (concerning organizational elements within the organism), and *motor aspects* (concerning the response system and the organism's "achievements"). The core of personality is the area of the central layer. Following Brunswik, Loevinger observes that predictions made within these areas or systems are less reliably made than are those that span the entire sequence. The human capacity to render disparate stimuli or responses as functionally equivalent interferes, then, with demonstrating simple S–R connections. Stimulus A may lead to response A, or to response B if responses A and B serve an equivalent function. Thus, those who predict an $S_A \rightarrow R_A$ relationship, or an $R_A = R_B$ invariant equivalence run the risk of doing poorly in their predictive task. Without a category schema that specifies in advance what functional equivalence program is to be applied at the center, the investigator will be at a loss in making predictions from the stimulus focal point to the distal effect, or among distal responses. This is precisely the place where a viable theory of personality—of what gets processed and how—can render useful service. It is the preoccupation with this problem at the conceptual level, at the measurement level, and at the level of prediction (workability), as well as the work that has evolved out of this attention, which Loevinger reviews in her chapter.

Loevinger's conceptualization of personality is broad in those areas of functioning that it encompasses but precise in its focus within these areas. She is concerned with the *process* of regulating input and output, as well as with the *structures* necessary to accomplish this. She is concerned with the organization of behavior by the perceiving, acting self and with the internal processes that render different external stimuli functionally equivalent. She believes that it is not in terms of isolated traits that one best charts personality development, but in terms of their organization. At the same time, she remains faithful to an empirically grounded theory even when this may lead for a time to empirical imprecision. She comments, "My conception is criticized because, unlike stages devised by the true-blue Piagetians, the stages are not defined in terms of strict logical coherence. I think my stages are just exactly as logically coherent as the people who serve as my subjects are" (p. 65). Loevinger, to use Murray's terminology, is neither a peripheralist nor a centralist, but recognizes the need to encompass both types of influence in formulating an inclusive science of personality.

Beyond these metatheoretical concerns, her chapter highlights two distinctly original themes. One is the differentiation between polar variables and milestone sequences. *Polar variables* are behaviors that vary in quantity—not quality—and that are not transformed as development progresses. Polar variables, such as abilities, are continuous variables; milestone sequences are not. *Milestone sequences* involve transformational change; they are the overt, disparate manifestations of an underlying common process, and are the basic variables of personality development. Ego development, in its successive stages, is an example of this latter process.

The second major proposition that Loevinger presents is a powerful and fascinating assertion: "*The dimension of individual differences in adult life is the trace of a corresponding developmental sequence*" (p. 63). Although evidence substantiating these propositions is still based largely on work coming from Loevinger and her colleagues and students, their potential for generating fruitful inquiry is large and hopefully will be tested by a wider group of investigators. The theory offers models for developmental inquiry that encourage the investigator to look for transformations that may reflect a common process even when superficial manifestations point in the direction of unrelatedness. It also explicitly directs personality researchers to think ontogenetically in order to understand more fully the mechanisms of individual differences.

Last, Loevinger's theory has direct relevance to a novel theoretical conception of aging phenomena. The theory implicitly suggests that the critical issue in age changes is not chronological age, but shift in developmental stage and its concommitants of qualitative as well as quantitative change. In other words, a series of milestone sequences is involved; when they occur, behavioral aging occurs, and when they are absent, aging does not occur. This formulation speaks directly and intriguingly to modern theories of aging, which take note of large individual differences that can be accounted for by neither the simple passage of time nor by conceptualizations of simple and linear decrement of function (e.g., Birren, Butler, Greenhouse, Sokoloff, & Yarrow, 1974; Siegler, 1980). In a more general vein, these propositions underscore the importance of Lewin's observations that there is nothing as practical as a good theory. In the present case, it leads in imaginative and potentially powerful directions.

References

Allport, G. W. *Personality: A psychological interpretation*. New York: Holt, 1937.

Birren, J. E., Butler, R. N., Greenhouse, S. W., Sokoloff, L., & Yarrow, M. R. Interdisciplinary relationships: Interrelations of physiological, psychological, and psychiatric findings in healthy elderly men. In J. E. Birren, R. N. Butler, S. W. Greenhouse, L. Sokoloff, & M. R. Yarrow (Eds.), *Human aging I: A biological and behavioral study*. Rockville, MD: Nat. Inst. of Mental Health, 1974.

Brunswik, E. The conceptual framework of psychology. In O. Neurath, R. Carnap, & C. Morris (Eds.), *International encyclopedia of unified science*. Vol. 1, Pt. 2. Chicago: Univ. of Chicago Press, 1952.

Garbarino, J. R., & Sherman, D. High-risk neighborhoods and high-risk families: The human ecology of child maltreatment. *Child Development*, 1980, *51*, 188–198.

Kenny, D. A. *Correlation and causality*. New York: Wiley–Interscience, 1979.

Moos, R. H., Finney, J. W., & Chan, D. A. The process of recovery from alcoholism: Comparing alcoholic patients and matched community controls. *Journal of Studies on Alcohol*, 1981, *42*, 383–402.

Siegler, I. C. The psychology of adult development and aging. In E. W. Basse & D. G. Blazer (Eds.), *Handbook of geriatric psychology*. New York: Van Nostrand–Reinhold, 1980.

White, R. W. Exploring personality the long way: The study of lives. In A. I. Rabin, J. Aronoff, A. M. Barclay, & R. A. Zucker (Eds.), *Further explorations in personality*. New York: Wiley–Interscience, 1981.

1

Personology for the 1980s*

Salvatore R. Maddi

Historical Background of Personology

In the first of the Michigan State University lectures honoring Henry A. Murray, Robert W. White (1981) depicted with grace and love the dazzling intellectual climate out of which *Explorations in Personality* arose in 1938. The Olympian figure of Murray was everywhere, daring to break old molds while reaffirming traditions of excellence, being fascinated by complexity rather than comforted by oversimplifications, retaining a sense of humanity in the midst of prevailing mechanistic views, inventing measures as needed instead of accepting what was available, and all the while moving steadfastly toward a grand scheme for understanding persons and the interactions with situations that constitute their lives. In those same lectures Daniel J. Levinson (1981) turned his special historical sensitivity toward illuminating the enormous influence Murray continued to exert on the generation of psychologists following that of White. At Berkeley, 3000 miles away, the young Levinson felt that Murray was his teacher long before they met. When Levinson arrived at Harvard in 1950 to teach, the major features of the community Murray founded were still intact, and its intellectual impact near and far was undiminished.

It is my honor to say something of Murray's impact on the third generation. When I arrived at Harvard to study clinical psychology in 1956, many changes were under way. Levinson had already left the Department of Social

*This work was supported in part by National Institute of Mental Health Grant #MH28839 to S. C. Kobasa and S. R. Maddi.

Relations for the Massachusetts Mental Health Center. The Psychological Clinic was still there on Plympton Street, with its famous library, memorabilia, and daily lunches. But White, who had inherited the directorship from Murray, was in turn relinquishing that post to David C. McClelland, who was just arriving from Wesleyan. Murray was deep into another research project centered at his Annex, and my fellow students and I saw him comparatively little. He was somehow still omnipresent, however, with his work and influence being ably transmitted by White and McClelland, each in his own way. White (1952) emphasized a multifaceted, holistic, autobiographical approach to studying persons' lives as they unfolded over time. Though more molecular in approach, McClelland (1951) insisted that for comprehensive understanding one must consider thoughts, feelings, and actions, and distinguish operants from respondents in each of those behavioral categories.

During the 3 years I spent at Harvard, even greater changes took place. The original Psychological Clinic was torn down (we gave it a tumultuous, sad farewell party), and Walter B. Cannon's old home on Divinity Avenue became the new Clinic. Murray appeared in this new setting less and less, and my classmates and I found our way to the Annex as infrequently. Nonetheless, we were vividly conscious of being in his tradition of combining research, clinical, and scholarly endeavors into a holistic view of the human condition. It was not just that those wonderful daily lunches persisted. Nor was it the mere presence in the library of that animated portrait in which Murray looks up at you over half-glasses perched jauntily on the end of his nose, as if he were just about to infect you with enthusiasm concerning some new finding contained in the papers he holds. What continued the tradition was the presence of a faculty that had been strongly influenced by Murray and that was articulate about it. In those years, White and McClelland were supplemented by such as Allport, Kluckhohn, Parsons, Whiting, Kelman, and Bruner. Given this heady day-to-day atmosphere, Murray's occasional appearances constituted an aperiodic schedule of reinforcement, and you know what that must have meant.

During the early 1960s, my classmates and I left Harvard, one by one, to take up academic, research, or clinical posts dotted around the country. We were proud, and perhaps a bit complacent, about being part of a tradition that had been so enormously influential. Within academic psychology, Murray's tradition emphasized the complexity of person–environment interactions, cataloging many *needs, press, thema,* and *need-integrates.* These catalogs were firmly established as the standard starting point for what personality tests were to measure. Within psychoanalytic theory, Murray's tradition was instrumental in shaping modern ego psychology in a humanistic direction, recognizing continual developmental change throughout the life span. Methodologically, there was the Thematic Apperception Test (TAT), that technique for studying operant imagination (McClelland, 1981) concerning person–environment interactions. Beyond that, Murray alerted us to the importance of securing information by various methods and over time in order to ensure accurate and comprehensive formulations. This tradition had even attempted a data language—you may remember Murray's "proceedings" and "serials"—that stands virtually alone in a field that too often assumes its data units are obvious. Further, Murray championed a good name—personology—for the tradition to indicate the emphasis on systematic study of perceptions, cognitions, emotions, and actions as they interact complexly, forming the holistic patterns we call personality.

But no sooner had we, the third generation, settled down to work than the person–situation debate broke out with the appearance of Mischel's (1968) book. I was quite surprised, as were some of my classmates. Dumbfoundedly, we heard the personological tradition criticized on conceptual grounds for supposedly emphasizing traits denoting a high degree of response repetition across situations and over time. The criticism was based on the empirical grounds that personality measures typically show only modest evidence of reliability and validity. The conclusion was reached that there probably was not greater reliability and validity to be found, the personological tradition being misguided from the start.

The modest correlations upon which this conclusion was based had been in the literature for quite some time. Why did raising them in 1968 have such an impact? This was an especially surprising development, given that the conceptual and empirical bases were already available for setting these seemingly disturbing findings into perspective without abandoning personality study. After all, as Bowers (1973) showed, several analysis of variance (ANOVA) studies had been reported prior to 1968, indicating that both situation and person factors, as well as the interaction between them, are empirically important in accounting for behavior. After all, Murray's (1938) definition of the need, with its five components, various possibilities for expression, and waxing and waning strength due to degree of satiation, makes clear that if test–retest situations do not precisely duplicate environmental and personal conditions (and how could they?), one should indeed expect only moderate reliability of measures. It is not a particularly new idea in psychology that the amount of reliability that is important to demonstrate (as long as there is some) is as much determined by the theory surrounding the variable as it is by psychometric considerations. McClelland (1981), in the first of these lecture series, mentioned research instances of validity coefficients higher than should have been possible from the conventionally calculated reliability of measures. Perhaps we need to learn how to estimate reliability better. After all, Murray's (1938) view that particular behaviors are so complex that no one personality factor will determine them completely, is relevant to the validity question. Behaviors are *overdetermined* by the interaction of several personality factors, to say nothing of multiple situational forces. What this means is that when you focus upon the validity of any one personality measure, you should not expect high correlations with behaviors, because these behaviors are also being affected by other person and situation variables. A long time ago, Cronbach and Meehl (1955) rendered this position psychometrically sound with the concept of construct validation, in which the validity of a measure is to be determined by its nomological network rather than its sheer degree of relationship to any particular behavior. After all, Murray's (1938) need concept does not predict simple response repetition either across situations or over time. Rather, the emphasis is on response coherence or pattern, as the person attempts to satisfy his or her multifaceted needs in changing situations and times. McClelland (1951, 1981) pinpoints this emphasis nicely in suggesting that the motive concept came into being specifically to explain the lawfulness underlying what appears to be response *inconsistency* across situations and over time. After all, from a similar personological vantage point, Allport (1937, 1961) early and steadfastly argued that common traits do not exist, being merely convenient fictions whereby researchers may be able to make modest sense out of aggregate data. To understand behavior more precisely, one must study *personal dispositions*, which are idiosyncratic bases for rendering sets of situations and actions functionally equivalent. One must engage in comprehensive idiographic study, he contended, in order to find the pattern in a person's functioning.

The personological message in all this, available in the 1930s and reiterated clearly in subsequent years, is that we should expect behavioral coherence rather than repetition, that we will not even find this unless we look in appropriate ways, and that personality theorizing is not cogent when restricted to simple trait notions. There should never have been any argument about this message, which could, and for some psychologists at some times did, provide a perspective for regarding the observations organized by Mischel (1968) without undue alarm. Even if many studies in an area do not reflect sophisticated theory and practice, that should not emerge as a basis for questioning the value of that area.

That this personological message did not soften the blow of Mischel's (1968) observations suggests that other factors were at play in the person–situation debate. Certainly, the lucidity of Mischel's exposition should be credited—his was a persuasive, spirited argument. Another factor may well have been the rise of a generation of energetic experimental social psychologists, homogeneous in education, committed to the search for general laws through experimental study, and firm in the conviction that social forces control behavior. Linking with behaviorists, who are of course similar in commitments, these social psychologists had intellectual reason to discredit personality study, with its seemingly softer emphasis on individual differences and correlational methodology.

In this regard, we should note that a kind of person–situation debate breaks out periodically in U.S. psychology. Earlier in this century, William McDougall and John Watson squared off concerning whether internal instincts or external stimuli control behavior. And somewhat before our most recent form of this debate was that in which Carl R. Rogers and B. F. Skinner took issue as to whether psychotherapy shapes behavior or merely serves as background support for the expression of inherent potentialities driven by the actualizing tendency. This long-standing tension in our field between inner and outer explanations of behavior continues unresolved because it is most likely unresolvable. That neither person nor situation alone provides sufficient understanding is the basis upon which our most recent form of the debate was called a pseudo-issue (Carlson, 1975). But do not think that this insight is new. Not only did Cronbach (1957) know it, but long before that William James (1890) talked about it in his doctrine of the transitoriness of instinct. For James, it made no sense to try to unravel what in behavior is due to instincts and to environment because from the second time an instinct is expressed, an interactional unit amalgamating both inner and outer influences is bound to be the most potent explanation.

I am not sure about all the reasons why person–situation debates spring up at particular times. But the reasons cannot be exclusively intellectual, as suggested by the early and continuing recognition in our field that such debates are probably unresolvable. Distasteful though it is, I raise the reason of political secondary gain, for this is inevitably intertwined with the more intellectual features of such issues. It cannot be overlooked, unfortunately, that it is to prevailing views and vigorous movements that important resources such as influential positions, high salaries, research grants, honorific posts, international conferences, and quality students are disproportionately allocated. Although such spoils of war are inevitable, participants in debates must scrutinize their motives carefully. As ours is a basically intellectual task, we cannot afford to be too swayed by the promise of political advantage. The saving grace is for each of us to insist that our work meet stringent criteria of intellectual worth, such as accuracy, internal consistency, and cogency. Even with a high level of self-scrutiny, however, we need the sobering effect of dialogue with others to keep our functioning on the highest plane.

It is in the spirit of dialogue that I express my worry concerning some persisting inaccuracies in the work of some interactional psychologists. Magnusson and Endler (1977) continue to define personology as trait theory, with all the attendant denotations of response repetition across situations and over time. But this is precisely what Murray and others in his tradition did not mean and the reason that he popularized the term personology. Further,

despite Allport's (1937, 1961) outspoken criticisms of common trait theorizing, he still is classified in many textbooks (e.g., Mischel, 1976; Feshbach and
Weiner, 1982) as a trait theorist, ironically criticized with his own criticisms.
I have tried in my textbook (Maddi, 1968/1980) and elsewhere (Maddi,
1963; Maddi and Costa, 1972) to correct these misinterpretations, as have
others, but apparently without complete success. It cannot pass unnoticed
that the effect of these erroneous definitions and interpretations is to give
interactional psychology the aura of a new and needed corrective. Interactional psychologists should take care lest their efforts appear too politically
motivated.

But when all is said and done, another reason that Mischel's statement was
so cogent in the late 1960s stems from the vulnerability of those of us
involved in personality study. Why were we so vulnerable? You may have
noticed that I did not call us personologists. That is a clue to my answer to
the question, for I believe the problem to be that not enough of us were
enacting Murray's tradition vigorously. Instead, we were busy studying to
death the correlates of individual personality variables, without much regard
for how these variables might interact with other person and situation variables to yield comprehensive understanding. We filled the literature with
correlations that were inconsequential, not so much because they were modest, but because they represented such a small corner of the whole terrain as
to amount to little by way of understanding. In reviewing the literature of
that period, Carlson (1971) could justifiably ask "Where is the person in
personality research?" Even less sympathetically, social psychologists were in
effect demanding to know "Where is the situation in human behavior that
occurs in a social context?" We were defenseless against the onslaught because we had lost sight of the main tasks and goals of personology.

The intellectual value of the person–situation debate is that it forced those
in personality study to reconsider their activities and views in order to respond cogently to the criticisms. In this process, there has been considerable
reaffirmation of the principles of Murray's personological tradition, laced
with methodological advances not available to him. Thanks to Mischel
(1968, 1973) we agree on the importance of interactional variables and
research designs. Following Block's (1971) lead, we now appear to believe
that the behavior of persons is rather stable over long periods of time, as long
as care is taken to equate behaviors reflective of the factors under consideration for life-span differences. For example, the same level of aggressiveness
may have to be expressed differently by children than by adults (Olweus,
1978). Further, we appear to believe that the closer we come to idiographic
study, with its multivariate, subjective measures, the greater behavioral consistency we find (Magnusson & Endler, 1977). We do not agree yet on
whether behavior shows consistency across situations (Mischel & Peake,
1981). But here, as this volume well exemplifies, an important shift has

occurred toward emphasizing the *predictability* rather than the sameness of behavior. Researchers from both sides of the recent debate are searching for situations and responses that are functionally equivalent for subjects (e.g., Bem & Allen, 1974; Bem & Funder, 1978; Mischel & Peake, 1981), recognizing that it is only in this way that the coherence or lawfulness of behavior can be judged. Further, we are resensitizing ourselves to the differing meanings and implications of different kinds of data. It is one thing to answer a questionnaire and quite another to engage in guided fantasy (McClelland, 1981). Both are very different from having your behavior rated by peers or the researcher (Magnusson & Endler, 1977). There is constructive resolve now to determine empirically the cross-situational coherence of these various kinds of data.

So the battle has largely subsided and an intellectual accord has descended. Although most personological effort seems narrowly directed toward demonstrating the scientific validity of the enterprise, intellectual bankruptcy has clearly been avoided. Even politically, personology is recovering something of its former status. Witness the new and very successful personality section of the *Journal of Personality and Social Psychology* (under the able editorship of Robert Hogan) and the new personality section of the APA Division of Personality and Social Psychology (struggled for by Alker, Carlson, Elmes, Epstein, Helson, Tompkins, and others). There is breathing space now for personologists to heed their recent vulnerability and to fashion a more vigorous endeavor for the 1980s. Current concern over the question of cross-situational consistency left unresolved during the recent debate is laudable in that there is much to be learned about how to predict behavior. But there is danger in exclusive investment in this primarily methodological concern. To make personology matter, we will need a broader conceptual and practical consideration of what is important to study and why. Only in this context will insights about how best to predict form a meaningful whole. Only by fashioning such a meaningful whole can we demonstrate that personology is not just alive but also quite well.

The following contributors to this volume admirably cover the issues of behavioral predictability; I will exercise the more general prerogatives given me and direct my remaining commentary to conceptual and practical matters of content and purpose for personology.

Critical Shifts in Emphasis

I will mention five shifts in emphasis that together would constitute a renewal of personology along lines viable for the next few years. Many times I will refer to trends already detectable. Other times, I will urge directions that seem needed. Throughout, you will easily discern the guiding spirit of Henry Murray.

Shifting from Construct Validation toward Important
  Phenomena

As I mentioned before, personality researchers have been preoccupied in recent years with studying personality constructs as they are expressed in various behaviors. Hundreds of studies of this sort have been reported concerning internal versus external locus of control, need for achievement, need for power, self-disclosure, Machiavellianism, androgyny, sensation-seeking, cognitive complexity, and the like. By and large, the impetus for these studies has been the way the personality construct is conceptualized, with the behavioral correlates being selected merely because they are relevant to that conceptualization.

If we try to fit this kind of research into some known strategy of inquiry, we find that it comes closest to construct validity (Cronbach & Meehl, 1955). Having conceptualized a personality construct, one engages in a gradual process of empirical test by building a theoretically relevant measure of the construct and determining whether its pattern of behavioral correlates matches the formulation. The more the pattern matches, the greater the confidence one is entitled to have in the formulation.

The construct validational strategy has been an important addition to the procedures available to psychologists. But, like everything else, it has pitfalls. One of them is the absence of guarantee that the behavioral correlates selected will be important natural phenomena. This is because the emphasis of the inquiry is more on the personality construct than on the behavioral correlates. Indeed, the behavioral correlates may be quite contrived, as long as they appear theoretically relevant. It is so easy to churn out study after study, each correlating the personality measure with some behavior that would be of little real interest were it not for the construct validational justification. This is just what happened in the personality area, and it contributed, over a period of time, to weakening the enterprise by rendering uncertain its relevance to major natural phenomena important for human welfare. To Carlson's (1971) question, "Where is the person in personality research?" might be added, "Where is real life in personality research?"

It may seem as if this point can be controverted by the fact that social psychologists could come on so strong in the recent person–situation debate. After all, they were experimentally based, and there is nothing so contrived and unnatural as an experiment. I contend that the recent vitality of social psychology is based less on its procedure of inquiry than on an insistence that the experiments be planned so as to facilitate inference to some significant natural phenomenon. In the studies, the overall aim has been to understand obesity, or criminality, or interpersonal attraction. If anything, the reliance upon an experimental strategy has carried with it a pitfall similar to that in construct validation. That pitfall is the oversimplification of natural phenomena that can easily occur when laboratory analogies have to be devised. By itself, the devotion to experimental methods would not have been enough to project social psychology into the limelight. The constant recognition of the importance of understanding natural phenomena has been an essential ingredient in this success.

I imagine a time when journal articles will routinely feature a justification of the phenomena focused upon, based on their importance in the day-to-day welfare of persons. An emphasis upon individual differences in these phenomena would mark the enterprise as relevant to explanations involving personality. Possible examples of important phenomena are legion; think of creativity–banality, health–illness, success–failure, love–hatred, wealth–poverty.

It is wise for us to insist that the importance of the phenomenon studied be authenticated in some fashion. There are two main authentication procedures: one is a process of social consensus and the other involves expert judgment. There are various ways of determining social consensus. A representative sample of persons could rate the prevalence and importance of a set of phenomena presented by the researcher. Or subjects could generate their own list through consideration of their lives, and the agreement across subjects could be determined. In any event, the phenomena emerging for study would reflect a kind of mandate from the people. The other authenticating process would involve experts (including psychologists) in arguing, on the basis of their special knowledge and skills, for the importance of behavioral phenomena. The argument would have to be clear and noteworthy, even if it did not convince everyone right away. Experts as authenticators could be valuable insofar as society might be conventionally oriented enough to miss the importance of some phenomenon too embarrassing or too painful to face.

It may appear that what I am saying is little different from what we have been doing. This is not so. Following the suggestions advocated here, the emphasis in deciding what research to do would shift from personality constructs to authenticated real-life phenomena. For some researchers, these advocated changes would not be objectionable in principle, and the extra work would be the only inconvenience. For them, the gain in relevance and vitality of personality study would, I suspect, far outweigh the inconvenience.

But for other psychologists, what I am advocating is no less than a retreat from the true path of science. Fiske (1974, 1977, 1978), for example, argues that when society or laymen are the source of the problems for personality study, that research is necessarily on the level of common sense. Common sense, used his way, implies group fictions, highly interpretive views of experience that bear only a tenuous relationship to anything real. In his own words (Fiske, 1977), investigators taking socially defined problems as a starting point should recognize that they are using "the perceptions and evaluative judgments of particular executives, clinicians, patients, or others, and not crude estimates of some underlying reality (p. 282)." Following from this, Fiske (1977) believes that these "concepts of the everyday world" force the investigator into observations that are so interpretive as to ensure distressingly low interscorer agreement. The whole thrust of this position is that studying socially defined phenomena is unscientific (Fiske, 1974), however much investigators have the laudable aim of helping their fellow humans. He regards the future of the personality area as bleak because it is so dominated by socially defined studies (Fiske, 1974). With the passage of a few years, Fiske (1977) has moderated his pessimism somewhat, suggesting peaceful coexistence between socially defined personality study and another sort he clearly favors. But the view of what is and is not scientific persists.

According to Fiske (1977), the other, scientific sort of personality study occurs when "the investigator determines the problem to be studied." That this is the road to objectivity for Fiske (1977, p. 283) is clear from the following statement:

> We should try to see what is there, instead of trying to find what we expect to find. I grant that researchers always have some expectations and cannot look at any set of phenomena without some a priori notions. We can, however, do our best to let the phenomena speak to us. The need for taking a fresh look is particularly great in the domain of personal phenomena, to which we bring so many preconceptions that have been reinforced by the greater or lesser success with which we have adapted to the world of people.

Not surprisingly, Fiske (1977) regards "uninterpretive" observation to lead to high interscorer agreement because it is pure and objective.

What Fiske calls socially determined phenomena bears some similarity to what I call natural and significant phenomena. One disagreement we appear to have, therefore, is about the frequency of such studies—he thinking them common and I, rare. It is admittedly difficult to quantify such impressions, but I tried, however sketchily. I looked at all the articles appearing in the *Journal of Personality* and in the personality section of the *Journal of Personality and Social Psychology* for 1980 and 1981. When I tried to do this also for the *Personality and Social Psychology Bulletin* there were so few studies concerning individual differences and personality formulations that it did not seem worthwhile to persist. As our main concern is with personology, it did not seem necessary to consider less central journals. In perusing the articles, I tried to identify the phenomena involved and the main impetus for the studies.

As illustrative of socially defined topics, Fiske (1977) mentions interpersonal distress, person–vocation fit, social program evaluation, productivity, satisfaction, maladjustment, and general distress. Classifying liberally, I found that only 21% of the articles concern these topics. Earlier, I mentioned creativity–banality, health–illness, success–failure, love–hatred, and wealth–poverty as possible illustrations of natural and significant phenomena. Only another 10% of the articles centrally concern these topics. And if we discount from this total of 31% those articles whose impetus is clearly construct validation, with the choice of behavioral phenomena being almost incidental, the percentage drops to 18. The list of topics mentioned by Fiske and me could be extended, no doubt, but the percentages mentioned would still remain small. The overwhelming majority of articles concern such presumably investigator-determined matters as androgyny theory, locus of control theory, attribution theory, the triangle hypothesis, personality complexity theory, facial feedback theory, and ego development theory, phenomena that seem far from anything lay persons would see as important in their lives. Other articles communicate particular theories of personality or concern methodological questions of research design, testing procedures, and statistical inference. Clearly, social consensus criteria of importance would not lead us to these topics.

But the infrequency of socially determined studies would not please Fiske. This is because the majority of studies, though in some sense investigator-determined, use concepts and theories still too reminiscent of everyday life for him. In his view the investigators are too concerned with illusory abstractions to be able to observe underlying realities. Fiske's emphasis here is reminiscent of radical behaviorism in two ways: the conviction that small, concrete data units are more real, and the association of objectivity with lack of interpretation or abstraction.

The argument that small data units are more real is based on the contention (Fiske, 1974, 1977) that they are inevitably associated with a higher level of interscorer agreement than are larger data units. The high agreement scores attending Duncan and Fiske's (1977) studies of nonverbal communication are cited as an example (Fiske, 1977). Apparently, however, scorers must work hard and long to achieve these high levels of agreement. Why should this be so, if smaller data units are so much more real? One might argue that it is because scorers must learn to discard their socially determined expectations before seeing the underlying truths. But such an argument, though admittedly difficult to disprove empirically, makes clear that the notion of reality as necessarily distorted by socialization is, in positions like that of

Fiske, an article of faith. There are, after all, numerous examples of scoring systems that he would call socially determined that can be used with agreement better than 85–90%. It is perfectly possible that with as much definitional and indoctrinational effort as has been expended on research approaches like that of Duncan and Fiske (1977), many more socially determined scoring systems could emerge as having high interscorer agreement. There is no compelling reason to believe that if bases for interpretation are made explicit, they cannot be used by open-minded persons who are willing to be trained.

Fiske's (1977) other view—the equation of objectivity with lack of interpretation—is particularly inhibiting of progress, however long its tradition in U.S. psychology. This tradition has saddled us with behavioristic formulations in which we must assert that animals are characteristically introduced into the experimental apparatus at two-thirds of normal body weight, not because we want them to be hungry but because it has been empirically observed that they are more active under these conditions. And we use food as a positive reinforcement not because hungry animals will do all sorts of things for the opportunity to eat but rather because it has been empirically observed that we can alter response rates using such a reinforcer. Did we really discover these things through uninterpretive observation in a laboratory? Did we not know them all along, as a function of having been socialized into our culture? I have argued elsewhere (Maddi, 1980) that the main reason why the experiments of radical behaviorists work is the hunches that lead them to plan as they do (but are then kept private for fear of appearing unscientific). Hunches are interpretations, and many of them are, in Fiske's terms, socially determined.

And is not Duncan and Fiske's work as interpretive as anyone's? It would undoubtedly be possible to scrutinize the relationship between their data and findings to discover, in their choice to observe just certain cues for initiating and ending speech, their own subjective construction of the environment. It would certainly also be possible to discern individual differences among interacting subjects in perception and action, even though Duncan and Fiske choose not to consider such matters. Similarly, Fiske's proposed direction for personology expresses a behavioristic preference on his part rather than a necessary conclusion for everyone else.

If anything, there is a strong argument to be made that, should objectivity mean anything at all, it must refer to observation guided by judgment and interpretation (e.g., Polanyi, 1964). While there may be an immutable thingness out there, we have only our perceptual systems with which to apprehend it. It is bad enough that this perceptual system has certain anatomical and physiological limitations (e.g., we do not have as sensitive olfaction or night vision as many other animals). But what compromises knowledge of thingness even more seriously is the influence exerted on perceptual systems by memories, beliefs, expectations, and values (e.g., Neisser, 1976). So it makes no sense to pursue the holy grail of thingness.

Fiske (1977) laments that there have been so few significant new ideas or findings in personology in the past 25 years and blames this on the absence of investigators who observe without interpreting. But the paradigm shifts (e.g., Kuhn, 1962) Fiske longs for come about precisely when observers interpret. Historians of science (e.g., Butterfield, 1957; Putnam, 1981) have long pointed out that Galileo, called the father of modern science, could never have escaped from Aristotelian doctrine to arrive at the law of gravity and to find a way of proving the heliocentric view of the cosmos by a merely "photographic" method of observation. Instead, he operated counterintuitively, apparently violating the immediate data of observation, and had to search long and hard for just those, and I might add rare, observations that would prove his points. Bowers (1977, p. 69) puts this process eloquently by maintaining "that abstraction is a *condition* for objectivity, not simply a distorted summary of "objective" facts . . . the scientist's powers of abstraction facilitate a deeper seeing, a more penetrating vision that goes beyond superficial appearances to the order underlying them [emphasis in original]." Bowers (1977) caps this argument by reminding us that brain-damaged persons become more concrete and uninterpretive but also less accurate in their interactions with the environment. Remember that Murray (1954) once dubbed the behavioristic insistence on uninterpreted observation "functional decortication," arguing steadfastly for grappling with complexities instead of oversimplifying in the slim hope of achieving a science that way.

You must not think that just because I believe interpretation to be valuable I favor the current trend in so-called investigator-determined studies. Most of these studies enact a construct-validational mode of inquiry. As such, the behavioral phenomena are relatively unimportant. In my little survey, attempts by the investigator to detail the bases upon which the behavioral phenomena were considered natural and important were extremely rare, to say the least. We must do better than this before investigator-determined research can serve as a balancing corrective on social consensus views of what is important to study.

Shifting from Single toward Multiple Explanatory
Constructs

Turning from the phenomena studied to the explanations pursued, my little survey also makes clear that personality research has recently emphasized single constructs (e.g., androgyny, locus of control, or *n* power). This appears so regardless of whether the phenomenon to be understood is complex or relatively simple. This approach, criticized long ago by Allport (1954) as "simple and sovereign theorizing," does not appear to require any justification, judging from the way research reports are written. If justification were requested, I suppose the responses would be not only pragmatic (e.g., space limitations in journals) but also principled (e.g., construct validation can be interpreted to refer to single constructs and their particular behavioral implications).

The emphasis upon single explanatory constructs has contributed as much as, and perhaps more than, any other single factor to the recently fragmented, meandering quality of personality research. Each subculture of personology has its own pet construct or two, and research reports appearing in neighboring journals—to say nothing of what is often within the very same journal—appear surprisingly disparate.

A typical behavioristic rejoinder to my criticism is that there is nothing to worry about in this apparent fragmentation because any true coordination can only scientifically be achieved through the accumulation of facts. The very research activities I decry, the story goes, will produce these facts, and when a certain critical mass is achieved, clarifying coordination will emerge naturally. This position has been reiterated throughout the history of psychology in the United States. Can anyone remember an area or time when any broadly recognized coordination could be traced to a critical mass of facts alone? How long must we wait before we conclude that this prophecy has failed? And if there is to be no statute of limitations, we are surely being regaled with faith rather than reason. Hopefully, this faith can be put to rest through recognition that, as I indicated earlier, paradigm shifts and other forms of clarifying coordination come about through interpretation, not mere accumulation of facts.

I wish I could at least say, with regard to recent personality research, that we have been learning more and more about less and less. The "less and less" would reflect the contrived nature of many of the phenomena we focus upon, as I mentioned previously. But there would at least be some cause for optimism if, on the explanatory side, there was high predictive power, however unimportant the phenomena predicted. Recall, however, all those modest correlations between a measure of a personality construct and a behavior loosely construed as relevant. The mere fact that there were many such reports in the literature did not decrease the vulnerability of personology to the situationist onslaught. One might be tempted to conclude that, in truth, we know less and less about less and less.

Fortunately, there does seem to be a small, developing trend toward including more than one explanatory construct in personality studies. The interactional accord, for example, is having the effect of encouraging investigators to study at least a situational variable along with a corresponding person variable. Also, recent feminist concerns are influencing the inclusion of gender along with what might otherwise have been only one explanatory variable. Hopefully, this trend will accelerate. Once or twice, the inclusion of several explanatory constructs does actually seem to have been prompted by the wish to explain more of the variance of a seemingly important phenomenon than was possible otherwise. Take as an example the evolution of the work of McClelland and his associates. Early on (e.g., McClelland, Atkinson, Clark, & Lowell, 1953), the emphasis was on correlating single need measures with whatever behaviors seemed supportive of construct validation. Then a shift took place (e.g., McClelland, 1961) toward emphasizing an important phenomenon, economic development. Although *n* ach (need for achievement) was supplemented as a measure of values in some analyses, the tradition could still be criticized for oversimplifying (e.g., Brown, 1965). Now, McClelland (1981) has turned to another important phenomenon, hypertension, and the attempt to predict it well is leading to reliance upon multiple explanatory concepts of different types. This evolution is a good illustration of how shifting the emphasis of research to important phenomena goes hand-in-hand with employing multiple explanatory constructs in the search for comprehensive understanding.

All in all, the beginning trend toward multiple explanatory constructs certainly seems valuable, even though it does not yet appear to derive reliably from systematically elaborated theories concerning the phenomena to be understood. At the very least, we should avoid the shotgun method of multiple variable inclusion and try instead to use discernment, judgment, and sensitivity. There are considerations of content and method that are relevant. For example, it is out of a first-order content concern that interactionists advocate including both person and situation variables in their studies. But it is out of method concerns that many of them (e.g., Mischel, 1973, 1977) have concluded that situation variables are more meaningfully measured idiographically, through each subject's individual judgments. There are, of course, two other measurement approaches you will recognize from my previous comments: the consensus of relevant social groups and the expert judgment of investigators. Mischel (1973, 1977) contends that whenever attempts have been made to measure social consensus about situations, rampant differences have emerged. For him, this demonstrates that situations have no objective status, being only subjective realities. This is certainly a position that traditional personality advocates, from Freud to Allport, could accept with enthusiasm.

Murray (1938) agrees that there is subjective construal of situations, calling this *beta press*, but still, in the concept of *alpha press*, advocates something less individualistic than this as well. While avoiding the snare of whatever might constitute objectivity, I would support the notion that there is more to say about situations than their most individual meaning. After all, the existence of individual differences does not, in and of itself, obviate social-consensus measures of situations. As long as the judgments of a sample of persons are normally distributed, the mean of this distribution can be taken as a meaningful estimate of group consensus. Also, the researcher is entitled to an expert judgment of how the situation is constituted as long as he or she does not insist that this is the objective view. If the researcher is at a loss as to how to construe situations, then this may well underscore the need for additional theory development.

Similarly, there are parallel ways to measure person variables. Persons may be described by themselves subjectively, by the consensus of persons with whom they interact, and by the expert judgments of the investigator. Having subjective, social-consensus, and expert views of interacting situations and persons opens up intriguing study of the importance of agreement and disagreement in these various kinds of estimates for understanding the phenomena under consideration.

There is another value to this tripartite approach to measurement beyond the wish to be comprehensive and the lure of intriguing studies. That is the combination of content and method that used to be called operationism. Personological constructs contain in their conceptualization directives for measurement that we have generally not taken seriously enough. These conceptual directives constitute legitimate bases for measuring in particular ways as opposed to other ways. For example, such Rogerian concepts as openness to experience should probably not be measured by expert opinion or social consensus, due to the strong subjectivistic bias in the theorizing. Once one accepts Rogers's (1961) remark that he "can never know persons as well as they know themselves," one is hard put to justify anything but subjective measurement approaches. In contrast, Freud (1960) believed that most of mental life is unconscious, virtually requiring for its explication the expert judgment of a trained psychoanalyst. Therefore, in operationalizing Freudian concepts, one would not rely upon either subjective or social-consensus approaches.

Some conceptual schemes incorporate various types of constructs calling for different measurement approaches. McClelland (1951, 1981), for example, considers both needs and traits. Because he regards needs as involving operant behavior, he advocates measuring them through unstructured fantasy tasks. In contrast, traits involve respondent behavior, and can best be measured through structured questionnaires. But some investigators, failing to heed this distinction, develop questionnaire measures of needs. Then the typically low correlations between questionnaire and fantasy measures is used as a criticism of need theory, on the grounds that there appears more method variance than so-called trait (more properly, we should call it "construct") variance. Such conclusions are confusing because the low relationship is indeed what McClelland would expect, as the questionnaires are probably getting at traits, no matter what label these measures are given by investigators. Indeed, taking the need for achievement as a case in point, we find that despite low relationships between fantasy and questionnaire measures, each has its own network of external correlates. That these correlates reflect the tendency to be influenced by the opinions of others for the questionnaire measures, whereas the fantasy measures relate instead to aspects of memory and performance, supports McClelland's contention (e.g., DeCharms, Morrison, Reitman, & McClelland, 1955).

There is an important implication in McClelland's view that should not go unrecognized, namely, that limits need to be placed on the use of multi-construct, multimethod matrices. One should not calculate method variance across all possible or even available measurement methods and use the results to reflect upon whether or not sufficient construct variance exists. The only methods that are relevant for this calculation are those that conform to the measurement implications incorporated in the construct under consideration. In McClelland's case, for example, one should only observe relationships among fantasy measures in attempting to reach a conclusion about the ratio of construct to method variance in the case of needs. That these necessary limits have usually not been imposed may well have exaggerated the inadequacy of existing construct measures.

Shifting from Cross-Sectional toward Longitudinal Studies

There are a number of recent demonstrations that personality constructs are quite predictive of behavioral regularity over many years. Indeed, Mischel (1977) insists that behavioral regularity over time was never really an issue in the person–situation debate. When the emphasis is on personality-test responses, the reason for greater predictability over time (which is recognizable in this case as reliability) is that agreement among a person's test responses increases with the number of test administrations (e.g., Epstein, 1977). When the emphasis is more on behavioral regularities rather than test responses per se, the reason for greater predictability over time is that observing persons in a wide variety of situations permits the emergence of the pattern or coherence in their functioning (e.g., Block, 1971; Olweus, 1978). Cross-sectional studies are at a disadvantage on both counts: they tend to measure personality only once and to incorporate only one situation, variously interpreted by subjects.

Many more longitudinal studies are needed, and this is not merely because they are conducive to greater predictability of behavior. Basically, such studies are infinitely more relevant to personality formulations than are cross-sectional studies. After all, personality theorizing is mainly concerned with the long-range effects of parent–child interactions on needs, traits, disposition, and conflicts, and the similarly long-range effects of such personality characteristics on career choices and goals, social and familial relationships, interactions with social institutions, and other aspects of lives. There is certainly a way of deriving from such conceptualizations hypotheses that can be studied cross-sectionally. But there is inevitably an air of inconclusiveness about such studies, and they would probably not be done so often except for reasons of practicality. Succumbing to the practicality of cross-sectional studies appears, however, to be a trap, if you add to their conceptual inconclusiveness the ambiguous evidence of predictability they generate. Once again, let us learn from our recent vulnerability in the person-situation debate.

Conceptually, longitudinal studies are especially crucial because they permit the test of causal formulations. Personality theorizing is largely causal, concerning as it does the developmental antecedents of personality characteristics and the behavioral consequences of these characteristics once formed. An ample time line in longitudinal studies is necessary for testing such causal formulations.

Viewing person and situation variables in a time line has led some interactionists to question whether causal formulations are possible. Magnusson and Endler (1977), for example, regard "dynamic interaction" as the most sophisticated view because it construes persons and situations as "inextricably interwoven in a continuous ongoing process (which) cannot be meaningfully discussed as a cause and effect relationship" (p. 21). Following the dialectical reasoning of Raush (1977), they cite the complexity of analyzing ongoing behavior when persons subjectively define and choose the situations they encounter, when the behavior of persons may serve as situational cues not only to others (who will then act toward them) but to themselves as well, and when these many relationships are changing over time. There is a danger for interactionism in this line of argument. However sophisticated it may seem, it finally ends in Magnusson and Endler's (1977) conclusion "that the individual is the active, intentional agent in [the] interaction process" (p. 22). Surely this is stark irony. Here are high priests of the interaction movement who have gone full circle and embraced what they originally found objectionable. Magnusson and Endler can call this position dynamic interactionism or anything else they like; it is nonetheless the very attribution of centrality to person variables that was found objectionable about some personological positions in the early days of the person–situation debate.

I think it neither necessary nor wise to abandon causal formulations. Even if situations could only be defined subjectively, it would certainly seem plausible that these subjective definitions, along with related actions, should be regarded as caused by person variables. But situational definition need not be restricted to individual subjectivity when social-consensus and expert-judgment measurement options are available. Using these measurement options opens up study of how situations subjectively chosen may, because of aspects of them definable through the other two options, have an influence on the chooser in ways unanticipated by him or her. Surely, this can be formulated causally. And with the three measurement options for defining person– situation interactions of developmental import, there is once again little reason to abandon causal formulations. Needless to say, today's dependent variable may become tomorrow's independent variable and vice versa. But there is no difficulty here as long as we avoid reifying these terms. Have not we always recognized that which variables get called dependent and which independent is an arbitrary—or theoretical—matter? The approach I am advocating, though pejoratively labelled "mechanistic interaction" by Magnusson and Endler (1977), may not only be all we have but all we need as a tool for understanding.

This brings me back to longitudinal designs. The logic of independent and dependent variables as tests of causal formulations when we are not dealing with the experiment proper really requires a time lag to be convincing. The supposed independent variables should be measured earlier in time than the supposed dependent variables. But this design feature of time lag does not wholly ensure the plausibility of causal inference. For example, the supposedly prospective demonstration that stressful life events in 1980 result in illness symptoms in 1981 might well reflect no more than a correlation between these events and illness symptoms in 1980 that persisted into 1981. Even worse, the illness symptoms of 1979 might have been just as highly correlated with 1980 stressful events as were the illness symptoms in 1980 and 1981. For such reasons, the data from longitudinal studies should be analyzed in a fashion that adds to the fact of time lag a statistical basis for prospective inferences. The method of cross-lagged panel correlations has recently achieved some popularity. But Rogosa (1980) has argued persuasively that this technique is unsuitable when there is reason to suspect reciprocal, or two-way, causality. Perhaps more justifiable is analysis of covariance where, to return to the example I just gave, the covariate would be illness level in 1980, thereby rendering the dependent variable to be illness *change* from 1980 to 1981. Responding to a similar problem, Alker (1977) suggests that we borrow from econometrics a two-stage least-squares technique for estimating strengths of relation when it is assumed that two variables reciprocally interact.

Shifting from Middle-Level toward Comprehensive Theorizing

It is fashionable in personality research these days to restrict conceptual effort to the middle ground, in the belief that the grand theories of the recent past are impediments to scientific advance. It is surely possible, even somewhat likely, that attempts at comprehensive conceptualizations will be vague and too abstract for useful empirical work. In warning of this, Murray (1959, p. 19) waxed eloquent about "those lazy white elephants of the mind—huge, catchall, global concepts signifying nothing." But this problem seems to me more in the nature of an avoidable pitfall rather than an inevitable concomitant of attempts to be theoretically comprehensive. Indeed, I believe that our scrupulous avoidance of any but middle-level approaches has cost us dearly in misunderstandings and wasted effort.

An unfortunate feature of a commitment to middle-level theorizing is the general distrust of any formulation that appears to have any surplus meaning. The only theorizing we will countenance must be absolutely needed in order to make the decisions permitting our research. This leads readily to reliance upon single explanatory concepts, which appears so parsimonious but really turns out not to be, as we must add more constructs each time we do another study. It also leads to a disinclination to consider whether the phenomena under consideration are important, lest we appear arbitrary, so we end by wasting time and effort. If I have convinced you at all about the limitations attending research on contrived phenomena and single explanatory concepts, then you should consider laying some of the blame at the doorstep of middle-level theorizing.

There is a specific example in current interactionist research that illustrates well the need to go beyond middle-level theorizing. The research question involved is whether behavior shows consistency across situations. Bem and Funder (1978) put forward the view that in order to predict behavioral consistency, one must match the personality of the person to the "personality" of the situation. When these two personalities match, person variables should be predictive of behavior in the situation. This certainly sounds like the voice of rationality and theoretical sophistication. But they go on to focus upon what they regard as a major implication of their view: namely, that only when situations have similar "personalities" should we expect to find high intercorrelations among behaviors displayed in them. Bem and Funder do not seem to recognize that once you have decided to go beyond superficial appearances to the underlying meaning of situations, you must be prepared to go all the way by doing the same thing for the behaviors involved. Ostensibly similar behaviors may mean different things in different situations and different persons. And ostensibly different behaviors may mean similar things in similar situations and similar persons. Prediction is simply more complex than the blithe assumption that observed behaviors in similar situations will be highly intercorrelated.

Despite this difficulty, Bem and Funder (1978) proceed to report findings from the comparison of two situations that appear conceptually equivalent, but emerge on the basis of Q-sorts to be functionally quite different. They then suggest that the absence of behavioral consistency shown across these two situations supports their view. But, as Mischel and Peake (1981) point out, these findings are actually irrelevant because a different set of subjects performed in each of the two tasks, even though the logic of the position would require the same set of subjects. Further, the clearest test of the position would have involved two or more situations that appeared dissimilar but emerged as functionally similar in the Q-sorts. Then one could at least have tested whether behavior was consistent across them, though, of course, the problem of behavioral meaning mentioned before would have persisted.

Mischel and Peake (1981) attempted a more adequate test of the Bem–Funder position by utilizing the same set of subjects in two performance situations, with many other features of methodology the same or similar. They found that not only did the two situations appear similar to the investigators, but they also emerged as functionally similar in the Q-sorts. The significant but low level of behavioral consistency across the situations appeared, therefore, to disconfirm Bem and Funder's prediction. Mischel and Peake (1981) seem almost surprised at these results, and spend effort trying to understand why behavioral consistency did not emerge. In critiquing aspects of sampling, procedure, and data combination, they indicate that one really should not do this kind of research without specific, articulated theoretical reasons to guide decisions.

I could not agree more, and would indeed go beyond the points raised by Mischel and Peake. There are many questions that have gone unanswered in these studies. Why were the mothers' Q-sorts about their children and the situations used, when it was actually the children who were performing? Although the mothers' views might well have accurately depicted *their* view of the situations, that may not be an accurate basis for how the children perceived the situations, or for that matter, what their personalities were like. The pragmatic answer that mothers are adults and therefore can be more articulate than children about things like Q-sorts is not in any sense convincing. It only raises the further question of why children were being used as

subjects in a study of behavioral consistency in the first place. Some personality theories consider children to have unformed personalities and, hence, to
be less stable in their behaviors and less definite in their construal of situations than they will be at a later age. Having gone this far, the question that
comes next to hand is why the delay of gratification performance seemed a
particularly relevant one with which to test the behavioral consistency notion.
Does not this behavior require a high level of ego control? And are not
children rather developmentally unformed? On these bases alone, one would
not expect much behavioral consistency, to say nothing of the crucial question already raised about the ostensible and underlying meanings of behavior.

I do not think we will get very far attempting to answer such questions
with middle-level formulations. Unless we wish to be dangerously implicit in
our theorizing, we must realize the large number of assumptions that have to
be made to answer any one of the questions. And as the whole set of questions need to be answered in a compatible manner for the sake of internal
consistency, what is actually called for is a comprehensive theory of personality, situations, and behaviors. We may say we do not yet have one, but we
should not say we really do not need one.

A contemporary research area where the dangers of middle-level theorizing
are even more apparent is intrinsic motivation. The basic phenomenon studied is the paradoxical decrease in performance of a preferred activity, which
takes place when an external reward is imposed. Many investigators have
proposed explanations of this phenomenon. Deci (1971) suggests a cognitive
evaluation theory emphasizing that if a reinforcer is perceived as controlling
behavior from an external source, then intrinsic motivation for performing is
reduced. Kruglanski (1975) proposed endogenous versus exogenous attribution, focusing on the reasons for instead of the causes of behavior. Then there
is the overjustification hypothesis of Lepper and Greene (1975), stressing
how behavior originally justified by intrinsic motivation becomes over-
justified with the addition of extrinsic reinforcements. Reiss and Sushinsky
(1975) offered a competing response hypothesis suggesting that subjects will
be less interested in playful activities to the extent that extrinsic rewards elicit
responses that interfere with play responses. There is even a delay of gratification hypothesis (Ross, Karniol, & Rothstein, 1976), which focuses on the
inhibiting effects of delay between promise and receipt of reward.

The empirical studies done in furtherance of these various hypotheses are
intriguing and sophisticated. Each hypothesis has its own kind of empirical
support. But, as DeCharms and Muir (1978) conclude in their review, the
great bustle of activity in this area has led to little consensus or accumulated
sense of understanding, and the problem may be the insufficient theoretical
elaboration of the many proposed explanations. By and large, the various
hypotheses involve middle-level theorizing. As such, they are rich in unelabo-

rated and implicit assumptions. I suspect that at the underlying level of implicit assumptions there is considerable similarity in these hypotheses concerning personalities, situations, and behaviors. We will not make significant headway until we theorize more comprehensively. Agreeing, DeCharms and Muir (1978, p. 107) suggest that we cease overlooking

> our major source of knowledge—a personal, nonobjective source which is at the heart of each mini-theory but not acknowledged. . . . Sophisticated as we are in manipulating rewards and contingencies, we still do not know why or even if experiences are engaged in for intrinsic reasons. We have personal knowledge of experiences that some of us label intrinsically motivated, but we try to explain away the experience with more "objective" terms such as self-perception and attribution.

The message in this is that middle-level theorizing is too fragmenting and distracting for real understanding, however much it is the source of experiment after experiment.

Thus far, I have tried to expose the limitations of middle-level theorizing even when the phenomena under consideration are simple, carefully controlled, laboratory performances. Picture how much greater the limitation imposed by middle-level approaches in considering naturally occurring phenomena important for human welfare. Such phenomena are typically complicated and multidetermined. Studying such phenomena should be an impetus to comprehensive theorizing about personalities, situations, and behaviors. In this regard, it is not surprising that the call is heard from within the interactional movement for more theorizing (e.g., Magnusson & Endler, 1977).

How shall we arrive at comprehensive theorizing? DeCharms and Muir (1978) certainly make a useful suggestion concerning fresh attempts to glean from the rich intuitions of our private experience conceptualizations that go beyond middle-level conventionalities. Our experiences of ourselves, our friends, our enemies, our clients, and our families are not to be overlooked. But what of the grand personality theories that were so relied upon years ago and seem discredited now, at least outside some clinical settings? Are not these theories the result of scrupulous, painstaking attempts to glean the wealth contained in private experiences from the various sources I just mentioned? Why not use the research implications of these existing theories as one starting point? Most of them qualify as comprehensive, and that is a great advantage.

At least with regard to personality formulations, it is becoming clear what it means to be comprehensive. As I have argued elsewhere (Maddi, 1968/ 1980), to be comprehensive, personality theories need peripheral, developmental, and core propositions. The peripheral propositions cover the major styles of life that it is possible to encounter and the particular dispositions that combine to form styles. The dispositions constitute bases for perceiving situations in particular ways and acting accordingly. In that sense, they are interactional variables. There are also implications for the meaning of particular behaviors in the disposition concept and in the organization of dispositions into the more genotypical styles. The core propositions cover the essential, unlearned nature of human beings, structured as overall directional tendencies and whatever entities or characteristics they imply. The developmental propositions cover the manner in which interaction with the environment leads to particular learned styles and dispositions. Locked in the developmental propositions are many assumptions about the nature of societies, groups, the family, and the learning process. Research that is to be informed by one or more of these theories must take into account that they constitute an integration of core, developmental, and peripheral propositions. It is poor practice, therefore, to study an isolated disposition here, or a partial developmental hypothesis there. All aspects of research—including sampling, raw data, data collection procedures, data reduction, procedural design, data analysis, and inferences from findings—must reflect the investigators' sensitivity to the implications of the overall theoretical approach at hand. In this fashion, we will be able to avoid the seemingly infinite methodological perturbations whereby inconclusive research is generated, such as that I mentioned concerning intrinsic motivation. Further, we will have a more solid, because comprehensive, basis for studying the complex, naturally occuring phenomena that should be the heartland of psychology.

I can imagine your groans now. Personological research has so recently freed itself from the deadweight of these grand theories, you will comment, and here I am advocating a capitulation. As far as I can tell, these theories felt like deadweight for two main reasons: they appear too fuzzy to permit clear, empirically testable hypotheses and they disagree with one another to a degree that seems dismaying. It is, of course, very easy for these two complaints to amount to the conclusion that grand theories are unscientific.

Let us consider first the complaint of fuzziness. It must be admitted that the grand theories paint with such a broad brush that it is difficult to extrapolate hypotheses concrete enough to be easily tested in research. It is difficult but not at all impossible, I would contend. And the effort expended in deductive elaboration with a view toward finding just the right test of a theoretical proposition is indeed worthwhile. But deductive elaboration is sometimes done poorly enough that the resulting research has contributed to giving grand theories a bad name. For example, Mowrer's (1940) classic experiment supposedly demonstrating the defense mechanism of regression created more confusion than it solved. What he showed was that under unavoidable punishment, rats will give up a newly learned but no longer effective habit and revert to an earlier-learned but presently more effective habit.

This study is a travesty on Freudian theory. In that theory, regression is linked to the specifics of fixation and psychosexual development. Also, it is linked to the presumed psychosexual nature of the human. How, then, could anyone justify selecting rats as subjects? Did Freud think they had sexual and aggressive instincts and went through Oedipal conflicts and the other aspects of psychosexual development? And in Freud's formulation, the behaviors involved in regression bear a specifiable relationship to sexual expression. How can lever-pressing and jumping in a rat be believably traced to sexual expression? Notice that Mowrer does not even try. What we are presented is a behavioristically aseptic demonstration of response substitution masquerading as the only version of the regression hypothesis that can be empirically tested. As such, it gives Freudian theory an unnecessarily bad name. Could not human subjects have been used? Could not the stress employed have been something with psychosexual significance rather than an electric shock? And could not the behaviors observed be less contrived than lever-pressing, in hopes of observing something more relevant to sexual expressiveness? It is easy to conclude that Mowrer was simply not taking Freudian theory seriously enough to do the admittedly hard work of relevant deductive elaboration and research planning.

Nor is this study an isolated instance. Take as an example the burgeoning research these days on birth-order effects on behavior (e.g., Falbo, 1981; Schachter, 1963; Staffieri, 1970). It appears that the majority of college graduates are first-born children and that last-born children are more gregarious and creative; various other interesting tidbits of this sort are also reported. Although several of the research reports refer to Adler in passing, there appears little appreciation of the extensive, provocative, and important things he had to say about birth-order effects. His theorizing in this regard about family constellation (Adler, 1956) seems eminently testable to me and far richer as a basis for hypotheses than the commonsense notions that seem to inform present research in this area. In addition, combining his statements about family atmosphere (Adler, 1956) with those about family constellation leads one to predict for which individuals birth-order effects will be pronounced or debilitating. Once again, we see the advantage of comprehensive theorizing.

The other complaint, that the grand theories disagree with each other too much, has been recently voiced by Fiske (1974). He argues that the disagreements among personality theorists concerning the definition and usage of what should be semantically similar concepts is a major basis for invalidating the concepts themselves. If there is so much confusion as to what a concept is, then the behavioral consistency the concept purports to describe probably does not exist, and the concept itself is an obstacle to clear observation. In a recent review article, Sechrest (1976) takes a similar view in an extremely pessimistic portrayal of the field. To me, the grounds for all this pessimism do not seem compelling. Once one recognizes that the various concepts in a comprehensive theory influence each other as to meaning, it becomes less surprising that a concept called by the same name in two different theories may have somewhat different connotations. Further, it has to be odd for theoretical disagreements to be used as the basis for charges of unscientific status. With the emphasis shifting from isolated concepts to comprehensive theories, it becomes possible to deal with disagreements constructively through a comparative analytic process I have outlined elsewhere (Maddi, 1968/1980). An appropriate and practical way of defining personology these days is in terms of major issues separating theories as they attempt to explain phenomena. In this fashion, the posing and resolving of issues can be legitimized as a normal part of research activity.

In psychology, there is little by way of theorizing about the nature of situations and behaviors that is comparably comprehensive to what the grand personality theories accomplish for persons. Although these personality theories are fairly rich in connotations for situations and behaviors, there may well be need for additional conceptual effort directed squarely at these matters.

Shifting from Actuality toward Possibility

Most psychologists see their task as determining what is actually there. In the search for facts, they use experimental designs in which it is assumed that subjects are interchangeable and individual differences unimportant. They take averages and majorities as estimates of the one true score. Unusual cases are regarded as "outliers" and either transformed to be more in line with the others or actually discarded as accidental occurrences. In so many ways, the bias is expressed that the more common something or someone is found to be, the greater the likelihood that the observations are real (Maddi, 1980). The prescriptive implication of this is that we should emulate everything common and distrust everything else in ourselves. For most psychologists, this is the way of science.

But the only way it makes sense for us to emulate the majority of persons and actions is if they can convincingly be regarded as ideal. After all, when the commonplace is the standard, there is no longer any basis for the kind of change that would alter majorities and the social institutions supportive of them. I do not think very many of the same psychologists who pursue actuality would try to argue that the commonplace is ideal. More likely, they would regard it as all we have. This is too narrow a view of psychology and science. Consider instead Murray's reason for shifting from physiology to psychology. With typical eloquence, he (Murray, 1959, p. 11) says that influential in some degree [was] the impression . . . that human personality, because of its present sorry state, had become *the* problem of our time—a hive of conflicts, lonely, half-hollow, half-faithless, half-lost, half-neurotic, half-delinquent, not equal to the problems that confronted it, not very far from proving itself an evolutionary failure.

Recall also Murray's (1962) impassioned condemnation of psychology, couched in the form of a dream that came to him under psilocybin (remember the magic mushroom?) wherein psychology is on trial, sometime in the future and beyond the clouds, for having failed to help persons improve their lives enough to circumvent nuclear holocaust. Psychology is also found guilty but not punished on the grounds that it was still so insecure of its status that it pursued a trivializingly narrow model of science, lest it be regarded as too loose.

Perhaps in the 1980s psychology will not be so immature. Among the fields of psychology, personology carries within itself the seeds of the needed corrective—a psychology of possibility (Maddi, 1980). It emphasizes individual differences, and that is an essential ingredient. If it also focuses upon phenomena important to human welfare, then the stage is set. Studies will identify individuals who are better off than others with regard to one or more important phenomena. Although those persons fortunate enough to be better off on many phenomena are bound to be few in number, they will be very important to understand. Once hypotheses explaining their good fortune have been derived from comprehensive theories and confirmed empirically, we will understand how they became what they are. Prescriptively, they can serve as models for the rest of us, and we will have bases for facilitatory reforms of education, child rearing, and psychotherapy. We will then have a true psychology of possibility without having abandoned science.

Some of you may object to this advocacy of the goodness and badness of phenomena on the grounds that science should be value-free. But the blunt reality is that psychology is an inherently ethical endeavor. Does Mischel study delay of gratification because he thinks it is neither good nor bad? Do those who study intrinsic motivation consider it neither good nor bad? And does Bandura spend so much time studying aggression and efficacy because they are neither good nor bad? Of course not. As researchers, we never operate in a value-free space. We should not be so critical, therefore, of the grand personality theories for delineating ideal and nonideal styles of life. Understood in the context of the inevitability of value judgments, these delineations are actually useful for their explicitness and theoretical sophistication. They go beyond the conventionality of common sense, serving as a guide for scrutiny and potential improvement of individuals and social institutions (Gergen, 1978; Moscovici, 1972; Tajfel, 1972). Thus, another reason for reconsidering the grand theories is the importance of developing a psychology of possibility.

As an illustration of how the psychology of possibility would work, consider what we know about the course of intimate relationships. Psychological research on this topic has been summarized (Gergen & Gergen, 1981) as indicating that passionate love results from high physiological arousal coupled with social cues that the associated person is attractive (Schachter, 1964). As the relationship consolidates, passion is regarded as receding, to be replaced by mutuality and stability (Levinger & Snoek, 1972). But with further prolongation, expressions of affection, sexuality, self-disclosure, and satisfaction decrease, the relationship becoming rather perfunctory (Blood & Wolfe, 1960). These conclusions are reached on the basis of averages, and fit well the common sense of our culture. But an investigator could—indeed, Blood and Wolfe (1960) did—identify among couples with long-standing intimate relationships those few that still showed vitality and closeness, in an attempt to understand how the usual atrophy was avoided. These investigators mention a factor or two, such as equality in decision-making power and division of labor, but fail to provide convincing overall understanding. They might have profited from recourse to such relevant comprehensive theories as existential psychology (Kobasa & Maddi, 1977), in which choosing the future constitutes a basis for renewal in relationships, or the individual psychology of Adler (1956), in which attempts to perfect oneself and others through the same set of actions is emphasized. Such a theoretically guided study of rare relationships could provide for the rest of us a sense of possibility in meaningful, long-term relationships of intimacy.

Conclusion: Implementing the Recommendations

To recapitulate, I have advocated multivariate, longitudinal study of significant human problems, in which explanatory effort expresses comprehensive theorizing and aims at models for the betterment of life. Because of the obvious practical complications involved, implementing these recommendations would mean research programs becoming larger but also fewer in number, with considerable coordination of investigators into teams or consortia. For the same reasons, published research reports would become more elaborate and extensive, but once again fewer and multiauthored.

On a day-to-day basis, the ongoing research activities of personologists would become, if anything, more rewarding. The teams and consortia, coupled with the longitudinal nature of the research, would lend a sense of scientific community which has been generally lacking since the heyday of Murray's annex. The emphasis on multivariate study and comprehensive understanding would foster a sense of intellectual completion. And focusing upon significant phenomena and possibilities for human betterment would be pragmatically satisfying. Thus, we would fashion a personology of sufficient vitality to carry us through the years ahead.

The danger in the plan is that it renders more difficult the flood of individually authored papers whereby investigators have heretofore made their reputations and ensured academic tenure. This is a significant obstacle, pinpointed forthrightly by Robert W. White (1981) in the Murray lectures presented in 1978. But I do not think we should let it hamper the development of personology. After all, fewer publications of greater scope and importance may indeed be a better way to have a long-run influence, and that prospect, properly understood, should cheer the individual investigator. As to the problem of academic tenure, those of us already in secure and influential positions need to educate department chairpersons and divisional deans about the unique contribution personology needs to make within the behavioral and social sciences, and how the reform of criteria for judging performance in this area can facilitate reaching that potential by rewarding young researchers for taking a chance on studies that are significant rather than merely numerous.

I have been very abstract in this discussion. Actually, there are some research programs currently in operation that fulfill reasonably well the recommendations I have made. Lest my position seem empty idealism, let me mention one of these research programs that I know the best. It was initiated by Suzanne C. Kobasa, then a graduate student and now a faculty member at the University of Chicago. As the project grew to proportions too large for any one investigator, I joined in, as did what is by now a close-knit, spirited group of 15 graduate assistants. The work has been funded for several years by the National Institute of Mental Health.

As to the first recommendation, the main phenomenon under investigation in this research program has been health–illness status, a conglomerate of physical and mental symptoms that certainly qualifies as a significant matter for human welfare. From the beginning, Kobasa's (1979) aim was to improve the modest but reliable ability to predict health–illness status from the stressful events in the person's life. Her inclusion of the personality style of hardiness as a moderator in the stress–illness relationship is consistent with the recommendation I made that multiple explanatory variables be studied. It is also relevant in this regard that stressful life events was measured both by social consensus (alpha press) and more subjectively (beta press). Further, several other possible moderators of the stress–illness relationship were also included (e.g., social supports, health practices, and constitutional predisposition). Since the first testing of our sample of business executives, which constituted Kobasa's (1979) Ph.D. dissertation, yearly retesting ses-

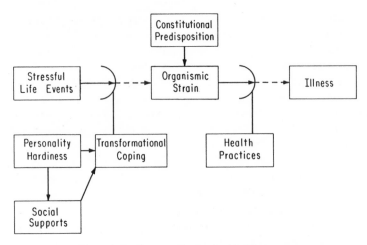

Figure 1.1   Factors affecting health–illness status.

sions have been carried out. Thus, the research program fulfills another of the recommendations by adding a longitudinal dimension of study.

Constituting a start on the recommendation for comprehensive theorizing, Kobasa (1979) viewed hardiness as a combination of the dispositions of commitment (vs. alienation), control (vs. powerlessness) and challenge (vs. threat), with the whole position derived from a more extensive existential personality theory. Briefly, this theory (Kobasa & Maddi, 1977) emphasizes the decision-making process at the core level, learning the rudiments of courage at the developmental level, and authentic versus conformist styles at the peripheral level. Hardiness is an adaptation of courage for coping with stressful events (Maddi, in press). Also relevant concerning comprehensive theorizing is a model (Figure 1.1) that relates the explanatory variables to each other and to illness. This model (Kobasa, 1982c) makes organismic strain the result of a complex interaction between stressful events and various moderating factors. Hardiness protects against strain both directly, through instigating transformational coping, and indirectly, through provoking a use of social supports that also facilitates this kind of coping. Transformational coping decreases the stressfulness of events by optimistic cognitive appraisal and decisive actions, which together alter the events and their sequels. We believe that, in contrast, persons low in hardiness engage, directly and in their use of social supports, in much more regressive coping, which involves pessimistic cognitive appraisal of stressful events and passive, avoidant actions. The minimal buffering effect of regressive coping permits organismic strain to mount and, if nothing else intervenes, when strain is sufficiently intense and prolonged, illness will result. The person's constitutional predisposition to illness determines the level of strain that is sufficient to undermine. Also, we believe that health practices, such as exercise and dieting, have a buffering effect by acting to reduce already present organismic strain, rather than by altering the stressfulness of events.

Although I cannot possibly detail the extensive results we have obtained in the last 7 years, a brief overview of major findings may suggest the power in research programs of this sort. In her dissertation, Kobasa (1979) showed that when there are many stressful events, health is better preserved if attitudes of commitment, control, and challenge are strong. Subsequently, Kobasa, Maddi, and Kahn (1982) combined time-lag data and analysis of covariance techniques controlling for prior level of illness to demonstrate that this buffering effect is indeed prospective. Hardiness has emerged as empirically independent of constitutional predisposition and exercise, but as mildly related to social supports. Kobasa, Maddi, and Courington (1981) showed that constitutional predisposition increases the likelihood of illness in the face of stressful events about as much as hardiness decreases it. Kobasa, Maddi, and Puccetti (1982) reported that exercise and hardiness have about equal buffering effects on stressful events and augment each other interactionally. As expected, Kobasa and Puccetti (in press) found the picture more complicated with regard to the widely claimed buffering effect of social supports. There is indeed evidence that subjects high in hardiness make more effective use of social support in buffering stressful events; but among subjects low in hardiness, the presence of social support is actually debilitating as stressful events mount. In organizing the various results together, we have considered stressful events and other mediating variables to be liabilities and assets with regard to health–illness status. In our sample, as liabilities mount and assets decrease, the probability of being high (above the median) in illness goes from 9 to 90% (Kobasa, Maddi, Zola, and Puccetti, 1983). This is a 10-fold increase in illness likelihood, certainly formidable evidence of predictability.

Lately, the research program has branched out in three additional directions, all now justified given the basic findings already obtained. In one direction, Kobasa (1982a, 1982b) is investigating the generality of the model shown in Figure 1.1 for women and for occupational groups such as lawyers, army officers, and priests. In the occupational emphasis, Kobasa's concern is with the differing role of hardiness and other moderating variables across various social institutions. A second direction elaborates hardiness as a personality style in ways that are conceptually important. Findings link hardiness at the physiological level to relatively low blood pressure, and at the psychological level to positive moods, exploratory behavior, alertness, and transformational rather than regressive coping (Kobasa, Maddi, Donner, Merrick, & White, 1983; Maddi, Hoover, & Kobasa, 1982). We also have interviews, experiential samplings, and thematic apperception stories on the subjects, although data analysis is just beginning. Finally, a third direction involves experimental intervention, whereby group training sessions are being used in the attempt to increase hardiness while decreasing various signs of illness risk. These experiments, coupled with interview data concerning past experience, may provide a basis for understanding how stress-resistant subjects got to be that way. Hopefully, this particular effort will culminate in a prescriptive basis for helping others to remain healthy despite stressful lives, thereby fulfilling the last of my recommendations.

I have tried to give you some concrete sense of what a currently viable personological research program would look like. That I have been involved in this program is relevant to these lectures. I was one of Kobasa's teachers; she is now the teacher of our research assistants. As Henry Murray was my teacher, his guiding spirit now extends to the fourth and even fifth generation of his far-flung band of students.

Acknowledgments

Suzanne C. Kobasa and the graduate students who form our research team have my gratitude for the many kinds of help they contributed to this chapter.

References

Adler, A. *The individual psychology of Alfred Adler* (Ansbacher, H. L., & Ansbacher, R., Eds.). New York: Basic Books, 1956.

Alker, H. A. Beyond ANOVA psychology in the study of person–situation interactions. In D. Magnusson & N. S. Endler (Eds.), *Personality at the crossroads: Current issues in interactional psychology*. New York: Wiley, 1977.

Allport, G. W. *Personality: A psychological interpretation*. New York: Holt, 1937.

Allport, G. W. The historical background of modern social psychology. In G. Luidey (Ed.), *Handbook of social psychology* (Vol. 1). Cambridge, MA: Addison–Wesley, 1954.

Allport, G. W. *Pattern and growth in personality*. New York: Holt Rinehart Winston, 1961.

Bem, D. J., & Allen, A. On predicting some of the people some of the time: The search for cross-situational consistencies in behavior. *Psychological Review*, 1974, *81*, 506–520.

Bem, D. J., & Funder, D. C. Predicting more of the people more of the time: Assessing the personality of situations. *Psychological Review*, 1978, *85*, 485–501.

Block, J. *Lives through Time*. Berkeley, CA: Bancroft, 1971.

Blood, R. O., & Wolfe, D. M. *Husbands and wives: The dynamics of modern living*. New York: Free Press, 1960.

Bowers, K. S. Situationism in psychology: An analysis and a critique. *Psychological Review*, 1973, *80*, 307–336.

Bowers, K. S. There's more to Iago than meets the eye: A clinical account of personal consistency. In D. Magnusson & N. S. Endler (Eds.), *Personality at the Crossroads: Current issues in interactional psychology*. New York: Wiley, 1977.

Brown, R. *Social psychology*. New York: Free Press, 1965.

Butterfield, H. *The origins of modern science*. New York: Free Press, 1957.

Carlson, R. Where is the person in personality research? *Psychological Bulletin*, 1971, *75*, 203–219.

Carlson, R. Personality. In M. R.Rosenzweig & L. W. Porter (Eds.), *Annual review of psychology*. Palo Alto, CA: Annual Reviews, 1975.

Cronbach, L. J. The two disciplines of scientific psychology. *American Psychologist*, 1957, *12*, 671–684.

Cronbach, L. J., & Meehl, P. E. Construct validity in psychological tests. *Psychological Bulletin*, 1955, *52*, 281–302.

DeCharms, R. C., Morrison, H. W., Reitman, W., & McClelland, D. C. Behavioral correlates of directly and indirectly measured achievement motivation. In D. C. McClelland (Ed.), *Studies in motivation*. New York: Appleton–Century–Crofts, 1955.

DeCharms, R. C., & Muir, M. S. Motivation: Social approaches. In M. R. Rosenzweig & L. W. Porter (Eds.), *Annual review of psychology*. Palo Alto, CA: Annual Reviews, 1978.

Deci, E. L. The effects of externally mediated rewards on intrinsic motivation. *Journal of Personality and Social Psychology*, 1971, *18*, 105–115.

Duncan, S. D. Jr., & Fiske, D. W. *Face to face interaction: Research methods and theory*. Hillsdale, NJ: Erlbaum, 1977.

Epstein, S. Traits are alive and well. In D. Magnusson & N. S. Endler (Eds.), *Personality at the crossroads: Current issues in interactional psychology*. New York: Wiley, 1977.

Falbo, T. Relationships between birth category, achievement, and interpersonal orientation. *Journal of Personality and Social Psychology*, 1981, *41*, 121–131.

Feshbach, S., & Weiner, B. *Personality*. Lexington, Mass.: D. C. Heath, 1982.

Fiske, D. W. The limits for the conventional science of personality. *Journal of Personality*, 1974, *42*, 1–11.

Fiske, D. W. Personologies, abstractions, and interactions. In D. Magnusson & N. S. Endler (Eds.), *Personality at the crossroads: Current issues in interactional Psychology*. New York: Wiley, 1977.

Fiske, D. W. *Strategies for research in personality: Observation vs. interpretation of behavior*. San Francisco: Jossey-Bass, 1978.

Folkman, S., & Lazarus, R. S. An analysis of coping in a middle-aged community sample. *Journal of Health and Social Behavior*, 1980, *21*, 219–239.

Freud, S. *The psychopathology of everyday life* (Vol. 6, std. ed.). London: Hogarth, 1960.

Gergen, K. J. Toward generative theory. *Journal of Personality and Social Psychology*, 1978, *36*, 1344–1360.

Gergen, K. J., & Gergen, M. M. *Social psychology*. New York: Harcourt Brace Jovanovich, 1981.

James, W. *Principles of psychology*. New York: Holt, 1890.

Kobasa, S. C. Stressful life events, personality and health: An inquiry into hardiness. *Journal of Personality and Social Psychology*, 1979, *37*, 1–11.

Kobasa, S. C. Barriers to work stress: II. The "hardy" personality. In D. Gentry (Ed.), *Behavioral medicine: Work, stress and health*. Stockholm, Sweden: Sijthoff & Nordhoff, 1982. (a)

Kobasa, S. C. Commitment and coping in stress resistance among lawyers. *Journal of Personality and Social Psychology*, 1982, *42*, 707–717. (b)

Kobasa, S. C. The personality and social psychology of stress and health. In J. Suls & G. Sanders (Eds.), *Social psychology of stress and illness*. Hillsdale, NJ: Erlbaum, 1982. (c)

Kobasa, S. C., & Maddi, S. R. Existential personality theory. In R. Corsini (Ed.), *Current personality theory*. Itasca, IL: Peacock, 1977.

Kobasa, S. C., Maddi, S. R., & Courington, S. Personality and constitution as mediators in the stress– illness relationship. *Journal of Health and Social Behavior*, 1981, *22*, 368–378.

Kobasa, S. C., Maddi, S. R., Donner, E., Merrick, W. A., White, H., & Zola, M. A. *The personality construct of hardiness.* Unpublished manuscript, 1983.

Kobasa, S. C., Maddi, S. R., & Kahn, S. Hardiness and health: A prospective study. *Journal of Personality and Social Psychology*, 1982, *42*, 168–177.

Kobasa, S. C., Maddi, S. R., & Puccetti, M. Personality and exercise as buffers in the stress–illness relationship. *Journal of Behavioral Medicine*, 1982, *4*, 391–404.

Kobasa, S. C., Maddi, S. R., Zola, M. A., & Puccetti, M. *The effectiveness of hardiness, exercise and social support as resources against illness.* Unpublished manuscript, 1983.

Kobasa, S. C., & Puccetti, M. Personality and social support in stress resistance. *Journal of Personality and Social Psychology*, in press.

Kruglanski, A. W. The endogenous–exogenous partition in attribution theory. *Psychological Review*, 1975, *82*, 387–406.

Kuhn, T. S. *The structure of scientific revolutions.* Chicago: Univ. of Chicago Press, 1962.

Lepper, M. R., & Greene, D. Turning play into work: Effects of adult surveillance and extrinsic rewards on children's intrinsic motivation. *Journal of Personality and Social Psychology*, 1975, *31*, 479–486.

Levinger, G., & Snoek, J. D. *Attraction in relationships: A new look at interpersonal attraction.* Morristown, NJ: General Learning Press, 1972.

Levinson, D. J. Exploration in biography: Evolution of the individual life structure in adulthood. In A. I. Rabin, J. Aronoff, A. M. Barclay, & R. A. Zucker (Eds.), *Further explorations in personality.* New York: Wiley, 1981.

Maddi, S. R. Humanistic psychology. In J. M. Wepman & R. W. Heine (Eds.), *Concepts of personality.* Chicago: Aldine, 1963.

Maddi, S. R. *Personality theories: A comparative analysis* (1st and 4th eds.). Homewood, IL: Dorsey, 1968, 1980.

Maddi, S. R. The uses of theorizing in personology. In E. Staub (Ed.), *Personality: Basic aspects and current research.* Englewood Cliffs, NJ: Prentice–Hall, 1980.

Maddi, S. R. Existential psychotherapy. In J. Garske & S. Lynn (Eds.), *Contemporary psychotherapy.* Englewood Cliffs, NJ: Prentice–Hall, in press.

Maddi, S. R., & Costa, P. T., Jr. *Humanism in personology: Allport, Maslow and Murray.* Chicago: Aldine, 1972.

Maddi, S. R., Hoover, M., & Kobasa, S. C. Alienation and exploratory behavior. *Journal of Personality and Social Psychology*, 1982, *42*, 884–890.

Magnusson, D., & Endler, N. S. Interactional psychology: Present status and future prospects. In D. Magnusson & N. S. Endler (Eds.), *Personality at the crossroads: Current issues in interactional psychology.* New York: Wiley, 1977.

McClelland, D. C. *Personality.* New York: Dryden, 1951.

McClelland, D. C. *The achieving society.* Princeton, NJ: Van Nostrand, 1961.

McClelland, D. C. Is personality consistent? In A. I. Rabin, J. Aronoff, A. M. Barclay, & R. A. Zucker (Eds.), *Further explorations in personality.* New York: Wiley, 1981.

McClelland, D. C., Atkinson, J. W., Clark, R. A., & Lowell, E. L. *The achievement motive.* New York: Appleton–Century–Crofts, 1953.

Mischel, W. *Personality and assessment.* New York: Wiley, 1968.

Mischel, W. Toward a cognitive social learning reconceptualization of personality. *Psychological Review*, 1973, *80*, 252–283.

Mischel, W. *Introduction to personality* (2nd ed.). New York: Holt Rinehart Winston, 1976.

Mischel, W. The interaction of person and situation. In D. Magnusson & N. S. Endler (Eds.), *Personality at the crossroads: Current issues in interactional psychology.* New York: Wiley, 1977.

Mischel, W., & Peake, P. In search of consistency: Measure for measure. In M. P. Zanna, E. T. Higgins, & C. P. Herman (Eds.), *Consistency in social behavior: The Ontario conference of personality and social psychology* (Vol. 2). Hillsdale, NJ: Erlbaum, 1981.

Moscovici, S. Society and theory in social psychology. In J. Israel & H. Tajfel (Eds.), *The context of social psychology: A critical assessment*. New York: Academic Press, 1972.

Mowrer, O. H. An experimental analogue of "regression" with incidental observations on "reaction formation." *Journal of Abnormal and Social Psychology*, 1940, *35*, 56–87.

Murray, H. A. *Explorations in personality: A clinical and experimental study of fifty men of college age.* New York: Oxford Univ. Press, 1938.

Murray, H. A. Toward a classification of interaction. In T. Parsons & E. A. Shils (Eds.), *Toward a general theory of action*. Cambridge, MA: Harvard Univ. Press, 1954.

Murray, H. A. Preparations for the scaffold of a comprehensive system. In S. Koch (Ed.), *Psychology: A study of a science* (Vol. 3). New York: McGraw-Hill, 1959.

Murray, H. A. Prospect for psychology. *Science,* 1962, *136,* No. 3515, 483–488.

Neisser, U. *Cognition and reality.* San Francisco: Freeman, 1976.

Olweus, D. *Aggression in the schools.* New York: Halsted, 1978.

Polanyi, M. *Personal knowledge: Toward a post-critical philosophy.* New York: Harper, 1964.

Putnam, H. *Reason, truth and history.* Cambridge, England: Cambridge Univ. Press, 1981.

Raush, H. L. Paradox levels, and junctures in person-situation systems. In D. Magnusson & N. S. Endler (Eds.), *Personality at the crossroads: Current issues in interactional psychology.* New York: Wiley, 1977.

Reiss, S., & Sushinsky, L. W. Overjustification, competing responses, and the acquisition of intrinsic interest. *Journal of Personality and Social Psychology,* 1975, *31,* 116–125.

Rogers, C. R. *On becoming a person.* Boston: Houghton Mifflin, 1961.

Rogosa, D. R. A critique of cross-lagged correlation. *Psychological Bulletin,* 1980, *88,* 245–258.

Ross, M., Karniol, R., & Rothstein, M. Reward contingency and intrinsic motivation in children: A test of the delay of gratification hypothesis. *Journal of Personality and Social Psychology,* 1976, *33,* 442–447.

Schachter, S. Birth order, eminence, and higher education. *American Sociological Review,* 1963, *28,* 757–767.

Schachter, S. The interaction of cognitive and physiological determinants of emotional state. In L. Berkowitz (Ed.), *Advances in experimental social psychology* (Vol. 1). New York: Academic Press, 1964.

Sechrest, L. Personality. In M. R. Rosenszweig & L. W. Porter (Eds.), *Annual review of psychology.* Palo Alto, CA: Annual Reviews, 1976.

Staffieri, J. R. Birth order and creativity. *Journal of Clinical Psychology,* 1970, *26,* 65–66.

Tajfel, H. Experiments in a vacuum. In J. Israel and H. Tajfel (Eds.), *The context of social psychology: A critical assessment.* New York: Academic Press, 1972.

White, R. W. *Lives in progress: A study of the natural growth of personality.* New York: Dryden, 1952.

White, R. W. Exploring personality the long way: The study of lives. In A. I. Rabin, J. Aronoff, A. M. Barclay, & R. A. Zucker (Eds.), *Further Explorations in Personality.* New York: Wiley, 1981.

2

On the Self and Predicting Behavior*

Jane Loevinger

Introduction: Must We Predict?

The topic of this volume is the contribution of personality theory to the prediction of behavior. Let me enter a demurrer to that assignment: Prediction is not everything, especially if one begins, as I do, with Egon Brunswik's (1952) conceptual framework of psychology. In this chapter, I demonstrate that important elements of Brunswik's view are shared by Henry Murray (1938). Next I discuss why personality traits seem unable to predict behavior, showing that this conclusion follows from the premises of Brunswik and Murray. As a substitute for trait theory, a theory of the self is emerging. I then present a précis of my own version of ego- or self-development stages, after which I deal with criticism from the Centralists and the Peripheralists, to borrow Murray's terms.

Must behavior be predicted? The idea that the psychologist must aim to predict behavior—predict and control is the usual phrase—has a utilitarian, almost technocratic ring. Surely *Explorations in Personality* (Murray, 1938) was aiming elsewhere, at depth of understanding. As Murray remarked, if one has a deep understanding, some otherwise enigmatic behaviors become predictable, but that is different from saying that prediction is the original purpose of investigating personality.

There are many obstacles to predicting behavior. One of those is the

*Preparation of this paper was assisted by a grant from the Spencer Foundation. The research reported here was supported by Grants M-1213 and MH-05115 and by Research Scientist Award MH-00657, all from the National Institute of Mental Health, U.S. Public Health Service.

obdurate originality and creativity of the human being. Govern conditions ever so carefully, and still someone will surprise you. Redmore (1976), for example, studied several times what would happen to our Sentence Completion Test (SCT) of ego development when individuals were asked to "fake good" or "fake bad" or to make a good or bad impression. I doubt that we have ever done such an experiment without at least one person clearly doing the opposite of what he or she was instructed to do—a phenomenon that no one else has acknowledged, so far as I know. Yet that creativity, as exasperating as it may be at times, is also one of the lovable things about our species. At best, then, we predict only probable behavior.

The question really is not, Can we predict perfectly? but, Can we predict any better than chance? Prediction a little better than chance does not give significant control, but it may signify or lead to understanding process. Poorly designed research or research done with too few cases to detect the effects being sought is guaranteed to yield negative results, as Block (1977) has persuasively argued. Examples showing that personality variables do not predict behavior are easy to produce—nothing could be easier.

On the other hand, if you wish to do good research on personality, you have to cope with a high degree of complexity—to wit, several variables measured in depth, each for that reason accounting for relatively little variance, hence requiring many cases to establish significant effects. The sheer economics of the situation dissuades some people from trying, but most researchers do try, except for one thing—getting enough cases. The importance of having enough cases is belittled for the very reasons it should be specially emphasized: namely, the complexity and variety of data.

Models of Behavior: Brunswik and Murray

Egon Brunswik was thinking about these problems at the time that Murray was working on *Explorations*. Brunswik, like Murray, had a large vision of psychology—something we often lose today, as we pursue our individual miniparadigms. (In arguing against construct validity, Maddi [Chapter 1, this volume] is, I suspect, really aiming at miniparadigms.) Brunswik showed how all systems of psychology could be depicted in terms of his *lens model* of psychology (Hammond, 1966). The basic element of the lens model is the schematic lens shown in Figure 2.1. Brunswik and Tolman (Tolman & Brunswik, 1935) found that this model described the work of both, Brunswik's on perceptual constancies and Tolman's on molar behavior and learning, or, as Hull (1934) called it, "habit family hierarchies." The point of the

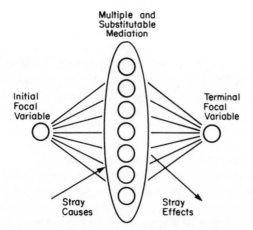

Figure 2.1   The lens model. From "The Conceptual Framework of Psychology," by E. Brunswik. In O. Neurath, R. Carnap, & C. Morris (Eds.), *International Encyclopedia of Unified Science* (Vol. 1, pt. 2). © 1952 by the University of Chicago. Reprinted by permission.

lens model is that causes and effects can be reliably related even when the mediating mechanisms are not fixed. There are alternative, mutually substitutable means, each of which is connected with cause or effect by only a low probability. Yet the connection between the distal causes and effects may be one of high probability.

The stream of behavior can be diagrammed in terms of two lenses, one on the perceptual side and one on the action side, as in Figure 2.2. When a child is looking at a piece of candy on a table, the candy is the distal stimulus, the pattern of light rays striking the retina is the proximal stimulus, the retinal image the peripheral perception, the movements of arms and legs as the child moves toward the table and reaches out are the proximal (or peripheral) responses, and eating the candy is the distal effect, or, as Brunswik would say, the "achievement." The "central layer" is the child's recognition of the candy and desire to eat it. Put a child in a room with the candy, and it is safer to predict that the candy will disappear than that any particular movement will be made by the child. In fact, at one time Brunswik felt that we could create a perfectly good "psychology without the organism," entirely in terms of distal causes and effects (1943). Later he became increasingly interested in what he called the "central layer," the constructs hypothesized within the organism to account for distal effects (Hammond, 1966). Throughout, he maintained that psychology should concentrate its efforts and its constructs not on the lens but on its focal points, that is, at the layer of the distal stimulus (i.e., the perceived stimulus), the distal effects (i.e., achievements), and the central layer, within the organism.

Rereading *Explorations*, I find that Murray was thinking in similar terms. (Both men, by the way, owed much to Heider's metapsychology.) Murray classified all personologists into two types—the centralists and the peripheralists. I will discuss some of his characterizations of these types later. He referred to the proximal–peripheral layer on the response side as "actones," a word that has not gained much currency, and he gave numerous reasons why the concepts of psychology should not be focused on that layer: "Practical experience has led me to believe that . . . classification [of conduct] in terms of effects organizes for our understanding something that is more fundamental than what is organized by the classification in terms of actones" (Murray, 1938, p. 56). Murray's argument against operational definition of need was exactly Brunswik's argument against being preoccupied with the lens of behavior.

One might suppose that the primary concern of personologists was the central layer, but there are and probably always have been and always will be those who, like Fiske (1978), think that the only way to be a true scientist is to concentrate on the lens itself. That is what Brunswik, following Alfred North Whitehead, called "misconceptions of exactitude."

Here is how Murray characterized the peripheralists:

> They are attracted to clearly observable things and qualities—simple deliverances of sense organs—and they usually wish to confine the data of personology to these. They stand upon the acknowledged fact that, as compared to other functions, the perceptions, particularly the visual perceptions—of different individuals are relatively similar, and hence agreement on this basis is attainable. . . . Since without agreement there is no science, they believe that if they stick to measurable facts they are more likely to make unquestionable contributions. Thus, for them the data are: environmental objects and physically responding organisms: bodily movements, verbal successions, physiological changes. . . . [They] usually come out with a list of common action patterns or expressive movements, though occasionally they go further and include social traits and interests. . . . The implicit supposition of this class of scientists is that an external stimulus, or the perception of it, is the origination of everything psychological [Murray, 1938, pp. 6–7].

Evidently the early writings of the social learning theorists also fall within Murray's category of peripheralists.

The peripheralists have had a heyday in recent years. They have attracted an enormous following among young psychologists, as Murray foresaw— even crying down the possibilities of personality psychology as contrasted with situational determinants of behavior. Recently, however, there has been a vigorous countermovement, whose tenets are in accord with the principles of Murray and Brunswik.

The attack on probabilistic approaches to personality has also come from the centralists, as Murray also foresaw. An interesting new example is that of Kohlberg (1981). He is not an intuitionist or a dynamicist, to use Murray's terms for certain of the centralists. But Kohlberg does believe, as does the typical centralist, that, in Murray's words, "by listening to the form and content of other people's speech" he will be "led directly" to the structure of their mental processes (Murray, 1938, p. 8).

Kohlberg harbors the illusion that whereas other testers see in a glass darkly what they aim to measure, he sees face-to-face. His way of stating this is to utilize Goodenough's (1949) distinction between test responses as signs and as samples. Referring to the structure of moral judgment, which his test aims to measure, Kohlberg states "The hypothetical structure is the principle of organization of the responses" (1981, p. 15), rather than an inferred entity.

> The responses of subjects to the dilemmas and their subsequent responses to clinical probing are taken to *reflect, exhibit,* or *manifest* the structure. They are the realizations of the "archetypal" structure in actuality, under special conditions. There may be disagreement by investigators concerning the correctness of the attribution of a certain structure, given certain responses (i.e., interrater reliability questions), but *there can be no error in the sense of a mistake in inferring* from a judgment to some state of affairs concurrent with, precedent to, or subsequent to the judgment. Thus, my procedure is not of the same order as that which one adopts in predicting from . . . an item on the MMPI to the conclusion of schizophrenia or hypochondriasis. [In the latter case] one is dealing not with reflections, exhibitions, or manifestations but with indices or signs [Kohlberg, 1981, p. 15; last emphasis added].

In terms of Figure 2.2, Kohlberg believes that he sees directly into the central layer.

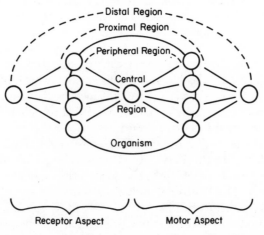

Figure 2.2 The functional unit of behavior. From "The Conceptual Framework of Psychology," by E. Brunswik. In O. Neurath, R. Carnap, & C. Morris (Eds.), *International Encyclopedia of Unified Science* (Vol. 1, pt. 2). © 1952 by the University of Chicago. Adapted by permission.

Thus both the peripheralists and the centralists want to deny or escape the fact that psychology is at best a probabilistic science; they are on what Dewey called a "quest for certainty." Brunswik pointed out that this is basically a hopeless, fruitless, and unpsychological quest:

> The probabilistic character of behavioral laws is not primarily due to limitations in the researcher and his means of approach but rather to imperfections inherent in the potentialities of adjustment on the part of the behaving organism living in a semi-chaotic environmental medium. In this sense even an omniscient infinite intellect, when turning psychologist, would have to adopt a probabilistic approach [Brunswik, 1952, p. 686].

Prediction by Traits

For many years it was assumed that traits were the dispositional constructs of choice "within" the organism. ("Within" is, of course, a metaphor, here meaning "pertaining to"; it is a metaphor, however, that is consonant with the Brunswik model of the organism and of the stream of behavior.)

If we put in Brunswik's terms the trait–situation controversy (now somewhat obsolete, as Loevinger and Knoll, 1983, point out), we see that the "proofs" that traits do not exist or that they fail to predict anything came in large part from concentrating on the lens of the lens model rather than on the foci, where the correlations are focused. Block's (1977) and Epstein's (1979, 1980b) suggestions that several alternative manifestations or several occasions of a given behavioral disposition be cumulated to arrive at predictive or predictable measures are one way of moving away from the lens toward its focus. If one thinks that "behavior" is predicted only when one has predicted the proximal–peripheral layer in Brunswik's model, then indeed behavior is not being predicted by the Block–Epstein device—which, of course, is the classic formula of psychometrics, first explained by Spearman in 1904.

Somehow, personality psychologists have failed to rally behind each others' banners with regard to lists of traits, which suggests that apart from the problem of prediction, all is not well for trait theory. Quite a few people do like Cattell's (1965) 16 PF (Personality Factor) traits; others find his neologisms indigestible and cut off from too many other significant insights and lines of research. His "universal index" of traits has not been universally adopted. Other trait theories have attracted equally specialized followings. All told, the number of traits that one or another psychologist thinks worth measuring must come close to a thousand, though not approaching the order of magnitude of Allport and Odbert's (1936) original estimate of 18,000 trait names.

The reason for the plethora of traits may be that not all people have every trait as an organized, coherent disposition. Kenrick and Stringfield (1980) provide evidence on this point. Beginning with common-language translations of Cattell's 16 PF traits, subjects were asked to nominate those most characteristic of themselves. On those self-selected consistent traits, their own judgment of where they rated on the trait correlated highly with their parents' and peers' judgments of where they rated. Correlations of own ratings with ratings by parents and peers were lower on traits they did not say were consistent.

Allport (1961) said that there were universal traits and unique traits. But he also recognized traits that characterize some but not all people. The Kenrick and Stringfield study, like the study of Conrad (1932) that Allport cited, is evidence for traits that characterize some but not all people. Dare we say this is evidence for types of people?

Self Theory

Whereas trait theory is, if not played out, winding down a bit, an alternative model for the central layer, self theory, is attracting an increasing number of adherents. To a remarkable extent many recent theorists have moved toward a model of the self that is virtually identical to Sullivan's (1953), which might be called the "anxiety-gating theory of the self." The Sullivanians include Epstein (1980a), and, with slight changes in terminology and provenance, Block (1982), Golding (1978), and Greenwald (1980). The philosophers Merleau-Ponty (1942/1963) and Fingarette (1963) enunciated basically the same theory some years ago, and Kuhn's (1962) theory of scientific revolutions has the same formal structure (Loevinger, 1976).

Let me put the theory in my words: What Sullivan calls the "self-system" acts as a kind of filter, template, or frame of reference for one's perception and conception of the interpersonal world. Any observations not consonant with one's current frame of reference cause anxiety; therefore, to avoid or attenuate the anxiety, such perceptions are either distorted so as to fit the preexisting system or they are "selectively inattended to," in Sullivan's phrase. Sullivan would go farther and say that the self system arises in the first place as a device for minimizing and managing anxiety in interpersonal relations.

There are, of course, many other ways of looking at self, ego, the I, and the me. Indeed, many psychologists operate with a pantheon, having separate definitions for two or three or four of those entities. I have not much patience with such distinctions, partly because even my rudimentary knowledge of foreign languages suffices to grasp that the differences do not survive translation. I also object because I am convinced that the self, ego, I, or me is in some sense real, not created by our definition. My purpose is to comprehend the way the person navigates through life, not to create artificially demarcated entities. In the past I have used the term "ego development" for the developmental trace of that construct, though the term is not entirely fortunate. No term is fortunate; there are objections to any term. Moreover, it is vain to hope that terminological precision will solve conceptual difficulties. Having taught elementary statistics a dozen times, I learned that those who complained about notation were those who didn't understand the statistics. Once you grasp the concepts, the terminology and notation are transparent; they no longer matter. Nonetheless, if I were starting anew, I would probably talk about the "development of the self," a term that accords better with the usage of other psychologists. What I have called ego development is, I believe, the closest we can come at present to tracing the developmental sequence of the self, or major aspects of it.

Development of the Self and Its Measurement

The earliest stage or stages of development of the self are shrouded in the mist of infancy. Psychoanalysts often confine the term *ego development* to this period alone, as if there were no development beyond that prehistory; I prefer to set this stage apart with the term *ego formation*. My conception (Table 2.1) takes hold with the next stage. During this *impulsive stage,* the small child's impulsive demands and emphatic "No!" help him or her to confirm a sense of separate identity, a sense of self. The child at this time is almost wholly dependent on others for control of impulses. At the following *self-protective stage,* there is some distance from impulse, some capacity for self-control, but functioning is still mainly in the service of the child's own short-term self-gratification. Thus this is still a highly egocentric stage in Piaget's sense.

Perhaps the most fateful and mysterious advance takes place as the person goes from the self-protective to the *conformist stage.* The conformist is still dependent on rewards and punishments for governance of behavior, but social rewards, such as approval and belongingness, are pre-eminent over the material and physical rewards of the impulsive and self-protective stages. Rules are obeyed by the conformist, not just out of fear of being caught but because the group sanctions the rules, and the conformist identifies self with the group.

TABLE 2.1

Stages of Ego (or Self) Development Measured by the Sentence Completion Test

Stage	Impulse control	Interpersonal mode	Conscious preoccupations
Impulsive	Impulsive	Egocentric, dependent	Bodily feelings
Self-protective	Opportunistic	Manipulative, wary	"Trouble," control
Conformist	Respect for rules	Cooperative, loyal	Appearances, behavior
Self-aware (transition)	Exceptions allowable	Helpful, self-aware	Feelings, problems, adjustment
Conscientious	Self-evaluated standards, self-critical	Intense, responsible	Motives, traits, achievements
Individualistic (transition)	Tolerant	Mutual	Individuality, development, roles
Autonomous	Coping with conflict	Interdependent	Self-fulfillment, psychological causation
Integrated	—	Cherishing individuality	Identity

Source: adapted from Loevinger, 1976, Table 1.

Another extraordinary and almost inexplicable leap takes the person to the *conscientious stage*. The person at this stage aspires to standards that are self-evaluated rather than merely imposed by membership in a group. There is an important intermediate or transitional level between the conformist and conscientious stages, which we call the *conscientious–conformist* or *self-aware* level. As Holt (1980) has shown, based on a nationwide survey by Yankelovitch, this is the modal level for the young adult population in our country.

The highest, *post-conscientious* stages are shrouded in mist, like the earliest stages, though for different reasons. The baby cannot tell us how he or she sees the world, and we have lost the capacity to think like babies. The people at the highest stages are articulate, but who is wise enough to say which is the highest stage? Each investigator in the field has a different idea of how the highest stage should be defined. In my research (Loevinger & Wessler, 1970; Loevinger, 1979b), we have devised methods for using data to bootstrap ourselves over this hurdle, but no such method is infallible.

To investigate ego development we have used a 36-item Sentence Completion Test (SCT), originally using stems such as "My husband and I ___," "A pregnant woman ___," and "When my mother spanked me, I ___." (None of those stems is used any more. They work less well than those we have retained, but the method assumes that stems are interchangeable, and that is close to being true.)

The basic technique in test construction has been to try to discern the level of the subject in each single response, taken out of context, with no identifying data. Then we estimate the level on the basis of the whole 36-item protocol. The total protocol rating is used as the criterion to improve the scoring manual for item ratings, by a process whose details are too intricate to relate here (see Loevinger & Wessler, 1970, Chapter 2). It is an adaptation of the classical method of internal consistency.

History of the Construct and Test

Let me interpolate here a brief history of how my colleagues and I came to this construct and test. I will try to convey to you how an essentially Brunswikian paradigm can illuminate psychological "traits" or processes. The crux of the argument is that low intercorrelations between bits of behavior, far from being uninteresting or unimportant, can be parlayed to reveal major insights into personality.

In the 1950s, when few psychologists deemed women worthy of study, I began to do research on mothers' attitudes. My colleagues (especially Blanche Sweet Usdansky) and I assembled a group of objective test items covering problems of family life, which we called the Family Problems Scale (Loevinger & Sweet, 1961). With the use of then-new computer capabilities, I intercorrelated every item with every other item. Anyone familiar with intercorrelations of single personality test items can imagine that the coefficients were very low, so low as to discourage the hope of discovering any meaning in them. Nonetheless, I decided to ignore their absolute value and to proceed to search for statistically coherent clusters (Loevinger, Sweet, Ossorio, & La Perriere, 1962).

Among the prevailing ways of characterizing mothers in psychiatric and clinical-psychological circles at that time were the trait terms "punitiveness–permissiveness" and "acceptance of the feminine role." Our results led us to question both of those concepts (though their subsequent decline in popularity undoubtedly had other causes).

The method for seeking homogeneous keys of a test (Loevinger, 1957; Loevinger, Gleser, & DuBois, 1953) requires assembling a pool of items whose content spans a domain broader than the trait or traits sought. Insight into the nature of the trait is obtained by examining not only the content of the items included in a cluster but also those excluded from it. Using this method, we looked for cluster-analytic evidence for existence of the above-named traits.

With regard to "acceptance of the feminine role," we found two separate clusters of items, which, in light of content both included and excluded, were called "acceptance of women's traditional social role" and "acceptance of women's biological role." The impressive finding was that when these clusters were keyed so that acceptance was the positive direction, they were negatively related: r (200) = $-.24$ in the original sample, and r (98) = $-.15$ in an independent sample. These item clusters have not proved to be robust traits in subsequent studies, but I believe that the demise of "acceptance of the feminine role" as a unitary entity is itself a robust finding.

Ernhart (Ernhart & Loevinger, 1969) showed that one variable being measured by the Family Problems Scale is robust under every circumstance we could contrive, and it is by far the most salient one in the test. Had we begun with the concept of punitiveness–permissiveness and stuck to the usual methods of refining tests by internal consistency, punitiveness– permissiveness would have been the characterization of this robust cluster. Because, however, we defined the domain more broadly, we discovered that many items directly referring to punishment were not included, and some items having no reference to punishment were excellent measures of it. For example, the item "A father should be his son's best pal" is hard to construe in terms of punishment or permissiveness, particularly because those who are high on punitiveness are those most likely to agree with it. In the light of all considerations, this cluster was called Authoritarian Family Ideology (Loevinger et al., 1962).

The sketch of those high on this dimension is similar to a sketch of those high on the "authoritarian personality" in the Berkeley studies (Adorno, Frenkel-Brunswik, Levinson, & Sanford, 1950). That is remarkable, considering that they began with an entirely social–political focus, whereas we had an entirely domestic focus, with no political items at all. In fact, the Berkeley group seems to have begun with the idea that particular psychosexual stages would determine particular syndromes or test responses. They found no such thing, but instead were driven by their data to give more importance to the capacity for inner life or "intraception" (to use a somewhat variant meaning of Murray's term) than they had anticipated. In both respects our results were similar; we found no evidence for clusters of items pertaining to psychosexual stages but much evidence for the centrality of "intraception," or rather, anti-intraception, in Authoritarian Family Ideology.

In investigating the nature of this variable, Kitty LaPerriere and Abel Ossorio convinced me that extreme, rigid authoritarian conformity is not the lower limit of a dimension that has liberal and tolerant personality traits and attitudes as its high extreme. Rather, authoritarian conformity is a midpoint, with a more chaotic, unstructured personality as the lower limit. This insight became a turning point in my intellectual history, changing me from a psychometric psychologist into a developmental psychologist.

To convey the significance of this transformation, another methodological digression is needed. Polar variables are dimensions that are described in terms of their extremes; milestone sequences, however, are dimensions described in terms of qualitatively different states or stages. For most purposes, abilities can be adequately described as polar variables. A further characteristic of abilities is that, in general, the developmental course is adequately described by the polar continuum. To describe the development of personality, however, we need to think in terms of qualitatively distinct milestones (as exemplified by the stages described in Table 2.1).

The Piagetian stages of intellectual development are, to be sure, a milestone sequence. A strict behaviorist could not have discovered preoperational and concrete operational logic. The more behavioristic one is, the more likely to see abilities the way Binet and Terman did, as so many correct answers, or as a proportion of average adult status. Piaget, on the other hand, lost interest in children as soon as they got the "correct" or adult answer, his interest being in kinds of childhood reasoning. His stages are in the first instance qualitative rather than quantitative ones. Thus there is an affinity between behaviorism and what might be called "psychometrism," both "isms" construing every trait as a polar variable. Both behaviorism and psychometrism are committed to taking responses at their least inferential level.

With personality, unlike abilities, the more behavioristic we are, the more we find ourselves measuring milestones; however, those milestones may be and commonly are misconstrued as polar variables. Conventional personality measurement, construing every trait as a polar variable—that is, as strictly, behavioristically quantitative—does not result in developmental assessment, as Binet-type ability tests do. To find the truly polar aspects of personality development requires an effort of inference, going beyond the obviously observable data (as ego development is the inferred continuum underlying the stages of Table 2.1).

To give a concrete example, conformity is a frequently measured personality trait, but it is neither a constantly increasing nor a constantly decreasing function of age. According to my conception, the highest level of conformity represents a way-station of ego development. This idea accords with the everyday observation of maximum conformity to peer pressure during adolescence.

That the logical extreme of a trait can be a developmental midpoint has one extraordinary consequence—namely, that two traits that are functions or signs of a single developmental dimension can have any correlation, even a zero or a negative one. This fact is illustrated in Figure 2.3. The abscissa is a developing personality structure, the ordinate the percentage of cases showing a given "sign," a term chosen to avoid the loaded terms "trait" and "behavior." Sign A peaks at Stage L, sign B at Stage M. Choose a sample that has persons who range from Stage L to Stage M, and these two signs of the same underlying dimension will be negatively related. Thus it is evidently

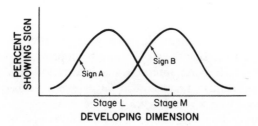

Figure 2.3   General model for two "signs" of a developing dimension.

fallacious to infer from the fact that two signs have a zero correlation that there cannot be an underlying psychological continuum of which they are both manifestations. Factor analysis, which deals only with rectilinear relationships, is helpless to overcome the problems that Figure 2.3 reveals. There is no substitute for insightful psychological hypotheses; no foreseeable machines or machinations will make them obsolete.

To test the hypothesis that Authoritarian Family Ideology is a developmental variable, LaPerriere tested a number of postpartum women in an analysis of variance design. She found that Authoritarian Family Ideology decreased with age, with experience in child-rearing (primiparous vs. multiparous women), and with education (grade school, some high school, finished high school, some college). Effects of education and parity were significant even with age covaried out. These and other results led us to postulate ego development as the underlying or "central" variable whose objective test manifestation was Authoritarian Family Ideology (Loevinger *et al.*, 1962).

Elizabeth Nettles, seeking to confirm the ego development interpretation of Authoritarian Family Ideology, initiated our first study of the Sentence Completion Test. Another SCT had been used by a group at the Camp Elliott Naval Retraining Command in San Diego, whose interest was the problem of delinquency in young men; their term for their dimension was "interpersonal integration" (C. Sullivan, M. Q. Grant, J. D. Grant, 1957). The late Virginia Ives (Word), a member of their research team, helped initiate ours, bringing a good deal of their accumulated wisdom to us. Again there is an impressive carry-over of psychological insights, not from political to domestic context in this case, but from a delinquent male population to a normal female one.

Initially we began by classifying each sentence completion into one of four stages, adapted from those of Sullivan *et al.* and corresponding about to what we now call impulsive, conformist, conscientious, and autonomous stages. The first scoring manual we constructed for that operation was an *exemplar manual,* listing all (repeated) responses under one of those four levels. Most projective test manuals are of this type. There is no way formally to use the results from one cycle of testing to improve such a manual. (The San Diego group studying interpersonal integration used an even more primitive kind of manual, a *reverse exemplar manual.* In this type, characteristic responses are given for each level, but the same response may appear in several levels, thus providing no guidance for raters in those instances.)

In order to use the data from one cycle of testing to improve the manual, we graduated immediately to a *categorized manual.* Each category at each level is given a name, and some examples are given, preferably including borderline examples. This kind of manual assists raters by calling attention to the features of the response that justify placing it at the given level.

Categories are also the vehicle of manual improvement. For each person whose response is in category A in some sample, there will be a total protocol rating. Almost invariably each category will have a distribution of total protocol ratings. Using that distribution (plus base rates for the sample; see Loevinger & Wessler, 1970), one can determine whether the category is placed at the correct level, whether it should be shifted, whether it should be split into two separate categories, and so on.

In successive cycles of testing, the manual is gradually improved by this bootstrap operation, using very small correlations, hardly better than chance. Since the number giving an answer in any category is usually small, most relationships are not statistically significant. Nonetheless, through repeated cycles, statistically reliable results can be obtained, as shown by a correlation between single items and total protocol ratings as high as .65 and rarely below .35 (Loevinger & Wessler, 1970). Indeed, comparable values were obtained in correlating single items of the Sentence Completion Test with Kohlberg's moral judgment test, in a dissertation done at another university (Lambert, 1972).

The main significance of this endeavor, however, does not lie in the technology of manual construction. It lies in the fact that in the course of revising the manual by this empirical process, our conception of the stages of ego development has been gradually revised, extended in scope, levels, and detail, and in several instances corrected, to its present detailed form. The method also leaves the avenue open to further revision.

The common element in these two projects—the objective test of family problems and the semiprojective SCT—is that our conception has been shaped by our data. In this interplay of theory and data (Loevinger, 1979b), an absolutely crucial element has been to take seemingly minute correlations seriously, although almost all of them are not statistically significant. When depending on such apparently fragile data, there must be some final proof that the results are not equally insubstantial. I will return shortly to the topic of the construct validity of the SCT.

The Centralist Critique

Kohlberg (1981) claims as a virtue of his Moral Judgment Instrument that it represents a *sample* of the domain that he is measuring. By contrast, he states, in the SCT responses are merely *signs* of ego development. Presumably we are meant to infer that either the concept of ego development or its measurement is more tenuous than that of moral judgment. There is, of course, a shade of truth to his assertion. My approach to test construction is firmly grounded on probabilistic considerations, whereas his—like that of the rest of the neo-Piagetian school of personality psychologists—is grounded primarily on the logical coherence of each stage. But suppose we look at it this way: Kohlberg's test uses moral judgment in hypothetical, farfetched, and improbable situations as signs of what moral judgment will be in real-world situations. The SCT, on the other hand, is designed to tap into a person's frame of reference, which is more or less synonymous with ego development as I use the term, and it does so by sampling that frame of reference. So perhaps it is the SCT that uses a sample and the Moral Judgment Instrument that uses signs. But no: every test response is, ipso facto, a sample of behavior, and no one would give a test unless it were a sign of some domain other than that of behavior in a test situation (Loevinger, 1957). Thus every test response is always and necessarily both a sign and a sample.

The many studies that have contributed to the construct validation of the SCT (Loevinger, 1979a) are too detailed to review here in any but a cursory fashion, but it is instructive to look at some of the issues involved. Contrary to what some of our psychometric–behavioristic colleagues may believe, theoretical considerations are essential to the evaluation of construct validity. Consider this example. Given the significant correlations between Kohlberg's Moral Judgment Instrument and our test of ego development, can one interpret them as evidence *for* or *against* construct validity of the two tests? That is, are the correlations between the two tests germane to convergent or discriminant validity? In fact, Kohlberg and I differ on this point. For Kohlberg (1981), the domain of personality is divided into several subdomains, joined by a necessary-but-not-sufficient relation.

My alternative conception is that ego development—or, as I would now prefer, development of the self—is a unity, partly ineffable, partly structural, partly substantive, and imperfectly coherent. The image, derived in part from data and from Perry's (1970) conception of intellectual–ethical development, is that of an amoeboid unity, proceeding by sending our pseudopodia, like an amoeba, to which the rest of the cell body then catches up. Where the Piagetians have described change in terms of that passe-partout label, *décalage*, Perry has an explicit and plausible description of change: One advances to a more complex conceptual level first in one special area—not necessarily the same area for everyone, however. Gradually the scope of higher-stage reasoning expands to greater and greater substantive areas, till finally the higher-stage reasoning is predominant, with only isolated pockets of lower-stage reasoning. The order of the subdomains depends on one's individual circumstances.

Not many data relevant to the choice between Kohlberg's model and mine are presently available, although many potential studies suggest themselves. Results such as those of Kurdek (1980) are on the whole on my side. More telling evidence comes from the dissertation of Lambert (1972), one of Kohlberg's students. The correlations that Lambert found for individual sentence stems on the SCT with overall score on Kohlberg's test are of exactly the same order of magnitude as the corresponding correlations between individual items and the total score on the SCT. By his data, the score on an item in the SCT could as well be an element of the Moral Judgment Instrument as in the SCT. This finding certainly needs to be replicated before any large conclusions are drawn, but for the moment it is provocative. (In fact, the item-total correlations for the SCT were drawn from a different sample than the item-total correlations for Lambert's study with Kohlberg's test, so the variance of the sample may be a factor in this result.) Perhaps Lambert's results are exceptional, for in other studies the correlation between two measures of ego development is somewhat greater than the correlation between a measure of ego development and one of moral judgment. For example, Ruth Lucas's (1971) dissertation correlated ego development as estimated from interviews with ego development as judged from the SCT; the correlation was about .6. E. V. Sullivan, McCullough, and Stager (1970) correlated ego development with moral judgment on a different sample, and found a correlation of .4.

Anyone who has worked with psychological tests for a while expects that two similar tests will correlate more highly than two tests designed to measure different traits. Note, however, that in Lucas's results the factor of test format, which Campbell and Fiske (1959) showed is usually more powerful than substantive content, did not operate to raise the correlation, since she was correlating an interview with a written test. Kohlberg's theoretical structure of numerous subdomains in the ego, or self, linked to each other by a necessary but not sufficient relation, raises the question: Does every new approach to the ego or self, every new test, every new definition of an observable slice of behavior require a new structure to be postulated? And if so, what is the purpose of a structure?

The Peripheralist Critique

The peripheralists, like the centralists, are a varied crew. There may be little that Fiske, Skinner, and such social learning theorists as Mischel and Bandura agree on, though I suspect that none of them would be interested in minor differences between Kohlberg and me.

Suppose that a psychologist were assigned the task of making a diagnostic study of two men: one, Richard Nixon or someone like him; the other, Elliott Richardson or someone like him. Most of us would agree that two such men differ with respect to their character structure. Just here one sees the point of the Brunswik model, for I imagine it would be hard to find in traditional psychological tests any evidence for the differences in their character, which played a fateful part in the recent history of this country. That is, their proximal responses might be indistinguishable, but their distal achievements differ vastly.

I find nothing in the transducers used by Fiske, Mischel, or Bandura that seems to me even to claim to capture such differences. That is the arena in which Kohlberg and I have set up our separate shops. Until Mischel (Chapter 7, this volume) described his recent work, I would have said that none of the behaviorists or social learning theorists even laid claim to that area. Mischel deserves credit for recognizing conscience as an area worthy of study. Were I raising a child, the items of his test of conscience might well be some of the behaviors I would try to instill; they represent an acceptable use of the word "conscience" in our language. However, they have no relation to what is called the conscientious stage in our study of ego development. Rather, they are characteristics one might expect to be at issue in the conformist stage, as well as others that may represent mild obsessive–compulsive behavior, fastidiousness, and so on. Psychometricians have known for decades that it is almost impossible to guess a priori which of such test items cluster together statistically (Meehl, 1945). Statistical clusters depend not only on apparent content but also on the exact wording of items, sometimes on unexpected details. That is why the MMPI (Minnesota Multiphasic Personality Inventory) was constructed with such ruthless empiricism. Indeed, statistical clustering can be exploited to further psychological theory (Loevinger, 1957).

Kohlberg's test and mine are put at a disadvantage by the fact that the same traditional psychometric tests that scarcely even recognize differences of character are held up by the psychology Establishment as ultimate criteria for the tests we have been working out.

In the first series of Murray lectures, McClelland (1981) made a point that is germane here. Behaviors can be ranged on a continuum, with respondent behaviors at one extreme and operant ones at the other. Objective tests and responses to laboratory tasks are close to the respondent extreme, whereas answers to projective tests are close to the operant extreme. Respondent behaviors are, by definition, situationally responsive. Personal consistency ought to be looked for primarily in operant behaviors; thus projective and semiprojective tests such as Kohlberg's and mine are appropriate.

Validity of the Ego Development Construct

Let me review briefly some of the conspicuous lines of evidence for the construct validity of the SCT, which are simultaneously evidence for the construct of ego development. To establish construct validity requires examining the substantive, structural, and external components (Loevinger, 1957), which correspond approximately to what are usually called content validity, homogeneity and reliability, and external or criterion validity.

Content validity, the *substantive* component, has ordinarily been examined in terms of an intuitive inspection of items included in the test. The format of the items can also be germane. To those considerations we have added several fairly rigorous studies of interrater agreement. The argument is that if our written materials, including practice exercises, can convey our scoring system to. new raters sufficiently to reach an adequate level of interrater agreement, there must be a coherent content that is being tacitly learned. The fact that this interrater agreement holds up for new items for which there is no explicit scoring manual, as two studies confirmed, is especially important.

Primary evidence for the *structural* component of validity is homogeneity or internal consistency. While we were constructing our scoring manual, we accumulated 543 new cases, which were sealed against inspection by any staff member until the entire preliminary version of the manual was completed. The new cases were then rated, as the major evaluation of the manual. Item ratings for the 36 stems were factor analyzed. The first principal component yielded an eigen value of 8.8; the second, only 1.2. The second component could not be interpreted, and its size is consistent with its being a chance deviation from unity (Loevinger & Wessler, 1970, Chapter 3).

The reason the SCT measures a unitary dimension, a conclusion for which there is much additional evidence, is methodological: A single conception of ego development guided the construction of all item manuals. Nonetheless, several investigators have tried to find subsets of items whose statistical relations corresponded to apparent differences in their content. The search proved fruitless (Blasi, 1971; Lambert, 1972).

An aspect of the structural component specially apropos for Piagetian or quasi-Piagetian developmental sequences is the criterion of sequentiality, on which Kohlberg primarily relies. Sequentiality requires that the stages always occur in the same order, that no stage can be skipped, and that progress is normally irreversible. The alternative hypothesis, usually advanced by social learning theorists and behaviorists, is that the order of acquisition of relevant behaviors, attitudes, and attributes is dictated by situational influences rather than the internal logic of development; therefore the order can be at times reversed. To test sequentiality rigorously, one would need a test free of error, frequent testing (at least as frequent as the least time needed to make measurable progress), and no effects of testing or retesting—obviously impossible conditions to meet. I claim no more than that the weight of evidence is consistent with sequentiality, not that it constitutes rigorous proof.

Evidence for sequentiality—all of it on balance favorable but none of it absolutely decisive—includes the following (reviewed in Loevinger, 1979a):

1. Cross-sectional studies show average increases by age and grade.
2. When cases are sorted by the total protocol ratings, the distribution of item ratings is more similar for adjacent than for nonadjacent stages.
3. Most samples studied longitudinally show significant average gain between test and retest; the gain is approximately proportional to the interval between test and retest, until the end of high school.
4. Test–retest correlations are significantly positive in longitudinal studies, even over intervals as long as 6 years.
5. Although attempts to raise ego level experimentally in a few weeks have not succeeded, experiments that have lasted 6–9 months have had statistically significant success.
6. Studies of faking have shown that people can lower their scores more reliably and more decisively than they can raise them.

The third component of validity is *external* correlations. Among the many relevant lines of evidence (reviewed in Loevinger, 1979a) the SCT has shown:

1. Substantial correlation with ego level judged from other behavior samples, including interviews and objective tests
2. Substantial correlation with measures of other theoretically related developmental variables, particularly Kohlberg's test
3. Predicted relations with several behavioral variables, such as delinquency and ratings of the level of responsibility shown in behavior.

Delinquency is correlated with low ego levels, as predicted. Predicted curvilinear relations with measures of conformity have also been shown.

One kind of study has yielded disappointing relationships for the students whose dissertations were patterned on its model. These studies (almost all unpublished but reviewed in Loevinger, 1979a) were of the following form. The descriptions of the several ego stages were scanned for terms that indicate traits for which somewhere in the psychological literature there is a putative measure. The latter measure was then correlated with ego level as measured by the SCT. Note that this method represents a partial retreat to a peripheralist approach. One must remember that the distinction between proximal–peripheral behaviors and distal behaviors (or behavioral effects) is a relative one; defining a single behavioral trait and measuring it in isolation is equivalent to retreating to the mediational details—that is, to the lens of the lens model. Judgment of ego level is never made on the basis of one trait, or one kind of behavior, however prominent. It always represents a pattern or gestalt. Any single trait, taken in isolation, can have a variety of meanings and signify various ego levels, depending on the gestalt in which it occurs. Thus the failure of this type of validational study to yield positive results does not invalidate my Brunswikian thesis. On the contrary, it backs it up.

Even discounting the last set of studies, however, the problem of external validity is complex. To demonstrate external validity requires correlations that are high enough with some variables and not too high with other variables, the latter being sources of distortion. The Campbell–Fiske matrix is a formal model for some consequences of this requirement. The trouble is that theory is not always clear as to which is which—that is, which correlations ought to be relatively high, which relatively low. Variables such as intelligence and socioeconomic status may be inextricably confounded with variables of major interest. Nature does not promise us an orthogonal universe. To the contrary, "To them that hath shall be given."

This consideration, that the significance of a finding is obscured by confounded variables, applies also to McGuire's (Chapter 3, this volume) demonstration of age differences in self-description. Perhaps these differences are primarily a function of mental age, with chronological age related only incidentally. They are exactly the kinds of differences we find for self-descriptions by persons of different ego levels within an age cohort, and that leads, shortly, to my final point.

Taking the worst case, which assuredly is untrue or at least an exaggeration, that ego level is *nothing but* a linear function of intelligence, socioeconomic status, and verbal fluency, it still represents an interesting set of data. There is nothing in the data of intelligence, socioeconomic status, and fluency that prepares us for the radical dialectic of stages of character structure that our analysis reveals.

A number of studies have been done since my 1979 review, and I missed a few at the time I compiled it, so that the evidence is on balance more strongly in its favor than represented there. I hasten to acknowledge, however, that not all predicted relations have panned out. Predictions are often guesses, only loosely related to premises. The SCT measure of ego development indexes an important constellation of traits, but it by no means overrides or outweighs all other situational and personal and interactive influences on behavior. What I want to add to that discussion is another line of evidence: one so important and overarching that, paradoxically, it is the last to present itself. My exposition of ego development, more than other expositions of related sequences, such as Kohlberg's of moral development, stresses the hypothesis that *the dimension of individual differences in adult life is the trace of a corresponding developmental sequence.* That makes the dimension in principle an abstraction. There are certainly characteristic differences between adults and children at a given stage. The definition of the stage, however, is precisely what they have in common. The concept is similar in this respect to mental age.

To support that hypothesis, which is the core of my conception, as sequentiality is the core of Kohlberg's (though each conception entails parts of the other), we must trace the characteristic sequences of child development found by those studying personality from a Piagetian framework. These sequences will be shown to be similar to the dimension we have traced on the basis of our work with adolescents and adults.

In this connection it is important to take into account that our method always was keyed to maximizing individual differences and never made any use of age differences. Indeed, raters were denied knowledge of age differences, so age could not have entered even subliminally. In the rare cases where they had some clue to age differences in the response, raters were explicitly instructed that age-contingent scoring was not permitted. The developmentalists, on the other hand, have been concerned almost exclusively with age differences and hardly at all with individual differences within an age cohort. While it would be unrealistic to expect us to come up with identical dimensions, any substantial evidence for concordance is evidence for construct validity.

Of the lowest stage in the child's conception of justice, Damon (1977) states: "The child's justice decisions do not extend beyond the egocentric referent of the child's own wishes" (p. 289). Correspondingly, of subjects at the impulsive stage of ego development, we have written: "People are seen as sources of supply, she [the subject] demands things from them, and *good* often if not always means *good to me*" (Loevinger & Wessler, 1970, p. 57). The stem "Women are lucky because ___" has a category of response at the impulsive level labeled simply "wishes," illogically related to the stem. Examples are responses such as "they get nice things" or "they wish for something" to the stem "Women are lucky because" (Loevinger, *et al.*, 1970, p. 121).

Here is another comparison: according to Damon,

At friendship level 1 . . . there is no sense that persons have stable characteristics and that friends may be chosen on this basis. . . . [During development] friends acquire

stable personality traits. . . . Reciprocal exchange as a criterion of friendship is understood even at level 1, but the recognized types of exchanges shift from material
sharing at level 1 to psychological interaction at level 3 [pp. 304–305].

We find a similar progression between ego stages. At the conformist stage,
we have stated, "Interpersonal interaction is described in terms of behaviors
rather than in terms of differentiated feelings, motives, or traits, as it is at
[higher levels]" (Loevinger & Wessler, 1970, p. 68). And, at the same level,
"There is an emphasis on concrete things" (p. 70).

Concerning the understanding of rules, Damon has stated: "At social reg-
ulation level 0, there is a fluctuating conception of one's obligation to defer to
rules or other expectations. There is no awareness of a stable collection of
regulations that transcend immediate situations or individual whims" (p.
304). At a slightly higher level, "Authority is thought of as an obstacle to the
child's desire. Thus, a conflict between the self and authority is perceived, and
obedience is considered a necessary means of resolving this conflict. When
obeyed, the authority figure is seen to be mollified" (p. 317).

Correspondingly, we have found at the impulsive stage that almost the
only identifiable category for the stem "Rules are ____" is a set of responses
that are concrete examples or admonitions, such as "Don't talk on the phone
too long and wash the dishes every night," or "to do as your [sic] told by a
cop." Thus, as Damon noted for children, there is no sense of a system of
rules. At the self-protective stage, "Rules are seen as loss of freedom" (Loevinger & Wessler, 1970, p. 62), corresponding to Damon's remark that
authority is conceived as an obstacle to desire. "Unqualified compliance with
authority is the dominant theme" at the conformist stage (Redmore *et al.*,
1978) which again parallels Damon's generalization about children.

These are but fragmentary examples of the similarity between the progression of ego stages derived from adolescents and adults and similar stage
sequences derived entirely from younger children. Of course no one says that
the two sequences are identical. Our adult subjects have logical capacities that
young children do not have, and they have sexual and other concerns that are
different from those of children. It is not altogether obvious how one could
study these parallels in a more rigorous, less impressionistic fashion, but I
suspect there may be some dissertations here for the ingenious.

Conclusion

Let me recapitulate my thesis. Prediction of fragmentary aspects of behavior
is not worthy of our efforts, nor of a lecture series honoring that grandfather

of modern personality theory, Henry Murray. Much of the thrust of the argument that trait theory has been a failure depended on evaluating the predictive value of traits against just such fragmentary or isolated behaviors or short-term effects. Gathering several instances of behavior reveals that what initially appears to have little or no predictive value, yields, when cumulated, characterizations that are about as predictive as one has any right to expect people to be.

My objection to trait theory is that it does not go far enough. Traits are too fragmentary. Damon has remarked that one best charts personality development not in terms of isolated traits but in terms of their organization. That organization is summarized in terms of development of the self or ego.

I have defended my conception of ego development and its measure against criticism from the centralists and the peripheralists, to use Murray's terms. On the one hand, my conception is criticized because, unlike stages devised by the true-blue Piagetians, the stages are not defined in terms of strict logical coherence. I think my stages are just as logically coherent as the people who serve as my subjects are. On the other hand, my measure is criticized because it does not predict behavior well enough. But no single behavior is a fair criterion of ego level. The sets of predictions that have consistently failed are those of isolated traits, as one ought to have expected, using a Brunswikian logic.

I have never heard anyone espouse the doctrine that behavior is predictable on the basis of personality alone, to the exclusion of situational considerations. Anyone unresponsive to situational demands would be, ipso facto, crazy. And if we believed that personality made no difference, that situational factors were all that there is, we ought to be social psychologists and abandon the field of personality altogether.

Numerous validational studies of the SCT show that certain behaviors are characteristic of lower ego levels; at higher levels no particular behaviors have been identified. What is predictable at higher levels is characteristic attitudes and values. Perhaps the predictability of behavior is itself negatively correlated with ego level.

My thesis, then, is that personality matters most for the larger aspects of behavior, which depend on character structure; these aspects have been and will always be difficult to capture in objective tests and laboratory studies. The cognitive developmentalists, an "invisible college" whose members include Kohlberg, Blasi, Selman, Rest, myself, and others, are working toward rendering measurable those larger aspects of personality. What I have tried to show here and in my work for the past three decades is that by appropriate statistical techniques, relationships so small as to be insignificant both statistically and practically can be parlayed into reliable tests and important theoretical insights.

References

Adorno, T. W., Frenkel–Brunswik, E., Levinson, D. J., & Sanford, R. N. *The authoritarian personality.* New York: Harpers, 1950.

Allport, G. W. *Pattern and growth in personality.* New York: Holt Rinehart Winston, 1961.

Allport, G., & Odbert, H. S. Trait names: A psycholexical study. *Psychological Monographs,* 1936, *47,* no. 211, 1–171.

Blasi, A. A developmental approach to responsibility training (Doctoral dissertation, Washington University, 1971). *Dissertation Abstracts International,* 1971, *32,* 1233B. (University Microfilms No. 71–19, 807)

Block, J. Advancing the psychology of personality: Paradigmatic shift or improving the quality of research? In D. Magnusson & N. S. Endler (Eds.), *Personality at the crossroads.* Hillsdale, NJ: Erlbaum, 1977.

Block, J. Some enduring and consequential structures of personality. In A. I. Rabin, J. Aronoff, A. M. Barclay, & R. A. Zucker (Eds.), *Further explorations in personality.* New York: Wiley, 1981.

Brunswik, E. Organismic achievement and environmental probability. *Psychological Review,* 1943, *50,* 255–272.

Brunswik, E. The conceptual framework of psychology. In O. Neurath, R. Carnap, & C. Morris (Eds.), *International encyclopedia of unified science* (Vol. 1, pt. 2). Chicago: Univ. of Chicago Press, 1952.

Campbell, D. T., & Fiske, D. W. Convergent and discriminant validation by the multi-trait–multimethod matrix. *Psychological Bulletin,* 1959, *56,* 81–105.

Cattell, R. B. *The scientific analysis of personality.* Baltimore: Penguin, 1965.

Conrad, H. S. The validity of personality ratings of preschool children. *Journal of Educational Psychology,* 1932, *23,* 671–680.

Damon, W. *The social world of the child.* San Francisco: Jossey–Bass, 1977.

Epstein, S. The stability of behavior. I: On predicting most of the people much of the time. *Journal of Personality and Social Psychology,* 1979, *37,* 1097–1126.

Epstein, S. The self-concept: A review and the proposal of an integrated theory of personality. In E. Staub (Ed.), *Personality: Basic aspects and current research.* Englewood Cliffs, NJ: Prentice-Hall, 1980. (a)

Epstein, S. The stability of behavior. II. Implications for psychological research. *American Psychologist,* 1980, *35,* 790–806. (b)

Ernhart, C. B., & Loevinger, J. Authoritarian Family Ideology: A measure, its correlates, and its robustness. *Multivariate Behavioral Research Monographs,* 1969, No. 69-1.

Fingarette, H. *The self in transformation.* New York: Basic Books, 1963.

Fiske, D. W. *Strategies for personality research.* San Francisco: Jossey-Bass, 1978.

Golding, S. L. Toward a more adequate theory of personality: Psychological organizing principles. In H. London (Ed.), *Personality: A new look at metatheories.* Somerset, NJ: Halsted, 1978.

Goodenough, F. L. *Mental testing.* New York: Rinehart, 1949.

Greenwald, A. The totalitarian ego: Fabrication and revision of personal history. *American Psychologist,* 1980, *35,* 603–618.

Hammond, K. R. (Ed.). *The psychology of Egon Brunswik.* New York: Holt Rinehart Winston, 1966.

Holt, R. R. Loevinger's measure of ego development: Reliability and national norms for male and female short forms. *Journal of Personality and Social Psychology,* 1980, *39,* 909–920.

Hull, C. L. The concept of habit-family-hierarchy and maze learning. *Psychological Review*, 1934, *41*, 33–54, 134–154.

Kenrick, D. T., & Stringfield, D. O. Personality traits and the eye of the beholder: Crossing some traditional philosophical boundaries in the search for consistency in all of the people. *Psychological Review*, 1980, *87*, 88–104.

Kohlberg, L. *The meaning and measurement of moral development*. Worcester, MA: Clark Univ. Press, 1981.

Kuhn, T. S. *The structure of scientific revolutions*. Chicago: Univ. of Chicago Press, 1962.

Kurdek, L. A. Developmental relations among children's perspective taking, moral judgment, and parent-rated behavior. *Merrill–Palmer Quarterly*, 1980, *26*, 103–121.

Lambert, H. V. A comparison of Jane Loevinger's theory of ego development and Lawrence Kohlberg's theory of moral development. Unpublished doctoral dissertation, University of Chicago, 1972.

Loevinger, J. Objective tests as instruments of psychological theory. *Psychological Reports*, 1957, *3*, 635–694.

Loevinger, J. *Ego development*. San Francisco: Jossey-Bass, 1976.

Loevinger, J. Construct validity of the sentence completion test of ego development. *Applied Psychological Measurement*, 1979, *3*, 281–311. (a)

Loevinger, J. Theory and data in the measurement of ego development. In J. Loevinger, *Scientific ways in the study of ego development*. Worcester, MA: Clark Univ. Press, 1979. (b)

Loevinger, J., Gleser, G. C., & DuBois, P. H. Maximizing the discriminating power of a multiple-score test. *Psychometrika*, 1953, *18*, 309–317.

Loevinger, J., & Knoll, E. Personality: Stages, traits, and the self. *Annual Review of Psychology*, 1983, *34*, 195–222.

Loevinger, J., & Sweet, B. Construction of a test of mothers' attitudes. In J. C. Glidewell (Ed.), *Parental attitudes and child behavior*. Springfield, IL: Thomas, 1961.

Loevinger, J., Sweet, B., Ossorio, A., & LaPerriere, K. Measuring personality patterns of women. *Genetic Psychology Monographs*, 1962, *65*, 53–136.

Loevinger, J., & Wessler, R. *Measuring ego development I. Construction and use of a sentence completion test*. San Francisco: Jossey-Bass, 1970.

Loevinger, J., Wessler, R., & Redmore, C. *Measuring ego development II. Scoring manual for women and girls*. San Francisco: Jossey-Bass, 1970.

Lucas, R. H. Validation of a test of ego development by means of a standardized interview (Doctoral dissertation, Washington University, 1971). *Dissertation Abstracts International*, 1971, *32*, 2204B. (University Microfilm No. 71-27, 335.)

McClelland, D. C. Is personality consistent? In A. I. Rabin, J. Aronoff, A. M. Barclay, & R. A. Zucker (Eds.), *Further explorations in personality*. New York: Wiley, 1981.

McGuire, W. J., & McGuire, C. V. The spontaneous self-concept as affected by personal distinctiveness. In M. D. Lynch, A. A. Norem-Hebeisen, & K. J. Gergen (Eds.), *Self-concept: Advances in theory and research*. Cambridge, MA: Ballinger, 1981.

Meehl, P. E. The dynamics of "structured" personality tests. *Journal of Clinical Psychology*, 1945, *1*, 296–303.

Merleau-Ponty, M. *The structure of behavior*. Boston: Beacon, 1963. (Originally published, 1942).

Murray, H. A. *Explorations in personality*. New York: Oxford Univ. Press, 1938.

Perry, W. G., Jr. *Forms of intellectual and ethical development in the college years*. New York: Holt Rinehart Winston, 1970.

Redmore, C. Susceptibility to faking of a sentence completion test of ego development. *Journal of Personality Assessment*, 1976, *40*, 607–616.

Redmore, C., Loevinger, J., & Tamashiro, R. Measuring ego development: Scoring manual for men and boys. St. Louis: Washington University, 1978. Unpublished manuscript.

Selman, R. L. *The growth of interpersonal understanding.* New York: Academic Press, 1980.

Spearman, C. "General intelligence" objectively determined and measured. *American Journal of Psychology,* 1904, *15,* 201–292.

Sullivan, C., Grant, M. Q., & Grant, J. D. The development of interpersonal maturity: Applications to delinquency. *Psychiatry,* 1957, *20,* 373–385.

Sullivan, E. V., McCullough, G., & Stager, M. A developmental study of the relationship between conceptual, ego, and moral development. *Child Development,* 1970, *41,* 399–411.

Sullivan, H. S. *The interpersonal theory of psychiatry.* New York: Norton, 1953.

Tolman, E. C., & Brunswik, E. The organism and the causal texture of the environment. *Psychological Review,* 1935, *42,* 43–77.

PART II

Phenomenological and Social Aspects of Behavior

The two chapters that are featured in this part allow readers to see how contemporary work in personality draws upon past accomplishments, solves earlier problems, and creates the groundwork for the next set of advances. Among their many valuable contributions, these chapters focus our attention on an important set of developments that have occurred in psychology in our part of the twentieth century.

The debate over the nature of the self—indeed, the very question of whether it was a proper subject for study—was one of the great controversies of the first phase of work in personology. At the time when Murray was attempting the great codification represented by *Explorations in Personality*, the study of the self was a topic that established one's credentials as a scientist or humanist (see Allport, 1937). It is a sign of marked progress that this is no longer a taboo topic nor does interest (or lack of interest) in the characteristics of the self broadcast the psychologist's existential stance. Both McGuire and Benjamin show us how well we can now combine studies that adequately record the "uniqueness" of the person with the proper concerns for the "quality" of the information required to form judgments about the person.

The investigation of most topics in the area of personality deals with two very different questions: (a) how best to account for the presence of specific elements in the larger structure and (b) how best to account for the organization among these elements. The two chapters that constitute this part provide excellent exemplars of two different contemporary approaches to research on the nature of the self. Each chapter reports the results, implications, and lessons for future research obtained from the authors' major programs of research. In the first, McGuire suggests an elegant principle to explain how many of the significant attributes that will become the self are selected by the individual. In the second, Benjamin presents a wide-ranging solution to the question of how to organize the disparate phenomenological and behavioral activities that seem to be required in a theory of the self.

McGuire launches his discussion of the "problem regarding individuated existence" in broad philosophical terms. This unusual form of introduction permits him to focus the reader's attention on the process through which the self can be understood to be an active, selecting agency. The primary observation that McGuire draws from this larger discussion is to propose that the person uses the set of attributes that are not present in him- or herself to help define the self. As McGuire states, in apparent paradox, "What makes me be 'me' . . . is not what I am but what I am not" (p. 76). "[It is the set] of absences that distinguish me from others . . . I am conscious of myself in terms of absences, my awareness of the distinctive features that individuate me from others by being absent in one of us" (p. 76). McGuire frames the end of the introduction with the statement of his primary observation in each of the two pillars of his intellectual heritage. As the student of philosophy he states, "Perceiving the self . . . involves recognizing the peculiar individuating ways in which it is not absolute being" (p. 78). As the student of the science of information processing he states, "The person has evolved as an efficient recognizer of absences in things, information . . . [as] distinctions made possible by absences" (p. 78).

McGuire's distinctiveness postulate is based on the assumption that human beings are "confronted by an astronomical amount of information." In order to cope with this "constant state of information overload," the human being has evolved a set of cognitive techniques, which include the capacity to focus attention on those attributes that discriminate between things. For personologists, this position is especially intriguing because we are most accustomed to finding cognitive mechanisms used as defensive techniques to control repressed contents. We have seldom explored the potential of precise cognitive strategies of this type to account for the development of important elements of personality. This direction is well worth pursuing, for perhaps the single greatest weakness in personology is the absence of clear, speculative models of how elements of the person are formed. Similarly, we can ask if this form of selective attention is a satisfying mechanism to account for all the elements of the self, for there does seem to be an analogical leap from distinctiveness as a short-term selective attention mechanism to its possible utility as a long-term basis for establishing the attributes of the self. For example, it would be interesting to examine the utility of this principle to account for the range of cognitive elements that Mischel (1973) suggested constitutes an alternative basis for the definition of personality. Up to this point McGuire has used his research to provide evidence for the existence of this mechanism rather than to demonstrate its range. Such issues offer promising directions for future research in personology.

Like McGuire, Benjamin uses an evolutionary perspective to justify the presence of a major principle in the development of personality. Her topic, however, deals less with how a particular element enters personality than with the underlying structure that permits the person to cope with experience. It is this structure that is used to account for a wide range of personality, developmental, social, and clinical phenomena. Benjamin's description of her work on the Structural Analysis of Social Behavior (SASB) allows us to underscore an obvious, although too infrequently noted, scientific principle. Prediction in the field of personality research, as elsewhere, is based on sets of antecedent variables, and more powerful predictions rely on the search for more important antecedents. The extensiveness of Benjamin's predictions shows us how much of human functioning can be derived from a rich set of antecedents.

The Structural Analysis of Social Behavior rests on a mature conceptualization of the coordinates of phenomenological and interpersonal space as the primary unit of analysis. This approach to the analysis of individual, social, and clinical phenomena has been explored by a variety of social scientists, such as Bales (1950, 1970), Leary (1957), Lorr and McNair (1963), Shaefer (1965), and Wiggins (1980). Benjamin's essential advance over their work is in conceiving this primary space to be simultaneously intrapsychic as well as interpersonal. This integration of approaches allows her to resolve apparent contradictions in the coordinates of the space that these earlier researchers have proposed. For example, the opposite pole to the usual "assertiveness" pole in some models is "submissiveness" and in other models is "passivity." Benjamin's distinctions show how both postulates are true, in that passivity is the appropriate opposite to assertiveness intrapsychically and submissiveness is the appropriate opposite interpersonally. Of even greater importance, Benjamin's model is not a simple notational scheme to classify a wide array of human events. Rather, this model includes a powerful set of postulates that results in an elegant theory of individual and interpersonal functioning. Benjamin shows how the dimensional approach can result in a dynamic model that predicts (for a specific behavior performed by a person) the nature of the interpersonal response that can be expected from another.

In her chapter, Benjamin describes several of the many uses that can be made of this model. For example, it can be viewed as a system for representing the details of human functioning; Benjamin shows its great utility in understanding certain person perception processes that have long been of interest to experimental work in personality. Similarly, the model provides a compact way to represent many of the classic forms of psychopathology as well as the intrapsychic processes that underlie them. Of even greater interest, Benjamin shows how the theory of interpersonal dynamics can be utilized to construct a theory of psychotherapy. For a given problem behavior in a client, the model predicts the specific form of behavior that is required from the therapist in order to elicit the desired changed state in the client. The chapter supplies some illustrative case materials to show how one can make easy transitions from the analysis of basic to the analysis of applied processes. Additionally, the chapter includes a description of the sophisticated technology that has been developed to obtain and analyze the data needed to examine the utility of this theory. This work is a rich and complex theory in the making. Benjamin's chapter, presenting the many facets of this theory, provides a secure base against which to evaluate the results of the many studies that this approach is sure to evoke.

References

Allport, G. W. *Personality*. New York: Holt, 1937.

Bales, R. F. *Interaction process analysis: A method for the study of small groups*. Cambridge, MA: Addison–Wesley, 1950.

Bales, R. F. *Personality and interpersonal behavior*. New York: Holt Rinehart Winston, 1970.

Leary, T. *Interpersonal diagnosis of personality: A functional theory and methodology for personality evaluation*. New York: Ronald Press, 1957.

Lorr, M., & McNair, D. M. An interpersonal behavior circle. *Journal of Personality and Social Psychology*, 1963, *2*, 823–830.

Mischel, W. *Personality and assessment*. New York: Wiley, 1968.

Mischel, W. Toward a cognitive social learning reconceptualization of personality. *Psychological Review*, 1973, *80*, 252–283.

Schaefer, E. S. Configurational analysis of children's reports of parent behavior. *Journal of Consulting Psychology*, 1965, *29*, 552–557.

Wiggins, J. S. Circumplex models of interpersonal behavior. In L. Wheeler (Ed.), *Review of personality and social psychology* (Vol. 1). Beverly Hills, CA: Sage, 1980.

3

Search for the Self: Going beyond Self-Esteem and the Reactive Self*

William J. McGuire

Introduction

The heart of any exploration of the person must be a search for the self. The self is easy enough to find: one does not have to be a depressive (though it helps) to realize that at times the self is all too much with us. There are dark nights of the soul when one can appreciate Gerard Manley Hopkins's (1933) feeling that "The lost are like this, and their scourge to be / As I am mine, their sweating selves; but worse" and to accept his position that to be surprised by joy or even to experience peace sometimes requires a release from this albatross of self which, like the world, is too much with us: "Soul, self; come, poor jackself, I do advise / You, jaded, let be; call off thought awhile / Elsewhere; leave comfort root room." This ambivalent intimacy is caught also by Valéry in his phrase "Myself, which I hate like a spouse." But though we know well enough where it is (all too close), the self requires search because we do not know what it is. Thinkers wise and unwise from Socrates to Wagner have asserted that the human imperative is to "know thyself," but most people live lives in which they wrestle through the night like Jacob locked in the grip of this adversary or savior whose nature they never learn.

Thousands of psychological studies of the self (Wylie, 1974, 1979) have left its secrets still intact, in large part because of the research's having been

*The research reported in this chapter was made possible by the support of Grant No. 5 RO1 MH32588-04 received from the Interpersonal Processes and Problems Section of the National Institute of Mental Health.

73

limited to the reactive self and to the self-esteem dimension. As a corrective, the studies reported here present a lower researcher profile to the participants, permitting them to disclose themselves more fully and meaningfully on dimensions of their own choosing, rather than limiting the person's self-descriptive options to placing him- or herself in dimensions chosen by the investigator, my associates and I elicited the spontaneous self-concept as the person phenomenally experiences it by presenting generalized probes such as "Tell us about yourself" or "Tell us what you are not" and then analyzing the elicited material so as to retain most of its informational content. Before reporting the findings I describe first the philosophical speculations out of which they grew and then the methodological innovations by which I attempted to correct imbalances caused by previous overemphases on the reactive self-concept and on self-esteem. Then I report the results of our empirical research stemming from the distinctiveness postulate that the salience in one's self-concept of one's various physical characteristics, ethnicity, gender, etc., is determined by how peculiar one is on that characteristic, that is, its information value in distinguishing oneself from other people. The remaining empirical sections describe how consciousness of self changes during the childhood years, primarily as shown by developmental trends and sex differences in the significant others and in the verb forms one uses to describe oneself.

Theoretical Bases of the Distinctiveness Postulate of Perceptual Salience

Among us laborers in vineyards personological, trampling out our vintage red and white, a substantial minority are closet philosophers no less than is Henry Murray; however, our empirical work often derives vaguely at best from our fundamental philosophical musings. The empirical work reported here is exceptional in this regard because it flows directly from my basic philosophical speculations on epistemological and even ontological issues, some of which are rather different from commonsense assumptions regarding the nature of knowledge and of existence. Since I wear a different school tie from most of my psychological colleagues, I am usually too shrewd to tell such tales outside of class but it seems within the spirit of the Murray lectures to risk a little and let some of my philosophical slips show, blinding some with a light too bright for their eyes and raising the eyebrows and suspicions of others that the academic underrepresentation of us Catholic ethnics (the sin that dare not speak its name) may be well deserved. Those who do not yet have tenure might wisely hesitate before following my example here in revealing their philosophical musings, even when more orthodox than mine. Lest this philosophical discussion immediately following drive the dust bowl empiricists to less windy environments, I give assurance that these speculations lead to recognizable empirical research with independent and dependent variables, massive data collection, familiar descriptive and inferential statistics, etc.

A Nonexistential Philosophy

Giving the term nonexistentialism to my philosophy is admittedly a bit perverse because it risks suggesting that I am quarreling with some Heidegger–Jaspers–Sartre existential dictum such as the precedence of existence over essence. Rather, I am using *nonexistentialism* to label an ontological and epistemological position that stands on its head, like Marx does Hegel, some commonsense notions of what exists and what does not.

Since one is urged to wax historical as well as speculative in Murray lectures, I shall explain how this nonexistential epistemology was developed in my college days when as a philosophy major I wrestled with the ontological problem of individuation within Aristotelian–Thomistic theory. I could then accept without logical anguish the assertion either that nothing exists or that something exists because neither produced an intrinsic contradiction (although the assertion that nothing exists raises an embarrassing Cartesian question about the domain of discourse in which such an assertion can be made). What did give me intellectual unease was to assert that more than one thing exists, since positing that being is multiple seems to impale us on a dilemma: That which distinguishes (individuates) separate beings must itself either exist or not exist. If it does not exist, then how could it distinguish other things? If it does exist, then it violates my intuition that being can never be heterogeneous to itself and furthermore raises the question of what distinguishes this discriminator from the first two beings, and so on in an infinite regress, a "turtles all the way down" solution that has always left me uncomfortable. Furthermore, my ontological problem regarding distinctive individuated existence seemed to be related to several bothersome cosmological issues. For example, cosmogonic speculations on the origins and limits of the universe (whether one takes a theological, big-bang, or bubble stance; and even Hoyle's continuous-creation position does not completely escape this problem) raise the issue of the existential status of the space within which the universe came into being or into which it is expanding. A number of other cosmological enigmas seemed to involve related dilemmas, such as how gravity and other forces can operate at a distance, how probabilistic physical particles can disappear and reemerge further on in their orbital passages, how electrons jump discontinuously between the orbital levels, and how electromagnetic waves can propagate through mediumless space (Grant, 1981; Cantor & Hodge, 1981).

My solution to this cluster of confusions involves a figure–ground reversal that stands the usual conception of being on its head by asserting that what exists is that which is conventionally regarded as the absence of being, whereas what are commonly regarded as entities are interruptions in reality. Thus homogeneous "empty" space is existent being, whereas the physical particles that interrupt this continuum (electrons or muons or whatever is one's preferred particle of the week) are holes in reality. This reversing of the conventional concepts of being and nonbeing makes more graspable cosmological conundrums such as those mentioned above: That particles disappear and reappear at a distance becomes more imaginable when they are seen as gaps rather than entities, and the propagation of electromagnetic waves through space becomes more comprehensible when space is seen as the existent medium rather than a void containing a scattering of hydrogen particles. As regards cosmogony, the origin of the universe is then seen not as a creation but as an annihilation when an almighty fiat produced a big bang that rent the seamless web of infinite homogeneous existence, introducing a gap of nonexistence that is metastasizing through space, making the multiplicity of entities possible through negation.

Individuation is thus accomplished, not by what the individual thing is (because being is one and cannot be heterogeneous to itself), but rather by what it is not. On the cosmological level, electrons are holes in reality; on the personality level, what makes me be "me" to myself and others is not what I am but what I am not, the consciousness of absences that distinguishes me from others. On the cognitive level, I am conscious of myself in terms of absences, my awareness of the distinctive features that individuate me from others by being absent in one of us. I exist to myself and others in terms of my differences. If a feature is always present it is never noticed, like the fish being the last to discover the ocean. It is absences that make me present to myself and others.

Before I apply this nonexistentialism to the nature of self and self-consciousness, the historical scholarship appropriate to or at least permissible in a Murray lecture calls for my mentioning possible progenitors of these philosophical speculations. Those very few psychologists who return my secret Catholic handshake may suspect that my nonexistential position derives from Duns Scotus's relentless struggles with the problem of individuality and its intelligibility. I perceive that he was slouching toward something profound in his haecceity solution (despite its obscurity having made his name contribute the word "dunce" to the language, a thoughtless and accepted pejorative like "hocus pocus" that linguistically symbolizes the intellectual elites' willingness to keep the Catholic ethnic in his or her place—and out of theirs). Still, I believe that his solution and mine differ radically although I do not rule out the possibility that the subtle doctor's opaque prose may have kept his secret intact from me. I am able to resonate with the cadences of Gerard Manley Hopkins's (1933) magnificent Scotist sonnet, "As Kingfishers Catch Fire, Dragonflies Draw Flame," which I believe to be the finest philosophical poem in English in catching so magnificently Duns Scotus's passion for individuation:

> Each mortal thing does one thing and the same:
> Deals out that being indoors each one dwells;
> Selves—goes itself; myself it speaks and spells
> Crying what I do is me: for that I came.

If my nonexistential formulation did derive from Catholic philosophical speculation it is more likely to have been influenced by Nicholas of Cusa's analysis of God as non-other (J. Hopkins, 1979). It is significant that God, even while being conceptualized as pure being, is defined in terms of negation in theologies as disparate as the Hindu Upanishads' depiction of Brahman as the not-this, not-that, etc., to Simone Weil's (1952) conception of God as present in creation under the form of absences. If the theologians find being in absences, can the literary and textual analysts be far behind? The notion was relayed by Nietzsche and Valéry (1934) that "the only proper object of thought is that which does not exist" to current textual critics like Foucault and Derrida (1967), who hold that "God" or other constructs can be understood only by admitting the absence of a referent, only in the erasure of the "transcendental signified," bringing them uncomfortably close to Popper's (1959) contention that the information content of a theory is a set of statements that are incompatible with the theory. Parallel structuralist traditions, precariously bridged by Heidegger, derive from de Saussure's (1916) relativistic epistemology that the meaning of a word can be grapsed only in terms of its opposite; for example, in Bloom's (1974) misreadings that there are no texts but only relationships between texts and in distinctive feature theory (Baltaxe, 1978). Obviously the classes and the masses have had no trouble thinking about and writing about nothing, even though philosophers from Parmenides to Wittgenstein have asserted that it cannot be done (Heath, 1967).

However, I believe that my own nonexistential position is intellectually closer to Isaac Luria's cabalism, as developed by Vital and Nathan of Gaza, in its doctrine of individuation and particularly in its depiction of the origin of things as involving annihilation more than creation, the world beginning with a *tzimtzum* or contraction of God, this recoil being needed to make room in which the universe of discrete beings could emerge. However, I feel more awe than agreement with the further Lurianic imaginative yoking of the terminal phase of human history with the return of the Jews to Israel as a terrestrial driving force for the cosmic ingathering of the individualized sparks that had been scattered by the breaking of the vessels, until once again at the end there will be nothing but light (Scholem, 1954, 1973). The interweaving of these strands that we have mentioned is illustrated by the fact that Martin Buber, long before he became interested in Hasidic cabalism, wrote his doctoral dissertation on the problem of individuation in Nicholas of Cusa.

These abstract ontological speculations lead even the "God in the quad" theologians to cognitive psychological theorizing through the "to be is to be perceived" principle. If the individuating essence of a being that makes it be itself is the distinctive absences that make it not be other things, then it follows that we perceive a thing not in terms of what is there but what is absent. Perceiving the self (or any other object) involves recognizing the peculiar individuating ways in which it is not absolute being and so differs from other specific things. The person has evolved as an efficient recognizer of absences in things, information being defined as perceived distinctions and distinctions made possible only by absences. This linkage to information theory allows our discussion to descend from the abstract philosophical level to the more familiar level of psychological theorizing, from our nonexistential ontology and epistemology to social cognition implications such as the distinctiveness postulate regarding what is salient in person perception.

Information Overload, Perceptual Selectivity,
    and the Distinctiveness Postulate

Given the vast number of entities in the world, each differing from others by multiple absences that constitute information on the basis of which individual objects can be discriminated and enter awareness, it follows that the perceiving person is confronted by an astronomical amount of information. To some extent humans are spared from being drowned in information by having evolved with quite limited sensory capacity. For example, we can directly sense only the narrow visible light band within the infinite range of the electromagnetic spectrum. Presumably species have evolved adaptively so that their sensoria put them in contact with a subset of information that is cost-effective in terms of the organisms' needs and capacities, alerting them to differences between objects that are important for their surviving and thriving and which can be picked up by a sensory apparatus economical to develop and operate.

This receptor insensitivity to vast ranges of energy differentials preserves humans from being completely swamped, but even within this limited sensory capacity we are in a constant state of information overload (Blumenthal, 1977). Humans have evolved with a sensory capacity for taking in much more information than they can process centrally (as can be illustrated by the armchair experiment of closing one's eyes and trying to recall the details of the visual scene that have just been in foveal vision). Other mammals also have evolved with this need for perceptual selectivity, rats not learning to use the crucial cues falling on their appropriate senses while traversing a maze unless they happen to be "hypothesizing" that the given cue may be relevant while they are running the path, as Krech (Krechevsky, 1932) demonstrated during the "continuity" controversy of the 1930s (Harlow, 1949; Riley & Leith, 1976). Apparently there is survival value in having sensory access at any given moment to vastly more information than one can effectively process, allowing one the flexibility of sampling a wide universe of environmental information constituted by the innumerable sensible differences among things.

General Modes of Coping with Information Overload Confronted with more information about the environment than can be effectively encoded, humans have evolved with the capacity to make good use of this embarrassment of riches in a variety of ways such as the eight listed in Table 3.1, seven of which will be mentioned in passing and only the eighth (selective perception) discussed more fully because of its relevance to the present empirical work. A first way of coping is to chunk or change grain size by using consciousness's "zoom lens" capacity such that as the number of trees gets overwhelming, one can take a broader perspective and perceive the forest as a whole. Like other modes of coping with information overload, chunking is not only an acute capacity of which the person can make varying use as need arises but is also a chronic, individual-difference dispositional characteristic in that people differ in their persisting tendencies to be levelers versus sharpeners, lumpers versus splitters, broad versus narrow categorizers. A second mode of coping with information overload is concept utilization or categorizing information so that a highly complex experience is reductively encoded as an instance of a familiar stereotype. A third way of coping is to utilize our flexibility for diverting cognitive capacity from one function to another; for example, lying abed in the dark hours fantasying the destruction of our enemies or other delights without paying much attention to the sounds around us, if something suddenly goes bump in the night we can cease our reflection and divert a large part of our cognitive capacity from fantasy reprocessing into receptive attention to subsequent external sounds.

A fourth mode of coping with information overload is to use several levels of cognitive storage as a cow does her several stomachs, so that in a particularly rich sensory environment we can stuff information temporarily into

TABLE 3.1

General Modes of Coping with Information Overload

Mode	Source
1. Chunking, changing grain size	G. A. Miller, 1956; Simon, 1974; Mueller, 1978
2. Categorical assimilation	Pribram & McGuinness, 1975; Shiffrin & Schneider, 1977; Rosch & Lloyd, 1978)
3. Diverting capacity from other functions	Kahneman, 1973
4. Temporary storage for later processing	Sperling, 1960; Blumenthal, 1977
5. Alternating attention from aspect to aspect	Moray, 1969; Hochberg, 1970
6. Parallel processing	Egeth, 1966; Smith, 1968; D. A. Taylor, 1976; Hinton & Anderson, 1981
7. Broadening and diffusing attention	Gardner et al., 1959; Treisman, 1969
8. Selective perception	See Table 3.2

push-down lists for later deliberative processing when the opportunity allows (dream work being one illustration of this reprocessing during quiet time). A fifth way of exploiting excessive sensory information is to shift our attention from one aspect of the object to another, as when we focus serially on different aspects of a complex visual field or think successively about various aspects of a complex problem. A sixth mode is to do parallel processing, for example, encoding some aspects of the situation auditorily and others visually, or doing separate encoding by left and right hemispheres in words and images. Diffusing attention so that ordinarily peripheral regions enter partial awareness, at some loss of attention to central concerns, is a seventh mode of coping with information overload. An eighth mode is selective perception, paying attention to some categories of incoming information and ignoring others, a mode that will be discussed more fully in the next section because it is the mode giving rise to the empirical self-concept work reported here.

Bases of Perceptual Selectivity as a Mode of Coping with Information Overload

One goes through life oblivious of most of the information that reaches one's senses: for example, we do not register in any meaningful way most of the visual information that reaches our appropriate retinal receptors. As an armchair experiment, consider giving a talk before a group of strangers and, after having been visually scanning your audience for a half-hour, suddenly being asked to close your eyes and answer a series of questions about the appearance of specific members of the audience. You would probably get an abominably poor recall score, often being unable to recall whether the person directly in front of you is wearing a jacket or sweater, what his or her hair color is, whether he or she has eyeglasses, or whether the end seat in the third row is occupied, etc., even though all of this information had just been in your foveal vision. Obviously we are conscious of and monitoring the audience but, shrewd public speakers that we are, we pay attention to certain things while ignoring others. Table 3.2 lists a dozen variables that affect what is selectively perceived; brief mention will be made of the first 11 before discussing in more detail the twelfth basis (distinctiveness), which bears directly on the empirical research reported here.

A first possibility is that one selects a subset of stimulus information randomly, an austerely elegant possibility which, despite its seeming conceptual vacuity, has been used creatively by stimulus-sampling theorists. A second possible determinant of what gets selectively noticed is transient need state: A person, asked where a letterbox can be found along a route walked a hundred times, is frequently unable to say, apparently having looked many times at mailboxes in passing without registering them. Yet if one often walks down the street with a letter in hand, one notices the mailboxes, and when walking

TABLE 3.2

Variables That Determine Which Aspects of a Complex Stimulus
Are Most Likely to Be Noticed

Basis of selective salience	Representative classical theorists
1. Random choice	Guthrie, 1952; Estes, 1950; Campbell, 1956
2. Transient need states (biological importance)	McClelland & Atkinson, 1948; Deutsch & Deutsch, 1963
3. Enduring values	McGinnies, 1949; Bruner, 1957; Tajfel, 1957
4. Expectancy (set, familiarity)	Solomon & Howes, 1951; Broadbent, 1958; Treisman, 1969; Mackworth, 1970
5. Stimulus intensity	Brown, 1943; Hull, 1952; Kessen, 1953
6. Past reinforcement for noticing	Harlow, 1949; N. E. Miller, 1959; Lawrence, 1963; Mackintosh, 1975; Chance & Larson, 1976
7. Availability (recency, retrievability)	Tulving & Thompson, 1973; Tversky & Kahneman, 1974; Nisbett & Ross, 1980
8. Encodability (pattern, context, categorizability)	Neisser, 1967; Battig & Montague, 1969; Norman, 1968; Biederman et al., 1973; Gombrich, 1979
9. Dimensional prepotency	Rorschach, 1921; Vigotsky, 1939; Garner, 1970
10. Vividness (concreteness, imaginability)	S. E. Taylor & Thompson, 1982
11. Satiation (fatigue, reactive inhibition)	Glanzer, 1953; Amster, 1964; Jakobovits, 1968
12. Distinctiveness (novelty, information)	See Table 3.3

down the same mean street with an appetite, one notices the restaurant signs. Another possible basis of selectivity, much studied in the midcentury "perceptual defense" era, is the perceiver's enduring values insofar as she or he tends preferentially to notice and recognize positive words from valued domains and blocks out disturbing words. A fourth determinant of what gets noticed is expectancy (set, familiarity), one tending to notice what one expected to find, as demonstrated in tachistoscopic laboratory experiments and in actual social situations where each person tends to notice aspects that conform to his or her own initial prejudices or to experimenter-established sets. This expectancy determination of selectivity appeals to theorists (Dember, 1974; Tomkins, 1981) who prefer to avoid affective constructs (like the transient needs and enduring values just considered), which the expectancy explanation reduces to purely cognitive processes by assuming that material from domains we most value are more easily recognized because we are most familiar with them. Stimulus intensity is an obvious fifth determinant of selectivity, as when bright lights or loud noises attract more notice than faint ones.

A sixth determinant, widely discussed in the era of "liberated" stimulus–response theory, is acquired distinctiveness of cue: One selectively perceives what in the past one has been rewarded for noticing or punished for not noticing, as when the new army recruit by the end of basic training attends closely to the various military insignia of rank which he or she would have disregarded in civilian days. A seventh determinant of perceptual selectivity is the currently fashionable "availability" heuristic that one notices aspects whose frequency, recency, etc., makes them readily retrievable. An eighth is encodability, as when regularity of pattern, meaningfulness of context, or categorizability captures and propels one's gaze. Dimensional prepotency is a ninth determinant in that some aspects of a stimulus are more likely to be encoded than others, either in general or for some types of situations and individuals, as when color versus form prepotency are used to diagnose chronic disposition by the Vigotsky (1939) and Rorschach (1921) tests or when children switch from color to form prepotency in the preschool years. Determinant ten is vividness insofar as concreteness, imageability, directness, etc. of the aspect attracts attention.

An eleventh determinant is satiation (fatigue, reactive inhibition), a central encoding analog of peripheral sense organ adaptation or nerve fiber refractory phase; after a long session in which the person has been encoding one aspect of a situation he or she tends to reach a point where further exposure lessens the likelihood of encoding that aspect (Peeke & Herz, 1972). Distinctiveness is a twelfth determinant in that novel, peculiar aspects of a situation tend to capture our awareness. The next section will be devoted to a fuller discussion of this distinctiveness basis of selectivity because the first series of studies reported here derives directly from it. Each of these last two determinants, satiation and distinctiveness, appears to contradict the fourth determinant, expectancy, which asserted that one is most likely to perceive the familiar, expected aspects of stimuli. Similarly, determinants seven and eleven, availability and satiation, seem to make opposite predictions about the effect of repetitive recent elicitations on salience. Such internal contradictions are no more unlikely or undesirable within science than in society, considering the complexities of human needs and modes of coping and how heuristically provocative of higher-order syntheses such contradictions can be, as discussed in the next section in terms of my contextualist philosophy of science (McGuire, 1983).

Vicissitudes of the Distinctiveness Postulate of Perceptual Selectivity The twelfth notion, that a characteristic's distinctiveness (novelty, unexpectedness) enhances perceptual salience, has been postulated decade after decade (as illustrated in Table 3.3) by diverse theorists who maintain that what gets noticed is not so much things as the distinction between them—their peculiar aspects, the ways in which they differ from one another, what is absent rather than what is there. In the 1920s the notion that distinctive aspects are preferentially noticed was explicit in Pavlov's (1928) concept of the orienting reflex (Maltzman, 1967; Kimmel et al., 1979) and was at least implicit in Head's (1926) concept of vigilance. In the 1930s it was central to Boring's (1933) theory that consciousness consists of making discriminations and that intelligence is the capacity to make them; to Lashley's (1934) position that what gets noticed is not objects but distinctions between them; and to Piaget's (1936) theory that the child's attention is drawn to objects that do not quite fit already existing cognitive structures and so offer manageable category accommodation and assimilation challenges.

Two ingenious perception theories made use of the distinctiveness notion

TABLE 3.3

Representative Theorists in Successive Decades Postulating That Distinctiveness Enhances the Probability of an Aspect's Being Noticed

Decade	Representative theorists
1920s	Head, 1926; Pavlov, 1928
1930s	Boring, 1933; Lashley, 1934; Piaget, 1936
1940s	Köhler & Wallach, 1944; Hebb, 1949; J. J. Gibson, 1950; Helson, 1948
1950s	G. A. Miller, 1953; Riggs et al., 1953
1960s	Berlyne, 1960; Fiske & Maddi, 1961; Fowler, 1965; Bieri et al., 1966
1970s, 1980s	McGuire et al., 1976, 1982; S. E. Taylor & Fiske, 1978; Zuckerman, 1979; Snyder & Fromkin, 1980

in the 1940s: Köhler and Wallach's (1944) figural after-effect theorizing, which modified classical Gestaltism by maintaining that it is neither figure nor ground but the contour between them that is critical to perceptual experience; and Gibson's (1950) gradient theory of perception which similarly stressed the importance of contours and discontinuities in determining interpretations of and reactions to space. Also relevant are Hebb's (1949) reverberating circuit concept of a need for background stimulation and Helson's (1948) concept that a departure from adaptation level is needed for perception. The distinctiveness notion was put forward in several innovative ways during the 1950s. Riggs et al. (1953) showed that a constant stimulus, even if quite intense in magnitude, soon fades from consciousness if it impinges constantly on the same retinal elements without any movement to vary whether a given receptor is excited from moment to moment. Information theory entered the psychological mainstream at about this time (G. A. Miller, 1953), incorporating the distinctiveness notion in its depiction of communication as the sender's telling the receiver what he or she does not mean rather than what he or she does mean. Sender and receiver are conceptualized as each having a code book with all possible messages, with communication consisting of progressively eliminating successive portions of the total universe of message as not being meant until the single intended message remains.

The distinctiveness notion particularly flourished in the 1960s (McGuire, 1966), when a variety of theories stressed its motivating power in humans and other mammalian species under such terms as the curiosity drive (Fowler, 1965), the need for varied experience (Fiske & Maddi, 1961), etc. This epistemic motivational formulation was most fully developed by Berlyne (1960), with more specialized treatments being found in work on need for novelty (Harlow, 1953), orientation (Dykman et al., 1959), alternation behavior (Dember & Fowler, 1958), cognitive complexity (Bieri et al., 1966), stimulus hunger, and sensation seeking (Zuckerman, 1979).

Surprisingly, the same 1960s decade that saw this flurry of theories stressing human need for the novel and unexpected also witnessed a flourishing of consistency theories. These stressed an opposite aspect of the person, the need for congruence and confirmation of the expected, as proposed in Osgood and Tannenbaum's (1955) congruity theory, Heider's (1958) balance theory, Newcomb's (1953) symmetry theory, Festinger's (1957; Wicklund & Brehm, 1976) dissonance theory, and the McGuire–Wyer probabilogic theory (McGuire, 1960, 1981; Wyer & Carlston, 1979), etc. It is not atypical that opposite views of the person flourish contemporaneously. Humans, being complex, are often guided by antagonistic tendencies whose ascendency varies across situations so that one tendency or its opposite may be the more powerful predictor in a given context, a point that is fundamental to my contextualist philosophy of science (McGuire, 1983). The paradoxical coexis-

tence of contradictory postulates, such as that expectedness and unexpectedness both enhance perceptual salience, is desirable because together they serve
as thesis and antithesis whose internal contradiction can provide heuristic
impetus to a powerful higher synthesis, as in the derivation that people seek
out intermediate levels of unexpectedness whose optimal level shifts predictably as a function of dispositional and situational factors (Berlyne, 1960,
1970; Kagan, 1970; Veroff & Veroff, 1980).

Salience of Characteristics in the Spontaneous Self-Concept The diversity of
these numerous formulations of the distinctiveness postulate provides reas-
suring evidence of the concept's utility but at the same time leaves its applicability in any specific situation ambiguous so we shall formalize the distinctiveness theory as used in our self-concept studies. The postulate asserts
that a person exists insofar as he or she is different and that he or she is
perceived by self and others in terms of those differences. When one thinks of
oneself generically as a human being, one thinks of characteristics by which
people are distinguished from other classes of beings; when one thinks of
oneself as an individual person it is in terms of ways that one is different from
other people, particularly from those with whom one comes in frequent
contact. Since one perceives oneself in terms of characteristics that differenti-
ate one from one's usual associates, then one's phenomenal sense of self will
change in predictable ways as one moves from one social setting to another.
For example, if a black woman serves on a jury with 11 black men, she will
think of herself as a woman; but if she then takes part in a committee meeting
with 11 white women, she will think of herself as a black. Richard Wright
wrote that one of his gains in moving from Chicago to Paris was that in
Chicago he was viewed by himself and others as a black, a characteristic
irrelevant to his vocation as writer; but in Paris he was perceived by others
and saw himself as an English-speaking person, an identity more in keeping
with and supportive of this vocation.

Distinctiveness theory's application to the spontaneous self-concept can be
illustrated by the self-perceptions of the people in a group consisting of a
black woman, a white woman, and three white men, each represented as a
column heading in Table 3.4. The row titles in Table 3.4 represent two
dimensions, gender and ethnicity, on which distinctions can be made among
the five persons in this group. The numerical entry in each of the 10 cells
indicates the number of other people in the group from whom the column
person differs on the row dimension. For example, in the gender row, because there are two women and three men, each woman gets a discrimination
score of 3 in her gender cell because her gender differs from that of the three
men, and each man gets a score of 2 in his gender cell since he is distinctive
from the two women members in this regard. The row totals, column totals,
and cell entries each yield salience predictions about what gets mentioned if

TABLE 3.4

Illustration of the Distinctiveness Postulate:
Salience of Gender and Ethnicity of Each Person in a Group
Including a Black Woman, a White Woman, and Three White Men

Dimension (j)	Person (i)					
	Black woman	White woman	White man	White man	White man	Σ
Gender	3	3	2	2	2	12
Ethnicity	4	1	1	1	1	8
Σ	7	4	3	3	3	20

we ask the five people in the Table 3.4 group to "Tell us about yourself." The row sums show us that gender is half again more likely to be mentioned by members of this group than is ethnicity; the column sums indicate that the women are twice as likely as the men to describe themselves in terms of these two characteristics; and the cell entries show, for example, that the black woman is 33% more likely to mention her ethnicity than gender, while the white woman is 300% more likely to mention her gender than ethnicity. In general, the probability of noticing a given entity's, i, aspect on dimension j (for example, the black woman's femaleness being noticed in this group), p_{ij}, is given by the following function:

$$ p_{ij} \propto \frac{N - n_{ij}}{\sum\limits_{j=1}^{x} \sum\limits_{i=1}^{y} (N - n_{ij})} , $$

where N is the number of people (or other objects) in the perceptual field and n_{ij} is the number of entities with i's aspect on the dimension j. It is this formulation that underlies the studies reported below on how a characteristic's distinctiveness determines its salience in the spontaneous self-concept. It can be seen from this formulation that the salience of a characteristic increases both with the number of discriminable categories on the characteristic and with the equipotentiality of the entities' (persons' or whatever) distribution among these categories.

Innovations Needed in Self-Concept Research

The person's sense of self is a quintessential psychological topic, and so it is not surprising that it has been one of the most heavily studied issues throughout the history of empirical psychology. Thousands of studies on the topic have been reviewed by M. Rosenberg (1979) and by Wylie (1974, 1979), the latter requiring 1200 pages to review accumulated research even though she has been highly selective as to topics covered. From so much labor, a disappointingly modest intellectual progeny has come forth. Scattered relationships of interest have been demonstrated (as have more numerous surprising lacks of relationships), but even those who have labored with love in the area express disappointment in their reviews. I attribute the meagerness of the yield to past research's having been very narrow in two regards: its having been limited to the study of the reactive self-concept and its almost exclusive preoccupation with the self-esteem dimension, each limitation calling for the brief discussion that follows.

The Limited Information Yield of Reactive Self-Concept Research

The reactive method that characterizes most psychological research has also dominated self-concept work in that the researcher almost always selects the dimension to be studied and asks the participants to place themselves on it. For example, the researcher presents a dimension in the form of such items as, "I am able to do things as well as most people," or "I give in very easily," or "Myself: fast . . . slow," and asks the participant to select the one response option that best locates him- or herself on this experimenter-chosen dimension. The chosen response reveals the "reactive" self-concept in the sense that the participant is simply reacting to dimensions presented by the experimenter; it could alternatively be called the "hypothetical" self-concept in that it provides "as if" information about where participants would think of themselves on the dimension were they ever to think about it, without revealing whether in fact the dimension is at all salient in people's thoughts about themselves.

The contextualist metatheory that I have been proposing (McGuire, 1983) calls for the researcher's being more permissive in allowing participants leeway in selecting dimensions on which to describe themselves (or otherwise respond). Such permissiveness yields important information that is lost in the reactive approach because the dimension that the respondent spontaneously choses for describing the self (or other stimulus object) reveals what is significant to the person, whereas the reactive approach reveals only where the person would think of her- or himself as falling on the researcher's dimension when and if she or he ever thought about it. Our research has gone beyond the reactive self, measuring the "spontaneous" self-concept by presenting participants with nondirective "Tell us about yourself" probes, which allow them to describe themselves in terms of the dimensions most cognitively available, thus providing information on the more psychologically significant issue of what are the dimensions in terms of which the person actually does think of self. Three other research traditions present a comparably low profile to the participants in order to collect information regarding what is actually salient in the self-concept, namely Kuhn's "Twenty Statement Test" (Kuhn & McPartland, 1954; Spitzer, Couch & Stratton, 1971), Bugental's "Who Are You" test (Bugental & Zelen, 1950), and Kelly's (1970; Pope & Keen, 1982) "Rep" test. However users of these procedures have been relatively few and have seldom exploited their information potential (Wylie, 1974). Our own program of research both collects data revealing the dimensions in terms of which the participants think about themselves and also makes fuller use of the rich information contained in the responses evoked.

Overpreoccupation with the Self-Esteem Dimension

Whether they are studying attitudes, person perception, the self-concept, or whatever, modern psychologists (and perhaps the whole "Protestant ethic" culture?) are obsessed with evaluating, investigating the good–bad dimension almost to the exclusion of all others, as if evaluation were the only dimension in people's meaning space. As a result, the reactive approach used in most self-concept research has for the past half-century exhibited the further restriction that the researcher-chosen dimension is usually confined to the self-evaluation dimension, to the extent that Wylie's (1974, 1979) two-volume review of the area might as appropriately have been called *Self-Esteem* as *The Self-Concept*. That students of the person and of society should be preoccupied so exclusively with the bottom line of how good or bad any object of thought is, ignoring any other aspect of the object, reflects upon the spirit of our age or at least upon the peculiar turn of mind of those drawn to social science research.

By moving our own research beyond this one overstudied dimension of evaluation we are not implying that self-esteem is a trivial aspect of the self but simply that it has been vastly overemphasized relative to other aspects. Only 5–10% of the material that people report in response to a nondirective "Tell us about yourself" probe is explicitly self-evaluation ("I'm a pretty handsome guy," "I am a slow reader," "I'm not a cut-up like most people in this class," "I cry too easily"). Over 90% of the elicited self-descriptive material is not explicitly evaluative but rather items like "I wish I had a dog," "My job is taking out the garbage," "I often go fishing with my father," "I may go to college." Although each of these statements could, with some interpretation, be scored on the evaluative dimension (S. Rosenberg, 1977), it also conveys further information about dimensions of the self other than the evaluative. Self-esteem deserves some attention but it is excessive to devote over 90% of the self-concept research to this single dimension that accounts for less than 10% of subjective self-space content, an excess that the work reported here is intended to correct.

Research on Characteristic Distinctiveness and Salience in the Self-Concept

Our first series of studies on the spontaneous self-concept tested derivations from the distinctiveness postulate that a person's characteristic will be salient in his or her phenomenal sense of self to the extent that her or his position on the characteristic is atypical, differentiating her or him from most other people in a customary social milieu. This distinctiveness postulate follows from my nonexistential epistemological speculations discussed above. Three distinctiveness studies will be reported, dealing successively with the salience of physical characteristics, of ethnicity, and of gender in people's spontaneous self-concept as a function of how distinctive the person is on a given characteristic. Before the predictions and results on each of these three topics are described in detail, a preliminary section will set forth the general method of data collection used in these spontaneous self-concept studies, the type of data obtained, and how the data are analyzed.

General Methods in the Spontaneous Self-Concept
   Studies

Data Collection Procedures Participants in this research included students, from first graders through college, who were asked to say anything that came to mind in response to a "Tell us about yourself" inquiry and given 5 minutes to respond, either orally for tape recording in individually run conditions or by writing in a booklet in a group-administered classroom situation. These response protocols were then content analyzed to obtain a measure of the dependent variables—the salience of the physical characteristics, gender, ethnicity, or whatever—as indicated by their spontaneous mention. After responding to the "Tell us about yourself" probe, the participant was given a structured interview to collect data on the independent variables, for example, the student's actual physical characteristics, ethnicity, gender, household sex composition, and so on, and to determine how peculiar the characteristic has been in the student's usual social milieu.

General Nature of the Obtained Responses and Content Analyses Content analysis of each participant's 5-minute response to the "Tell us about yourself" probe involved three steps: (1) dividing the prose into 3-unit (subject–verb–object) segments, (2) pre-editing the participant's prose constructions slightly into a standardized grammar (for example, the rare passive voice expressions were transformed to active) that better fit this 3-unit structure, and (3) translating his or her words into a standardized vocabulary provided by a dictionary of about a thousand concepts, which retains much of the essential information in the original response protocol but simplifies it somewhat to facilitate computer analysis (for example, by eliminating intensifiers like "very" and by translating specifics like "Great Dane" into the more generic "dog").

In the written condition, the children responded with an average of 14 3-unit segments in the 5 minutes allowed, the length increasing progressively with age from 9 segments by fifth graders to 15 segments by twelfth graders and with a sex difference such that boys produced an average of 12 segments and girls, 15, both age and gender differences being significant at the .05 level. An illustrative written protocol by a ninth-grade female is the following:

> Well, I am not very smart in some areas. I am not very pretty. I like almost all kinds of activities, especially summer sports. I like to have a good time at parties and get-togethers. I like dogs very much and horses. I do not have very many friends but the ones I have I like and get along with very well. I like to play my records while I am doing my homework and in my spare time I have a baby-sitting job. I am 14 and I have my problems too.

The 5-minute self-descriptions in the oral condition were of course considerably longer, averaging 28 3-unit segments. Again response length increased with age, from 22 segments for the first graders to 34 segments for the eleventh graders, the age trend being significant at the .05 level. However, whereas the girls' protocols were longer than the boys in the more difficult written condition, in the more assertive oral condition the boys were slightly more verbose than the girls, boys and girls averaging 29 and 27 segments, respectively. An illustrative oral response, written by an eleventh-grade female, is the following:

> Well, I enjoy kids and I like to type and I enjoy coming to school and I like some subjects but some aren't so hot that I like to go to them. And I really want a job as a secretary; if I can't get that, I'd

like to work with kids. And if that's not possible, I'd like to work in a store. And I like any kind of music that's good. I like to go out on weekends and have fun. And I really enjoy my parents. They try to understand me when I've got problems and when there's a problem at home, I try to understand that. If, like, I can't go where I want, and my mother has to yell at me for some reason, I understand. And, I don't know, I really get along with my family and my friends at school. And I really like some of the teachers they have in school. Some of them are very understanding. Some are just, I don't know, you don't understand what they're talking about. And they say, "Ask questions," and when you ask questions, they get so pissed. But Mrs. [name deleted] is very nice and Mr. [name deleted] and a whole mess of other teachers; but some of them just, I don't know, I just can't stand them. And I like all of my friends. They try to help one another, you know, when we're in trouble. And I like to help my friends if I can and if I can't, well I try to tell them why I can't . . . and if it's impossible . . . if I can find a way, I always try to help them. If they need money and I have it, I give it to them. And, I don't know, I guess that's all. I really enjoy kids, though.

Salience of Distinctive Physical Characteristics

Because physical characteristics occur fairly frequently in the spontaneous self-concept and their distinctiveness is easy to score objectively, our first study of distinctiveness postulate predictions focused on them. Most people in responding to the "Tell us about yourself" probe report some physical characteristics in describing themselves, the most commonly mentioned being height, weight, hair color, and eye color, so these four were included among the ones to be studied. We also studied the frequency of mention of two less salient characteristics, wearing eyeglasses and handedness, and of two commonly mentioned quasi-physical characteristics, age and birthplace (McGuire & Padawer-Singer, 1976; McGuire & McGuire, 1981, 1982).

In the most elaborate of these studies (McGuire & McGuire, 1981) we obtained written "Tell us about yourself" responses from 1000 school children including 100 boys and 100 girls at each of five grade levels—the fifth, seventh, ninth, eleventh, and twelfth grades (fifth graders being the youngest who could complete the writing tasks without noticeable discomfort). The children were tested in their regular classroom settings and given 5 minutes to write down all the thoughts that came to mind in response to the "Tell us about yourself" probe; their responses were content analyzed to measure the dependent variable, salience in self-space of the various physical characteristics. Initially we scored salience on a 4-point scale with a score of 3 for more than one mention of the physical characteristic; 2 for one mention occurring during the first half of the protocol; 1 for one mention occurring during the second half of the protocol; and 0 for no mentions. However, the frequency of mentions was too low to justify this refined 4-point scale, so in the discussion that follows the salience dependent variable is scored on a simple dichotomous scale, 1 for any mention versus 0 for no mention of the characteristic.

After they wrote out their 5-minute spontaneous self-descriptions, the children were given a structured questionnaire asking for their actual height, weight, hair color, etc., so that we could calculate their independent variable distinctiveness scores. Since responses on the structured questionnaire gave every participant's actual position on each of the physical characteristics, it was easy to calculate the child's distinctiveness on any characteristic within his or her usual social milieu, which we defined as the students in the same school on his or her gender and grade level.

Salience of Height and Weight Height was spontaneously mentioned by 19% of the children and weight by 11% during their 5-minute self-descriptions, so these two physical characteristics are fairly salient. Each is mentioned about equally often by boys and girls; as regards age trends, height is equally salient across grade levels but weight becomes progressively more salient with age. The distinctiveness hypothesis that a trait's salience is greater for those with atypical or extreme positions on that dimension was confirmed for each of these two characteristics. As regards height, 27% of very tall or very short children (5 inches above or below the mean height for their gender and grade level) spontaneously described themselves in terms of their height; but only 17% of children close to average height spontaneously mentioned their height. As regards weight, 12% of the heavy and light children (those whose weight deviated by 14 pounds above or below the grade level mean for their gender) spontaneously described themselves in terms of weight as contrasted with only 6% mention by children of normal weight. Overweight children were especially likely to mention their weight, while tallness and shortness were equally likely to provoke self-description in terms of height.

Salience of Hair and Eye Color These two characteristics were almost as salient as height and weight, hair color being mentioned by 14% of the respondents and eye color by 11%, both significantly more often by girls than by boys and by younger than by older children. The salience of hair color confirmed the distinctiveness postulate prediction: significantly ($p < .05$) more of the blonde- and red-headed minority spontaneously described themselves in terms of their hair color than did the black- and brown-haired majority. The distinctiveness prediction was not confirmed as regards eye color: slightly more of the blue-eyed minority mentioned their eye color than did the brown-eyed majority, but the difference was of trivial statistical magnitude.

Salience of Birthplace and Age Age was highly salient to these students, 31% mentioning it as part of their self-description (girls and younger children significantly more often); birthplace was mentioned by only 6%, without significant gender or grade differences. Birthplace salience confirmed the distinctiveness prediction but age salience did not. As regards birthplace, only 3% of the great majority of participants who were born in the state (and usually the city) in which the research was done mentioned their typical birthplace. By contrast, 15% of the minority who were born outside the state (and 18% of the smaller minority born outside the United States) spontaneously described themselves in terms of their birthplaces. As regards age, there was only a trivial effect of atypicality on salience: 33% of the atypically older or younger children (those more than 6 months different from their grade level's age mean) spontaneously mentioned their age, which is only slightly and nonsignificantly more than the 30% mention by the more typically aged children (those within 6 months of their grade level mean).

Salience of Wearing Eyeglasses This "acquired" physical characteristic has low salience in the self-concept: Although 31% of the children reported wearing eyeglasses at least occasionally when they were later asked explicitly if they wore glasses, fewer than 2% spontaneously mentioned their wearing glasses in response to the "Tell us about yourself" probe. Even at this low base rate of responding, the distinctiveness postulate was supported in that in classes where eyeglass-wearing was relatively rare (less than 30% of the class-mates reporting that they used glasses), 8% of the wearers spontaneously mentioned their wearing eyeglasses in response to the "Tell us about your-self" probe, whereas in classes where eyeglasses are more common (30% or more of the classmates reporting wearing them) significantly fewer, only 1%, of the wearers spontaneously mentioned using them.

Salience of Handedness Handedness has very low salience in school-children's self-concepts, with only one of the participants in the just-discussed study spontaneously mentioning it in response to "Tell us about yourself." It became more salient when we went from the general to the physical self-concept, elicited by asking "Tell us what you look like." In response to this probe, handedness was sufficiently salient to allow analysis, showing a trend significantly ($p < .05$) in accord with the distinctiveness prediction: A van-ishingly small percentage of the right-handed schoolchildren as contrasted to 2% of the left-handers spontaneously mentioned their handedness as part of their self-perception of what they looked like. Handedness is somewhat more salient among college students, and their responses similarly confirm the distinctiveness postulate. When 291 introductory psychology undergraduate students responded to the general "Tell us about yourself" probe, of the 14% who were left-handed 8% spontaneously mentioned their sinistrality while fewer than 1% of the 86% who were right-handers spontaneously mentioned their dexterity, a significant difference in accord with the distinctiveness postulate (McGuire & McGuire, 1980).

In general, these results regarding the salience of physical characteristics in the spontaneous self-concept are in reasonable agreement with the distinctiveness postulate. The trends for all eight of the physical characteristics investigated came out in the direction predicted by the distinctiveness postulate and the relationship was significant above the .05 level for six of the eight characteristics. On several of these characteristics the distinctiveness prediction was confirmed even though it went against an opposite social desirability prediction, as when people who were overweight or were foreign-born described themselves in terms of these stigmatized oddities more often than did people of the more acceptable (but so typical as to go unnoticed) average weight and local birthplace.

Salience of Ethnicity as a Function of School Racial Heterogeneity

The remaining two studies on the distinctiveness postulate turned from physical characteristics to two politically sensitive demographic characteristics, the salience in self-space of one's ethnicity and one's gender. The extent to which ethnicity is salient in person perception (self and others) has been a matter of social concern during the past half century. Ethical and esthetic feelings on the issue are complex and ambivalent, in that liberal people usually think it desirable for person perception to be color-blind, but on the other hand are tolerant of the argument that racial consciousness is a "good thing" for members of nondominant groups although perhaps deplorable if it occurs in the dominant group. The distinctiveness postulate suggests an additional dilemma by implying that racial integration heightens the tendency of the people brought together to perceive self and others in terms of ethnicity because as one's group becomes more racially heterogeneous, one's ethnicity becomes more informative by its distinctiveness. If so, those who favor school integration and also wish that people would perceive one another on dimensions other than ethnicity will have to settle for a trade-off because school integration, by increasing racial heterogeneity and therefore informativeness, also increases the extent to which the school children will perceive themselves and each other in terms of their similar or contrasting ethnicity. McGuire, McGuire, Child, and Fujioka (1978) tested the distinctiveness predictions about how school ethnic heterogeneity affects the salience of ethnicity in the students' self-concepts.

Method The participants were 560 public school students in a middle-sized city in the northeastern United States—70 boys and 70 girls from each of four grade levels (the first, third, seventh, and eleventh). The eleventh graders included those in one of the two large high schools in the city, the seventh graders were from two junior highs that fed into that high school, and the first and third graders were from three elementary schools that fed into the two junior highs; thus similar neighborhoods were sampled at all grade levels. Within each school, virtually all of the students at any given grade level were included in the study except for those who were chronically absent. Students were called individually from their classrooms and during an oral interview were requested to "Tell us about yourself." The student had 5 minutes to say all of the thoughts that came to mind; these responses were later transcribed and content analyzed for mentions of ethnicity, which was scored as a dichotomous "mention versus no mention" dependent variable. The independent variable, distinctiveness of the child's actual ethnicity in his or her school, was measured by having the interviewer judge, on the basis of appearance, accent, name, etc., the ethnicity of each child; then, after the ethnicity of all students in a school had been judged, the distinctiveness of each ethnicity was scored in terms of the proportion of students in the school who were of other ethnicities.

Results The interviewers classified the children into four ethnic categories including the majority white English-speaking (82%), and the minority black (9%), Hispanic (8%), and other and uncertain (1%). The basic distinctiveness postulate prediction that ethnicity will be more salient in the minority than the majority group was confirmed: Of the white English-speaking students, only 1% spontaneously mentioned their ethnicity during their 5-minute self-descriptions while 14% of the Hispanic and 17% of the black students spontaneously mentioned their ethnicity in describing themselves ($p < .01$ for this majority vs. minority difference). A more subtle prediction is that within any one ethnic group, the salience of ethnicity will decline to the extent that this group becomes a more preponderant part of the total student body. This prediction was supported in the total participant population in that for all three ethnic groups combined, it was found that children were less likely to mention their ethnicity spontaneously when their ethnic group representation in their classroom exceeded than when it fell short of their ethnic group's representation in the city's total student body. This prediction was also confirmed separately for the white English-speaking students and the Hispanics; for example, when the white English-speaking students constituted less than 80% of their class, 4% of them spontaneously mentioned their ethnicity, but when they constituted more than 80%, less than 1% spontaneously mentioned their ethnicity ($p < .01$ for the difference). However, for the blacks analyzed separately an opposite relationship was found: When the blacks constituted less than 10% of the students in their class, only 5% spontaneously mentioned their ethnicity, whereas when they became a more substantial minority constituting more than 10%, 26% spontaneously mentioned ethnicity. Perhaps this exceptional behavior of the black subgroup represents some special historical situation such that currently black consciousness-raising interventions are more likely to occur when the size of the black minority increases to some critical mass in excess of 10%.

Salience of Gender as a Function of Household Sex Composition

Just as the reactive self-concept in general has been amply (even excessively) studied, its special subarea of gender identity has also received massive research attention but usually as regards its affective and conative manifestations, to the neglect of its cognitive aspects. That is, most of the research has concentrated either on affective considerations of how satisfied the person is with her or his feminine or masculine identity, or the conative, role-taking consideration of how well the person's behavioral pattern matches the conventional gender role ascribed to her or his sex. The spontaneous self-concept approach allows investigating the neglected cognitive aspect of gender identity by considering how salient the person's gender is in her or his sense of self. The hypothesis derived from the distinctiveness postulate is that the person is more conscious of her or his gender to the extent his or her gender tends to be in the minority in her or his significant social settings (McGuire & Padawer-Singer, 1976; McGuire, McGuire, & Winton, 1979).

Method We used the responses to the "Tell us about yourself" probe obtained from 560 students used in the ethnicity-salience study just described to measure also the dependent variable of gender salience. Each child's spontaneous mention of gender was scored on a dichotomous scale of gender mention versus no-mention in his or her 5-minute oral self-description. The independent variable of gender distinctiveness in the child's accustomed social settings was measured with respect to the home rather than school setting because the classes varied little from gender equipotentiality, it apparently being school policy to balance each class as regards sex ratio. Chronic gender distinctiveness was measured in terms of the preponderance of other gender in the child's household. After giving his or her 5-minute self-description, each of the students was interviewed regarding the makeup of his or her household. They were asked whether the mother and the father (or their surrogates) were present, which siblings of each gender were present, and the gender of any other people currently living in the household. In this way it was possible to measure the extent to which each child was currently living in a household in which his or her own gender predominated or was in a minority (McGuire, McGuire, & Winton, 1979).

Results Gender was substantially more salient than ethnicity in the spontaneous self-concepts: 9% of the 560 children reported their being boys or girls as part of their self-descriptions while only 3% mentioned their ethnicity.Gender became progressively more salient with age, being mentioned by only 3% of first graders, increasing to 5 and 10% for third and seventh graders, and to 19% for eleventh graders. Gender was mentioned slightly more often by girls than boys, but the difference is of trivial statistical significance and there was no appreciable sex-by-age interaction effect on gender salience.

To test the distinctiveness postulate prediction we partitioned the children into three groups: those from female-majority households (33%), those whose households contained equal numbers of each sex (29%), and those from male-majority households (38%). That the results support the distinctiveness prediction can be seen in Figure 3.1: Boys spontaneously mentioned their being boys most when they came from female-majority households and least when they came from male-majority households, while girls mentioned being girls least when they came from female-majority households and most when they came from households with male majorities ($p < .05$ for each gender).

Another distinctiveness postulate implication regarding gender salience in the self-concept is that father's absence from the household should increase a boy's consciousness of his being male, a prediction that may seem to conflict with the social learning theory prediction that a father's absence will interfere with the boy's attaining a masculine identity. The results tend to confirm the distinctiveness postulate prediction: 33 of the boys in our sample came from households in which the mother but not the father was present and 18% of these mentioned that they were male as part of their spontaneous self-concepts; while among the 227 boys in our sample who came from homes in which both mothers and fathers were present, a significantly ($p < .05$) lower 7% spontaneously mentioned being boys. (Father presence or absence made no difference on the extent to which girls spontaneously mentioned their femaleness, and there was not a sufficient number of households with fathers present and mothers absent to make a meaningful test of whether mother absence affects gender salience.) The Moynihan (1965) report, *The Negro Family,* like many other studies on the effects of father absence, assumes that

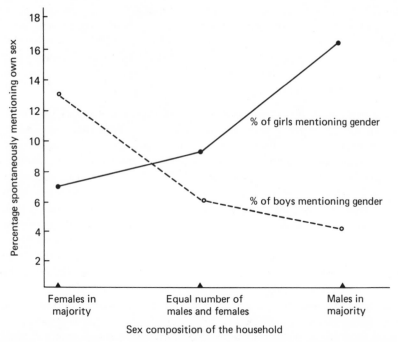

98   William J. McGuire

Figure 3.1   Increasing salience of gender in the spontaneous self-concept as the other gender's numerical predominance in one's household increases. Reprinted with permission from *Self-concept: Advances in theory and research.* © 1981, Ballinger Publishing Company.

boys growing up in fatherless households tend to have a deficiency in masculine role identity, but our data indicate that actually such boys are more conscious of their maleness than those from homes with fathers present, in accordance with the distinctiveness postulate's implication that in the absence of a father in the home, the boy's maleness becomes more distinctive and hence more noticed by him and others in the household. Of course, the two predictions can be reconciled: Our distinctiveness postulate makes predictions regarding the cognitive salience of gender in sense of self, one's consciousness of being a male or a female; the social learning theory predictions deal more with the conative aspect, the gender appropriateness of one's role playing, predicting that boys from fatherless homes, lacking the paternal role model and reinforcer of masculine behavior, will behave in ways that less closely match the socially prescribed masculine behavioral pattern. It may be that boys from fatherless homes are more aware of being male (our predicted and obtained cognitive effect) but less happy about it and less knowledgeable regarding what to do about it (the affective and conative effects usually predicted from social learning theory). Past neglect of the cognitive salience of gender is unfortunate since gender identity may develop first, prior to the learning of role-prescribed behavior (Kohlberg, 1966; Ullian, 1976).

The Affirmation versus Negation Self-Concept

So far we have been discussing the "Tell us about yourself" probe as a measure of the self-concept in general. However, to avoid ambiguity we should call responses to this specific probe by the narrower term of *affirmation self-concept*, to distinguish it from the *negation self-concept* given in response to a "Tell us what you are not" probe or a *physical self-concept* given in response to a "Tell us what you look like" probe. It is the negation self-concept that particularly concerns us here. People are interestingly inefficient at processing negative information; for example, in concept formation it is found (Hovland, 1952) that humans make less use of negative than positive instances even if one adjusts for the relative amount of information they contain. The nonexistential epistemology underlying the distinctiveness postulate raises an interesting question regarding the negation self-concept: If according to the postulate the person acquires a sense of self by noticing what he or she is not, then how does the person perceive what he or she is not? To explore the nature of the negation self-concept we asked the 560 children who had responded orally to the affirmation self-concept "Tell us about yourself" probe also to respond to the negation self-concept probe, "Tell us what you are not." Here we shall describe some obtained differences between affirmation and negation self-concepts as regards the salience of ethnicity and of gender.

Salience of Ethnicity in the Negation Self-Concept   Ethnicity is more salient in the negation than affirmation self-concept: Only 3% of the young people spontaneously mentioned their ethnicity in their 5 minutes of self-description in response to "Tell us about yourself," but over 6% spontaneously mentioned not having ethnicities other than their own in the 3-minute responses to the "Tell us what you are not" negation self-concept probe. The distinctiveness postulate implies an interaction prediction as regards ethnicity salience between affirmation versus negation self-concept and whether the person is in the majority or the minority group. As mentioned in an earlier section, in the affirmation self-concepts minority group people are much more likely to describe themselves in terms of their ethnicity than are the majority group members by a 15 versus 1% ratio, as predicted by distinctiveness theory. The theory predicts an opposite effect of majority versus minority group membership on ethnic salience in the negation self-concept. The affirmation self-concept's "Tell us about yourself" probe focuses one's attention on peculiarities in the self, so that it is the black and Hispanic children in New England who are more likely to notice their peculiar lack of the typical white ethnicity and thus define themselves in terms of their blackness or Hispanic status. On the other hand, the negation self-concept "Tell us what you are not" probe focuses one's attention on people other than oneself, so that one notices the peculiarities in other people that one does not share, and therefore it is the majority group members who are more aware of minority ethnicity as being a distinctive feature that does not characterize them.

The results confirmed this tortuously derived interaction prediction. The white majority group, with a vanishing 1% spontaneous mention of their ethnicity as part of their affirmation self-concepts, were much more conscious of their not having minority ethnicity, 5% mentioning their not being black or Hispanic as part of their negation self-concept, the increase from 1% to 5% being significant at the .01 level. For the black and Hispanic minority students, on the other hand, as predicted, the salience of ethnicity declined from the 15% who mentioned their own black or Hispanic ethnicity as part of their affirmation self-concept to only 7% who mentioned white ethnicity in their negation self-concept as something they were lacking.

Salience of Gender in the Negation Self-Concept Gender, like ethnicity, is more salient in the negation than affirmation self-concept: Whereas only 9% of the children mentioned that they were boys or girls in response to the "Tell us about yourself" probe, 25% reported not being a member of the other sex in response to "Tell us what you are not," a difference significant at the .01 level. Also, there is an interaction effect between own gender and type of self-concept in that there was only a trivial difference between boys and girls in salience of gender in the affirmation self-concept mentions, but in the negation self-concept girls were much more likely to mention they were not boys than boys were to mention they were not girls ($p < .05$ for the sex difference). Although these main and interaction effects—that one thinks of the other gender (and ethnicity) as something one is not more than one thinks of own gender as something one is and that this tendency is especially pronounced in females—are not derivable from the distinctiveness postulate, they are of interest in their own right and illustrate the serendipitous findings that can emerge when the open-ended spontaneous self-concept approach is used instead of the usual reactive approach.

The Social Self: Significant Others in Self-Space

The distinctiveness research just described and the social-self research to which we now turn illustrate contrasting divergent and convergent strategies

(McGuire, 1969, 1983) of using theory in research. The divergent style used in the distinctiveness studies involves starting with a single theoretical notion (here, the postulate that aspects of complex stimuli like the self are noticed to the extent they have information value by being distinctive, atypical, unpredictable) and applying it divergently to a wide variety of manifestations. The social-self research, on the other hand, uses the contrasting convergent style of starting with a phenomenon to be explained (in this social-self case, the extent to which people define themselves in terms of other people) and bringing a variety of theoretical postulates convergently to bear on the phenomenon to be explained. The divergent style uses a single theoretical insight to explain a small amount of the variance in each of a wide variety of relationships; the convergent style uses a wide variety of theories to explain much of the variance in a single relationship. These contrasting explanatory aims result in radically different research strategies being used by divergent and convergent theorists, who at many choice points in the empirical process elect opposite options. McGuire (1983) describes how a better appreciation of these contrasting explanatory aims would help resolve some long-continuing controversies about optimal research methods.

It is predictable that a sizable proportion of the person's phenomenal self-space is occupied by thoughts of the self in relation to other people. Freud (1921) observes that not only when one is engaged in interpersonal activity but even in one's most autistic thinking another person is always involved as a model, helper, rival, or whatever. Our social-self research on the salience and identity of the significant others in terms of whom one describes oneself when asked to "Tell us about yourself" uses theories eclectically to predict age trends and gender differences in the social self, the significant others in terms of whom one forms one's identity.

Methods in the Social-Self Research

Participants in this research were 560 students in the public school system of a medium-sized inland New England city including 70 boys and 70 girls from the first, third, seventh, and eleventh grades, with mean ages of 7, 9, 13, and 17 years, respectively. Each student was asked during an individual oral interview the question "Tell us about yourself" and her or his answer was recorded for 5 minutes. The participants and procedures are described more fully in McGuire and McGuire (1982).

Each participant's tape-recorded response to the "Tell us about yourself" probe was transcribed and scored for mentions of significant others, whether specific individuals or categories of people, for example, mentions of George, Mrs. Jones, my mother, kids, teachers, everyone, people, etc., were all scored. To facilitate this content analysis, each student's transcribed response was partitioned into 3-unit (roughly, subject–verb–object) segments and the proportion of all first- and third-unit (subject and object) entries that mentioned significant others was scored in order to obtain dependent variable measures of which significant others were salient enough in the child's self-space so that they constituted part of her or his self-definition in response to the "Tell us about yourself" probe. The child's birthdate and gender were recorded during subsequent structured interviews to provide measures of the age and gender independent variables.

Results Regarding Developmental Trends in the Social Self

The Social Nature of the Spontaneous Self-Concept As expected, children's self-concepts turn out to be highly social in that many significant others were mentioned by children called upon to "Tell us about yourself." Of the over 30,000 noun concepts elicited in the 560 children's spontaneous self-concepts (that is, the contents of the first and third "subject" and "object" units of the segments), over 7000, or 23% of the total, were mentions of significant others. Of these 7000 significant other mentions by all participants, including both boys and girls across all four age levels, almost half (47%) were mentions of kin, one quarter (24%) mentions of friends, 8% mentions of school-connected individuals or groups of teachers or students, 11% mentions of broader categories of people (one's family in general, adults in general, human beings in general, etc.), and 11% mentions of nonhuman animals. The big 47% kinship category included 42% nuclear-family and 5% extended-family mentions. The 42% nuclear-family mentions included 20% mentions of siblings, 14% of parents, and 7% mentions of the nuclear family in general. The 5% extended-family mentions included 2% cousin, 1% grandparent, and 1% uncle or aunt mentions. The breakdown of the 11% of all significant other mentions that referred to nonhuman animals is discussed below in connection with age trends.

Four general hypotheses about age trends in the social self were investigated, beginning with a basic salience prediction that other people become less important in one's self-definition as one grows older. Further, as regards which significant others are most salient at various age levels, it was predicted that during childhood and adolescence the significant others in self-space become increasingly peer-oriented and increasingly cosmopolitan. Finally, it was predicted that nonhuman animals become progressively less salient in self-space as the child grows older. The derivation of each of these four hypotheses and the several specific predictions each yields will be considered in turn as the relevant empirical results, summarized in Table 3.5, are reported.

TABLE 3.5

Developmental Trends in Defining Oneself in Terms of Significant
Others

	Participants' age (in years)			
Predictions	7	9	13	17
A1.1 Sig. other nouns ÷ all nouns	.29	.27	.24	.16*
A2.1 General "humans" ÷ all sig. others	.06	.05	.10	.27*
A2.2 General "relatives" ÷ all kin nouns	.11	.18	.22	.29*
A2.3 General "students" ÷ all students	.03	.04	.40	.69*
A2.4 General "teachers" ÷ all teachers	.09	.04	.13	.36*
A3.1 Enemies ÷ (friends + enemies)	.04	.08	.09	.13*
B1.1 Sib. ÷ (sib. + parents)	.56	.60	.69	.58
B1.2 Cousins ÷ all extended family	.40	.38	.54	.32
B1.3 Students ÷ (students + teachers)	.66	.65	.26	.58
C1.1 Parents ÷ (parents + teachers)	.95	.78	.67	.58*
C1.2 Sibs. ÷ (friends + students + sibs.)	.63	.42	.51	.30*
C1.3 Extended family ÷ all nonkin	.19	.11	.07	.02*
D1.1 Animals ÷ all sig. others	.09	.19	.10	.03

*Monotonic age trend significant above the $p < .05$ level.

Contraction of the Social Self with Age Our most basic developmental postulate regarding the social self is that as the child matures during childhood and
adolescence, becoming less dependent on others and developing a richer
cognitive capacity and content, he or she will define him- or herself less and
less in terms of other people. The most obvious prediction following from
this postulate is that mentions of significant others should constitute a progressively smaller proportion of all nouns used in self-descriptions as the child
grows older. The results shown in the A1 row of Table 3.5 clearly support
this prediction: The proportion of all subject and object entries that were
mentions of significant others declined progressively from 29 to 16% as the
children matured through the four age levels from 7-year-olds to 17-year-
olds. A second indication of this lessened interest in other people is that as the
child grows older, references to others become deindividuated, involving
mentions of more generic categories of people rather than specific individuals; from this implication four predictions follow, all of which were
confirmed as shown in the A2 rows of Table 3.5. For example, self-definitions in terms of "people in general" as a proportion of all significant-other
mentions of individuals or of less universal sets of individuals increases from
6% in first graders to 27% in eleventh graders. As regards self-definitions in
terms of kin, references to "relatives" or "family" in general increased with

age as a proportion of all kin mentions from 11% in first graders to 29% in eleventh graders. As regards school-related significant others, self-definitions in terms of students in general constitute only 3% of all student mentions for first graders but 69% for eleventh graders; and mentions of "teachers in general" increase from 9% for first to 36% for eleventh graders as a proportion of all mentions of teachers. A third implication of this postulated de-socialization of the self as the child matures is that mentions of significant others become less positive with age. As can be seen in row A3.1 of Table 3.5, this prediction was also confirmed in that "enemy" mentions increase as a proportion of all friend or enemy mentions from 4% for first graders to 13% for eleventh graders. All the age trends mentioned are significant beyond the .05 level.

Effect of Age on Peer Orientation A second developmental postulate is that as children become older and spend more time outside the home in cohesive groups of age peers and beyond adult supervision, they define themselves progressively more in terms of people of their own age. This postulate yields three predictions, none of which was supported by the data, as can be seen in the B rows of Table 3.5. As regards self-descriptions in terms of nuclear family members, the postulate predicts that as the child grows older, her or his self-descriptions should increasingly be in terms of siblings rather than parents, but as can be seen in Table 3.5 there is no such trend. In the case of school-related significant others, there is no evidence of the predicted increase with age of mentions of peer students relative to authority teachers. Perhaps the predicted increasing age-peer association with age is washed out by a counterbalancing concomitant developmental increase of socialization pressures to think of oneself in terms of adult roles.

Increasing Cosmopolitanism with Age Choice of Significant Others A third developmental postulate regarding the social self is that the broader social environment that one encounters as one matures through childhood and adolescence will broaden the range of significant others in terms of whom one describes oneself. This cosmopolitanization postulate yielded three predictions, each of which was confirmed by a significant monotonic trend as shown in the C rows of Table 3.5. As regards mention of the two major adult categories, the domestic parents and the more cosmopolitan teachers, parents supplied 95% of mentions for first graders but declined progressively to 58% for eleventh graders; as regards mentions of the three main groups of age contemporaries (siblings, friends, and classmates), brothers and sisters constitute 63% of such age-peer mentions for the first graders but only 30% for eleventh graders. Finally, members of one's extended family declined in salience relative to nonkin others, dropping from 19% of the latter for first graders to 2% for eleventh graders.

Salience of Nonhuman Animals in the Social Self Across the four age groups, nonhuman animals are quite salient in the phenomenal self, constituting no less than 11% of all significant other mentions. Even though all of the children had mothers and not all had pets, pets constituted 8% of all mentions of significant others and mothers only 7%. As regards which animals are salient, 78% of the self-definitions in relation to nonhuman animals involved pets and only 22% nondomesticated species, most often fish, birds, and insects (especially bees), a distribution comparable to Bowd's (1982). As regards pets, these children tended to be dog people somewhat more than cat people (30 vs. 23%), while small mammals such as gerbils supplied another 8% of animal mentions, birds 6%, and horses 5%, with only incidental mentions of other pet species such as goldfish and turtles.

We postulated that self-definition in terms of nonhuman animals is a primitive process, perhaps representing an infantile Freudian identification of the young child with these nonhuman small and dependent creatures that would be progressively outgrown, but this postulate was not supported by the empirical results. As can be seen in Figure 3.2, there was a consistent inverted-U nonmonotonic age trend, with third graders being particularly prone to define themselves in terms of nonhuman animals, no fewer than 19% of all their social self-definitions involving mentions of nonhuman animals, as compared with 9% for the first graders and 10% and 3% for the seventh and eleventh graders. This nonmonotonic age trend, peaking in third graders, occurred not only when all species are aggregated but also appears in each of the four major classes of nonhuman animals (dogs, cats, other pets, and wild animals) taken separately. I have long ago argued (McGuire, 1961, 1968) that such nonmonotonic, inverted-U relationships indicate the operation of two counteracting mediating processes. It is my post-factum conjecture that interest in animals does lessen with age because the child decreasingly identifies with these small beings and may even actively repress them as he or she grows to appreciate the human exploitation of animals as in food production; for example, among 5-year olds, 84% know the origin of milk but only 16% know the origin of meat (Bowd, 1982). On the other hand, I hypothesize that there is a counterbalancing decline in fear of these animals. As a result of these two opposite mediating processes, preoccupation with animals peaks at the intermediate age of 9.

Gender Differences in the Social Self

Turning from age to gender as the independent variable, predictions regarding how boys and girls will differ in defining themselves in terms of other people derive from three general postulates: that the social self occupies

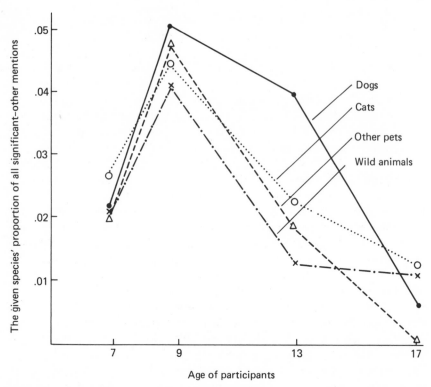

Figure 3.2 Nonmonotonic developmental trend in the salience of nonhuman animals in the spontaneous self-concept.

a greater proportion of total self-space in females than males; that females are more local (that is, family- and peer-oriented) in choosing significant others in terms of whom to describe themselves; and that children tend to define themselves in terms of same-gender parent and other-gender siblings. The theorizing behind each of these three postulates and the several predictions that each one yields are described in the following section as the relevant empirical findings are presented.

Significant Others More Salient in Girls Our basic gender postulate is that females are socialized to be more interpersonally sensitive and concerned than boys, yielding as its most direct prediction that females' self-descriptions involve more mention of other people than do males'. The results shown in columns in row E1 of Table 3.6 confirmed this prediction in that mentions of significant others supplied 24% of all first- and third-unit content for girls and only 17% for boys. A less direct implication is that girls, being more interpersonally concerned, will more than boys individuate the significant others in terms of whom they define themselves, citing specific individuals, whereas boys describe themselves more in terms of deindividuated broader groupings of people. All three predictions yielded by this implication were confirmed, as shown in the E2 rows of Table 3.6. For example, when girls did refer to groups of people, they differentiated them on the basis of age by specifying them as either adults or children 35% as often as they referred to undifferentiated people in general, whereas boys differentiated on the basis of age only 5% of the time; also girls gender-differentiated people into males or females 24% of the time in their grouped-people mentions while boys did so in only 6% of theirs. As regards family mentions, girls described themselves in terms of specific family members rather than the family in general in 84% of all family mentions, but boys only in 78%. A less direct implication of this social orientation postulate is that the social selves of females are more positive than those of males: As can be seen in row E3 of Table 3.6, of all self-definitions in terms of "friends" and "enemies," 94% referred to friends for girls and 87% for boys. All of these differences are significant beyond the .05 level.

TABLE 3.6

Gender Differences in Defining Oneself in Terms of Significant Others

		Participants' gender	
Prediction		Boys	Girls
E1.1	Sig. others nouns ÷ all nouns	.17	.24*
E2.1	"Adults," "child" ÷ all categ. others	.05	.35*
E2.2	"Males," "females" ÷ all categ. others	.06	.24*
E2.3	Specific family members ÷ all family	.78	.84*
E3.1	Friends ÷ (friends + enemies)	.87	.94*
F1.1	Kin mentions ÷ all human references	.49	.55*
F1.2	Nuclear family ÷ all family	.90	.90
F1.3	Romantic friends ÷ all friends	.11	.14*
F1.4	Pets ÷ all animals	.68	.88*
G1.1	Sib. age-peers ÷ all household	.52	.62*
G1.2	Student age-peers ÷ (students + teachers)	.48	.66*
G2.1	Own-gender kin ÷ all kin	.53	.53
H1.1	Mother ÷ (mother + father)	.40	.67*
H1.2	Brother ÷ (brother + sister)	.49	.56*

*Gender difference significant above the $p < .05$ level.

Girls' Social Self More Local (Domestic- and Peer-Oriented) Than Boys' Assuming that the relatively "overprotected" socialization of females would narrow their social experiences, it was postulated that girls would be more parochially local than boys in their choice of others in terms of whom to define themselves, choosing more domestic and more similar-to-self significant others than would boys. Three of the four derived domesticity predictions were confirmed at the $p < .05$ level of statistical significance as can be seen in the F rows of Table 3.6. Of all self-definitions in terms of other people, 55% of the girls and only 49% of the boys involved mentions of kin. As regards mentions of friends, 14% of the girls' but only 11% of the boys' mentions involved romantic friends; and of all mentions of animals, 88% of the girls' but only 68% of the boys' mentions were of household pets. The one disconfirmation of a "domesticity" gender prediction is the finding that mentions of nuclear (as opposed to extended) family members constitutes a practically identical 90% of both boys' and girls' mentions of family.

The peer-orientation implication that girls more than boys would define themselves in terms of people like themselves yielded three predictions, two of which were statistically confirmed ($p < .05$) as can be seen in the G rows of Table 3.6. As regards all nuclear family (parent or sibling) self-descriptions, similar-to-self siblings constituted 62% of girls' and only 52% of boys' mentions. As regards the school domain, mentions of age-peer students constituted 66% of student-plus-teacher mentions for girls and only 48% for boys. However, the parochialism prediction that girls would define themselves in terms of own-gender others more often than would boys was not confirmed: Both boys and girls defined themselves in terms of own-gender people in 53% of all gender-specified mentions.

Self-Definition in Terms of Parents and Kin An analysis of biologically and culturally imposed role-acquisition tasks of boys and girls suggests that children will tend to define themselves in terms of the same-gender parent and the other-gender sibling. Socialization procedures make it adaptive for children in observing adults (parents) to focus on their own-gender parent in order to learn prescribed adult roles (Flake-Hobson *et al.*, 1980); as regards age peers, on the other hand, the press to prepare for heterosexual procreative relationships with other-gender age peers makes it more adaptive for children to focus on siblings of the other gender. The results shown in the H rows of Table 3.6 are in keeping with this prediction. As regards self-definition in terms of parents, girls describe themselves in terms of their mothers in 67% of the parental mentions and boys in only 40% of parental mentions. On the other hand, as regards self-definition in terms of siblings, girls define themselves in terms of brothers in 56% and boys only in 49% of all sibling mentions.

Future Directions of Our Spontaneous Self-Concept Research

Further research on the phenomenal self can be illustrated by brief descriptions of five other lines of work in progress, including three further studies on the affirmation self-concept, one on the negation self-concept, and one on the physical self-concept.

Research on the Ontogeny of Verbs

A quite different type of research allowed by the open, nonreactive approach to the self-concept focuses on an assumption that the verbs people use to describe themselves disclose their conceptualizations of the self–world relationships. This research has proceeded far enough so that preliminary results can be described here.

Modes of Self–World Relating and Their Verb Manifestation The classification of verb types that I developed and my predictions about how age affects the relative usage of the various classes of verbs by children in describing themselves were derived from assumptions about how environmental stresses and human capacities for meeting them change during maturation, and about the verb types that manifest these changes. I postulate that the most basic dichotomy of self–world relationships is into actions versus states, as expressed in the classic grammatical division into verbs of action versus verbs of state. Childhood cognitive development involves a shift from observation and direct action to reflection and increasing use of abstraction, so that the growing child shifts progressively from perceiving the self as acting on and being acted upon by the environment to perceiving self and world in terms of states. Hence, it is predicted that the verbs used in self-descriptions will show a progressive shift during childhood and adolescence from verbs of action to verbs of state.

Furthermore, these two basic modes of perception (and their corresponding verb types) can be analyzed into subsets about which additional ontogenetic predictions can be made. For example, within the more primitive mode of perceiving the world as the arena of action, the action can take the form of overt acting on the world or a more mature covert reacting to it. The former includes perceiving the self as physically acting on the world (moving, possessing, handling, etc.), and socially interacting with the world (associating, conversing, contending, etc.). As the child grows more autonomous and reflective in his or her self-consciousness, he or she will tend to inhibit such direct action on the physical or social environment and instead increasingly react to it mentally, both affectively and cognitively. It is predicted that as the child matures, verbs of covert reacting, both affective (e.g., liking, feeling, etc.) and cognitive (e.g., knowing, learning, etc.), will become increasingly preponderant over verbs expressing physical and social overt actions. State verbs can be comparably subdivided but this will not be discussed further here.

Methods in the Verb Ontogeny Research The affirmation self-concept was elicited by asking participants to respond for 5 minutes to the probe, "Tell us about yourself." Oral responses were obtained from 560 school children, including 70 boys and 70 girls from each of four school grade levels—the first, third, seventh and eleventh. Written responses were obtained from 1000 children, including 100 boys and 100 girls from each of five school grade levels—the fifth, seventh, ninth, eleventh, and twelfth. The oral responses were tape-recorded and later typed on standard sheets and the hand-written responses were also typed on standard sheets.

An elaborate content analysis was developed to retain as much as possible of the idiosyncratic information in the child's response while at the same time standardizing it sufficiently to permit aggregation of data and computer analysis. We found that it was possible to divide each participant's total response into 3-unit segments roughly corresponding to subject–verb–object constructions. After the person's self-description was divided into such basic thought segments, each segment was pre-edited into an approximation of this 3-unit format. For example, if a child said, "My father works at Dalkey Tools," it would be pre-edited as "father–works at–factory," and if the child said, "One thing I would really love to have is a ten-speed bicycle," this would be pre-edited into "self–wants–bicycle." Some information is lost in this process since all of the units are pre-edited into the active voice even in the rare cases when the child used the passive; the workplace is described generically as a factory and the desired object is identified generically as a bicycle, losing the information that a ten-speed was specified; and by recording the verb as "want," the intensity of the "really love to have" expression is lost. After this pre-editing of the segments, the content of each unit of pre-edited prose was translated into a basic dictionary of about 1000 frequently used concepts, each with a numerical label to facilitate computer analysis. The basic 1000-word vocabulary included 100 verb types and their negations worked out by a priori logical analysis and by prestudy experience as allowing encoding of all the children's prose without major loss or distortion of information, these 100 verbs being classified in the basic types discussed above. For each segment, the middle unit was supplied by one of these 100 verbs and the first and third units by one of the other (noun and modifier) concepts in the 1000-concept dictionary.

This content analysis procedure, from the basic decision to partition the responses into 3-unit standard segments to the final dictionary of about 1000 concepts, was developed by starting with an a priori system and then modifying it a posteriori on the basis of prestudy experience with the information actually contained in people's spontaneous self-concepts. For example, our a priori dictionary contained our own list of rational categories and categories used in previous thesauruses of human concepts. Hence, this a priori list contained a rich set of terms for social attitudes and values and only a few generic terms for animal species; however, when we collected data on the content of children's and adolescents' self-space, it turned out to be much more occupied by animal species and less by attitudinal concepts than we had anticipated. So, to improve information coding efficiency, the dictionary was revised to distinguish among more animal species while overrefined attitude and value concepts were grouped into broader categories.

Once the content analysis system was worked out and the children's spontaneous self-concept responses were collected, research aides who were unfamiliar with the hypotheses used the system to encode the response protocols. The coded information was then entered in a computer, and for this verb study we extracted all the segments whose first unit was "self" in order to ensure that we were analyzing self-descriptions. For example, if the child responded "I love my mother. She works at Whartons," we included the verb from the "self–likes–mother" segment in the analysis but not the verb from the "mother–works at–store" segment. The included "self" segments constituted about 60% of all segments in the affirmation self-concepts. Cross-tabulations were then obtained for the proportion of all verbs that fell in each of the six broad classes, including four action classes (physically acting on, socially interacting with, affectively reacting to, and cognitively reacting to) and two state classes (states of being and states of becoming) at each grade level, allowing us to calculate the ontogenetic trends in use of the six classes of verbs.

Results We shall report here only the results on the basic postulate that as the person matures through childhood and adolescence he or she progressively shifts from perceiving the self in terms of actions to seeing him- or herself in terms of conditions. As can be seen in Figure 3.3, there is a highly regular age trend in shifting from action to state verbs in describing the self, both in the oral and written modalities. In the oral-response condition, verbs of state constitute only 12% of second-unit content for first graders and increase progressively until they occupy 38% of self-space for eleventh graders. The young people in the written-response condition show, not only the same trends but also the same levels, verbs of state furnishing 31% of all self-descriptive verbs for fifth graders and increasing progressively with age until they supply 43% of the twelfth graders' verbs. Also found, but not shown in

William J. McGuire

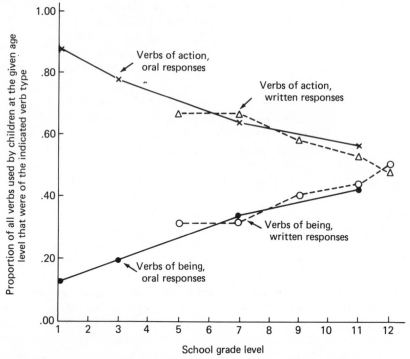

Figure 3.3 Decline of action verbs and growth of state verbs in self-descriptions as the child matures from age 7 to 18 years.

Fig. 3.3, are the predicted age trend with action verbs, a shift from verbs of overt physical and social action to covert affective and cognitive reaction, and other predicted within-group verb shifts.

Further Spontaneous Self-Concept Studies in Progress

A further affirmation self-concept study currently in progress investigates age trends and sex differences in the noun concepts that occupy self-space by analyzing the first- and third-unit contents of the segments comparably to the analyses of the second-unit contents in the ontogeny of verbs study just described. Susequent studies will investigate the sequence of thought by more complex analyses of the transitions from segment to segment to account for the order in which thoughts arise as one proceeds through a self-description. For example, whether the sequence of thought is more guided by nouns or by verbs will be investigated: If the person giving his or her spontaneous self-concept reports, "I like my father," does the noun guide the stream of thought so that the child is more likely to be propelled into a series of thoughts on the father such as, "My father and I go fishing together. He works at Murray Tools"? Or does the verb "to like" channel the thought so that subsequent segments might continue with, "I like my dog, I like sports, but I don't like school"?

Other studies on the research agenda go beyond the affirmation self-concept to other types of self-concepts. An investigation of various hypotheses about how the affirmation self-concept differs from the negation self-concept, some preliminary aspects of which have been mentioned above in reporting the research on distinctiveness and salience, is planned. Also planned is an investigation of the physical self-concept, contrasting the self-image as expressed in words and in drawings of the self along with how responding in one of these modes affects subsequent responding in the other. An already completed study (McGuire, Fujioka, & McGuire, 1979) investigated how the proportion of self-space occupied by school-related thoughts grows during childhood, so that by age 17 years more of the young person's self-definitions are related to school than to any other domain, such as friends or family.

Thick Texture of the Phenomenal Self-Concept

We have been discussing the content and structure of self-space analytically, as befits nomothetic thinkers interested in describing relationships between abstract variables who are willing to lose specific information about the concrete situation in order to abstract general principles that have wide, even if only vague and inexact, applicability to concrete cases. To retrieve some of the information lost by our abstract level of discourse, I shall close this chapter with some idiographic, thick description (Geertz, 1973) in concrete protocols obtained in this spontaneous self-concept research. While the self-descriptions of any one participant are of limited generalizability, they do give a fuller depiction of a concrete case that has heuristic power for provoking generalized insights. One participant whose self-descriptions I find particularly evocative and provocative is a seventh-grade male in the written-response condition whose touching response to our "Tell us about yourself" probe was

> I am a kid that has nothing and gets nothing. When I born I born trouble. My mother said to me that I was born just for trouble. I was born in New York. I used to think to myself that I should be

dead. I never had a good time for long. When I come home I just
get fust at. I was born just to be born. I am a kid that is hardly
known to the world. I am a human just like everybody you know
and should be treated like one. Please be my friend.

His response to our "Tell us what you look like" probe was even more
depressing:

I have blue eyes, brown hair, black eyelashes. I am a kid that looks
like a stupid donkey. I say deep down in my heart I am no good.

Nor was he much happier in his response to our "Tell us about your past life"
probe:

When I was growing up I had a hard life but I will tell you why.
When I was born my parents said that I would grow with a hard life
and I did. I had the hardest life. Thank you.

Yet in his response to our "Tell us about your family" request, this young
man showed an appreciation of and ferocity for love that many do not grasp
even in their maturity:

My family is the nicest parents in the world. Sometimes they can be
mean and I think they no good. My mother said she hated me so I
thought I shouldn't like her but I do. I love her very much and she
loves me but she doesn't know it.

And his response to our "Tell us what you like best" probe shows that his
heart could soar in the presence of beauty:

I like Trudy Greenberg because when I went to school and saw her
I said I like her. And I do like her because she pretty. I like her.

It was our request for his negation self-concept that surprisingly elicited his
most affirmative response. He replied to the "Tell us some of the things you
are not" probe as follows:

I am not a hero or prince or king. But I can do some things well
maybe better than anybody. Some people can do things better than
me but I can top people in sports. I am not a prince, hero or king.
But I am a kid that lives.

Few sets of responses are as poignant as this boy's, but any child can be
expressive when one presents a low enough profile to the participants that
allows them to express themselves in their own terms rather than restricting
them to making check marks on semantic differential polarities presented by
the researcher. Allowed to express themselves in their own words, people

give rich material, too rich to avoid the necessity of data reduction to allow aggregation across cases if one seeks for general principles but leaving it to the researcher to choose the level of abstraction. It allows one to pause on the thick description before riding off in one or more analytical directions, beholding an individual human realizing her- or himself at a certain moment in time as one manifestation of the infinite variety of possible human epiphanies. Our seventh grader in this case shows himself to be a troubled boy, perhaps feeling a little too sorry for himself or perhaps entitled to every bit of his sadness. And yet from his valley of despondency he shows a capacity not only to be surprised by joy but an active avidity to "let joy seize at God knows when to God knows what." His self-descriptions do not leave one sure that he will grow and prevail or even to feel certain that he has survived until this reading. But his rich self-descriptions put us in the presence of a self at a moment fully lived, a self that can look at a face of truth and seek something finer, a self that makes selves worth studying.

Acknowledgments

Important contributions to the research were made by Claire McGuire, Jason Cheever, Anders Thompson, and Joyce Ghiroli.

References

Amster, H. Semantic satiation and generation: Learning? Adaptation? *Psychological Bulletin,* 1964, *62,* 273–286.

Baltaxe, C. A. M. *Foundations of distinctive feature theory.* Baltimore: University Park Press, 1978.

Battig, W. F., & Montague, W. E. Category norms for verbal items in 56 categories. *Journal of Experimental Psychology Monograph Supplement,* 1969, *80,* No. 3, part 2.

Berlyne, D. E. *Conflict, arousal and curiosity.* New York: McGraw-Hill, 1960.

Berlyne, D. Novelty, complexity and hedonic value. *Perception and Psychophysics,* 1970, *8,* 279–286.

Biederman, I., Glass, A. L., & Stacy, E. W., Jr. Searching for objects in real world scenes. *Journal of Experimental Psychology,* 1973, *97,* 22–27.

Bieri, J., Atkins, A. L., Briar, S., Leaman, R. L., Miller, H., & Tripodi, T. *Clinical and social judgment: The discrimination of behavioral information.* New York: Wiley, 1966.

Bloom, H. *A map of misreadings.* New York: Oxford Univ. Press, 1974.

Blumenthal, A. L. *The process of cognition.* Englewood Cliffs, NJ: Prentice-Hall, 1977.

Boring, E. G. *The physical dimensions of consciousness.* New York: Century, 1933.

Bowd, A. D. Young children's beliefs about animals. *Journal of Psychology,* 1982, *110,* 263–266.

Broadbent, D. *Perception and communication.* London: Pergamon, 1958.

Brown, J. S. The generalization of approach responses as a function of stimulus intensity and strength of motivation. *Journal of Comparative Psychology,* 1943, *33,* 209–226.

Bruner, J. S. On perceptual readiness. *Psychological Review*, 1957, *64*, 123–152.

Bugental, J. F. T., & Zelen, S. L. Investigations into the self-concept—The W-A-Y technique. *Journal of Personality*, 1950, *18*, 483–498.

Campbell, D. T. Perception as substitute trial and error. *Psychological Review*, 1956, *63*, 330–342.

Cantor, G. N., & Hodge, M. J. S. (Eds.). *Conceptions of ether: Studies in the history of ether theory.* New York: Cambridge Univ. Press, 1981.

Chance, M. R. A., & Larsen, R. R. (Eds.). *The social structure of attention.* New York: Wiley, 1976.

Dember, W. N. Motivation and the cognitive revolution. *American Psychologist*, 1974, *29*, 161–168.

Dember, W. N., & Fowler, H. Spontaneous alternation behavior. *Psychological Bulletin*, 1958, *55*, 412–428.

Derrida, J. *La voix et le phénomène.* Paris: Presses Universitaires de France, 1967. [*Speech and phenomena.*] Evanston: Northwestern Univ. Press, 1973.

Deutsch, A., & Deutsch, D. Attention: Some theoretical considerations. *Psychological Review*, 1963, *70*, 80–90.

Dykman, R. A., Reese, W. G., Galbrecht, C. R., & Thomasson, P. J. Psychophysiological reactions to novel stimuli: Measurement, adaptation and relationship of psychological variables in the normal human. *Annals of the New York Academy of Science*, 1959, *79*, 43–107.

Egeth, H. E. Parallel versus serial processing in multidimensional stimulus discrimination. *Perception and Psychophysics*, 1966, *1*, 245–252.

Estes, W. K. Toward a statistical theory of learning. *Psychological Review*, 1950, *57*, 94–107.

Festinger, L. *A theory of cognitive dissonance.* Stanford, CA: Stanford Univ. Press, 1957.

Fiske, D. W., & Maddi, S. R. *Functions of varied experience.* Homewood, IL: Dorsey, 1961.

Flake-Hobson, C., Skeen, P., & Robinson, B. E. Review of theories and research concerning sex-role development and androgeny with suggestions for teachers. *Family Relations*, 1980, *29*, 155–162.

Fowler, H. *Curiosity and exploratory behavior.* New York: Macmillan, 1965.

Freud, S. [*Group psychology and the analysis of the ego.*] New York: Norton, 1959. (Originally published 1921.)

Gardner, R. W., Holzman, P. S., Klein, G. S., Linton, H. B., & Spence, D. P. Cognitive control: A study of individual consistencies in cognitive behavior. *Psychological Issues*, Monograph 4. New York: International Universities Press, 1959.

Garner, W. R. The stimulus in information processing. *American Psychologist*, 1970, *25*, 350–358.

Geertz, C. *The interpretation of cultures.* New York: Basic Books, 1973.

Gibson, J. J. *Perception of the visual world.* Boston: Houghton Mifflin, 1950.

Glanzer, M. Stimulus satiation: An explanation of spontaneous alternation and related phenomena. *Psychological Review*, 1953, *60*, 252–268.

Gombrich, E. H. *The sense of order: A study of the psychology of decorative art.* Ithaca, NY: Cornell, 1979.

Grant, E. *Much ado about nothing: Theories of space and vacuum from the middle ages to the scientific revolution.* New York: Cambridge Univ. Press, 1981.

Guthrie, E. R. *The psychology of learning.* New York: Harper, 1952 (rev. ed.).

Harlow, H. F. The formation of learning sets. *Psychological Review*, 1949, *56*, 51–65.

Harlow, H. F. Mice, monkeys, men and motives. *Psychological Review*, 1953, *60*, 23–32.

Head, H. *Aphasia and kindred disorders of speech.* New York: Macmillan, 1926.

Heath, P. L. Nothing. In R. Edwards (Ed.), *The encyclopedia of philosophy* (Vol. 5). New York: Macmillan, 1967.

Hebb, D. O. *The organization of behavior*. New York: Wiley, 1949.

Heider, F. *The psychology of interpersonal relations*. New York: Wiley, 1958.

Helson, H. Adaptation-level as a basis for a quantitative theory of frames of reference. *Psychological Review*, 1948, 55, 297–313.

Hinton, G., & Anderson, J. A. (Eds.). *Parallel models of associative memory*. Hillsdale, NJ: Erlbaum, 1981.

Hochberg, J. Attention, organization, and consciousness. In D. Mostofsky (Ed.), *Attention: Contemporary theory and analysis*. New York: Appleton-Century-Crofts, 1970.

Hopkins, G. M. *Poems of Gerard Manley Hopkins* (2nd ed.). (R. Bridges, Ed.). London: Oxford Univ. Press, 1933.

Hopkins, J. *Nicholas of Cusa on God as non-other*. Minneapolis: Univ. of Minnesota Press, 1979.

Hovland, C. I. A "communication analysis" of concept learning. *Psychological Review*, 1952, 59, 461–472.

Hull, C. L. *A behavior system*. New Haven: Yale, 1952.

Jakobovits, L. A. Effects of mere exposure: A comment. *Journal of Personality and Social Psychology*, 1968, 9, No. 2, Part 2, 30–32.

Kagan, J. Attention and psychological change in the young child. *Science*, 1970, 170, 826–832.

Kahneman, D. *Attention and effort*. Englewood Cliffs, NJ: Prentice-Hall, 1973.

Kelly, G. A. A brief introduction to personal construct theory. In D. Bannister (Ed.), *Perspectives in personal construct theory*. New York: Academic Press, 1970.

Kessen, W. Response strength and conditioned stimulus intensity. *Journal of Experimental Psychology*, 1953, 45, 82–86.

Kimmel, H. D., van Olst, E. H., & Orlebeke, J. T. (Eds.). *The orienting reflex in humans*. Hillsdale, NJ: Erlbaum, 1979.

Kohlberg, L. A cognitive-developmental analysis of children's sex role concepts and attitudes. In E. E. Maccoby (Ed.), *The development of sex differences*. Stanford, CA: Stanford Univ. Press, 1966.

Köhler, W., & Wallach, H. Figural after-effect, an investigation of visual processes. *Proceedings of the American Philosophical Society*, 1944, 88, 269–357.

Krechevsky, I. "Hypotheses" in rats. *Psychological Review*, 1932, 39, 516–532.

Kuhn, M. H., & McPartland, T. S. An empirical investigation of self-attitudes. *American Sociological Review*, 1954, 19, 68–76.

Lashley, K. S. Learning: III. Nervous mechanisms in learning. In C. Murchison (Ed.), *A handbook of general experimental psychology*. Worcester, MA: Clark Univ. Press, 1934.

Lawrence, D. The nature of stimulus: Some relationships between learning and perception. In S. Koch (Ed.), *Psychology: A study of a science* (Vol. 5). London: McGraw–Hill, 1963.

Mackintosh, N. J. A theory of attention: Variations in the associability of stimuli with reinforcement. *Psychological Review*, 1975, 82, 276–298.

Mackworth, J. F. *Vigilance and attention: A signal detection approach*. Harmondsworth: Penguin, 1970.

Maltzman, I. Individual differences in "attention": The orienting reflex. In R. M. Gagné (Ed.), *Learning and individual differences*. Columbus, OH: Merrill, 1967.

McClelland, D. C., & Atkinson, J. W. The projective expression of needs: I. The effect of different intensities of hunger drive on perception. *Journal of Psychology*, 1948, 25, 205–222.

McGinnies, E. Emotionality and perceptual defense. *Psychological Review*, 1949, 56, 244–251.

McGuire, W. J. A syllogistic analysis of cognitive relationships. In C. I. Hovland & M. J. Rosenberg (Eds.), *Attitude organization and change*. New Haven: Yale Univ. Press, 1960.

McGuire, W. J. A multi-process model for paired-associates learning. *Journal of Experimental Psychology*, 1961, 62, 335–347.

McGuire, W. J. The current status of cognitive consistency theories. In S. Feldman (Ed.), *Cognitive consistency*. New York: Academic Press, 1966.

McGuire, W. J. Personality and social influence. In E. F. Borgatta & W. W. Lambert (Eds.), *Handbook of personality theory and research*. Chicago: Rand-McNally, 1968.

McGuire, W. J. The nature of attitudes and attitude change. In G. Lindzey & E. Aronson (Eds.), *Handbook of social psychology* (Vol. 3) (2nd ed.). Reading, MA: Addison–Wesley, 1969.

McGuire, W. J. The probabilogical model of cognitive structure and attitude change. In R. E. Petty, T. M. Ostrom, & T. C. Brock (Eds.), *Cognitive responses in persuasion*. Hillsdale, NJ: Erlbaum, 1981.

McGuire, W. J. A contextualist theory of knowledge: Its implications for innovation and reform in psychological research. In L. Berkowitz (Ed.), *Advances in experimental social psychology* (Vol. 16). New York: Academic Press, 1983.

McGuire, W. J., Fujioka, T., & McGuire, C. V. The place of school in the child's self-concpet. *Impact on instructional improvement*, 1979, *15*, No. 1, 3–10.

McGuire, W. J., & McGuire, C. V. Salience of handedness in the spontaneous self-concept. *Perceptual and Motor Skills*, 1980, *50*, 3–7.

McGuire, W. J., & McGuire, C. V. The spontaneous self-concept as affected by personal distinctiveness. In M. D. Lynch, A. Norem-Hebeisen, & K. Gergen (Eds.), *Self-concept: Advances in theory and research*. Cambridge, MA: Ballinger, 1981.

McGuire, W. J., & McGuire, C. V. Significant others in self-space: Sex differences and developmental trends in the self. In J. Suls (Ed.), *Social psychological perspectives on the self*. Hillsdale, NJ: Erlbaum, 1982.

McGuire, W. J., McGuire, C. V., Child, P., & Fujioka, T. Salience of ethnicity in the spontaneous self-concept as a function of one's ethnic distinctiveness in the social environment. *Journal of Personality and Social Psychology*, 1978, *36*, 511–520.

McGuire, W. J., McGuire, C. V., & Winton, W. Effects of household sex composition on the salience of one's gender in the spontaneous self-concept. *Journal of Experimental and Social Psychology*, 1979, *15*, 77–90.

McGuire, W. J., & Padawer-Singer, A. Trait salience in the spontaneous self-concept. *Journal of Personality and Social Psychology*, 1976, *33*, 743–754.

Miller, G. A. What is information measurement? *American Psychologist*, 1953, *8*, 3–11.

Miller, G. A. The magic number seven, plus or minus two, or, some limits on our capacity for processing information. *Psychological Review*, 1956, *63*, 81–97.

Miller, N. E. Liberalization of the basic S–R concepts: Extensions to conflict behavior, motivation and social learning. In S. Koch (Ed.), *Psychology: A study of a science* (Vol. 2). New York: McGraw-Hill, 1959.

Moray, N. *Selective attention: Selective processes in vision and hearing*. London: Hutchinson, 1969.

Moynihan, D. P. *The Negro family: The case for national action*. Washington, D.C.: U.S. Department of Labor, 1965.

Mueller, J. H. The effects of individual difference in test anxiety and type of orienting task on levels of organization in free recall. *Journal of Research in Personality*, 1978, *12*, 100–116.

Neisser, U. *Cognitive psychology*. New York: Appleton–Century–Crofts, 1967.

Newcomb, T. An approach in the study of communicative acts. *Psychological Review*, 1953, *60*, 393–404.

Nisbett, R. E., & Ross, L. *Human inference: Strategies and shortcomings in social judgment*. Englewood Cliffs, NJ: Prentice-Hall, 1980.

Norman, D. A. Toward a theory of memory and attention. *Psychological Review*, 1968, *75*, 522–536.

Osgood, C. E., & Tannenbaum, P. H. The principle of congruity in the prediction of attitude change. *Psychological Review*, 1955, *62*, 42–55.

Pavlov, I. P. [*Lectures on conditioned reflexes.*] New York: International, 1928.

Peeke, H. V. S., & Herz, M. J. (Eds.). *Habituation* (2 vols.). New York: Academic Press, 1972.

Piaget, J. [*The origins of intelligence in children.*] Original French edition, 1936. New York: International Universities Press, 1952.

Pope, M. L., & Keen, T. R. *Personal construct psychology and education.* New York: Academic Press, 1982.

Popper, K. *The logic of scientific discovery.* London: Hutchinson, 1959.

Pribram, K. H., & McGuinness, D. Arousal, activation and effort in the control of attention. *Psychological Review,* 1975, *82,* 116–149.

Riggs, L. A., Ratliff, F., Cornsweet, J. C., & Cornsweet, T. N. The disappearance of steadily fixated visual test objects. *Journal of the Optical Society of America,* 1953, *43,* 495–501.

Riley, D. A., & Leith, C. R. Multidimensional psychophysics and selective attention in animals. *Psychological Bulletin,* 1976, *83,* 138–160.

Rorschach, H. [*Psychodiagnostics: A diagnostic test based on perception.*] 1st German edition, 1921. Berne: Huber, 1942.

Rosch, E., & Lloyd, B. B. (Eds.). *Cognition and categorization.* New York: Halsted, 1978.

Rosenberg, M. *Conceiving the self.* New York: Basic Books, 1979.

Rosenberg, S. New approaches to the analysis of personal constructs in person perception. *Nebraska Symposium on Motivation,* 1977, *24,* 179–242.

Saussure, F. de [*Course in general linguistics.*] Originally published, Paris, 1916. (Trans. W. Baskin.) New York: Philosophical Library, 1959.

Scholem, G. *Major trends in Jewish mysticism* (3rd ed.). New York: Schocken, 1954. (1st ed., 1946.)

Scholem, G. [*Sabbatai Sevi: The mystical messiah.*] Princeton: Princeton Univ. Press, 1973. (Original Hebrew edition, 1957.)

Shiffrin, R. M., & Schneider, W. Controlled and automatic human information processing: II. Perceptual learning, automatic attending and a general theory. *Psychological Review,* 1977, *84,* 127–190.

Simon, H. A. How big is a chunk? *Science,* 1974, *183,* 482–488.

Smith, E. E. Choice reaction time: An analysis of the major theoretical positions. *Psychological Bulletin,* 1968, *69,* 77–110.

Snyder, C. R., & Fromkin, H. L. *Uniqueness: The human pursuit of difference.* New York: Plenum, 1980.

Solomon, R. L., & Howes, D. H. Word-probability, personal values, and visual duration thresholds. *Psychological Review,* 1951, *58,* 256–270.

Sperling, G. The information available in brief visual presentations. *Psychological Monographs,* 1960, *74,* (11, Whole No. 498).

Spitzer, S., Couch, C., & Stratton, J. *The assessment of self.* Iowa City: Sernoll, 1971.

Tajfel, H. Value and the perceptual judgment of magnitude. *Psychological Review,* 1957, *64,* 192–204.

Taylor, D. A. Stage analysis of reaction time. *Psychological Bulletin,* 1976, *83,* 161–191.

Taylor, S. E., & Fiske, S. T. Salience, attention and attribution: Top of the head phenomena. In L. Berkowitz (Ed.), *Advances in experimental social psychology* (Vol. 11). New York: Academic Press, 1978.

Taylor, S. E., & Thompson, S. C. Stalking the elusive "vividness" effect. *Psychological Review,* 1982, *89,* 155–181.

Tomkins, S. S. The quest for primary motives: Biography and autobiography of an idea. *Journal of Personality and Social Psychology,* 1981, *41,* 306–329.

Treisman, A. M. Strategies and models of selective attention. *Psychological Review,* 1969, *76,* 282–299.

Tulving, E., & Thomson, D. M. Encoding specificity and retrieval processes in episodic memory. *Psychological Review*, 1973, *80*, 352–373.

Tversky, A., & Kahneman, D. Judgment under uncertainty: Heuristics and biases. *Science*, 1974, *185*, 1124–1131.

Ullian, D. Z. The development of conceptions of masculinity and femininity. In B. Lloyd & J. Archer (Eds.), *Exploring sex differences*. London: Academic Press, 1976.

Valéry, P. *Mauvaises pensées*. 18e ed. Paris: Gallimard, 1934.

Veroff, J., & Veroff, J. B. *Social incentives: A life-span developmental approach*. New York: Academic Press, 1980.

Vigotsky, L. S. Thought and speech. *Psychiatry*, 1939, *2*, 29–54.

Weil, S. [*Gravity and grace.*] (Trans. A. Wills.) New York: Putnam, 1952.

Wicklund, R. A., & Brehm, J. W. *Perspectives on cognitive dissonance*. Hillsdale, NJ: Erlbaum, 1976.

Wyer, R. S., Jr., & Carlston, D. E. *Social cognition, inference and attribution*. Hillsdale, NJ: Erlbaum, 1979.

Wylie, R. *The self-concept*. Lincoln: Univ. of Nebraska Press. Vol. 1, 1974; Vol. 2, 1979.

Zuckerman, M. *Sensation seeking: Beyond the optimal level of arousal*. Hillsdale, NJ: Erlbaum, 1979.

4

Principles of Prediction Using Structural Analysis of Social Behavior*

Lorna Smith Benjamin

Introduction

According to Murray (1938), personology is a science that studies persons as whole units, emphasizes intrapsychic variables more than externally observable variables, and is characterized by concern with the dynamic, goal-directed, adaptive character of behavior. Prediction of behavior is more likely to be successful if one can clearly formulate the subject's needs and the subject's view of the world in relation to those needs. Like the psychoanalysts, Murray holds that how a person sees the world (Beta press) is more relevant to prediction than how the world actually is (Alpha press). In important ways, therefore, personology emphasizes phenomenology; this means that if one is to predict behavior using a personologist's point of view, one must be able to "get inside the subject's head," to empathize, and to see and experience the world as she or he does. To interpret properly another person's phenomenology, one must be fully aware of one's own mental structure, and so Murray, like Freud, recommended that students of personology have their own successful therapy.

Murray made it clear that it is preferable to understand a small sample of individuals in depth rather than to study, with superficial concepts and measures, large numbers of people. His is a biological and developmental view, in which the basic inherited structure of the person is shaped by the individual's

*This report was supported in part by Grant No. MH-33604 from the National Institute of Mental Health.

121

developmental history and by his or her goals for the future. "By conserving some of the past and anticipating some of the future, a human being can, to a significant degree, make his behavior accord with the events that have happened as well as those that are to come" (Murray, 1938, p. 49). The view is like Heidegger's (1960) notion of "*Dasein* coming back upon itself": the optimal state of adjustment fully represents being in the moment and possessing an acute awareness and deep understanding of the past as well as of where one will end in the future if one continues on the present course. Prediction by personology, then, must include assessment of both the past and present needs and anticipations.

Murray had great faith in the power of scientific method, but he objected to psychology's move toward narrowness and rigidity in its enthusiasm for applying scientific method to the study of behavior. "We have been more ashamed of triviality than of disagreement," he said (Murray, 1938, p. 250). In short, Murray wanted to understand the person in a dynamic, phenomenological, inner-oriented fashion, and yet, like Freud, he wanted to invoke the methods and power of the scientist to the fullest extent possible. If clinical complexity went beyond what science could handle, Murray opted in favor of discussing clinical complexities.

Rather than survey the work of personologists since Murray (see McLemore & Benjamin, 1979), this chapter focuses on the results of an extensive research project, the Structural Analysis of Social Behavior (SASB), on which I have been long engaged. I hope to show how SASB is compatible with the personological approach and that its internal structure permits the generation of a wide range of predictions about the social behavior of human beings.

In keeping with the tradition of Murray lecturers, a few personal remarks about the development of SASB are in order. It is probably not possible to know all that goes into causing a person to devote a lifetime to "some grids on a piece of paper." But the inherent attractiveness of a concept that can enrich understanding and experiencing by organizing and clarifying everyday transactions surely has something to do with my sustained interest. SASB is an attempt to provide a behavioral classification system that has the attributes of an hypothetical construct; the SASB classification scheme generates an infinitude of ideas and predictions that then can be checked by observation. Often the clarity of SASB classifications gives one the feeling "Of course— why didn't I see that before?" and then the observation seems trivial because it is so familiar. For example, "Of course my poor self-concept comes from all those times my older sister told me I was stupid," "Yes, my husband is interpersonally just like my mother," and "It does make sense that the patient will become defensive if you tell him he is not assertive enough" all sound sensible, but readers unfamiliar with SASB could not know the connection between the "sense" of these observations and the SASB model. The advantages in having a theoretical model based on clinical data for generating, organizing, and clarifying such observations are many. The potential for enhanced teaching, research, and clinical practice through reference to such a model is significant.

The ambition to operationalize and study behavior scientifically, just as chemists and physicists study the physical universe, is an old dream. Sometimes such an idea has had negative associations; the behavior scientist is viewed as an inhuman mechanist who wants to reduce the richness of human experience to a heap of numbers buried in a stack of computer printouts. But just as there is paradox in becoming free to make more choices through understanding determinism, there also is a paradox in becoming humanistically richer through having a deep and benign understanding of the scientific lawfulness and order in human social interaction.

For me, the idea of finding a model for social interaction that is concrete enough to be tested and proven wrong, yet abstract enough to have broad and meaningful clinical applications, is over 30 years old. At Oberlin College in the early 1950s, I first was awed by the chemists' periodic table of the elements and then was impressed by George Heise, my introductory psychology professor, who had just come to Oberlin from Harvard and who steadfastly held that B. F. Skinner had some really good ideas about how there could be a science of behavior.

To pursue the quest for a table that could serve a science of behavior, I chose to go to graduate school at the University of Wisconsin, where there was a strong empirical tradition with emphasis on acquiring technical skills. This was followed by 4 years of clinical training at the University of Wisconsin Department of Psychiatry. Then followed a period of several years of professional isolation associated with the political realities of the 1960s, and while I was relegated to the periphery of the professional community with only books, paper, pencil, ideas, and about $300 a year in computer time available as research support, SASB evolved. Probably the isolation and freedom from distraction were important in allowing SASB and its software to develop. Now SASB has a life of its own. SASB was not created; it was discovered. The model keeps generating new ideas for me and for others, and there is reason to expect that even more concepts and applications can be forthcoming in the future.

This chapter focuses explicitly on the SASB model and its associated technology in order to show how they can be used operationally to define and measure the phenomenology of the person and to use those definitions to make predictions about social behavior. Structural Analysis has evolved from Murray's work via the contributions of Schaefer (1965), Leary (1957), Lorr and McNair (1963), and others. SASB is far more complex than preceding models, but this subjective disadvantage is offset by its ability to define operationally and measure a wide variety of difficult clinical problems.

The present exposition is limited to those aspects of SASB that relate directly to the advantages of approaching the study of psychiatric and psychological problems through description of the person's phenomenology. There will be a demonstration of how SASB's operationally defined and rationally organized description of a person's experiencing of his or her social milieu can be helpful in accounting for behavior. In addition, there will be special emphasis on some psychometric issues inherent in measuring social phenomenology. Problems such as the discrepancy between self-description and observations by others, variations in moods or states, the presence of different behaviors from the same person in different relationships, and failed test–retest reliability that nevertheless makes sense clinically are all examples of the issues dealt with here.

To be consistent with Murray's preference for dynamic, goal-oriented formulations and his belief that it is important to understand a person's developmental history as well as his or her goals for the future, this chapter also shows how the SASB's descriptions of early social learning experiences and resultant self-concept can serve to keep a person always headed toward a "maladaptive" posture. The interpretation explains self-destruction without invoking the tautological notion of a basic drive toward self-destructiveness—in Murray's terms, need-masochism, and in Freud's terms, Thanatos. The exposition of the SASB model itself will necessarily be brief. (For a more complete, leisurely exposition, see Benjamin, 1979a.)

Psychometric issues will be illustrated with clinical materials, some of which came from an Interpersonal Diagnostic Project (see page 125) and some of which came from my private practice. The emphasis on clinical material reflects the belief that personality theory should be kept very practical and close to the clinical realities faced by clinicians on an everyday basis.

The construct validity of the SASB model has been formally explored and discussed elsewhere (Benjamin, 1974, 1980b). Briefly, the validity of SASB structure has been tested by techniques of factor analysis, autocorrelational analysis, circumplex analysis, and a dimensional ratings procedure. Published applications of the model have included an exposition of how it can be used to formulate a treatment plan and measure change during therapy (Benjamin, 1977), how it can be used to define the common clinical problem of differentiation failure (Benjamin, 1979a), how it can be used to characterize patient–therapist interactions and study sequences in individual therapy using Markov chaining logic (Benjamin, 1979b) and/or family therapy (Benjamin, Foster, Giat-Roberto, & Estroff, in press). The model has successfully been used to characterize disturbance on the power dimension in couples having an alcoholic member (Chiles, Stauss, & Benjamin, 1980).

Presently a large-scale interpersonal diagnostic project is under way to determine whether the SASB model can either (1) add its operationally defined measures of self and social milieu to the *Diagnostic and Statistical Manual of Mental Disorders* (DSM-III) so that DSM-III would be more explicit about the behavioral and intrapsychic difficulties experienced by psychiatric patients; and/or (2) whether the SASB model might provide the basis of a meaningful alternative nosology organized primarily around social behavior and self-concept. An illustration of how an interpersonal nosology might work clinically is provided in a recent work (Benjamin, 1982) wherein the phenomenology of a suicidal man is shown to account for his psychiatric "symptomatology."

There are many potential advantages in using a technology like that offered by SASB rather than a traditional diagnostic nomenclature. Special features include an ability to include an individual's strengths as well as weaknesses in the initial assessment, highly individualized treatment of each person through the flexibility and comprehensiveness of computer analysis, rational organization of social concepts having implications for social etiology and treatment, and emphasis on what frequently is of interest to most psychiatric patients themselves, namely self-concept and social behavior (see Benjamin, 1981). SASB is accompanied by parallel models Structural Analysis of Affective Behavior (SAAB) and Structural Analysis of Cognitive Behavior (SACB). These parallel models have already been sketched briefly (Benjamin, 1981). The language of SASB can relate meaningfully to language used by many different "schools" of psychotherapy, and SASB theory and method are being summarized in a monograph (Benjamin, in preparation).

Highlights of the Model for Structural Analysis of Social Behavior

Effective use of the SASB model requires three different types of understanding: (1) the structure of the model itself; (2) the statistical parameters generated from SASB questionnaires corresponding to the model; and (3) the sequence of steps used to code any observed interaction in terms of the SASB model. Coding may be done on an informal basis, as in clinical practice, or on a very formal basis suitable for subsequent sequential analysis by computer, as in research.

What is SASB?

SASB is a formal model for scientifically defining and measuring social behaviors and self-concept. It classifies interpersonal activity in terms of the *focus* of the event and the two interpersonal dimensions of *affiliation* and *interdependence*. By way of these constructs the SASB model provides a clear description of relationships that define who is like whom and in what respect (the concept of *similarity*). It is explicit about which behaviors tend to elicit each other (the concept of *complementarity*), how social milieu affects the self-concept (the concept of *introjection*), and what to do to optimize conditions for behavioral change in a specific desired direction (the concept of *antithesis;* the Shaurette principle).

Focus

The first step in classifying any transaction is to identify the focus of the event. Figure 4.1 shows that the SASB model identifies three major types of

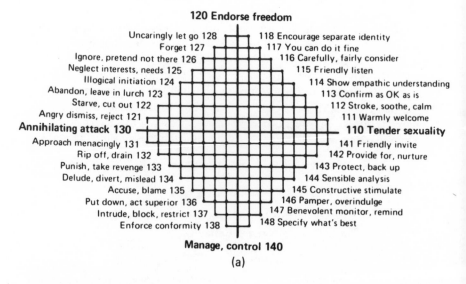

Figure 4.1 Full model for Structural Analysis of Social Behavior (SASB). The SASB model allows a transaction or a relationship to be classified in terms of focus, friendliness, and interdependence. The theory is explicit about what a given interpersonal posture is likely to draw from another person (complementarity), what the impact of the social milieu is upon the self-concept (introjection), and what can be done to get the opposite of what you have (antithesis; Shaurette principle). The three diamonds or surfaces reflect three types of focus: (a) interpersonal, focus on

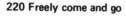

220 Freely come and go

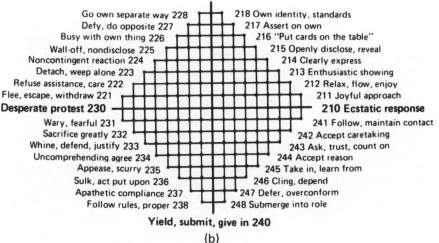

Go own separate way 228	218 Own identity, standards
Defy, do opposite 227	217 Assert on own
Busy with own thing 226	216 "Put cards on the table"
Wall-off, nondisclose 225	215 Openly disclose, reveal
Noncontingent reaction 224	214 Clearly express
Detach, weep alone 223	213 Enthusiastic showing
Refuse assistance, care 222	212 Relax, flow, enjoy
Flee, escape, withdraw 221	211 Joyful approach
Desperate protest 230	**210 Ecstatic response**
Wary, fearful 231	241 Follow, maintain contact
Sacrifice greatly 232	242 Accept caretaking
Whine, defend, justify 233	243 Ask, trust, count on
Uncomprehending agree 234	244 Accept reason
Appease, scurry 235	245 Take in, learn from
Sulk, act put upon 236	246 Cling, depend
Apathetic compliance 237	247 Defer, overconform
Follow rules, proper 238	248 Submerge into role

Yield, submit, give in 240

(b)

320 Happy-go-lucky

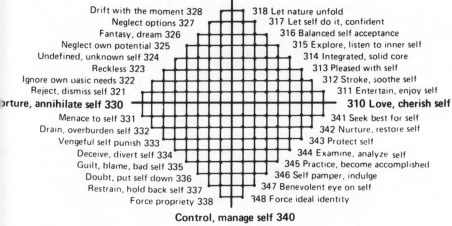

Drift with the moment 328	318 Let nature unfold
Neglect options 327	317 Let self do it, confident
Fantasy, dream 326	316 Balanced self acceptance
Neglect own potential 325	315 Explore, listen to inner self
Undefined, unknown self 324	314 Integrated, solid core
Reckless 323	313 Pleased with self
Ignore own basic needs 322	312 Stroke, soothe self
Reject, dismiss self 321	311 Entertain, enjoy self
orture, annihilate self 330	**310 Love, cherish self**
Menace to self 331	341 Seek best for self
Drain, overburden self 332	342 Nurture, restore self
Vengeful self punish 333	343 Protect self
Deceive, divert self 334	344 Examine, analyze self
Guilt, blame, bad self 335	345 Practice, become accomplished
Doubt, put self down 336	346 Self pamper, indulge
Restrain, hold back self 337	347 Benevolent eye on self
Force propriety 338	348 Force ideal identity

Control, manage self 340

(c)

other; (b) interpersonal, focus on self; and (c) intrapsychic, focus on other turned inward upon the self. The horizontal dimension represents affiliation, with all points on the right side of the model being friendly and all points on the left side being unfriendly. The vertical dimension represents interdependence, with all points on the upper halves of the model representing independence and points on the lower halves representing interdependence. From "Structural Analysis of Differentiation Failure" by L. S. Benjamin, *Psychiatry*, 1979a, *42*, 1–23. © 1979 by the William Alanson White Psychiatric Foundation. Reprinted by permission.

focus for an interpersonal event: focus on the other, the self, and the intro-jected other. Each of these types of focus is represented in the SASB model as a diamond created by the interaction of the orthogonal interpersonal dimensions of affiliation and interdependence described later. The first dia-mond or surface of the SASB model describes focus on another person (focus on other), ánd this is defined (see Benjamin, 1979a) in terms of transitive action toward a direct object. The second surface of the SASB model describes focus on the self and is defined as an intransitive state of being, or more loosely speaking, a reaction to another person. The third surface of the model represents focus on other or transitive action turned inward upon the self. More dynamically speaking, the third surface describes introjection. The first two surfaces of the model are interpersonal, and the third is intrapsychic. Although the clinical world has neglected the concept of focus, attention to this dimension is highly useful in guiding psychosocial assessments and interventions. The folk wisdom in the distinction between transitive and intransitive verbs, interpreted as focus by the SASB model, has substantial but heretofore unrecognized psychological usefulness. Under-standing and appreciating the focus dimension or the transitive–intransitive distinction can come with practice in applying the SASB model. Although clinicians and researchers usually work with SASB a while before they really understand focus, linguists usually understand it quickly. Transitivity is an elusive but powerful concept.

Prototypically speaking, focus on others (doing something to, for, or about the other person) is characteristic of parents, whereas focus on self (being in a reactive state) is characteristic of children. In an ideal adult rela-tionship, focus is well balanced with equal amounts of focus on other and focus on self. In other words, in a good intimate relationship one attends to one's own needs, reactions, and states about as often as one focuses on those of the other person. There are some situations in which imbalance of focus is appropriate and defined by the role. A common example of role-defined imbalance of focus is that the psychotherapist should be focusing mostly on the patient. Similarly, the patient should be focusing mostly on him- or herself.

Affiliation

The second decision to be made in classifying any interaction in terms of the SASB model is to identify its attributes along the interpersonal dimen-sion of affiliation. In Figure 4.1, this is represented in all three diamonds by the horizontal dimension. All of the points on the right-hand sides of the three surfaces are positively affiliative (friendly) while all of those on the left-hand sides are negatively affiliative (hostile). A transaction can be rated on a 9-point scale for friendliness (0 to +9) or hostility (0 to −9).

Interdependence

The third decision to be made in classifying any interaction in terms of the SASB model is to identify its attributes along the interpersonal dimension of interdependence. In Figure 4.1, this is represented in all three diamonds by the vertical dimension. All of the points on the lower half of each diamond represent interdependence or "enmeshment" and all the points on the upper half of each diamond represent independence or differentiation. The vertical scales are different for each type of focus, but all range from 0 to +9 for degrees of independence and from 0 to −9 for degrees of enmeshment.

Classification

A transaction is classified by a three-step decision process. For example, if person X says to person Y, "sit down," the first decision is that X is engaged in a transitive action toward Y (X is "up to something"). Next, it seems the statement is mildly unfriendly, say −2 on a scale ranging from 0 to −9. Finally, the statement is recognized as quite interdependent or enmeshed. More specifically, the vertical scale for focus on other ranges from "manage control" (−9) to "endorse freedom" (+9), and the statement "sit down" is quite controlling, say −7 on the 9-point scale. With these three decisions complete, one classification from the total of 108 on Figure 4.1 has been selected. It is on the focus on other surface, −2 units on the horizontal axis and −7 units on the vertical axis. On Figure 4.1, it can be seen the classification is point 137, "intrude, block, restrict."

Code Numbers on the SASB Model

Each point on the model has a code number that follows a simple logic. Knowledge of code numbers facilitates application of predictive principles of the model. The first digit identifies the surface to which the point belongs, with the 100s belonging to the first surface, the 200s to the second, and the 300s to the third. The middle digit describes the quadrant: 1, 2, 3, or 4 as shown in the center of Figure 4.2a and 4.2c, and the last digit describes the subdivision of each quadrant and ranges from 0 to 8. Points ending in 0 describe the axes.

The Definition of Opposites in the SASB Model

Each of the points on any of the three surfaces is made up of the interaction of the underlying dimensions of affiliation and interdependence. There are a number of implications of this mathematical and logical structure that have important consequences for psychological explanation. First, this model permits psychological, geometric, and logical *opposites* to be defined. An opposite of any of the behaviors on the three surfaces can be found by moving 180°

from that point. The *opposite* of a point is identified with the code number ending in the same units digit. Opposites for a given type of focus are defined precisely as a reversal of sign of the (*X,Y*) coordinates. For example, 137, "Intrude, block, restrict," has coordinates (−2/9,−7/9), meaning that it is located 2 units in the hostile direction on the *X* axis and 7 in the enmeshed direction on the *Y* axis. The opposite of this point is (+2/9,+7/9), point 117, "You can do it fine," 2 units in the friendly direction and 7 units in the independent direction. Thus, the opposite of point 137, "Intrude, block, restrict," is point 117, "You can do it fine." Later, it will be shown that this definition of opposites permits the derivation of statistical definitions of ambivalence, conflict, and double-bind.

Levels of Complexity in the SASB Model

All systems that categorize human behavior can be defined in terms that are more or less inclusive. As a coding system is written in more detailed individual terms, the system as a whole becomes more complex. Figures 4.2a–4.2c present three levels of complexity (or specificity of individual elements) of the SASB model for each level of focus. In the center of the figures, each diamond is divided into four quadrants that are defined by the combination of the poles encompassed by the quadrants. For example, Quadrant III, located between the attack and the control pole, is called "hostile power." The quadrant version of the SASB model is the simplest to understand. At a higher level of complexity, in the center of the figures, are the names of eight clusters of specific items. In the outer ring, the individual points from the most complex version of the model are enclosed in boxes that define the intermediate (or cluster) version of SASB.[1] The first cluster appears at the top of each diamond in the box located at 12 o'clock, and clusters are numbered sequentially in clockwise succession. For psychometric purposes, the intermediate level of complexity (involving subdivision of each surface into eight clusters) is the most useful form of the SASB model. One example of the psychometric usefulness of the cluster version is that the interpretive computer program (discussed later) is able to generate a paragraph applicable to a relationship if 75% or more of the items in a given cluster are endorsed at an above-median level. In addition, the clusters provide enough data points to permit some very powerful curve-fitting techniques. These also will be described later.

Use of Figures 4.2a–4.2c allows one to work with the intermediate level of complexity represented by the blocks of items shown in the clusters; the cluster boxes contain text from individual items on the 1983 version of the

---

[1] The cluster labels were prepared in collaboration with Clinton W. McLemore.

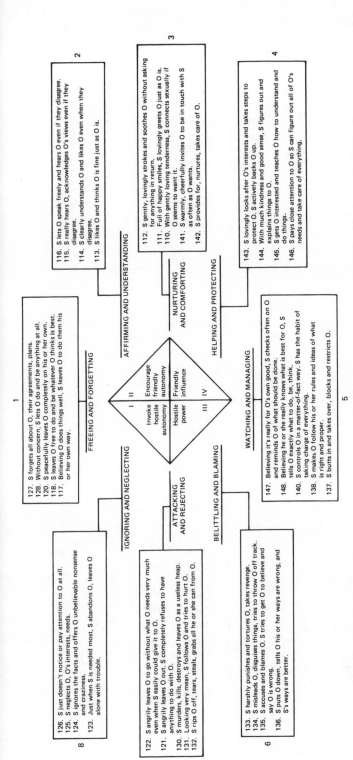

Figure 4.2a The SASB model, interpersonal other (O) focus. The quadrant version appearing at the center of the figure simply divides each type of focus into four sections. The middle ring provides names for eight clusters or subdivisions for each type of focus. The outer ring contains eight boxes corresponding to each of the eight clusters; the boxes contain 1983 questionnaire items for each of the model points from Figure 4.1 belonging to a cluster. The clusters are numbered from 1 to 8, starting at 12 o'clock on the top of each surface and proceeding clockwise. Familiarity with cluster numbers is important in interpreting the cluster profiles to be described subsequently. The quadrant model is from "Structural Analysis of Differentiation Failure" by L. S. Benjamin, *Psychiatry*, 1979, *42*, 1–23. © 1979 by the William Alanson White Psychiatric Foundation. Copyright on the cluster model has been registered by INTREX Interpersonal Institute, Inc., 1981; copyright on the questionnaire items, by Lorna Smith Benjamin, 1983. Reprinted by permission.

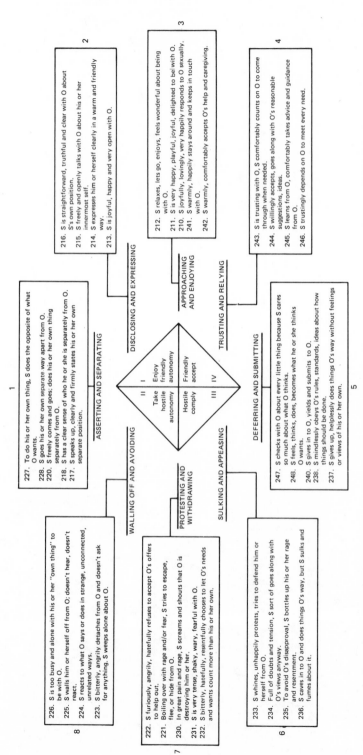

Figure 4.2b The SASB model, interpersonal self (S) focus. See Figure 4.2a legend for explanation. © 1979 by the William Alanson White Psychiatric Foundation. Copyright on the cluster model has been registered by INTREX Interpersonal Institute, Inc., 1981; copyright on the questionnaire items, by Lorna Smith Benjamin, 1983. Reprinted by permission.

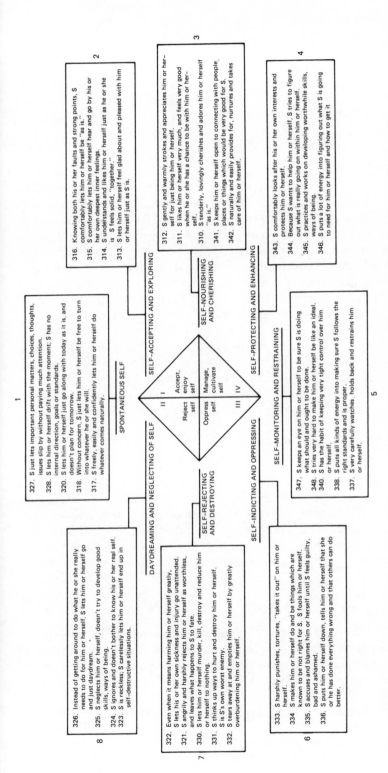

Figure 4.2c The SASB model, intrapsychic focus: introject (I) of other to self. See Figure 4.2a legend for explanation. Figures 4.2a, b, and c each show three levels of complexity of the SASB model: the quadrant version (4 categories), the cluster version (8 categories), and the full version (36 categories). © 1979 by the William Alanson White Psychiatric Foundation. Copyright on the cluster model has been registered by INTREX Interpersonal Institute, Inc., 1981; copyright on the questionnaire items, by Lorna Smith Benjamin, 1983. Reprinted by permission.

133

SASB questionnaires and therefore provide enough detail to give very specific and concrete understanding of what behaviors are included in each cluster. Items are published in a randomly determined order in questionnaire format by INTREX Interpersonal Institute, Inc.

Complementarity in the SASB Model

Through the principle of complementarity, the SASB model provides a number of inferences about the responses expected from others in reaction to any given interpersonal posture. The principle of complementarity states: *If the speaker is focusing on other, there is a strong draw for the listener to react by focus on self at the same point in interpersonal space.* In other words, if I talk to you about yourself, it is natural for you to reflect upon yourself, and there also is a tendency for our interdependence and affiliation dimensions to be matched. Geometrically, if one makes a classification on one of the two interpersonal SASB surfaces, its complement can be found at the same place on the other surface. In the example at hand, the complement of point 137, "intrudes, blocks, restricts person," is point 237, specified on the INTREX questionnaire as "gives up, helplessly does things O's way without feelings or views of his or her own." Put more informally, sheer "control" is best complemented by affectless compliance. If two persons are in complementary positions, their dyadic relation is stable, much as a chemical compound can represent the combination of two elements of opposite charge.

Instability in Interpersonal Space

There is maximal instability if two persons attempt to occupy the same point in interpersonal space. There is, for example, great instability if two people are trying to control (power struggle), if there are two blamers, if there are two listeners, if there are two emancipators, if there are two rejectors, and so on. In brief, if both people have the same, rather than complementary focus, there is no "connection." If I focus on you and you focus on me, we're not talking about the same thing and we're not going to have a stable transaction.

Introjection and the SASB Model

Sullivan (1953) and Mead (1934) suggested that we treat ourselves in the way that important other people have treated us. The third diamond in Figure 4.1 outlines the various aspects of self-concept that result from treating the self as important others have. It outlines what happens if focus from others is turned inward.

SASB predictions of impact of milieu on the self-concept are based on the subject's *perception*, not the reality. Self-concept is affected more by how we experience the world, than by how it really is. According to the full version of the SASB model, there are 36 different messages one can give oneself as a result of introjecting perceived focus from others inward upon the self. In general, one can predict that if messages described by the top surface are directed toward and perceived by another person, potential effects on self-concept can be described by the introject surface.

Antithesis, the SASB Model, and the Shaurette Principle

The SASB model can be used to explain how the social milieu can influence and change an individual. The concept of antithesis describes the behavior to be selected if the subject desires a type of behavior from another person that is the opposite of what is being experienced.

Specifically, antithesis is defined in SASB as the opposite to the complement of a specific behavior. For example, the antithesis of 137, "intrudes, blocks, restricts person," is 217, "assert on own." If you attempt to block me, and I show a nonattacking, differentiated self-disclosing response, the chances are maximized that you will permit me to proceed: 117, "you can do it fine."

Giving the antithesis does not always draw out the predicted complement, but the SASB model suggests that chances are optimal in a relationship that has normal flexibility. Exceptions are easily seen in rigid personalities and also with more severely disturbed people. For these situations, the Shaurette principle is recommended. Very briefly, the Shaurette principle states: Severely disturbed individuals do not have the interpersonal flexibility to respond directly to antithetical messages. To "connect" with these persons, one must first use the principle of complementarity to match the maladaptive behavior in the hostile regions of interpersonal space, and then, in stepwise fashion, proceed counterclockwise toward the desired antithesis. Limitations of space preclude further exposition of this difficult but important principle here (see Benjamin, 1982; Benjamin, Foster, Giat-Roberto, & Estroff, in press; and Benjamin, in preparation).

Comparison of SASB with Earlier Models of Interpersonal Space

The earliest version of the SASB model appeared in 1973 with an exposition of the relation of the model to previous work, including most especially that of Schaefer (Schaefer, 1965). A more complete discussion of the relation of the SASB model to other circumplex models and Murray-based models appeared in 1974 (Benjamin, 1974). Because the Murray-based Leary model is better known and far more easily understood (Leary, 1957), there will be an attempt here to show why SASB's added complexity is, in fact, worth the trouble.

One major difference between the SASB model and the Leary model is that SASB includes the concept of focus. Focus, shown by the three distinct surfaces in Figures 4.1 and 4.2a–4.2c, permits the definition of complementarity and resolves the dilemma posed by the fact that Leary called submission the opposite of dominance, whereas Schaefer called emancipation the opposite of dominance. Both opposites make sense, but both cannot be true. With SASB, submission is the *complement* of dominance, and the two combine to make a stable dyad. Emancipation is the *opposite* of dominance; both focus on other, but the sign of the control dimension is reversed.

A second major difference is that the introduction of the independence poles creates a whole new segment of interpersonal space not covered systematically by the Leary model and, incidentally, not understood by many pathological families. Recognition of this region of differentiated or independent interactions permits the important distinction between assertiveness and dominance. Friendly independent focus on the self represents a domain of interpersonal space that is needed when successful outcome in psychotherapy is measured. The nonadversarial autonomous self is well defined and doesn't need to oppress others in order to feel "OK." SASB theory defines friendly autonomy as healthy (see Benjamin, 1979a).

The concept of introjection, shown on the bottom surface of Figure 4.1 and in Figure 4.2c, frees one from the need to postulate a primary self-destructive drive such as Leary's need-masochism. Details of this feature are discussed in a later section, "The Dynamics of Misery."

The SASB model rationally defines opposites, complements, introjections, and antitheses. These predictive theoretical features are explicit enough to be scientifically testable and have clearly stated implications for etiology and treatment. In addition, SASB questionnaires, behavioral coding system, and software provide a large number of psychometrically sound parameters that can be applied to any number of clinical problems.[2] None of the other interpersonal models is so explicit about stable combinations, about what to do to move toward desired change, or so specific about the impact of social milieu upon self-concept. None offers such an array of software for operationalizing and testing dynamic clinical hypotheses.

---

[2]Manuals for coding typescripts and video or audiotapes are available through the author. In addition, most of the SASB software is available at cost to qualified researchers and teachers.

Measurement and Higher-Order Categorizing with the Structural Analysis of Social Behavior Model

Perception can be classified by individuals themselves or by an observer listening to an individual. A more formal means of measurement of perception is available through a series of SASB questionnaires called the INTREX Questionnaires.

Getting the Data

Each item on the INTREX questionnaire describes one point on the SASB model in Figure 4.1; the essence of the items in the questionnaire appears in the cluster boxes of Figures 4.2a–4.2c. Any relationship or series of relationships can be rated by using different forms of the questionnaire which appropriately substitute he, she, they, I, and use the present or past tense, depending on the desires of the investigator. Items appear in a randomly determined order, and for each relationship, the rater gives each item a score ranging from 0 to 100 in terms of frequency and aptness of fit. The scale is marked at 10-point intervals with 50 defined as the boundary between true and false.

Maps

For patient and clinician feedback, the MAP program generates maps like the diamond shown in Figure 4.3. Program INTERP adds interpretive comments to the map; these are shown in the cluster analysis section in Figure 4.3. Use of the maps alone compares to plotting an MMPI profile, whereas use of INTERP compares to using a computer-generated interpretation of an MMPI. INTERP simulates clinician function in reading the maps. In the present exposition, space does not allow for a review of all the features of INTERP; interested readers may wish to refer to earlier papers (Benjamin, 1980a, 1981, 1982) for more detail.

Creation of the map involves unscrambling the items, finding the median, and printing out phrases from those items that received above-median endorsements. The ratings in Figure 4.3 are from Patient 046 of the interpersonal diagnostic project, reporting on her perception of how she behaved in relation to staff on the inpatient service. It can be seen that most of her above-median endorsements were on the friendly side of the SASB model and the interpretive text generated by INTERP confirms this impression in the clus-

138

Lorna Smith Benjamin

```
PATIENT NUMBER 046. FEMALE. MARCH, 1981.
RATING NUMBER   2  WAS OF YOUR PERCEPTION
AS I SEE MYSELF IN RELATION TO STAFF (I AM RATED)

BEHAVIORS SHOWN INVOLVE FOCUSING ON ANOTHER PERSON. THERE IS ACTIVE
INITIATION, ACTION, OR PARENTLIKE BEHAVIOR
THIS IS THE FIRST OF TWO PARTS FOR THIS RATING
```

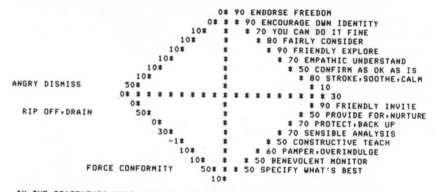

```
                                    0* 90 ENDORSE FREEDOM
                                 0* * * 90 ENCOURAGE OWN IDENTITY
                            10*    *    * 70 YOU CAN DO IT FINE
                           10*     *      * 80 FAIRLY CONSIDER
                          10*      *        * 90 FRIENDLY EXPLORE
                         10*       *         * 70 EMPATHIC UNDERSTAND
                        10*        *          * 50 CONFIRM AS OK AS IS
                       10*         *           * 80 STROKE,SOOTHE,CALM
ANGRY DISMISS         50*          *             * 10
                      0* * * * * * * * * * * * * * * * * 30
                       0*          *           * 90 FRIENDLY INVITE
RIP OFF,DRAIN         50*          *          * 50 PROVIDE FOR,NURTURE
                        0*         *         * 70 PROTECT,BACK UP
                       30*         *        * 70 SENSIBLE ANALYSIS
                      -1*          *       * 50 CONSTRUCTIVE TEACH
                     10*           *      * 60 PAMPER,OVERINDULGE
                    10*            *    * 50 BENEVOLENT MONITOR
FORCE CONFORMITY   50* * * 50 SPECIFY WHAT'S BEST
                   10*
```

```
IN THE STATEMENTS WHICH FOLLOW, THINK OF 'I' AS THE SUBJECT AND THE
LISTED IMPORTANT PERSON AS THE OBJECT OF THE DESCRIPTIONS. FOR EXAMPLE,
IF THE REPORT SAYS: 'IGNORES THE OTHER PERSON, NEGLECTS HIS/HER INTER-
ESTS', READ: 'I IGNORE HIM/HER, NEGLECT HIS/HER INTERESTS'. YOU ARE
DESCRIBING YOURSELF AND THE SOURCE IS THE 'I' FORM OF THE QUESTIONNAIRE.

*****************************************************************************
                            CLUSTER ANALYSIS

AFFIRMING AND UNDERSTANDING. THE PERSON RATED IS DESCRIBED AS
APPRECIATING, UNDERSTANDING, AFFIRMING AND SHOWING EMPATHY FOR THE
OTHER PERSON. ADDITIONAL BEHAVIORS THAT MAY BE PRESENT INCLUDE FAIRLY
TREATING THE OTHER PERSON AND ACTIVELY LISTENING EVEN IF THERE IS
DISAGREEMENT.

HELPING AND PROTECTING. THE PERSON RATED IS DESCRIBED AS ACTIVELY
HELPING THE OTHER PERSON THROUGH PROTECTION, SUPPORT, CONSTRUCTIVE
ADVICE AND POSSIBLY TEACHING. SUCH ACTIVE HELP GIVING MAY, IF PUSHED TO
EXTREMES, TAKE ON THE CHARACTERISTICS OF PAMPERING AND PERHAPS
OVERINDULGENCE.

*****************************************************************************
```

Figure 4.3   Part of the output from INTERP summarizing Patient 046's self-description of her behavior on the ward with psychiatric inpatient staff. When focusing on others, she saw herself as quite friendly and reported herself as "affirming and understanding" and "helping and protecting."

ter analysis shown at the bottom of Figure 4.3. The perceptions of Patient 046 are to be described later on, in more detail, in the next section.

SASB   Parameters

There are a number of parameters that can be generated by the MAP and QUAD programs, using the data illustrated in Figure 4.3. These include a weighted affiliation–autonomy vector (X,Y), which is a 2-space summary score of the average thrust on the affiliative axis (X) and on the interdependence axis (Y). A coefficient of internal consistency (see Benjamin, 1974, 1980a, and 1980b) describes the degree to which items that are supposed to be similar are given similar ratings; those that are supposed to be orthogonal or independent are given uncorrelated ratings, and those that are supposed to be opposite are given opposite ratings.

Other parameters, available as output from the QUAD program, include average quadrant scores, the number of true items in each quadrant, the number of above-median items in each quadrant, a measure of systematic contradiction (180° coefficient), and still more. For the present exposition, emphasis will be on output from the FIG program, which (1) graphs the average cluster scores for every rating, (2) identifies a best-fit theoretical curve that comes closest to describing the curve graphed, (3) correlates the actual curve with the theoretical best-fit curve and provides a test of the statistical significance of the best-fit curve, and (4) provides three numbers describing the degree to which the graphed curve shows attack, control (or submission), and/or conflict. These three numbers—called the attack, control, and conflict pattern coefficients, respectively—also may be tested for statistical significance. These three pattern coefficients may or may not include the curve that was the best fit.

To illustrate the function of FIG, the cluster-pattern profile for a medical student's description of psychiatric inpatient 046 focusing on staff is presented on the left side of Figure 4.4, and the cluster pattern from the patient's perception of the staff focusing on her is shown on the right side of Figure 4.4. Curve-fitting techniques are presented in the remainder of this section, and illustration of clinical and psychometric meanings follows.

In Figure 4.4, the solid circles represent the average scores for each cluster from the medical student's ratings of the patient (left) and from the patient ratings of staff (right). The stars in Figure 4.4 (connected by lines) represent the best-fit theoretical curves for these two data sets. Visual inspection suggests that the theoretical best-fit curves are similar to the average cluster score ratings. Both student doctor and patient seem to be describing hostility; both have higher ratings for the hostile clusters and lower values for friendly clusters. Accordingly, for both parts of Figure 4.4, the attack pattern coefficient is high and positive (.949 and .946, respectively). In addition, the control pattern is quite high (although not significant) for the medical student's perception of the patient whereas the control pattern is significant in the *negative* direction for the patient's perception of staff. The logic of the SASB model provides that a significantly negative control pattern would mean significant giving of autonomy. With these coefficients establishing that the patient perceives significant attack and autonomy-giving from staff, it becomes reasonable to say she experiences staff as very rejecting (Quadrant

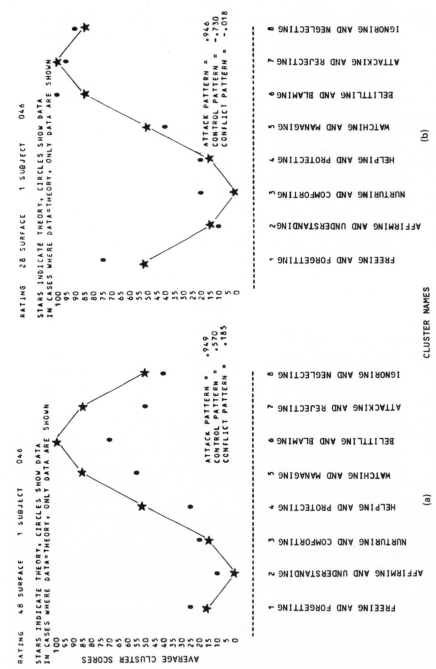

Figure 4.4 Output from FIG showing circumplex order in individual ratings. On the left, the average cluster scores for the medical student's rating of Patient 046 relating to staff appear in dark circles. On the right, Patient 046's perception of staff is shown in dark circles. The theoretical curves connected by lines are explained in the text in conjunction with Figure 4.5.

II). The medical student's perception of the patient is also unfavorable, but is more aptly described as hostile with a tendency to control (Quadrant III). The pattern coefficients provide considerably more information than can be obtained from the general impression of "hostility" to be gained from mere inspection of Figure 4.3 or Figure 4.6. In summary, pattern coefficients on the right side of Figure 4.4 reflect significant attack and rejection components, and those on the left side reflect significant attack and some control.

Understanding of the pattern coefficients is facilitated by knowledge of how they are computed. Twenty-one different theoretical curves describing possible cluster scores are correlated with the actual average cluster scores obtained for each cluster. These 21 different theoretical curves include several cosine curves transformed by linear interpolation from the cosine range of −1 to +1 to the SASB questionnaire range of 0 to 100. The different cosine curves represent various degrees of displacement (i.e., the cosine curve is moved to the right). In addition, other theoretical curves were created from the complete set of orthogonal polynomials for eight points, and still others were selected composite curves created on an ad hoc basis because they had been observed to occur frequently in practice. For example, a curve combining pure affiliation plus pure power is often the best-fit curve for describing childhood memory of mother. A complete exposition of all 21 curves is beyond the scope of this presentation, but key types are shown in Figure 4.5, and named in Table 4.1.

The rationale of the names in Table 4.1 for the curves in Figure 4.5 is based on circumplex logic. Circumplex logic, mathematically described by Guttman (1966), refers to an underlying space of two dimensions which permits arrangement of a set of points in a circle. If there is circumplex order, movement in one direction, say clockwise, provides for an increase in the representation of the dimension on the axis being approached and a decrease in the representation of the dimension on the axis behind. In stepwise fashion one can move around a circumplex through opposite points and end up back where one started. The three surfaces of SASB conform to circumplex logic except that they use absolute values of the underlying dimension rather than the squares; this is why SASB surfaces appear as diamonds rather than as circles.

If circumplex ordering is obtained in a set of SASB cluster scores, then any given cluster will have a maximal level of endorsement; those farther away will have progressively lesser endorsements, and the minimal level of endorsement will appear at the opposite cluster. The maximum and minimum points can appear at any place on the SASB surface, and if circumplex order is found for any given rating, it is appropriate to name that rating in terms of where the maximum endorsement was observed.

For example, the top part of Figure 4.5 shows curves having maxima at or

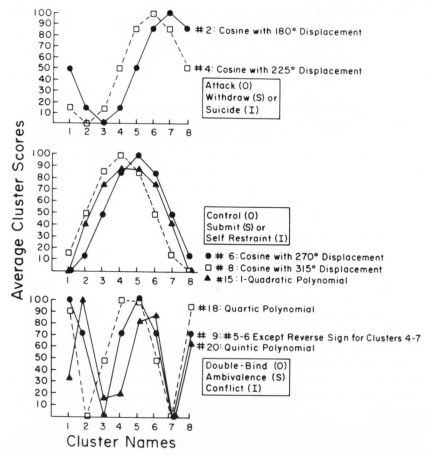

Figure 4.5 Key examples of theoretical curves; these can be fitted to actual curves by FIG. O denotes "other," S denotes "self," and I denotes "introjection." Correlations between various theoretical curves and actual curves yield the "best-fit" curve. If $r > .71$, the best fit characterizes the actual curve at the .05 level. Such fits permit the naming of specific relationships as "controlling," "attacking," "submissive," "withdrawn," and so on.

near the hostile poles of the SASB model, and Table 4.1 suggests these may be named "attack" if the rating involves focus on other, "protest and withdrawal" if the focus is on self, and "suicide" if introjection is being rated. If the sign of the attack coefficients is reversed by subtracting the respective values of the ordinate at the top of Figure 4.5 from the quantity 100, then the attack coefficient becomes a "friendliness" coefficient as shown in the last three entires in the "Attack" column of Table 4.1.

The middle part of Figure 4.5 shows the three theoretical curves that appear in the shape of an inverted-U as required by SASB theory for circum-

TABLE 4.1

Names for Significant Pattern Coefficients[a]

		Pattern coefficient		
	Focus	Attack	Control	Conflict
Image (positive sign of the pattern coefficient)	Other Self Introject	Attack Protest & withdraw Suicide	Control Submit Self-restraint	Power double-bind Ambivalent differentiation Conflict: self-control vs. let go
Reverse image (negative sign of the pattern coefficient)	Other Self Introject	Friendly (N) Friendly (N) Self-love (N)	Give autonomy Take autonomy Free self	Attachment double-bind Ambivalent attachment Conflict: self-love vs. self-hate

[a] Program FIG outputs an attack, control and conflict coefficient for each surface rated. If a pattern coefficient is greater than .71, it is significant at the .05 level or better. The name of the interpersonal posture associated with the significant coefficient depends on the surface rated (i.e., focus) and on the sign of the coefficient. Positive coefficients are called "image" in this table, and negative coefficients are called "reverse image." For example, the negative image of a significant attack coefficient is a significant friendliness coefficient. The fact that normative ratings usually produce a significant friendliness pattern is reflected by marking these patterns as (N).

plex ordering centering on clusters 4, 5, and 6. Table 4.1 shows that these coefficients describe "control" if focus is on other, "submission" if focus is on self, and "self-restraint" (control directed inward) if introjection is being rated. Cluster profiles resembling the best-fit curves shown in the middle of Figure 4.5 will have high control coefficients. If the sign of the control coefficient is reversed by subtracting the respective values at the ordinate in the middle of Figure 4.5 from the quantity 100, then the circumplex ordering centers on the autonomy pole and Table 4.1 suggests the names "give autonomy" if focus is on other, "take autonomy" if focus is on self, and "free self" if there is introjection.

The bottom part of Figure 4.5 shows what happens if circumplex order is *systematically* violated by high endorsement of opposites located on the vertical axis of the SASB model. Table 4.1 suggests the names "power double-bind" (conflict between "control" and "give autonomy") if focus is on other, "ambivalent differentiation" (conflict between "submit" and "take autonomy") if focus is on self, and "self-control vs. let go" if there is introjection. If the respective values of the ordinate at the bottom of Figure 4.5 are subtracted from the quantity 100, negative conflict coefficients are generated. Table 4.1 suggests these may be named "attachment double-bind" (conflict between "attack" and "nurture") if focus is on other, "ambivalent attachment" (conflict between "approach and enjoy" and "protest and withdraw") if focus is on self, and "self-love versus self-hate" if there is introjection.

In summary, FIG, which created Figure 4.4, graphs the cluster scores and computes the best of 21 possible theoretical fits. That best fit is graphed on the same scale as the actual cluster scores, and the correlation between best fit and actual data is given. In addition, the program reports the maximum absolute value for each of three theoretical sets of curves representing attack, control, and conflict:

1. The attack pattern coefficient is high and positive for relationships that are hostile; it is negative for relationships that are friendly.

2. The control pattern coefficients yield high positive coefficients for relationships that are controlling if focus is on other, submissive if focus is on self, and self-control if introjection is involved. Autonomy is reflected on the respective surfaces by negative control pattern coefficients.

3. The conflict pattern coefficients represent cluster profiles that show high endorsements at opposing poles—either interdependence or attachment. If focus is on other, conflict coefficients describe double-binds. If focus is on self, they describe ambivalence. If focus is introjected, the interpretation is of a conflicted self-concept. A summary of names for the three types of curves shown in Figure 4.5 appears in Table 4.1.

The orderly patterns shown by data in Figure 4.4 and described by the pattern coefficients are *typical* of individual subject ratings on SASB, and the finding of such recurrent order is yet another demonstration of the validity of the circumplex structure of SASB. Nearly every rating for every individual fits some pattern coefficient or other; the question usually is not whether the SASB-described circumplex exists, but rather, where is it centered: around friendliness? control? submission? withdrawal? conflict? Once the centering is identified by the best-fit coefficient, additional precision is available by considering the values for the attack, control, and conflict coefficients as was illustrated when comparing the left and right sides of Figure 4.4. Both relationships were perceived as attacking, but control coefficients suggested one was rejecting whereas the other was controlling.

The $N = 1$ Technology

The pattern coefficients give the investigator and the clinician a means of defining perception of a given relationship in familiar clinical terms such as controlling, withdrawn, submissive, autonomous, or friendly. The pattern coefficients also provide a test of statistical significance of these descriptions for $N = 1$. Not only does this technique operationalize useful and familiar clinical concepts, but it also gives the researcher freedom from the necessity of testing a hypothesis under conditions where everyone must show the same dynamic in order to confirm the hypothesis. For example, one dissertation researcher hypothesized that college females would relate to their boyfriends as they saw their mothers relate to their fathers. This is a reasonable hypothesis, but it might not be confirmed in the sample as a whole. The clinician might observe that some people could relate to their boyfriends as did their mothers, whereas others might identify interpersonally with their fathers. Still others might do the opposite of what their mothers did; some might maintain with their significant other their own complementary position with the mother. All may be showing the effects of early learning on the love relationship, but not the same way, so any one of these hypotheses might not be confirmed in an analysis of the sample as a whole.

With the introduction of an $N = 1$ test of whether parental and marital relationships were perceived as dominant, controlling, submissive, and so forth, and with average cluster scores from one relationship available to correlate with others, one is in a position to define sample subsets of subjects who identified with their fathers, subjects who identified with their mothers, subjects who did the opposite of either parent, and those who did none of the above. When the null hypothesis can be rejected at the $N = 1$ level, we have a technology suitable for the classification of individuals that opens the way to deal with the more heterogeneous patterns that people show in the real world.

It should be noted that some statisticians object in general to hypothesis testing on single subjects because, they argue, the sampling of data points within subjects is not independent. However, on the SASB questionnaires, each item is rated independently; nothing in the procedure forces the subject to connect one item to another. The alternative hypothesis tested by the proposed $N = 1$ procedure is: Do the patterns shown by the theoretical clusters correspond to the patterns shown by the empirical clusters? The square of the correlation between theoretical and empirical data points represents the variance shared. If $r = .71$ is the critical value of $p < .05$, then $r^2 = .5041$. Therefore, if $r \geq .71$, it can be said that over half the variance is accounted for by the correlation between data and theory. If desired, one who objected to hypothesis testing under these conditions could name the curves by using the criterion "over half the variance" rather than the criterion $p < .05$.

Clinical Utility of the Structural Analysis of Social Behavior Model

In this section, data from a specific clinical event are presented and explored as they highlight the utility of the SASB model in understanding difficult interactions. The case was selected because it illustrates a clinical need for prediction and shows how the SASB model helps explain an unpredicted event. The example implies that use of the SASB model in similar cases in the future might permit better clinical prediction.

The Unexpected Clinical Event

The unpredicted event was precipitated by a psychiatric patient who had been diagnosed as manic and maintained on lithium. With no apparent provocation, he arrived at the clinic and began to punch his psychotherapist in the head savagely. The therapist said afterwards that he felt like a battered spouse because someone he had known well and trusted had severely abused him for reasons he did not understand; the major initial feeling was one of disbelief.

The clinical history had included several hospitalizations for manic attacks, a well-planned program of lithium maintenance with varying and questioned degrees of compliance, and about 2 years of psychotherapy of a supportive type. Therapeutic communications had mostly to do with management of daily affairs with special emphasis on difficulties at work. Two of the patient's hospitalizations had been involuntary, the commitments being associated with verbal threats; he had never acted on any of these threats and at the time of this incident, there had been no threats toward the therapist nor even any indication that there was any anger. The traditional interpretation of the incident would be that this kind of nonsensical, unpredictable irritability is, in fact, one of the attributes of mania. There is presumed to be a defective biochemistry and periodically the manic person simply gets out of control. This, of course, is not the interpretation offered by the phenomenologist who attends carefully to the patient's perception of his or her world. Manics usually feel quite justified and have explanations for their behavior that seem entirely satisfactory to them. This patient, for example, maintained for several days after the event that he felt really good about punching his therapist out. Even a week later, he said: "I regret hitting him but, I don't know, for some reason I can't quite regret it as much as I might have done with a different situation." Limitations of space preclude an exposition of what was meant by "a different situation," although it is an interesting digression. The point here is that nearly a week after the incident, the patient still had his own privately acceptable reasons for the behavior, and punching the therapist was not exactly what an analyst might call ego-alien.

The resident and staff remained puzzled about the severely aggressive behavior, but the patient's reasoning become more clear during a 45-minute phenomenological clinical interview that was conducted according to the guidelines presented by Benjamin (1982). This type of structured interview focuses on assessing self-concept and important social relationships in terms of the SASB model. Bits and pieces of the clinical interview will be used to illustrate features of the SASB model, and then an integrative hypothesis explaining the event from a phenomenological point of view will be offered. Consider, for example, the manic patient's explanation of the punching incident:

> Oh, things had been building up. A lot of things related to the therapy, but things elsewhere like [a situation where the patient was called upon to perform] . . . and I was resenting all my duties at the time, and I guess what touched it off . . . was I was contacted through my landlords that Dr. S. wanted to see me, so I said okay, let's go see what Jack wants now [Jack S.]. And it was just one of those days when everybody wanted something right away . . . they all wanted something so I came up and uh, Dr. S. kind of, in my view kind of, kind of ordered me into the back. It wasn't a very, um, didn't seem to be, seemed to be hostile for some reason and he's not usually like that. So I just said come over here and I started hitting him. . .

The perception immediately preceding the attack on Dr. S. was summarized by the phrase "[he] kind of ordered me back into the back [office]." To classify the patient's perception of SASB, one must first identify within the content of the message the source of the transaction (called the X referent) and the recipient of the transaction (called the Y referent). In this phrase, X is Dr. S. and Y is the patient. SASB codings are always made from the point of view of X. Dr. S. is to be classified in order to characterize the patient's perception of the moment. When ordering the patient to step back into the office, Dr. S. is engaging in focus on another (namely the patient).

As noted earlier, the second decision to be made in classifying any interaction in terms of the SASB model is whether it is friendly or unfriendly. In the example in question, the patient reported that he experienced Dr. S.'s order-giving as hostile—more hostile than the reality warranted. From Dr. S.'s point of view, the request to see the patient was not hostile and probably is best characterized in the region on the friendly side of dominance, say, point 147 ("benevolent monitor, remind") of the top surface of Figure 4.1.

However, the patient did not experience the friendliness in the request; he said Dr. S. was "hostile." The patient also experienced Dr. S., who was focusing on other, as very controlling. The composite picture of focus on other, plus some hostility, plus much influence suggests that the classification for the patient should be in the region of mildly hostile (-1 or -2), strong influence (-8 or -7) on the focus-on-other surface. These observations would place the transaction at point 138 ("makes O follow his rules and ideas of what is right and proper") of Figure 4.1, or at point 137 ("butts in and takes over, blocks, restricts person"). As noted earlier, there are other considerations and factors in making classifications, but space limitations preclude more elaboration of these finer details. (For further exposition on coding procedures, see Benjamin, Giat, & Estroff [1981] and Benjamin, Foster, Giat-Roberto, & Estroff [in press].) For the purposes at hand, the informal coding conclusion can be that the patient experienced Dr. S. as interfering or blocking, that is, as exerting unwelcome control.

The principle of complementarity states that if the speaker focuses on other, there is a strong draw for the listener to focus on its complement, namely focus on self, at the same point in interpersonal space. In the present example, the complement of point 137 ("intrudes, blocks, restricts person") is point 237, specified on the SASB questionnaire as "Just does things person's way without feelings of one's own, is apathetic." Put more informally, sheer "control" is best complemented by affectless compliance. If in this instance the patient had complemented his perception of Dr. S., he would then have obediently and wordlessly followed Dr. S. back into his office. The patient's appearance at the clinic in response to the message from the landlord was, in itself, a kind of compliance, but when he came face-to-face with Dr. S., the move toward compliance ceased. He did not give the expected complementarity to Dr. S.'s monitoring. More information is needed to understand the failure of complementarity.

Using Developmental History to Understand
   the Unpredicted Response

It has been established that the patient experienced Dr. S. as intrusive and restrictive (point 137). He felt demanded of and controlled by "everyone" and was resenting his duties. In addition, the structured interview established there had been a series of difficult interactions with his boss that had involved the boss showing extremely tight monitoring of a project that the patient considered his own. Previously the boss had no interest in the project, but now was seeming to take it away and claim credit for it. In addition, the boss had contacted Dr. S. and enlisted his cooperation in a plan that involved, among other things, forcing the patient continually to bring to his boss a note signed by Dr. S. indicating that the patient had in fact kept each of his appointments. Finally, it should be noted that the landlord did not know about the patient's difficulty with mania. Having been previously evicted from two other living situations, the patient was threatened by having his landlord learn of any contact with mental health helping-professionals.

At this point, one's interpretation of the "biological" meaning of aggression becomes important. According to SASB's evolutionary-based logic, aggression is a set of behaviors that has evolved for the purpose of controlling space, time, persons, and supplies. If there is to be a fight, there will be a winner and a loser, with the loser either submitting or leaving. If aggression is viewed as an instrument for controlling or for resisting control, being left alone, and allowed to go free, it becomes easier to understand the patient's urge to attack Dr. S.

Nonetheless, most civilized persons do not attack people physically, especially helping authority figures. To understand why the patient went beyond these normal limits, it is helpful to know something about his early history. Very briefly, he had lost his father at an early age and acquired a stepfather whom he did not like. His mother used to discipline him by punching him in the head; this continued over a period of time until one day the patient decided he was big enough to punch his mother back—very hard, several times. This counterattack ended her abuse of him. He repeated this behavior 2 years later with the disliked stepfather and again was extremely successful in stopping the undesired behavior. He also hit a teacher and felt that this was successful. In short, the patient had modeling of punching from a very important early care-giving authority figure and had himself had major successes in defending himself against what was perceived to be overcontrol. It is no wonder then, that when he felt cornered, he repeated this coping mechanism and showed no particular remorse about it. Rather than giving antithetical assertiveness, he used attack to attempt to fend off the perceived overcontrol.

Predicting the Correct Treatment

Superficial application of the principle of antithesis to attack would be useless in this case. The antithesis of battering is loving approach. If Dr. S. were to respond with loving approach, most clinicians would predict disaster (even though many misguided parents do try to give more "love" to correct misbehaving children). Rather, the correct treatment approach is suggested by the recognition that the aggression or attack was not the primary issue. *The problem was the patient's perception of being overcontrolled.* He needed to exhibit the antithesis of control, namely assertiveness. He needed skills in how to express his state of being in an autonomous, highly differentiated fashion. In short, the patient needed assertiveness training (the antithesis of 137, "intrude, block, restrict"). Note that in SASB language, assertiveness represents autonomous focus on self, not controlling focus on other. Dominance is not assertiveness (compare cluster No. 2 on the focus on self surface with cluster No. 5 on the focus on other surface in Figures 4.2a–4.2b). This patient had very little experience with self-disclosure in a differentiated, non-hostile fashion. Had he been able to articulate his perception that the boss was appropriating his work, describe his fear about the landlord becoming alienated, and express his resentment of Dr. S.'s apparent alliance with the boss, he might well not have had to resort to punching.

Learning theory teaches us that providing a constructive alternative response (such as assertiveness) is optimal for changing behaviors. However, in some cases there also has to be punishment for the undesired behavior in order to break up the pattern and motivate the learning of the better alternative. In this case, punishment for the battering may have been needed. The loss of Dr. S. (whom the patient did like) as a therapist might teach that punching is generally unacceptable in civilized society. On the other hand, it could be that, in addition, formal filing of charges would be necessary for behavior change, since the patient heretofore had perceived physical assault as a successful coping mechanism. Such punishment would be coded in Quadrant III; it illustrates application of the Shaurette principle with a more severely disturbed person. At first, by therapist use of punishment, the patient is met in his familiar region of interpersonal space in order to begin the process of behavior change. Gradually, a therapeutic clockwise movement could unfold toward more friendly control followed later by therapist movement toward friendly separating.

In sum, understanding of the patient's phenomenology provides an explanation and "post"-diction of the unpredicted behavior. If the therapist had known that this person had a history of successful battering of care-giving authorities and that the therapist was being perceived as engaging in hostile control and as collaborating with the controlling boss, then the therapist could have predicted he was a likely target. One could predict the therapist would continue to be a vulnerable target until there was evidence that the patient had learned alternate ways of experiencing and coping with (asserting to) authorities whom he perceived as restricting his freedom.

If the Subject's Perception Is the Best Predictor, What about Defensiveness and Response Sets?

Are Some Patients "Invalid"?

Psychoanalysts and personologists hold that how a person sees the world determines largely how he or she responds to it. This necessarily means that subjects' own views must be a major part of personality assessment. Yet for many years there was extreme concern among theorists of personality measurement (e.g., Berg, 1967) that self-descriptions were highly suspect and even invalid because of distortion. This was attributable to response sets such as social desirability, acquiescence, nay-saying, and the like. If individuals are invested in presenting a "good image" of themselves, then their self-descriptions may not relate well to "reality."

One of the methods for dealing with response set is to attempt to disguise "undesirable" traits in socially desirable form (technically speaking, to match items for social desirability). But this technique has the drawback of requiring inference that the disguised form does in fact measure the underlying trait. Another device is to present some socially undesirable items that nevertheless are true of everyone and assume that if the subject denies these he or she must be lying in order to present a more favorable picture. The MMPI Lie Scale uses this approach. Such a measure can then be used as an index for identifying "invalid" profiles. A problem with this approach is that it leads nowhere once you have established test invalidity. What do you do with patients who are (inferred to be) liars? They can't truly be said to be "invalid" clients.

If You Want to Know What's Wrong, Ask

Personologists are more inclined to follow the old medical axiom: "If you want to know what's wrong with the patient, ask him or her." The professionally responsible intake interviewer asks the patient questions like: "Have you ever thought of hurting yourself?" "Have you ever thought of hurting anyone else?" The inquiry about suicide and murderous impulses surely is not socially "desirable," and yet in the medical setting it is considered malpractice to ask such questions in a disguised form.

Murray and his colleagues took great care to establish rapport with their subjects, and indeed apparently were able to obtain much sensitive information in the research setting. With such respectful collaboration between investigator and subject, there was not much concern about deceptiveness. The SASB approach has been compatible with Murray's in that there is emphasis on assuring that there is rapport, understanding, and mutuality between the subject and the investigator. In research studies the SASB is given with the offer of feedback, so subjects have an opportunity to enhance their self-awareness and personal growth by participation in the research. Except for unconscious defensiveness, the motivation for feedback often is adequate to elicit candor; such cooperativeness appropriately approximates the ideal medical setting wherein the person is presenting him- or herself for help and has everything to lose and nothing to gain by deliberately obscuring information.

Under the assumption of good faith, a desire for feedback, and self growth, the SASB forms elicit a wide variety of information, some of it socially "undesirable," from a wide range of subjects. On the average, normal volunteers and other nonpsychiatric respondents show self-ratings that are closer to those obtained when subjects are asked to rate their very best perception of themselves or their spouse, than to ratings obtained when they are asked to rate their very worst moments. Rather than falling in the middle of the range defined by the best and worst ratings, the unspecified ratings fall at about the 75% point in the direction of "best" or ideal. These ratings show that what is socially desirable is also affiliative in terms of the SASB model. But since the primate adapts by being sociable, it would be pathological for what is most adaptive, namely friendliness, to be socially undesirable. In other words, there likely is a major overlap between what is socially desirable and what is adaptive. If social desirability is eliminated from one's measurement system, one runs the risk of introducing a cure that is worst than the disease.

When Distortion Is Itself Pathognomic

If one accepts the idea that distortion in itself is important diagnostic information and that not all individuals are characterized by distortion, the problem takes on new form. For some people, distortions in self-image, whether delibarate to create an image or through unconscious defensiveness, should serve as descriptors. One method of measuring such distortions is to have the subject rated by "objective observers" as well as by him- or herself. Comparisons are possible when the same SASB forms are used by self and by other observers.

An example of such pathognomic discrepancy is Patient 046. This woman, in her early 30s, had a long history of depression and other symptoms. She was admitted for evaluation of an apparent suicidal potential. Her first hospitalization for depression was at age 12, and the illness had persisted intermittently ever since. Throughout the years she had been taking appropriate doses of antidepressants. Several other members of the family had also been hospitalized and treated for depression, and the father was alcoholic. One of the key events in her recent history had been that she had received a promotion on the job; this had caused an increase in the depression. The diagnosis was major depressive disorder with psychotic features. The interpretive output for Patient 046's description of herself focusing on the staff was presented in Figure 4.3. It is clear from inspection of Figure 4.3 that 046 saw herself as quite friendly and helpful in relation to the staff. Her attack pattern coefficient was $-.88$, indicating that the friendliness shown in this rating is sufficiently close to the theoretical curve to reach the .01 level of statistical significance.

This patient's self-description contrasts dramatically with the medical student's perception of her focusing on staff, presented in Figure 4.6. The interpretive output of Figure 4.6 shows that the medical student experienced 046 as exerting much hostile control, which at times came very close to outright attack. The coefficient of attack for the medical student's view of 046 was .949, as shown in the left side of Figure 4.4.

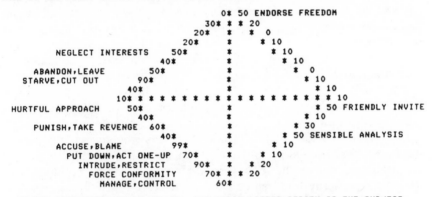

```
PATIENT NUMBER 046. FEMALE. MARCH, 1981.
RATING NUMBER    7  WAS OF YOUR PERCEPTION
MEDICAL STUDENT RATES PATIENT IN RELATION TO STAFF

BEHAVIORS SHOWN INVOLVE FOCUSING ON ANOTHER PERSON. THERE IS ACTIVE
INITIATION, ACTION, OR PARENTLIKE BEHAVIOR
THIS IS THE FIRST OF TWO PARTS FOR THIS RATING

                                  0* 50 ENDORSE FREEDOM
                         30*  *  * 20
                      20*    *    *  0
                   20*       *       *  10
     NEGLECT INTERESTS    50*       *       *  10
              40*        *       * 10
    ABANDON,LEAVE     50*       *       *  0
    STARVE,CUT OUT   90*       *       * 10
              40*        *              * 10
             10* * * * * * * * * * * * * * * * * 10
    HURTFUL APPROACH  50*       *              * 50 FRIENDLY INVITE
              40*        *              * 10
    PUNISH,TAKE REVENGE  60*       *            * 30
              40*        *            * 50 SENSIBLE ANALYSIS
      ACCUSE,BLAME         99*       *      * 10
      PUT DOWN,ACT ONE-UP  70*       *      * 10
         INTRUDE,RESTRICT     90*    *    * 20
         FORCE CONFORMITY    70* * * 20
         MANAGE,CONTROL       60*

IN THE STATEMENTS WHICH FOLLOW, THE FIRST LISTED PERSON IS THE SUBJECT
OF THE DESCRIPTIONS AND THE SECOND LISTED PERSON IS THE OBJECT.  FOR EX-
AMPLE, IF THE RATING WAS OF MOTHER IN RELATION TO FATHER WHEN YOU WERE
AGE 5 TO 10 YEARS, AND THE REPORT SAYS:  'IGNORES THE OTHER PERSON, NE-
GLECTS HIS/HER INTERESTS', READ:  'MOTHER IGNORED FATHER, NEGLECTED HIS
INTERESTS.'  YOU ARE DESCRIBING ONE PERSON IN RELATION TO ANOTHER.


***********************************************************************
                          CLUSTER ANALYSIS

BELITTLING AND BLAMING.  THE PERSON RATED IS DESCRIBED AS BELITTLING,
BLAMING AND POSSIBLY MANIPULATING THE OTHER PERSON THROUGH DECEIT.
THERE MAY BE EFFORTS TO OBTAIN ADMISSIONS OF WRONGDOING FROM THE OTHER
AND IN THE EXTREME A DEDICATION TO EXACTING REVENGE AND INVOKING
PUNISHMENT.


*********************************************************************** **
BRIEF TECHNICAL REMARKS
    THE RATINGS FOR THIS GROUP OF BEHAVIORS ARE INTERNALLY CONSISTENT.  SUCH
    INTERNAL CONSISTENCY USUALLY INDICATES THAT THE BEHAVIORS DESCRIBED ARE
    MOSTLY ORIENTED AROUND THE TRENDS DESCRIBED IN THE CLUSTER ANALYSIS.
    IF NO CLUSTERS WERE IDENTIFIED, THE MEDIAN MIGHT BE HIGH.
```

Figure 4.6 INTERP summarizes the medical student's view of Patient 046 in relation to the inpatient staff. A comparison of Figure 4.6 with Figure 4.3 shows that the medical student observer had a very different impression of Patient 046 than she did of herself.

In sum, 046's self-description had a very high coefficient suggesting friendly behavior ($-.88$), whereas the medical student's view of the patient in the very same context showed an extremely high coefficient of attack (.95). The descriptions are diametrically opposed and statistically significant in opposite directions. The correlation between the two views was $-.87$; there could hardly be greater disagreement about this patient's interpersonal orientation when focusing on staff.

Now the problem is to determine whether this person was faking to present a good image or whether her self-description represented some kind of defensiveness. At the research case review conference, the project associate observed that "she would be friendly enough if things were going her way, but if she got crossed she became very angry and demanding and lashed out." An example was offered: The medical student at first was perceived by the patient as being a really good guy. Later on, when it turned out the patient wasn't going to be able to stay in the hospital as long as she wanted, she became very angry and critical of him. Interestingly enough, four months after this hospitalization the patient had to be rehospitalized following a verbal explosion at her outpatient psychotherapist, whom she felt was not handling her case properly. The next admission also was for increasing depression and suicidality.

Here, then, is a case where objective observers would agree; the patient was hostile in relation to persons having a care-giving and authoritarian role, but she did not describe herself as hostile. How are the phenomenologist and the psychometrician using self-descriptions to solve this problem? The first step is to obtain ratings by self and by observers and to make comparisons of the two (as in Figures 4.3 and 4.6). The next, and more novel, step is to measure systematically the subject's perception of the world around him or her. Patient 046's ratings of staff focusing on her, shown in the right-hand side of Figure 4.4, had an *attack* coefficient of .95! There also was a significant negative control coefficient, which, combined with the high attack coefficient, suggests "very hostile rejection" and would characterize 046's perception of staff. Her cluster analysis by INTERP suggested that she saw the staff as "freeing and forgetting," "belittling and blaming," "attacking and rejecting," and "ignoring and neglecting" her. A psychoanalyst might call the pattern of attack coefficients projection: The subject attributes her own hostile behavior to those around her and describes herself in a diametrically opposite fashion. This is not an unreasonable interpretation. In fact, methodologically speaking, Figures 4.3, 4.4, and 4.6 display ways of operationally defining the defense of projection.

One might be content to have an operationally specified method of defining projection. One could build these observations into a diagnostic system: Select persons who have significant negative attack coefficients (indicating friendliness) in their self-descriptions but also are described by objective observers as attacking. If such persons also inappropriately perceive others as hostile, they can be said to project hostility. People having these attributes can be grouped together and studied in an effort to understand the origin of the mechanism of this particular defense. But the personologist who is interested in the phenomenology of the situation can pursue the question still further. Patient 046's rating of her interpersonal history on the INTREX forms yielded a description of her mother not unlike the right side of Figure 4.4. The attack coefficient for 046 rating mother focusing on her was .89; this also reached statistical significance at the .01 level. Now it can be said that the patient saw and experienced the staff as she experienced her mother.

Further information was available from a recording of 046's SASB staffing interview. During this routine interview, discussion about her relationship with her mother revealed that many messages were sent to her concerning how "defective and inadequate" the patient was. She said, for example:

> My mother likes to read me articles about every sickening situation she can find in the newspaper that might pertain to me . . . so she'll sit there and read me these articles and get really upset with me if I tell her I don't want to listen . . . Time and time again since I was a kid, you know, before I was the "sickie" (became depressed), I had allergies and my mother blew them all out of proportion. Made them a lot worse than they were.

Then the interview had turned to 046's involvement with her mother and father when they had fights. It seems that this patient would sometimes unlock the door for her father to get back in at night when her mother had locked him out. The mother's response to this was to lock her daughter out and say, "Great. You can go and live with him." The patient noted that her parents were always in the process of getting divorced and that she was constantly in the position of having to decide whom she was going to live with, even though she didn't want them to get a divorce at all.

At this point the personologist has little difficulty in understanding 046's tendency to do what ward personnel call "split." Splitting means the patient sees one person as all good and another as all bad. This patient's ratings in the interpersonal history showed the father to be all good, in as much excess as the mother was all bad. The same split was observed in relation to the medical student who had been transformed from a good guy into a bad guy quite easily. The patient's early living situation was chronically chaotic, and monumental life decisions were being made and unmade every evening, during which the patient had to judge who was right and who was wrong, whom she would go with and whom she would reject. In this context one can see how the patient could get in the habit of developing extreme and firm perceptions that flip-flop from moment to moment. In addition, this person had responsibility for taking care of both parents and her younger siblings. She also had the not uncommon fantasy that if she wasn't perfect, her father, who had a heart disorder, probably would have a heart attack and die. As the details of the early family history unfolded, it became easier to see why this person felt very angry with and critical of her care-givers and why she tended to produce ratings as all good or all bad.

Patient 046's case has illustrated that the personologist can deal with defenses by comparing ratings of self with ratings of others. Further, the subject's perception of those around him or her can provide some insight into the behavior observed. If 046 really did see the staff as rejecting, attacking, and controlling, then it's no wonder that she would be hostile in return. Further, the phenomenological measurements showed that this in fact was her experience of care-givers in authority, and so her misperception of staff may have been, in part, a matter of stimulus generalization. One might extrapolate the following working hypothesis: If the world is perceived as hostile and attacking, chances are the subject will behave in ways consistent with that perception even when he or she may not describe himself or herself in those terms. In other words, if self-description fails, measurement of perception of those around may do better at predicting a subject's behavior.

What about Different Moods? The Problem of Within-Subject Variability

Even folk wisdom recognizes that many people have variations in personality called mood changes. Raters taking the SASB forms will say, "I think the results would be different if I'd done it on another day." Such variability leads, in psychometric terms, to poor test–retest reliability; this is usually presumed to be "bad" and a fault in the psychometric instrument. Standard psychometric theory holds that if the internal consistency of a rating is high, then one can presume that the test–retest stability will also be high. The psychometric logic has been that if an instrument or a person doesn't give the same results on repeated occasions, then the data are not useful for predicting and the results cannot be valid. Recently this all-or-none view has been softened by renewed discussion supporting the idea of keeping the instrument and discarding only subjects whose reliability is poor (Bem & Allen, 1974; reviewed by Tellegen, Kamp, & Watson, 1982).

But such thinking presumes that good psychometrics and good subjects are not variable. As a matter of fact, pursued to its extreme, this logic would suggest that the most rigid of personalities are the best because their test–retest reliability would be highest. However, many clinicians recognize that rigidity itself can be pathological; flexibility is regarded as an index of health.

Beyond the observation that rigidity in behavior across situations and across time may not be "desirable" in any sense other than the traditional psychometric one, there is the additional fact that variability, or unpredictability, is in itself an important parameter descriptive of behavior. Do we not characterize destructive parenting in some contexts as "inconsistent"? If so, then one would not want to eliminate such parents from a sample. An important descriptive parameter is that some syndromes (such as mania) are characterized by variability and unpredictability. Rather than disregarding subjects and/or measuring instruments when high reliability coefficients are not obtained, there should be a study of the conditions under which high reliability is and is not obtained. Psychiatric patients are, as a group, characterized by less internal consistency as measured by SASB techniques (e.g., Benjamin, 1974). Lack of reliability is itself a matter of interest when describing persons.

Measuring Variability with Conflict or Contradiction Coefficients

The conflict pattern coefficient reflects the degree to which the endorsements of opposing clusters on the axes of the SASB model are correlated. The 180° coefficient performs a similar operation on raw scores (see Benjamin, 1980b); because it measures opposition off the axes as well as on them, the 180° coefficient is a more general measure of contradiction.

A significant conflict pattern coefficient ($r = .77$) is presented in Figure 4.7. The cluster pattern in the figure is for the manic patient previously mentioned; in the data presented here he is rating his reaction to his girlfriend under the instruction to describe himself when he was at his worst. Inspection of Figure 4.7 shows that when reacting to his girlfriend, this patient had a tendency to show the opposites: trusting and deferring (i.e., being interdependent) versus asserting and walling off (i.e., being very separate). His statistically significant conflict coefficient suggests he was ambivalent about interdependence (intimacy–distance) with his girlfriend. Especially noteworthy is the fact that he received a very low score for "disclosing and expressing" himself, and that, for his ratings of himself focusing on his girlfriend at his worst, he reported battering her (attack coefficient = .88). Again, there is a suggestion that lack of assertiveness appears in a context where there is battering.

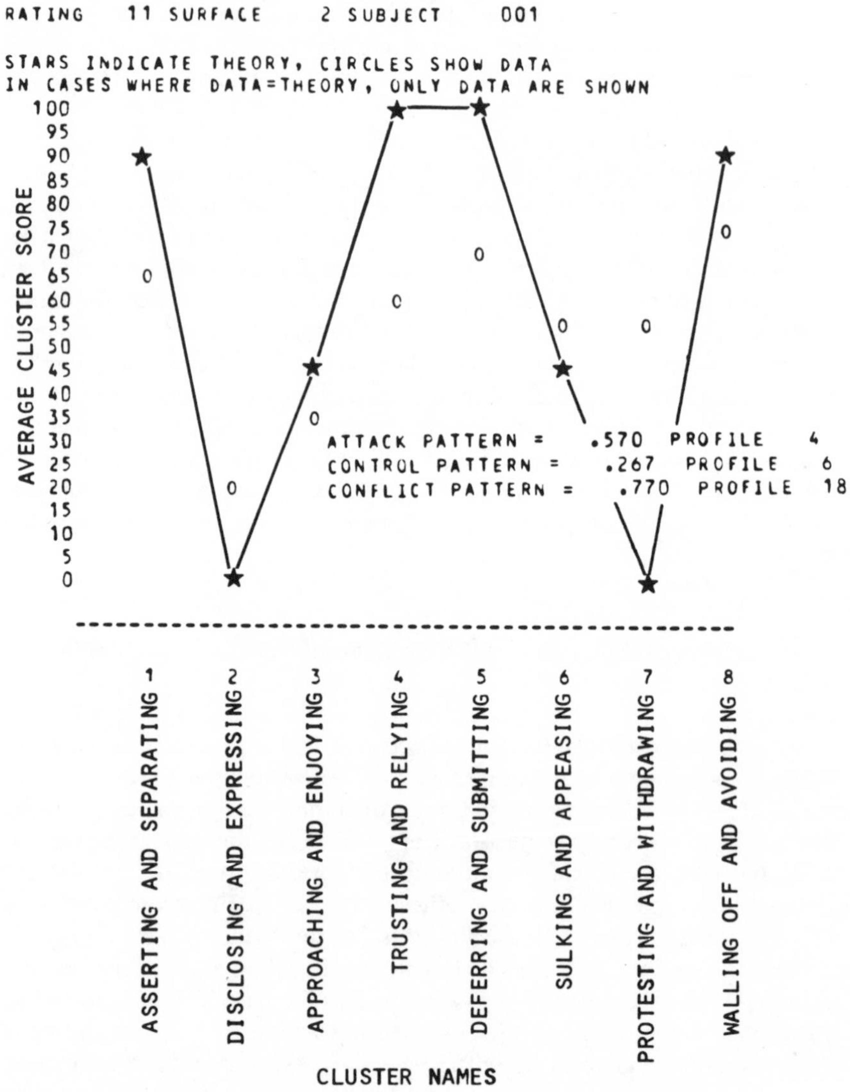
RATING 11 SURFACE 2 SUBJECT 001
STARS INDICATE THEORY, CIRCLES SHOW DATA
IN CASES WHERE DATA=THEORY, ONLY DATA ARE SHOWN
100
95
90
85
80
75
70
65
60
55
50
45
40
35
30
25
20
15
10
5
0
AVERAGE CLUSTER SCORE
ATTACK PATTERN = .570 PROFILE 4
CONTROL PATTERN = .267 PROFILE 6
CONFLICT PATTERN = .770 PROFILE 18
1 ASSERTING AND SEPARATING
2 DISCLOSING AND EXPRESSING
3 APPROACHING AND ENJOYING
4 TRUSTING AND RELYING
5 DEFERRING AND SUBMITTING
6 SULKING AND APPEASING
7 PROTESTING AND WITHDRAWING
8 WALLING OFF AND AVOIDING
CLUSTER NAMES

Figure 4.7 Cluster-pattern profile illustrating a significant conflict coefficient. The manic patient provided these ratings of himself when reacting to his girlfriend at his worst state. The conflict coefficient is .77; inspection of Figure 4.7 shows that the conflict is between "trusting and deferring" (being very compliant and interdependent), or "asserting and walling off" (being highly autonomous).

Pilot analyses of the data from the interpersonal diagnostic study suggest that persons in some diagnostic categories do in fact get significantly higher ratings than others on both the conflict coefficient and the 180° coefficient. Conflicts are different for different diagnostic categories.

Rating the Best and Worst States

Besides using the coefficient of internal consistency to make an inference about test–retest stability, the INTREX questionnaires can be adapted directly to measure variation in moods. Most often this variation has been done by having subjects rate themselves and others twice. The first time the rating is for when they or the other person are in their "best" state, and the second time the rating is made for the "worst" state. This procedure is named the best–worst form. Most subjects respond willingly to the opportunity to rate themselves at their most favorable, and then again when they are in a bad mood or "weirded out." Even normal subjects show an intuitive understanding of mood, or natural variabilities. One would expect that in a normative sample the range between best and worst would be small and significantly smaller than in a psychiatric sample. However, in a recent study of volunteer students from a personality class,[3] normal subjects showed a surprisingly wide range in self-concept: their "best" introject had an average attack coefficient of −.80; their "worst," of .06! This finding suggests the presence of quite a bit of intrapsychic pain in the form of self-attack in a normal sample. When these same normal subjects provided descriptions of themselves focusing on significant others, results were more in line with the expectation they would be less variable: Their average attack coefficient in their best state was −.91 and in their worst state, −.66. In other words, they were very friendly at their best, and even at their worst, they still saw themselves as fairly friendly to their significant other person.

Variation in an individual patient's ratings in the best and worst states is illustrated in Figures 4.8 and 4.9. The introject for Patient M. when she was depressed (Figure 4.8) can be compared and contrasted with her introject when she was not depressed (Figure 4.9). The figures were generated by INTERP and the differences are like night and day. When depressed, Patient M. was quite suicidal, self-neglectful, and very oppressive of herself; this hostile introject was maintained with a high level of internal consistency (.99). In addition, the weighted affiliation–autonomy vector (−113, −100)

[3]Thanks are expressed to Daniel Kirschenbaum and his students of personality in the University of Wisconsin Department of Psychology. Their willingness to contribute time and effort to the generation of normative data are much appreciated.

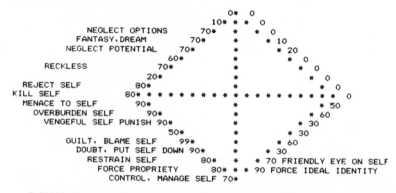

```
RATING NUMBER    1   WAS OF YOUR PERCEPTION
HOW I TREAT MYSELF WHEN I AM DOWN

                                        0*   0
                                   10*  *  *  0
               NEGLECT OPTIONS    70*    *  *  0
               FANTASY,DREAM       70*     *    0
            NEGLECT POTENTIAL     70*      *    * 10
                         60*               *    * 20
        RECKLESS            70*             *      *  0
                   20*                      *      *  0
     REJECT SELF        80*                 *          *  0
  KILL SELF          80* * * * * * * * * * *  * * * * * * * * *  0
    MENACE TO SELF      90*                  *        * 50
     OVERBURDEN SELF     90*                 *         * 60
      VENGEFUL SELF PUNISH 90*               *        * 30
                    50*                      *        * 30
          GUILT, BLAME SELF    99*           *        * 60
          DOUBT, PUT SELF DOWN 90*           *       * 30
            RESTRAIN SELF       80*    *     * 70 FRIENDLY EYE ON SELF
            FORCE PROPRIETY       80* * * 90 FORCE IDEAL IDENTITY
            CONTROL, MANAGE SELF 70*
```

THEORETICALLY THIS RATING REPRESENTS WHAT HAS BEEN DONE TO YOU BY EARLY
AND/OR CURRENT SIGNIFICANT OTHERS SUCH AS PARENTS, SPOUSE, CHURCH, IM-
PORTANT SIBLING, SPECIAL CHILD AND SO FORTH. TOWARD THE END OF THIS RE-
PORT, THERE WILL BE AN ATTEMPT TO CHECK THIS THEORY. IF THE INTROJECT
DESCRIBED HERE DOES NOT RELATE MEANINGFULLY TO THE OTHER PERSONS RATED
IN THE SERIES, PERHAPS AN IMPORTANT SOMEONE ELSE SHOULD ALSO BE RATED.

****
                          CLUSTER ANALYSIS

SELF MONITORING AND RESTRAINING. THE PERSON RATED IS DESCRIBED AS SELF
REGULATING AND CONTROLLING. THERE IS MUCH GOAL-DIRECTED SELF
DISCIPLINE. THIS MAY INVOLVE CAREFULLY KEEPING AN EYE ON ONE'S OWN
BEHAVIOR MUCH OF THE TIME TO INSURE CONFORMITY TO IDEALS, AND MUCH SELF-
MANAGEMENT TO MOVE TOWARD SELECTED GOALS. IN ITS MORE NEGATIVE FORM,
THIS INCLUDES CONSIDERABLE SELF RESTRAINT, EVEN SELF-COERCION.

SELF INDICTING AND OPPRESSING. THE PERSON RATED IS DESCRIBED AS SELF
OPPRESSING. INTERNALLY DIRECTED ACCUSATIONS OF INADEQUACY ARE LIKELY,
ALONG WITH GUILT AND SHAME. UNCERTAINTY AND GUILT MAY BLEND INTO 'FOOL-
ING' THE SELF BY DOING WHAT IS KNOWN TO BE NOT GOOD FOR THE SELF.
VICIOUS SELF PUNISHMENT MAY BE PRESENT AND THE POSSIBILITY OF SELF DES-
TRUCTIVE BEHAVIOR PROBABLY SHOULD BE DISCUSSED WITH A THERAPIST.

SELF REJECTING AND DESTROYING. THE PERSON RATED IS DESCRIBED AS VERY
HURTFUL OF SELF. THIS MAY INCLUDE IGNORING ILLNESSES AND INJURIES,
OVERBURDENING AND DEPLETING THE SELF; REJECTING AND DEPRIVING THE
SELF; GENERALLY BEING ONE'S OWN WORST ENEMY. IN ITS HARSHEST FORM, THIS
MAY INCLUDE TORTURE AND ANNIHILATION OF THE SELF. THE POSSIBILITY OF
SELF DESTRUCTIVE BEHAVIOR SHOULD BE DISCUSSED WITH A HEALTH PROFESSIONAL

DAYDREAMING AND NEGLECTING OF SELF. THE PERSON RATED IS DESCRIBED AS
SELF NEGLECTING. THIS MAY INCLUDE DAYDREAMING, AND FANTASIZING, UNDER-
DEVELOPMENT OF SKILLS AND POSITIVE POTENTIALS. IN THE EXTREME, UNWAR-
RANTED OR ILLOGICAL IDEAS ABOUT THE SELF MAY GO UNEXAMINED, THE PERSON
MAY BEHAVE RECKLESSLY, AND END UP IN SELF DESTRUCTIVE SITUATIONS. IT MAY
BE APPROPRIATE TO DISCUSS THE POSSIBLITY OF SELF HARM WITH A THERAPIST.

****

Figure 4.8   Subject M. rating herself at her worst. INTERP made it vividly clear that there was
relentless self-attack when she was depressed. The coefficient of internal consistency for this
rating was .99 and the weighted affiliation–autonomy vector was (−113, −100), indicating
extreme hostile self-oppression.

RATING NUMBER   4   WAS OF YOUR PERCEPTION
HOW I TREAT MYSELF WHEN I AM UP

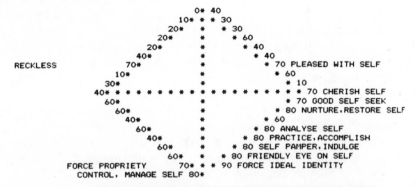

```
                                    0* 40
                                 10* * * 30
                              20*   *   * 30
                           20*      *      * 60
                        20*         *         * 40
                     40*            *            * 40
      RECKLESS       70*            *               * 70 PLEASED WITH SELF
                  10*               *               * 60
                30*                 *                * 10
             40* * * * * * * * * * * * * * * * * * * * 70 CHERISH SELF
                60*                 *                * 70 GOOD SELF SEEK
                  60*               *                * 80 NURTURE,RESTORE SELF
                    40*             *             * 60
                      60*           *          * 80 ANALYSE SELF
                        40*         *        * 80 PRACTICE,ACCOMPLISH
                           60*      *      * 80 SELF PAMPER,INDULGE
                              60*   *   * 80 FRIENDLY EYE ON SELF
            FORCE PROPRIETY      70* * * 90 FORCE IDEAL IDENTITY
              CONTROL, MANAGE SELF 80*
```

THEORETICALLY THIS RATING REPRESENTS WHAT HAS BEEN DONE TO YOU BY EARLY
AND/OR CURRENT SIGNIFICANT OTHERS SUCH AS PARENTS, SPOUSE, CHURCH, IM-
PORTANT SIBLING, SPECIAL CHILD AND SO FORTH. TOWARD THE END OF THIS RE-
PORT, THERE WILL BE AN ATTEMPT TO CHECK THIS THEORY. IF THE INTROJECT
DESCRIBED HERE DOES NOT RELATE MEANINGFULLY TO THE OTHER PERSONS RATED
IN THE SERIES, PERHAPS AN IMPORTANT SOMEONE ELSE SHOULD ALSO BE RATED.

****

                            CLUSTER ANALYSIS

SELF PROTECTING AND ENHANCING. THE PERSON RATED IS DESCRIBED AS SELF
PROTECTIVE AND ABLE REALISTICALLY TO EXAMINE THE SELF. THERE IS AN
ABILITY TO TAKE CONSTRUCTIVE STEPS ON ONE'S OWN BEHALF, ACTIVELY TO
DEVELOP ABILITIES AND OTHER ASSETS IMPORTANT TO SELF-REALIZATION. THIS
MAY EXTEND TO PUTTING MUCH ENERGY INTO GETTING EVERYTHING NEEDED OR
WANTED.

SELF MONITORING AND RESTRAINING. THE PERSON RATED IS DESCRIBED AS SELF
REGULATING AND CONTROLLING. THERE IS MUCH GOAL-DIRECTED SELF
DISCIPLINE. THIS MAY INVOLVE CAREFULLY KEEPING AN EYE ON ONE'S OWN
BEHAVIOR MUCH OF THE TIME TO INSURE CONFORMITY TO IDEALS, AND MUCH SELF-
MANAGEMENT TO MOVE TOWARD SELECTED GOALS. IN ITS MORE NEGATIVE FORM,
THIS INCLUDES CONSIDERABLE SELF RESTRAINT, EVEN SELF-COERCION.

****
BRIEF TECHNICAL REMARKS
THE RATINGS FOR THIS GROUP OF BEHAVIORS SHOWED EXTREMELY HIGH INTERNAL
CONSISTENCY. SUCH HIGH INTERNAL CONSISTENCY USUALLY INDICATES THAT THE
BEHAVIORS DESCRIBED ARE PREDICTABLY AND CONSISTENTLY ORIENTED AROUND THE
TRENDS DESCRIBED IN THE CLUSTER ANALYSIS. IF NO CLUSTERS WERE IDENTI-
FIED, THE MEDIAN MUST BE HIGH.

INTERNAL CONSISTENCY WAS GOOD ENOUGH TO PERMIT A SUMMARY OF
THE INTERPERSONAL ORIENTATION-
  THE PERSON RATED IS DESCRIBED AS CULTIVATING AND GUIDING HIM/HERSELF.
  SELF-DISCIPLINE, SELF PROTECTION AND SELF ENHANCEMENT ARE PRESENT OFTEN.

COEFFICIENT OF INTERNAL CONSISTENCY =   .993
THE SCORE   60 IS MEDIAN
  WEIGHTED AFFILIATION - AUTONOMY VECTOR=(39., -82.)

****

Figure 4.9 Subject M. rating herself when she was not depressed. INTERP showed that she
could exhibit a great deal of self-discipline and even direct some warmth toward herself. The
coefficient of internal consistency was high (.99) but is in dramatic contrast to M.'s equally
consistent worst self-concept, shown in Figure 4.8.

indicated hostile self-oppression in the extreme. In contrast, when not depressed the patient's self-concept was described by the interpretive program as "self-protecting and enhancing" plus "self-monitoring and restraining." These behaviors were maintained also with a high degree of internal consistency (.99). Speaking more informally, when depressed, she was highly consistent in her orientation around self-attack, and when not depressed she was consistently oriented around warm self-restraint. In pilot analyses, this pattern appears to be characteristic of inpatients carrying the diagnostic label of major depression, nonpsychotic type. An interesting problem for psychometric theory is that these self-concepts were reported by the same person at a given time, recalling different states. The moods are very different and internally consistent. Perhaps personality theory should give more attention to the problem of multiple personality—to changes of mood.

Is Multiple Personality Just a Change of Moods or Vice Versa?

Figures 4.8 and 4.9 demonstrate that the same individual can perceive himself or herself as being in very different states at different times and that the internal consistency at any given time can be extremely high. Here excellent internal consistency, combined with poor test–retest reliability, is due to clear differences in state or mood. The formal concept that comes closest to reflecting these differences is that of multiple personality, which, according to *The Diagnostic and Statistical Manual of Mental Disorders* (DSM-III) (American Psychiatric Association, 1980, pp. 257–259), is characterized by:

> a) The existence within the individual of two or more distinct personalities, each of which is dominant at a particular time. b) The personality that is dominant in any particular time determines the individual's behavior. c) Each individual personality is complex and integrated with its own unique behavior patterns and social relationships.

Multiple personality is rarely diagnosed these days, although the concept may become more fashionable again if personology gains broader acceptance. An interesting theoretical question would be, when does getting into a different "mood" cross the boundary into the category "multiple personality"?

Another relevant concept here is that of set. It may be normal and common for a certain sequence of events and/or contexts to put a person into an interpersonal *set* that is associated with a self-concept and behavioral propensities that are very different from another set equally accessible to the same normal individual. A familiar example might be the variation between self-concept and interpersonal responsiveness when one is on vacation and when one is trying to get everything in order just before vacation. It is not at all unusual for a person to comment, "How different I feel" when on vacation or even when moving from work to home on an ordinary day. In the latter case, if a person fails to change set, there can be significant interpersonal problems: loved ones at home often don't feel that behaviors appropriate to the work setting are what are wanted in the home. The point here is that varying moods, states, or situations are common and normal and probably underconceptualized both in clinical and psychometric theory. Personology and measurement of phenomenology are going to be important in studying and better understanding variability in mood or state.

What about Test–Retest Reliability for Different Moods?

If there is to be tolerance for describing personality in terms of different moods and states, then test–retest technology also needs to be reformulated. Subjects can rate themselves in, say, their best and worst states on one occasion and then do it again at a later time. A subgroup of 18 normal subjects showed an average test–retest $r = .87$ for 22 different moods and relationships.

Inpatients are expected to be less stable with test–retest r. There are illustrative test–retest data available on Patient 046 and on the manic patient discussed earlier. Subject 046 was measured in the SASB series for two of her hospitalizations, which were about 4 months apart. The specific measure of test–retest stability is the product–moment correlation between the average cluster scores for a given SASB surface with the average cluster scores on retest. The correlation between 046's ratings of her introject in her best state for the two hospitalizations was .55 and for her introject in the worst state was .64. Neither of these reaches the 5% significance level; nor did her ratings of herself with her significant other in best and worst states show significant test–retest r.

The most stable phenomenological measurements for 046 were of the memory of the past: her perception of her relations with her mother and father and of their marital relationship all showed significant positive test–retest r. Her perceptions of the best and worst of her relationship with the same significant-other person were extremely unstable between hospitalizations, with some of the correlations actually being negative. Her best and worst self-concepts also did not correlate well. However, different medical students assigned to her for the two hospitalizations did show significant agreement in their perception of her behavior on the ward.

Not Everybody Has the Same Kind of Instability

The manic patient presented a different picture of test–retest stability than Patient 046. His memory of his mother and father during childhood showed no significant correlations except for mother focusing on him (.71). On the other hand, his introject-best and introject-worst showed significant test–retest correlations (.71 and .78, respectively). Both sets of his ratings of himself with staff showed significnat test–retest r (.80 for focus on other, .83 for focus on self), as did his view of himself with other patients (.95, other; .73 self). The medical students also agreed with each other in their ratings of him with staff (.87, other; .75, self.).

In sum, it is possible to measure test–retest for different states, and variability in the stability can itself be pathognomic. Patient 046 had a stable memory of her early childhood, but the manic patient did not. The manic patient did provide stable descriptions of himself in his best and worst states. It seems possible that these differences have primary clinical meaning, but a definitive characterization requires larger sampling.

The Dynamics of Misery

The phenomenologist is potentially able to explain transitions from one mood to another and to explain why some poeple predictably gravitate toward the same state even though that state may be self-destructive. Freud was so impressed by the tenaciousness with which people retain and return to self-destructive states that he postulated Thanatos, a death instinct. Murray, also an acute clinical observer, developed a related concept and named it need-masochism. The postulation of a self-destructive drive contradicts the fundamental biological postulates (Murray, 1938, p. 118) that behaviors can be classified in terms of whether they avoid harm or allow the organism to seek benefits. However, need-masochism had to be introduced because Murray defined needs (Murray, 1938, p. 54) as "a hypothetical process, the occurrence of which is imagined in order to account for certain objective and subjective facts." The fact of self-destructive behaviors is undeniable.

Misery Is a Gift and a Tribute to Loved Ones

The thesis proposed here is simple and is based on introjection: *If we abuse ourselves, there must be a perception that we have been or are being abused by important others*. With self-oppression, we are doing unto ourselves as we have been done unto by others. Frequently it is possible to find, at some level, that the self-destructive behavior is or is imagined to be desired by a very important other person or persons or institution. The phenomenologist knows that introjection is the mental residual of previous experiences, and is not necessarily related to reality. It is the patient's perception of how it was that affects his or her self-concept (Beta press). Reality (Alpha press) is less important, except when the health care provider is working with family members in the present to try to change old destructive introjections by replacing them with newer and more benevolent ones.

To return to Patient 046, we find a reversal of the norm that the rating of the self in the best state is more friendly than the rating of the self in the worst state. Her introject for the worst state during her first hospitalization had a weighted affiliation–autonomy vector of $(-24, 96)$, whereas the introject for the self in the best state had the vector: $(-60, 26)$. In other words, there was more self-attack, neglect, and oppression when she was in the best than in the worst state. This case of "feeling worse when she was feeling better" was explained during her clinical interview.

In the interview, Patient 046 demonstrated at several points that she had the perception that her parents thought her role was to do poorly:

> *Patient*. It was a very good job, it was very challenging and it required a lot of responsibility and a lot of decision-making and I wanted to do it.
> *Interviewer*. Um, hm. Did you do it?
> *Patient*. Ya, I did it for four years.
> *Interviewer*. Did you do it well?
> *Patient*. Yes, I got a promotion and then I started getting depressed.
> *Interviewer*. Did you tell your parents about the promotion?
> *Patient*. No, I don't think so. I don't remember.
> IIInterviewer. What might they have said?
> *Patient*. I think they just didn't say much of anything, you know.
> *Interviewer*. What did you feel like?
> *Patient*. Oh, sort of discouraged, I guess. More than discouraged. Discouraged is a mild word. You know there isn't any point in trying to please them. There isn't anything I'm going to do to please them other than to be a complete basket case.
> *Interviewer*. To be a complete basket case would please them?
> *Patient*. Yes. I think that I am their way of getting help for themselves, you know . . . I was just being used as a reason for getting all these people involved in their lives because they don't want to say they've got problems.

Interviewer. Um, hm. So they get personnel around for you and then tell them their troubles.
Patient. Right.
Interviewer. So they made you into a basket case.
Patient. Right. You know, it's real clear to me. I see what's going on. I can see it but I'm not sure I can change it.

The patient went on to describe her more overt care-giving to her parents; one can see that the patient's role in the family was to be inadequate outside the home. Her pathology was her gift to the family, and from this frame of reference her "sickness" was not self-destructive. It was her ticket to fitting in, to being needed and wanted and accepted by the family. So when she was depressed and down on herself, and not doing well at the job and needing to live at home, she was where she was "supposed to be" and felt "better." This phenomenon may be characteristic of cases of self-destructiveness that are very persistent and unresponsive to usual treatment interventions.

Operationally Measuring the Dynamics of "Resistance"

Measures available for Patient 046 were restricted by the uniformity of the research protocol. However, when using the SASB technology on individuals in psychotherapy, it is possible to measure the subject's perception of him- or herself in different states and different relationships and even to measure different parts of the self. Theoretically, the possibilities are limited only by the imagination and the energy level of the patient and of the therapist.

Patient M., whose introject ratings are shown in Figures 4.8 and 4.9, was highly educated and successful professionally, but suffered from chronic major depression. Her developmental history was tragic and included multiple suicides within the family and extended family, including one parent and one sibling. In addition, her mother was alcoholic to the point of having been unable to keep up responsibilities of housekeeping, not to mention childcare. Having had some limited but vital amounts of support from a grandmother, the patient had enough strength to try to parent her mother. But of course, she was never able to make things better; no matter how hard she tried to keep the house orderly and take other corrective measures for all the problems that her mother chronically complained about, the mother's functioning did not change. Fortunately for M., the mother did approve of doing well in school, and so she had permission to develop herself in this way. Other maternal messages were that other people treat you poorly, that people can't be counted upon, and that the only safe place and real intimacy are to be found at home.

When M. started therapy she was actively resisting a tendency to feel guilty about the two suicides in her immediate family (probably she didn't do enough, she reasoned). She remembered her mother as an unhappy woman who was mostly withdrawn into her bedroom. She knew she had tried hard to please and make her mother better, that it had never worked; she also knew that she was important to her mother. The patient herself was a suicidal risk and most of the time she felt depressed. Her boyfriend was domineering and abusive, and she thought he probably was justified. She was evaluated for medications by an expert diagnostician, and though she showed the classic vegetative signs of endogenous depression, the decision was that medications should not be primary in treatment. The reasoning was that there was enough in her life history to account for the depression. There was, nevertheless, a brief trial of antidepressants, but these proved ineffective.

During most of therapy Patient M. was almost completely unable to discuss her mother in any terms other than with understanding and compassion. This, of course, is admirable and a form of high-level functioning, but it did not help her get rid of her own self-destructive tendencies, which are so clearly shown in Figure 4.8. Eventually, though she was willing not only to rate herself when depressed and when not depressed, but also to rate her perception of her mother at such times. Figure 4.10 was developed in collaboration with M.; it summarizes these ratings and also shows why she had such difficulty in avoiding depression. As shown at the left of the figure, she started from a baseline state of loneliness, which easily became associated with a bad self-concept ("No one loves me; I am unlovable"). When she was in the depressed state, her ratings suggested that her mother was able to provide nurturance and understanding (along with the punishment and blaming). But when the patient felt better about herself, this nurturance and understanding disappeared, attacks were increased, and rejection became blatant.

The transition between the states is also outlined in Figure 4.10. While in a depressed state, the patient said she felt calm. Her self-descriptions on the INTREX questionnaires revealed that she was extremely submissive (weighted autonomy score = −104). Pleasing her mother in this way made her feel better about herself and so she would move toward a state that she called hope—which, nevertheless, she still classified as depression. She would drift along in this state, basically thinking of herself as connected with the introjected representation of her mother, and something would happen that ought to have made her feel better. The most potent event was success in a relationship with another person, especially a man. Success at work was helpful too, although it seemed to be less potent, because much positive feedback from work was likely to be screened out or ignored. In any event, whenever M. began actually to feel good about herself, she became anxious very quickly and expected the world to reject and attack her.

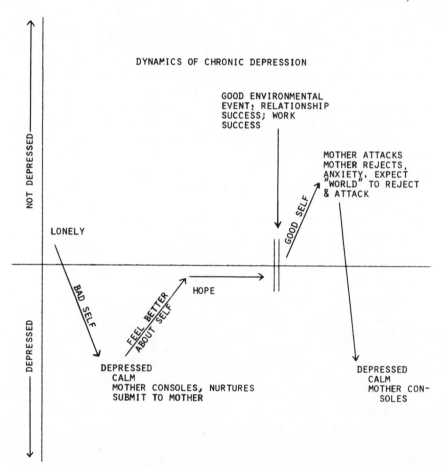

Figure 4.10 The dynamics of chronic depression. Patient M. helped prepare this figure to show her transitions among depressed and nondepressed states. Her introjection of her mother was more consoling and nurturant when the patient was depressed and was extremely attacking and rejecting when she was not. This interpretation was formally documented by ratings of her fantasy of her mother when the patient was in the different states.

Patient M.'s ratings of her mother when M. was not depressed were summarized by the interpretive output: [mother is described as] "facilitating freedom and independence in an uncaring manner. Neglect and rejection are present often." The coefficient of internal consistency was .99. By contrast, the description of the mother when the patient was depressed was very inconsistent (coefficient = .03), and the interpretive text read: "The ratings for this group of behaviors showed essentially no consistency. There probably is extreme unpredictability with frequent changes from moment to moment. In general it can probably be said that this group of behaviors is not stable or 'together.' In many cases, the word 'chaotic' would be appropriate." That is, the patient had a clear sense of how the mother would focus on her if she was not depressed (mother would be consistently rejecting), but was more confused about her mother's treatment of her when she was depressed. The confusion is directly reflective of the mixed picture of nurturance, understanding, punishment, and attack perceived from the mother during these times.

Despite all the insight offered by the discussions in therapy, by viewing the output, and by the joint preparation of Figure 4.10, M. for a long time was unable to free herself from the power of the maternal introject. She understood it intellectually, but commented: "Although it comes from inside, it feels like it's out of control. *To challenge it is too anxiety-provoking.* I had a dream the other night in which I was singing to a child and the child said 'Stop it.'" Associations to the dream established a connection to the idea of her being an inadequate parent (the patient didn't parent her mother properly). M. also stated: "I have a compulsion to put myself down. The wish to destroy myself is out of control. When I fight this, it gets bad . . . I seem to be weak against it. It's more strong than I am." Then she continued, "That's the way it was with Mother. She really came down on me hard if I got up." Such fear of constructive change has been noted by others (e.g., Kepecs, 1982).

In summary, Patient M. was socialized in an extremely restrictive world in which her "protector" was, in fact, her oppressor. This is a technique well developed by brainwashers. There was a chance of some reward and intrapsychic comfort if she remained depressed, but the INTREX measures showed that the internal attack and rejection were consistent if she dared to stop being depressed. The correlation between the memory of the mother focusing on her when she was nondepressed and her introject when she was nondepressed was $-.87$, establishing at the .05 level of statistical significance that the mother was doing to M. the opposite of whatever M. was doing for herself when not depressed. This opposition is illustrated graphically in Figure 4.11. The left side presents the cluster profile for M.'s perception of herself (and presumably also her treatment of herself) when she was not depressed; the right-hand part shows her perception of how the mother focused on her at this time. Inspection of the figure shows that the right side (mother's focus) has a U-shape, whereas the left side (introjection) is in the shape of an inverted-U. Curve-fitting coefficients establish at better than the .01 level of confidence that when M. was not depressed, there was self-directed control (.92), and that the maternal introject engaged in autonomy-giving (.92) plus attack (.84). This combination of attack plus autonomy-giving amounted to consolidated and highly consistent rejection. Another way of operationalizing internal maternal rejection is to note that the weight-

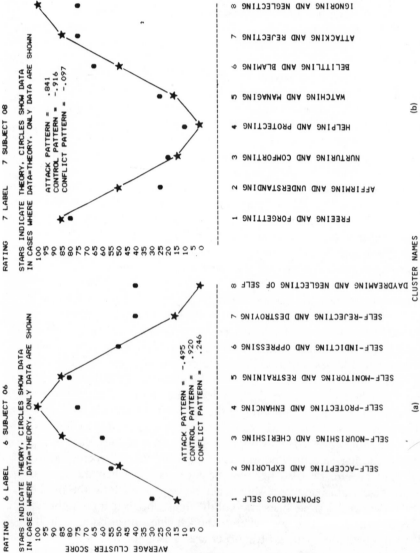

Figure 4.11 Patient M. rating her self-concept when she was not depressed (a), and her perception of her mother's focus on her when she was not depressed (b). The inverse relation between the "good" self-concept (a), and the attacking, rejecting input from the maternal introject when M. feels good about herself (b) enhance understanding of why it is so hard

ed affiliation–autonomy vector for the mother's focus on M. in this state is (−113, 78), with an internal consistency of .99. In other words, when the patient was at her best (left side of Figure 4.11), the maternal introject (right side) contradicted all the good self-talk.

The treatment approach for this situation was to do everything possible to help M. detach from the destructive introject and replace it with more constructive representations. This was attempted through facilitating constructive relationships with important others. The first step in that chain was to help M. extricate herself from the abusive relationship with her boyfriend, which she did. Her next boyfriend was similar in his needs to control, but his put-downs were more subtle and less lethal. In addition she was referred for group therapy.

The attachment between M. and the therapist remains, and always will be, very important. The insight provided by the dynamic analysis and operationalized by the ratings and the statistical parameters outlined the task, but the insight was not the cure itself. The change came with everyday experiences with people who were more loving and more pleased when she was nondepressed than when she was compliant and depressed. M. chose a course of successively approximating this transition in different relationships. Each new friend (male or female) tended to be more friendly and less controlling and attacking. Eventually she married a man who was very good to her. A year after the termination of therapy, she wrote: "I consider myself an example of successful psychotherapy."

The personologist can predict that when M. has success, she is likely to feel better at first and then to become anxious. Despite the successful treatment, she will remain vulnerable to rejection and fear of rejection. She may be potentially suicidal at times when something hoped for doesn't work out (just as her mother predicted). Her major change required toleration of the anxiety associated with abandoning the internal representation of her mother and letting the good relationships in her present world become more important. If the present "betrays" her, she will be vulnerable to regression back to the internal representation of mother and the depression.

Conclusion

Murray underscored the need for intensive, high-quality, in-depth study of the whole person. He emphasized "inner variables" and the dynamic or goal-directed character of behavior. Reference to the individual's developmental history and his or her goals for the future is an important part of dynamics.

The phenomenology, or experiencing state of the subject (Beta press), is thought to be more relevant to the task of prediction than is reality itself (Alpha press).

Structural Analysis of Social Behavior (SASB) is a derivative of Murray's work and implements many of his values for the study of the person. SASB is a rational theory, developed since 1968 with repeated revisions and refinements that were dictated by empirical results. SASB permits the classification of social interactions in terms of focus, affiliation, and interdependence. Classification of a subject's perception in terms of SASB can sharpen the understanding of the meaning of the social event. For example, the classification in terms of underlying dimensionality can deepen the therapist's reflection of the patient's communication and heighten the level of intensity and understanding. Classification by SASB also permits a number of inferences about antecedent and consequent social events (via the principle of complementarity), about the impact of a social event on the self-concept (via introjection), and about what to do to optimize the possibility of desired change (the Shaurette principle and the principle of antithesis).

There is a formal SASB coding system accompanied by computer software that permits a study of sequences by Markov chaining.The SASB questionnaires, named the INTREX questionnaires, permit measurement of the subject's perceptions, and these in turn can be compared and contrasted to observer ratings on the same scales. Such comparisons can provide a means of operationally defining defenses such as projection.

Software associated with the rating scales yields a number of parameters, suitable for feedback to subjects, to facilitate their own interpersonal learning; other software yields within-subject research parameters that permit the characterization of relationships as dominant, submissive, withdrawn, friendly, hostile, at a statistically signifiicant level for $N = 1$. These parameters include statistical definition of nonlinear clinical concepts such as conflict, ambivalence, or double-bind. The powerful within-subject parameters also allow statistical definition of subpopulations (e.g., reaction formers, identifiers, complementers) so that dynamic hypotheses can be tested without requiring that they apply to everyone in the sample. The flexibility of the SASB questionnaires means that methodologically difficult clinical realities, such as variable moods and the fact that people can be different in different relationships at different times, can be handled. This flexibility also permits an in-depth, rich view of complicated persons in real life. The uncovering of unconscious introjections during psychotherapy can be followed by SASB ratings of the perception of important others in different states. Such specific ratings can operationalize the dynamics of self-destructive behavior in terms of affiliation with an oppressive introject. Specifying a connection between subject perception of valued but destructive others and self-destruction precludes the need to postulate the existence of primary maladaptive drives such as a death instinct or need-masochism. All of these ideas need further development. To illustrate, it is not known why some persons identify with one parent and not the other, why some persons relate to a spouse as they related to their parents, and why others relate to a spouse as they saw one parent relate to the other. It is not known why some people develop the defense of projection, whereas others favor repression or denial. It is expected that such questions can be answered by the in-depth, highly operationalized study of individuals and that ordinary principles of social learning will help answer many of the questions. There is promise that the SASB technology, applied in the ways illustrated here, will permit the scientific study of difficult dynamic clinical issues along the lines articulated so well by Murray. The outer limits and possibilities have not yet been approached.

Acknowledgments

Thanks are expressed to Patients 046 and 099, who participated in the Interpersonal Diagnostic research; to Patient M., who helped prepare Figure 4.10; and to Dr. S., who provided valuable feedback. Thanks too are due Paula Machtinger and Rob Jones for their diligent and skillful acquisition of ratings from patients in the interpersonal diagnosis study. Sara Edwards, Patricia Hanson, and Sandra Tetzloff were unerringly accurate in their preparation of the massive data files from the project. Hanson and Machtinger also were vital to the development of our research procedures for reliably defining DSM-III categories. The editors were helpful in revising this manuscript to improve communication. Dee Jones, who always is infinitely pleasant, patient, and accurate in her typing of manuscripts and computer programs full of demanding detail, also is acknowledged with gratitude.

References

Allport, G. W. *Personality*. New York: Holt, 1937.
American Psychiatric Association. *The diagnostic and statistical manual of mental disorders* (3rd ed.). Washington, D.C.: Author, 1980.
Bem, D. J., & Allen, A. On predicting some of the people some of the time: The search for cross-situational consistencies in behavior. *Psychological Review*, 1974, *81*, 506–520.
Benjamin, L. S. A biological model for the study of individual differences. In J. Westman (Ed.), *Individual differences in children*. New York: Wiley, 1973.
Benjamin, L. S. Structural analysis of social behavior. *Psychological Review*, 1974, *81*, 392–425.
Benjamin, L. S. Structural analysis of a family in therapy. *Journal of Abnormal Psychology*, 1977, *45*, 391–406.
Benjamin, L. S. Structural analysis of differentiation failure. *Psychiatry: Journal for the Study of Interpersonal Processes*, 1979, *42*, 1–23. (a)

Benjamin, L. S. Use of structural analysis of social behavior (SASB) and Markov chains to study dyadic interactions. *Journal of Abnormal Psychology*, 1979, *88*, 303–319. (b)

Benjamin, L. S. *INTREX users manual*, Pts. I and II. Madison: INTREX Interpersonal Institute, Incorporated, 1980. (a)

Benjamin, L. S. *Internal validity of structural analysis of social behavior.* Unpublished manuscript, 1980. (b)

Benjamin, L. S. A psychosocial competence classification system. In J. D. Wine and M. D. Smye (Eds.), *Social competence.* New York: Guilford Press, 1981.

Benjamin, L. S. Use of structural analysis of social behavior (SASB) to guide interventions in psychotherapy. In J. Anchin and D. Kiesler (Eds.), *Handbook of interpersonal psychotherapy.* Elmsford, NY: Pergamon Press, 1982.

Benjamin, L. S. *Interpersonal diagnosis and treatment: The SASB approach.* New York: Guilford Press, in preparation.

Benjamin, L. S., Foster, S. W., Giat-Roberto, L., & Estroff, S. Coding videotapes of family interactions by structural analysis of social behavior (SASB). In L. Greenberg and W. Pinsoff (Eds.), *The psychotherapeutic process: A research handbook.* New York: Guilford Press, in press.

Benjamin, L. S., Giat, L., & Estroff, S. *Coding manual for structural analysis of social behavior (SASB).* Unpublished manuscript, 1981.

Berg, I. A. *Response set in personality assessment.* Chicago: Aldine, 1967.

Chiles, J., Stauss, F., & Benjamin, L. Marital conflict and sexual dysfunction in alcoholic and nonalcoholic couples. *British Journal of Psychiatry*, 1980, *137*, 266–273.

Guttman, L. Order analysis of correlation matrixes. In R. B. Cattell (Ed.), *Handbook of multivariate experimental psychology.* Chicago: Rand–McNally, 1966.

Heiddeger, M. *Sein und Zeit.* Tübingen, West Germany: Max Niemeyer, 1960.

Kepecs, J. *Beyond neurosis.* Unpublished manuscript, 1982.

Lorr, M., & McNair, D. M. An interpersonal behavior circle. *Journal of Abnormal and Social Psychology*, 1963, *67*, 68–75.

McLemore, C., & Benjamin, L. S. Whatever happened to interpersonal diagnosis: A psychosocial alternative to DSM-III. *American Psychologist*, 1979, *34*, 17–34.

Mead, G. H. *Mind, self, and society.* Chicago: Univ. of Chicago Press, 1934.

Murray, H. A. *Explorations in personality.* New York: Oxford Univ. Press, 1938.

Leary, T. *Interpersonal diagnosis of personality: A functional theory and methodology for personality evaluation.* New York: Ronald Press, 1957.

Sullivan, H. S. *The interpersonal theory of psychiatry.* New York: Norton, 1953.

Schaefer, E. S. Configurational analysis of children's reports of parent behavior. *Journal of Consulting Psychology*, 1965, *29*, 552–557.

Tellegen, A., Kamp, J., & Watson, D. Recognizing individual differences in predictive structure. *Psychological Review*, 1982, *89*, 95–105.

PART III

The Predictability and Stability of Personality

This part, consisting of the chapters by Holt, Epstein, and Mischel, focuses upon the major theme of the present volume: the issue of personality stability and consistency, or, from a slightly different vantage point, the prediction of behavior.

Holt's chapter attacks the very philosophical underpinnings of the issue of predictability of behavior. Although prediction of behavior apparently implies a deterministic orientation that is incompatible with a notion of freedom of will, Holt argues that we can find an accommodation between the two so that we need not surrender exclusively to either the unpredictability of free will or the compulsion of determinism. Holt adopts the position "that determinism is not only fully compatible with freedom, but that the latter is inconceivable without the former" (p. 180). He goes on to explain as follows: "What good would it do me to be free to choose any course of action that appealed to me if I lived in a social world in which the behavior of other people was wholly unpredictable, because not subject to lawful determination?" (p. 180). However, Holt points out that the choice of behavior made by people most often involves "the balancing of several values," and although it "is determined even when free," it is not helpful in predicting it. He adopts a somewhat pessimistic view regarding the personologist's ability to predict behavior ("only indifferently well") and believes that the obstacles are "intrinsic"; behavior is never completely predictable—even under the most compelling conditions there is some freedom to choose. Thus, as Holt tries to accommodate the notion of free will with that of determinism, he comes to the inevitable conclusion that some behavior is predictable, albeit imperfectly, some of the time.

Seymour Epstein continues to address the issues introduced by Holt. Epstein has for some time questioned Mischel's conclusions regarding the stability and consistency of personality and behavior. Like Holt he is critical of single-item measures of behavior for which low levels of reliability have been demonstrated. However, numerous studies reviewed in his contribution

175

illustrate the methodological strategy of aggregation that, he argues, solves the problems noted by Mischel. By aggregating behavior over time Epstein demonstrates high levels of consistency in the responses of his subjects in daily ratings of emotions experienced and, more generally, of dispositions across situations. Epstein claims the effectiveness of not only temporal aggregation but of cross-situational aggregation as well, and concludes that "Behavior is to some extent situationally unique and to some extent cross-situationally general" (p. 212).

Epstein reasons that any response to a situation tends to contain a situationally specific element and a more general component. Since the situationally specific component is dominant at any one assessment, aggregation is necessary to obtain a measure of the general component. Thus, according to him, a high degree of situational specificity does not rule out the existence of broad dispositions, such as intelligence, honesty, ego resiliency and ego control, social competence, aggression, etc. And, as a result of aggregation over situations, "common variance is compounded and situational uniqueness cancelled out; hence cross-situational dispositions" (p. 222).

Furthermore, in another series of studies Epstein demonstrates the effectiveness of the aggregation method with laboratory data to achieve high coefficients of reliability. He goes beyond temporal aggregation and shows that aggregation is also effective, though in varying degrees, in studying the relationship between self-rated emotional states (e.g., happy–sad, secure–threatened, calm–jittery) and scores on personality inventories (e.g., sociability, extension) as well as psychophysiological reactions. Finally, within the same experimental design, he actually identifies certain emotional states (e.g., fear, boredom, anger) and correlates them with a large variety of experimental variables utilizing disparate measurement operations (self-rated emotions, psychophysiological measures, and motor behavior) in order to demonstrate "that there is widespread cross-situational stability of behavior across the different situations of the experiment" (p. 236).

These and other results lead Epstein to criticize laboratory experiments as traditionally conducted in psychology. He notes that a major weakness is their limited generality and the lack of replicability of their findings. Epstein sees this as a product of their failure to sufficiently "sample stimuli or situations" and of the confusion in these studies of meaningful experimental variance with incidental variance. He argues that the solution to this problem is aggregation over instances, rather than establishing a statistical criterion of presumed replicability.

Mischel begins his presentation by disavowing any rejection of, or disbelief in, the stability and continuity of personality that may have been attributed to him. He lists many instances of successful prediction, based on the understanding of the environment (e.g., child-rearing variables) on "relevant past behavior," self-reports etc. However, he believes that most personologists, including himself, "care less about prediction of behavior than about its analysis to enhance our understanding of basic psychological processes and to clarify the distinctive nature and structure of human personality itself" (p. 275). He further points out the tendency of personologists to ignore situations or the environment, which is the root of the difficulty in predicting behavior. In order to predict behavior psychologists must take "serious account of the psychological environment rather than relying exclusively on context-free dispositional inference . . ." (p. 279).

Mischel reports the results of a recent study, which investigates conscientiousness in 63 Charleton College students, to illustrate a different approach to temporal stability and cross-situational consistency. In this study, students were assessed by their friends and parents and were observed in a number of situations relevant to the studied trait, which was broken down to 19 behavioral measures (e.g., class attendance, assignment punctuality, room neatness). The percentage of significant coefficients of temporal stability for a single occasion was 46; when single occasions were aggregated, the mean coefficient was .61. Some cross-situational consistency was obtained, but Mischel concludes "it is just as clear . . . that behavior is also highly discriminative and that broad situational consistencies remain elusive even with reliable measures" (p. 288). Methodologically, we can see here an agreement with Epstein regarding the effectiveness of aggregating observations over occasions, but less confirmation of the achievement of cross-situational consistency.

Most important is Mischel's attempt at a "theoretical reconceptualization of the issues that will unify the analysis of person characteristics with the analysis of cognitive-learning processes, allowing the person and the situation to be analyzed in light of the same psychological principles" (p. 293). He believes that the mere "search for consistencies without an appropriate theoretical framework can become an ultimately uninteresting hunt for statistically significant coefficients" (p. 293). In the proposed reconceptualization, the focus shifts from what Mischel calls "global traits," describing "situation-free people," to person variables originating in cognitive social learning theory. Specifically he proposes five classes of person variables: *construction competencies* (abilities to construct diverse behaviors under appropriate conditions), *encoding strategies* (grouping and constructing events, self, and situations), *expectancies, goals, and values,* and *self-regulatory systems.* In addition to these variables that constitute the *person structure,* he proposes a model of *person operations* that will address the interaction issue of person structures and their integration "into a coherent functioning system." A "self-system" is seen as part of such an overall design. He also suggests that to understand the person operations "may require the development of a grammar of the individual or the 'self'" (p. 296). Mischel ends this extensive discussion of the structural underpinnings of personological research by turning once again to the examination of the major theoretical problem that a concern with prediction has attempted to solve. He concludes that for psychology to best understand the behavior of the human being and to produce thereby the most highly predictable (and thus most valid) science of personality, we must have a workable theory of the structure for such behavior, as well as a way to discern it. Mischel goes on to suggest that "the roots of such structure may be in the occurrence of temporally stable but cross-situationally discriminative features that are prototypic for the particular behavior category as perceived by the particular individual" (p. 300).

5

*Freud, the Free Will Controversy, and Prediction in Personology**

Robert R. Holt

Introduction

I begin by giving some brief answers to the two questions posed to contributors to this volume. First: How well can personologists now predict behavior? Only indifferently well, at best. Moreover, I do not look for great improvements. It is difficult to think of any specific obstacle to better prediction that can be removed by means of improved instruments, better training, shrewder judges, or the like. Rather, the obstacles to predicting behavior seem to be intrinsic. Instead of categorizing them, let me simply refer you to the list of 20 reasons why it is hard to make a scientific psychology that Meehl (1978) tells us he jotted down after "10 minutes of superficial thought."

Let us turn, then, to the second question: What factors facilitate or constrain our ability to accomplish this task? Surely there are many. I want to concentrate upon one, however, which has so far been little mentioned in the literature on clinical and statistical prediction—the problem of freedom. For decades, the silent consensus seemed to be that free will was an illusion, the very nature of scientific psychology requiring the assumption of determinism, which was interpreted as incompatible with human freedom to choose among possible courses of action. Hence, it required little discussion.

I have discovered one sure way to predict a trend in at least one form of

*The preparation of this chapter was supported by a U.S. Public Health Service Research Career Award, Grant No. 5-KO6-MH-12455, from the National Institute of Mental Health.

human behavior: the fads in personology. If I believe that I have arrived at an original insight or hit upon a fresh approach, I have only to look around me carefully for a few months to discover that I am part of a social movement among psychologists of personality. That is how it has been with this issue. About a decade and a half ago, the problem of freedom attracted me, and I wrote a couple of papers about it (Holt, 1967, 1972), only to discover that several of my friends were doing likewise. By now, one could assemble a respectable little shelf of psychologists' books on free will, choice, and related topics (de Charms, 1968; Deci, 1980; Easterbrook, 1978; Rychlak, 1979).

It is a striking, perhaps ironic fact that a closely related topic, self-control, came into great prominence recently among behavior modification psychologists, directly stimulated by Skinner. In his 1953 book, Skinner gave his blessing to the study of self-control and provided what Kanfer and Goldfoot (1966) call "a general paradigm" for self-control research: he "defined self-control as a process in which a person makes a response that alters the probability of the occurrence of another response" (p. 79). That, seemingly, makes such an act of freely exercised will power an acceptable subject for behaviorists to study and to incorporate into their therapeutic practices. In about a decade, a few papers were appearing giving instances of procedures by means of which patients (e.g., smokers who wanted to quit) could get control over their own behavior (Goldiamond, 1965; Nolan, 1968; Bandura & Perloff, 1967). Twenty years after Skinner's book, papers on self-control were becoming frequent enough so that *Psychological Abstracts* introduced it as an index heading, with 18 entries. In the second index of 1973 the count jumped ahead to 43; but it dropped to 26 and 22 in the next two volumes, followed by 29 and 42 in the two volumes for 1975, after which I stopped counting, for there was nearly a full page in Volume 55 (1976; not quite 40 items make up a column, with two columns to a page). The high point was reached in 1978 and 1979; in each of those years there was a total of almost three pages of indexed papers on self-control!

In the mid-1970s, I had another chastening experience: after the exhilaration of discovering a solution to the dilemma of free will versus determinism, I learned after publishing it that it was one of the standard positions in the philosophical literature. Nevertheless, I still liked it and was pleased to find that my friends Isidor Chein (1972) and Brewster Smith (1971) had independently arrived at similar ideas. The kernel of our position is that determinism is not only fully compatible with freedom, but that the latter is inconceivable without the former. What good would it do me to be free to choose any course of action that appealed to me if I lived in a social world in which the behavior of other people was wholly unpredictable, because not subject to lawful determination? I realized, moreover, that I feel maximally free when I have plenty of time to decide and am under minimal external constraints, so that my decision is determined primarily by realistic considerations interacting with my own conscious values, which are closely connected to or part of my sense of identity. Note the word conscious: If I respond in terms of an unconscious wish or fear, acting out some infantile fantasy, I am not likely to feel particularly free even though I am not neurotic enough to feel in the grip of an ego-alien compulsion. It follows, then, that if you know my value system and know the situation I am in, you should be in a pretty good position to predict my choices. Offer me a choice between an opportunity to speak at a meeting in honor of Harry Murray or one in honor of Fred Skinner, and you do not have to know me very well to be sure which invitation I will accept. I will confess, however, that if I had to choose between giving a Murray lecture and giving the same lecture to a large audience of behaviorists for an honorarium an order of a magnitude larger, I might decide that it would be a good idea to beard a few lions in their dens and preach to the unconverted for a change.

The example is fanciful, of course, but with it I wish to make a simple point: All too often, the choices people must make are not simple and involve the balancing of several values. Hence, my concession that behavior is determined even when free does not solve many of the problems of predicting it.

As I write these words in the summer of 1981, I imagine myself reading them in East Lansing. Having made the commitment to give the lecture I feel fairly confident that I can predict my own behavior; but only *fairly* confident. The combination of invitation, sentiments, wishes, and values that led to my acceptance created a firmer than usual intention (backed up by a conviction that a commitment must be honored), even a determination that I will do it. No matter, now, if the Psychonomic Society were to lure me with implausible and wholly unlikely offers and inducements to address them elsewhere on the same day; it is too late. The die is cast. Yet I know that a thousand things could happen to prevent my appearance: I could be killed in an auto accident; I could fall seriously ill and be immobile at the time of the lectures; a serious accident at the Zion nuclear plant coupled with just the right (or perhaps I should say, wrong) wind pattern might require the evacuation of East Lansing's vicinity; strikes in the transportation industry might make travel between New York and Michigan out of the question; and—God forbid most of all—the nation could be involved in a war crisis. I will not weary you with other scenarios, like personal family problems that could preclude my coming and all the rest that spring to mind. The point, I am sure, is made: good will and firm intentions cannot guarantee a successful follow-through.

So far I bring you nothing new. As I was writing the previous paragraph I suddenly recalled a passage in Meehl's *Clinical vs. Statistical Prediction* (1954), in which he gave the example of an unexpectedly broken leg as spoiling a prediction of the moviegoing behavior of a person whose taste in entertainment was accurately known. In the more recent paper already cited (Meehl, 1978), he has addressed these issues in a much more sophisticated fashion, bringing out the extent to which human behavior resembles a "random walk," responsive as it is to a host of environmental events that are likely to be unpredictable by a persönologist.

Who Says Behavior Is Predictable?

In the past decade, more heat than light has been contributed by the controversy initiated by Mischel's attack (1968) on the conception of traits. His move was not wholly unjustified, even though I have little sympathy for the way he went about it. It is undeniably true that clinical psychologists, psychoanalysts, psychiatrists, and other clinicians have had a pervasive occupational disease—exaggerating the extent to which behavior is intrapsychically determined. When Freud was stung by the failure of his seduction theory, he overreacted, losing interest not only in the legitimate possibility that neuroses might be caused at least in part by traumatic experiences in early childhood, but even tending to deny that the real circumstances in which a child lived had *any* role in pathogenesis. So deeply did he immerse himself in the study of dreams, fantasies, and symptoms interpreted in terms of unconscious fantasies and so-called transference paradigms that he seemed to lose interest in reality altogether. After all, the real situation was what everyone else, overlooking the unconscious determinants, had always stressed; psychoanalysis would now correct all that by unmasking the truly responsible villains: the patient's unconscious wishes and fears.

It is easier to understand and forgive Freud's defensive exaggeration than to feel equally benign toward his many followers who adopted his errors along with his insights, unnecessarily repeating mistakes they need not have made had they been less blinded by adulation. True, their principal adversaries, the behaviorists, never tired of reiterating the simplistic $S-R$ formula and seeking with Skinner to shape behavior by controlling the stimulus situation. By the extremism of their advocacy, they put a curse on the stimulus for many a clinician, confirming the latter's tendency to exaggerate the consistency of behavior and its predictability from a knowledge of the person alone.

For all his fascination with techniques for studying fantasies and early memories, however, Murray never forgot to give equal weight to the outer and the inner determinants of behavior. Thematic analysis, you may recall, requires that we look for configurations of press and need. Mischel originally said, in effect, that we should forget about need and concentrate on press, since the evidence was so poor that there are any consistent intrapersonal tendencies such as needs or traits. Now surely there are situations so pressive that an enormous majority of people will respond to them in the same way; under the incredible pressures of a Nazi concentration camp, the vast majority of inmates conformed to orders, even when to do so was to prepare their own deaths. Yet it is instructive to notice that behavior is never 100% predictable even under circumstances when every vestige of choice has seemingly been taken away from the actors. Some of the persecuted did fight back even against impossible odds; some of them escaped; some retained self-respect under systematic attempts to undermine and humiliate everyone. There was a popular saying during World War II that every man has his breaking point; it was used by many clinicians in an effort to prevent civilians from being contemptuous of those with traumatic neuroses and other such casualties. Yet I vividly recall hearing a lecture shortly after the war's end by the chief psychiatrist of the British army, who cited repeated examples of men who withstood truly incredible hardships, terrorizing dangers, and stressors of every kind, maintaining both sanity and adaptive, even heroically selfless behavior until only death itself stopped them. The range and extent of psychological differences among individual human beings can hardly be overestimated.

Mischel's practical mistake was to overlook the poor quality of a lot of the research he cited. When something is not easy to find, it is dangerous to conclude from the failures of a few ineffectual search parties that it does not exist. Behavior is, manifestly and undeniably, a function of the situation, but also of the person. It therefore follows that if one of these dependencies is to be studied, the other must either be held constant or its influence not allowed to conceal or confound that of the other. As Fishbein and Ajzen (1974) pointed out and as Epstein (1980) has demonstrated so cogently, one of the fallacies of many unsuccessful attempts to predict behavior is that they have been innocent of psychometric theory; for their criterion or dependent variable, they have sampled a behavioral realm with a one-item test. Putting a person in one situation and obtaining one type of response from him or her is, from the standpoint of measurement theory, exactly analogous to the attempt to measure a trait by an inventory containing one single item. But if you put people in a variety of situations and examine their behavior from the standpoint of a given trait, you have a much more defensible measure of it. Better yet, observe them in a *representative* sample of situations, as Brunswik (1956) urged many years ago, and you can obtain an ecologically valid sample of their behavior, one from which you can logically and practically have a better chance of predicting their usual response.

One of the strengths of Murray's Thematic Apperception Test (TAT) is that its pictures present a person with a substantial sample of varieties of press that are important and recurrent in most people's lives, and that many respondents tell elaborate enough stories so that they introduce other types of press that are significant for them. From the press–need configurations— themas—found in the stories, one can predict that *if* a press of a given kind arises, specific needs will show themselves. Yet we have only to think about the test in Brunswikian terms to realize how far it is from providing a relevant selection of situations for everyone and how thinly we can sample the repertory of possible themas a person may manifest, using a manageable number of stories.

In speaking about sampling situations, notice that I quickly switched to the shortcut of the TAT. For a criterion measure, however, nothing less than the behavior in question will do, observed in its actual life setting. Consider the work of Barker and his associates on "psychological ecology." To record the behavior of one boy during one day took a large team of highly trained observers, and the result was enough raw data to fill a book (Barker & Wright, 1951). That boy's behavior *was* sampled in all relevant behavioral settings, but for only a period of one day. Surely we need to allow for day-to-day variation in behavior, too.

The attempt to predict human behavior is a shooting match with a constantly moving target. That endlessly paradoxical creature, the human being, is forever changing and yet remains recognizably the same; moreover, some people are reliably more changeable than others! Complete consistency is rigidity to the point of rigor mortis, just as the only completely reliable watch is the one that won't run. Yet most of the classical research on the consistency of behavior completely lacked awareness of these commonsense truisms. Someone would define a type of behavior, and then solemnly set about trying to discover if it is a trait—that is, do people always manifest the same amount of it? What an absurd question! Yet it is easier to see how little can be learned from asking it in that way than it is to say how to study consistency more meaningfully, a topic I leave to Epstein in Chapter 6.

The more I think about these matters, the more I begin to feel that our whole orientation to the problem somehow fails us; we have asked the wrong questions. Does it really make much sense to ask how well anyone can predict behavior? Is one form of behavior of equal interest to another? Some kinds are easier to predict than others, but they may be trivial from the standpoint of practical affairs. A man's decisions as a business leader may affect the lives of millions, but be much less easily predictable than his choice of neckties or his nervous mannerisms; does it matter, as far as theory goes? Presumably to rout the null hypothesis of the naysayers, any kind of prediction will do to make the point that it is, in principle, possible.

Suppose I were to present to you a patient with a tic whom I had observed long enough to be rather confident that he would demonstrate his characteristic grimace 15 times per hour, plus or minus 2; is that good enough? Or might a skeptic not justifiably object that no real prediction had been accomplished, only a crude statistical approximation? No *single* ticlike movement had been predicted; no understanding of the behavior and what determined it would necessarily have been achieved. Of course, the same can be said for most statistical prediction: however successful a team of actuaries may be, they need not understand any of the behavior they successfully predict once given the desired data about the subjects. They do not have to know anything about how the behavior is organized and determined, what significance it has in the lives of the persons involved, or how it could be affected in any way; nor is their work likely to yield anything of the kind—only reasonably effective predictions. Clinicians, by contrast, are full of hypotheses about these psychologically more nutritious matters, but are typically unable to frame them in testable fashion or to adduce any evidence that these hypotheses are right or wrong.

The Metaphysical Approach to Behavioral Studies

When I first approached the problem of prediction, I was a good deal younger and brasher than I feel now. It seemed obvious to me that clinicians had done badly, for correctible reasons having little to do with the validity of clinical methods and theories, when compared with statistical predictive systems. It was hard to keep one's footing in an arena so liberally scattered with red herrings (there is no fish more slippery), and it has taken me a long time to discern what makes this such an insoluble problem. It certainly did not work to label it a pseudoproblem, one couched in the wrong terms; it just doesn't disappear, even though many people have lost interest, on the mistaken supposition that the statisticians had won long ago (Holt, 1978).

In a certain sense, I am willing to concede that there are natural advantages to the statistical approach, which give it a commanding lead in any race—especially, the capacity of modern computers to process enormous quantities of data without becoming bored or losing interest and motivation. If you want to set up a system for predicting something more or less behavioral, like college grades, year in and year out for thousands of students, you would be very ill-advised to hire a staff of clinicians for the purpose. But, as I have argued before, one can hardly understand the amount of interest stirred up by the controversy over a few decades on the supposition that psychologists have been faced with a lot of demand for such predictive systems. Instead, psychologists have had the mistaken impression that somehow through a comparison of the predictive validities of judgmental and nonjudgmental predictions we were going to get answers to much larger and more fundamental issues.

Today, I would formulâte the underlying disagreement as metaphysical—a difference in world hypotheses, to borrow a phrase from Pepper (1942). If your hair is as gray as mine, you were perhaps taught in graduate school that metaphysics is at worst nonsense, at best something like poetry—to be viewed indulgently as an off-hour diversion, but not the sustained concern of serious people. After all, metaphysics is not testable, so it must be inconsequential. The favorite example of a metaphysical problem was the scholastics' disputation over the number of angels who could dance on the point of a pin. In fact, that hardly qualifies as a metaphysical issue at all, but it served the purpose of those who needed a straw man who could be dismissed with a gust of derisive laughter. Then they could get back to their empirical studies with the smug delusion that they had freed themselves from any need to consider such messy, difficult, and indeterminate questions as, What is to be considered real? How do we get valid knowledge about anything? What is Man's place in the universe? By what values and ideals should we guide our conduct?

In my own experience, it was the logical positivists who led the attack on metaphysics, scorning it as mere poetry or a harmless pastime that had absolutely no implications for the real world. But the heyday of positivism is over. Philosophers of science in increasing numbers agree with Popper (1962) that it is discredited if not actually dead. Psychology's most respected methodologist, Donald Campbell, has explicitly renounced logical positivism. Whereas various passages in the influential book on research design by Campbell and Stanley (1963) had a noticeably positivistic flavor, that is no longer true of his more recent book (Cook & Campbell, 1979), which adopts a Popperian line of thought.

In a generally thoughtful and useful paper, Westcott (1977) makes a distinction between three types of questions concerning free will: "First, there are metaphysical questions about universal truth; second, there are theoretical questions for the construction of ethical theory and psychological theory; third, there are empirical psychological questions about behavioural and experiential phenomena" (p. 254). I thoroughly agree that these are different realms of discourse and should be carefully distinguished, but cannot accept Westcott's further proposal "that the metaphysical question is not the business of psychologists, as psychologists; it is not a realm to which they bring any particular competence, and to which they have brought only confusion" (p. 254). I think he is not quite on target as to what the metaphysical issue is (hardly "universal truth") and alas, he makes the usual non sequitur in concluding that psychologists should simply turn away from metaphysics to concentrate on their own work. That easily becomes a formula for evading the responsibility to acknowledge the importance and necessity for clarifying and making explicit our metaphysics even though we have no competence to settle the questions or contribute to their final answers.

Let me try to say rather briefly and simply what metaphysics is and why we should be concerned with it. It traditionally begins with ontology, the systematic concern for what is to be considered real. No one can carry on a life—not even a psychotic one—without some implied idea of what is real. Consider, for example, the fear of ghosts. Primitive people and vast numbers of Europeans up until about a century ago believed that spirits of the dead not only existed but were responsible for many of the miseries of mankind; hence, many believers devoted important resources to magical attempts to propitiate or ward off these and other malevolent spirits and neglected to learn realistic ways of solving their problems. Coming closer to the present day, some radical behaviorists used to argue in effect that mental phenomena were not "really real"; lacking any place in a world of things and stuff, matter and energy, they not only could but should be ignored. In so doing, those writers were adopting a materialist ontology, saying that only the subject matter of physics could be considered real, the rest being illusory. I hope these examples make it clear that this branch of metaphysics has major implications for what scientists and other people do in the world.

Yet it remains true that there is no way of *settling* the question, "What is real?" You may stoutly believe in a spiritual realm of God, angels, and souls of the dead inhabiting a heaven, and although I do not, I have no way of disproving it and no logical means of converting you to my secular (though not materialistic) ontology. Too many people have concluded from such standoffs that because metaphysical questions allow many equally defensible answers and because the disputes cannot be settled by rational or empirical means, the questions themselves are idle or even meaningless. That is a major fallacy, a true non sequitur. Again and again in history, metaphysical issues have been matters of life or death. Wars have been fought over them, and even today a major political confrontation is shaping up over questions that are actually metaphysical. Consider the entry into politics of religious fundamentalists trying to enact into law their convictions about undecidable questions on which they take a dogmatic stance—for example, cosmological issues like the ultimate origin of the universe.

We can see in the controversy over creationism another important way in which metaphysics has major practical effects via the issue of epistemology. That formidable word means a sustained concern with the question, "How do we gain true knowledge?" Virtually all religions contain some version of the following answer: "by accepting the word of God, as expressed in his sacred book and as interpreted by wise and holy men who have been in-spired—that is, to whom he has revealed some of the Truth." To be sure, if human beings had never had any other way of attaining knowledge, it seems likely that they would have died out as a nonviable species. But human intelligence and the human anatomical–physiological system for receiving and processing information about the world have made it possible to develop a very different epistemology. People survived because they could form a perceptual world of stable objects arrayed in a way that made possible effec-tive locomotion and adaptive action. In fct, the scientific method is little more than the deliberate sharpening and elaboration of ways of getting knowledge that are guaranteed by our evolutionarily shaped genes. It is hard to imagine that any responsible person would seriously advocate abandoning this overwhelmingly successful epistemology. If we truly believed what was long taught, that it is impious arrogance to pretend that mere mortals can find the truth without a direct appeal to God or the intercession of his appointed earthly ministers, we would have to give up not only our worldly goods but also our weapons, following a truly Christian way of humble poverty, loving surrender, and glad obedience to any enemy or oppressor. I am not foolish enough to argue that we would necessarily be worse off to do so; I merely note the fact that extraordinarily few people who consider them-selves Christians are willing to follow this line of reasoning to its logical end. For our whole social and economic system is founded on an implicit accep-tance of the epistemology of science, without which we could not have our material affluence with its ominous technologies that make it possible, even likely, that we shall destroy ourselves. Let me hasten to add that I do not believe that the only alternative to self-destruction is a return to early Chris-tianity; but I am getting ahead of myself.

The other major subdivision of metaphysics is cosmology, a set of answers to questions about the nature of the universe and our place in it. The "chief world systems" about which Galileo (Galilei, 1632/1953) wrote were intended to be more narrowly cosmological than metaphysical; he meant mainly to compare the Ptolemaic and the Copernican models of the solar system. The term cosmology today is used by astronomers in a similar re-stricted sense, referring to theories about how the observed universe of stars, galaxies, clouds of gas and dust, etc. came to be. Philosophers use the word in a larger sense, going back past the big bang, for example, and developing ideas about the possible role of a creator, about human beings and their concerns in the cosmos, and the possible meanings or purposes of it all. It is less obvious how questions of this type could have practical implications, although it became painfully evident to Galileo that he could not develop his cosmological ideas with impunity when they conflicted with those of other more powerful persons. Today, an even more dreadful threat than excommunication or even the tortures of an Inquisition hangs over all of us: ther-monuclear extinction. That is made possible only because of Einstein's revolution in physics; without $E = Mc^2$ there would have been no atomic and hydrogen bombs, and his majestic equation depended on his first having developed fundamentally new ideas about the nature of space and time—issues that had always been an important part of cosmology. Newton's universe was in many ways dramatically different from the one postulated by the predominant world picture of religion, but agreed with it in conceiving of space and time as fixed and absolute, a first principle that seemed so self-evident and necessary that it took a Newton to make it explicit. Yet the entire structure of modern physics could not have been imagined without replacing this kind of absolutism. The question is not whether we are better off with the new knowledge and the awesome technologies it permits, but simply to note what a tremendous difference to all living things it may make that one man was able to produce a new cosmology.

Let me just underline by repetition my first main point. The logical positivists, who taught us to sneer at metaphysics, overlooked two important facts: We all do have positions on metaphysical questions—there is no way to avoid it—whether we are conscious of them or not; and the positions we assume have extensive and extremely important consequences for our scientific work and our very lives.

The next major point I want to make is that metaphysical ideas do not exist as isolated fragments but as parts of ideological systems which, following the philosopher Pepper (1942), I shall call *world hypotheses*. Those in turn do not just exist as isolated sets of metaphysical propositions. It is easy to show that ideas of the kinds we have been discussing so far usually exist in intimate association with beliefs about morality or ethics. They tend also to carry implications about the social and political order, as I have tried to indicate near the bottom of Table 5.1, where I have set down, in a perhaps misleadingly simple and skeletal format, some of the chief world systems that have seized the imaginations of people during the past millenium or so. I am painfully aware of the vast oversimplification of this scheme, yet I believe that it contains a helpful first approximation to the truth, a way of thinking about matters that I have found highly useful. Hardly anything in it is original; its sources are numerous and diverse; but I do want to acknowledge the important help I have gotten from Pepper's book, and the initial stimulation to think this way came to me from Yankelovich and Barrett (1970) and Ackoff (1974).

At times, I have used the currently voguish term *world view*. Unfortunately, however, this translation of the German term *Weltanschauung* has no precise meaning, being employed in a variety of senses by many contemporary authors. Reflecting on my own usages, I realize that it would be better to use

TABLE 5.1

Summary Formulations Concerning Major Successive World Hypotheses

Issues	Animism (supernaturalism)	Mechanism (materialism)
Cosmology		
Origin of universe	Created by omnipotent, omnipresent God	No beginning or end; or indeterminate
Nature of space and time	Finite; time began, no end; both are absolute	Both are infinite, fixed, separate dimensions
Man's place in cosmos	At center in all respects (geocentric)	No special place
Ontology		
What is real?	The spiritual; temporarily, the material world	Substance, simply located in space and time
Mind–body problem	Dualism/absolute idealism/ interactionism	Materialist monism: epiphenomenalism
Voluntarism problem	The soul is spontaneous, free from determinism	Freedom denied: everything is determined
Epistemology		
How do we gain knowledge?	By revelation from God; tradition; consulting authorities	By observation, experiment, logic, reason, and mathematics
What can be known?	Little, but absolute truth	Much, as asymptotically approached truth
Methodology	Logic; study texts; have faith	Analysis; reductionism; objectivity the goal
End point	God's laws	Scientific laws
Organization of disciplines	Hierarchical, theology first	Hierarchical, physics first
Ethics		
Nature of morality	Obey God's commandments, interpreted by the church	Science will yield a new morality (or, none)
Meaning of life	Serve God; his purposes alone supply meaning	Question lacks meaning or undecidable by science
Implied structure of society	Authoritarian	Authoritarian
Root metaphor	Man (parent–child)	Clockwork machine

two other slightly less familiar terms for which I might have more hope of assigning controlled definitions. Let me refer to the *ethos* of, for example, nineteenth century science, when I am referring to a rather broad and encompassing cultural trend, like the spirit of mechanism and materialism and of faith in rational and empirical investigation as the key to material progress and the conquest of nature, which prevailed then. The Germans call it *Zeitgeist*, the spirit of the times. In a more restricted sense, when referring to the set of philosophical assumptions underlying the endeavors of the age of science

Pragmatism (relativism)	Systems philosophy (organismic humanism)
All cosmological questions are indeterminate and unknowable; each observer his own center and views	Has developed in cycles and stages; origin uncertain Closed, 4-D, nonfixed framework
	Man of special interest and dignity
Context, pattern, process, change	Patterns, relationships, recursively nested systems
A matter of one's viewpoint (context)	Not a problem; monism/pluralism
A matter of one's viewpoint (context)	Both attainable freedom and determinism are affirmed
Pluralistic, eclectic	Invariant laws attainable by systematic decentering transformations
Truth is relative and uncertain	Much: many relative truths, some invariances
Contextualism	Analysis *and* synthesis; emergence; objectivity *and* subjectivity
No firm laws (None?)	Scientific laws, other truths Nonhierarchical structure of disciplines
Moral relativism	Invariances: universal humanistic principles, developmental sequences
Existentialism; local/individual illusions of meaning	Meaning intrinsic and relational, does not have to be given
Democratic	Democratic
Experienced events	The human person

that began about 1600, assumptions implicit in the writings and the practice of most empirical scientists of the nineteenth century, I will adopt Pepper's term, the mechanistic *world hypothesis*.

Whether the concept of a world view is interpreted as an ethos or as a world hypothesis, one curious and inconvenient fact about it needs to be faced right away: We are dealing with constructs, or ideal types, not concrete doctrines promulgated in full by any one author. They have, therefore, an uncomfortably abstract and inferential kind of existence and should certainly not be treated as causal agents. The ethos is not usefully defined as a "world soul" or "group mind" that manipulates individuals like puppets to bring about some vast plan. Although that kind of thinking seemed quite acceptable to many in the last century, including Freud, it does not stand up to methodological scrutiny of the kind Popper (1957) has given it. Rather, I believe that the spirit of an age is conveyed to its people through ordinary sensory channels of informational input; it is just that there are so many such channels, and some are so subtle that many tender-minded thinkers are tempted to assume some mystical, extrasensory process. Moreover, we must assume that a good deal of the process of transmission takes place without conscious awareness on the part of either the transmitter or the recipient. That too need not trouble the hardheaded: If in answering a child's questions, a parent constantly responds in terms of a coherent set of assumptions, he or she need never teach those underpinnings as such—they are conveyed quite effectively anyway.

That appears to be the way world hypotheses are taught and diffused throughout a culture in which only a few persons in a thousand ever read or discuss metaphysics as such. Consider, for example, the Middle Ages, a time when the Christian ethos dominated European thought. Very few people could read or write; there were no newspapers or magazines, the few books being hand-copied and treasured by a tiny band of scholars—monks and priests of the Catholic church. The one great organ of communication, the church, did not deliberately teach ontology and epistemology to its congregations. Nevertheless, everything we know about the mental life of those times agrees that there was virtually universal belief in the spiritual. Anything out of the ordinary—disease, famine, eclipses, earthquakes, even unusually bad weather—was explained as the intervention of a supernatural power, for no naturalistic explanation was at hand. Everyday superstitions, attributing "bad luck" to various failures to perform ritual actions or the violations of taboos, conveyed—and still convey—the animistic world hypothesis as effectively as any specific teachings from the pulpit.

Pepper (1942) notes that the animistic or supernatural explanation of the universe does not differ in its essentials from one religion to another. All world hypotheses seem to embody a root metaphor, he believes, in this instance that of the ordinary human being. I see his point, but want to emphasize the guiding image of the patriarchal family. By analogy, the adult seems as powerless before the blows of a hurricane as the child is before those of the punishing parent. The more the prevailing family structure puts power in the hands of the father, the more likely a culture's religion is to be monotheistic. Freud saw this strong emotional root of religion, which gives it an enormous hold on the nonrational core of most people's lives. The wonder is not that the religious world view has predominated everywhere at all times, but that others have nevertheless been able to arise and challenge it as success-fully as they have.

Sources of Freud's Ideas about Free Will

In my somewhat discursive way, I have edged into a discussion of the world hypothesis of Christianity, which was in active conflict with that of science at the time when Freud was forming his basic intellectual orientations. As a bright and bookish adolescent, he belonged to a group of friends—school-mates in his *Gymnasium*—all budding intellectuals who read and passed from hand to hand the best-sellers of their time (Knoepfmacher, 1979). I spent a good part of one summer following their paper trail through a group of five books from which, I might remark, I learned a good deal. The first thing that may strike you as odd—I was surprised by it—is the fact that two of them were works on theology, and by Christians at that! You probably know the name of the more famous author, Ludwig Feuerbach, because of his influ-·ence upon the young Marx; David Strauss, the other, was also a liberal Protestant rebel who, like Feuerbach, was heavily influenced by science and wrote very well. Their books were widely read all over Europe at midcentury.

Their two books, *The Essence of Christianity* (Feuerbach, 1841/1957) and *The Old Faith and the New* (Strauss, 1872/1873), appealed to the bright youths of the *Sperlgymnasium* because they were liberal, democratically ori-ented, scientifically informed attacks upon the established orthodoxy of official religions, and perhaps because they were attempts to come to terms with the mechanistic and materialistic ideology of science without giving up the *Geist-lich*, the spiritual side of man. Oddly enough, they have a great deal in common with one of the other books, which one might expect to have been bitterly opposed to them. That is the notorious *Force and Matter*, (1855/1884) by Ludwig Büchner. (This book, incidentally, made a powerful impression on the mind of another gifted adolescent a few years later: Albert Einstein.) Before discovering that Freud had read these books, I had come across Büchner's name in works on intellectual history, in which he was depicted as one of the most extreme of materialists. I approached his book, then, half expecting a nineteenth-century version of either La Mettrie's *L'homme machine* (1748/1966) or Skinner's *Beyond Freedom and Dignity* (1971). I found, instead, a popular science writer who was at the same time a romantically ·inclined German *Gelehrter*, immersed in the humanistic classics, constantly quoting poetry (some of which he confessed in later editions he had written himself), and admiringly citing the works of Feuerbach and Strauss! He was no behaviorist at all, and not even a consistent materialist; where he did take a consistent stand was in rejecting any belief in a god or a supernatural realm. That is, after all, the fundamental tenet of the animistic world hypothesis. This failure to be completely consistent, which was sufficient to exclude Büchner from serious consideration as a major philosopher, shows up also in Büchner's (1855/1884) discussion of free will. He begins his chapter on the topic, as always, with a series of epigraphs. One, a quotation from Lavater, reads: "Man is free as a bird in a cage: he can move within certain limits" (p. 366). Büchner then goes on not to deny free will but to minimize it: "We can only speak of volition and free decision in a very limited sense" (p. 462); "All human actions are everywhere dependent in the last resort on the fixed necessities of nature or on external and internal influences, and . . . in each individual instance there remains only a very small scope, and often times no scope at all, for free volition" (p. 463).

You might be interested to hear how Freudian his ideas sound, this forgotten German physician who gave up his practice to write best-sellers about science and philosophy and Darwinism:

> How often does it happen that a man knows himself and his mental and peculiar characteristics sufficiently well to see what faults he is likely to commit, and yet is unable to successfully resist this internal pressure. He repeats the same faults over and over again; and gets again and again into the same scrapes; for it is quite an exception for the powers of imagination and thought to gain the victory over a man's perceptive faculties and appetites. The youthful man or the sensualist, as a rule, sacrifices everything to his passion. . . . A man of a violent temper, while in a rage, commits acts of which he would deem himself incapable in quieter moments [p. 470].

A clue to Büchner's mixed position on free will may be found in this passage: "Within this boundary represented by natural laws, he [i.e., Man] doubtless enjoys sufficient free scope so long as more sensible views get the better of less sensible ones, or reason and reflection gain the day. . ." (p. 473).

Consider also some of his examples of the many ways in which behavior is determined: The statistics of suicides and marriages, he says, show us lawful regularities. It is evident that Büchner made the common mistake of confusing a scientific law with a statistical generalization, overlooking the fact that a true law brooks no exceptions. Likewise, in the context of discussing evolution, he uncritically adopted the prevailing historicist notion of a natural law of progress: "This progress of the organic history of the earth . . . proves . . . that a perfecting and evolving principle, due partly to internal, partly to external physical conditions, is universally active, spurring on the individual forms to an ever higher development" [p. 195]. Quite a nature-philosophical remnant in the work of a man thought to be leading the pack of the antithetical mechanistic materialists! It is not difficult to trace this kind of idea, which was so characteristic of Ernst Haeckel and Lamarck, back to religion: In the animistic world hypothesis, life and the whole history of the universe has a meaning, one given by the (usually inscrutable) purposes of the Creator. Slightly secularized, the same thought appeared in the *Naturphilosophie* of the early nineteenth century as "Nature's purposes" or "natural design." With only minor changes, it could be made seemingly consistent with the scientific ethos by interpreting the same notion as a law of history—as H. T. Buckle did in another of those books that made a profound impression on Freud: *History of Civilization in England* (1871/1934).

Subject to such influences as soon as he began to develop serious intellectual interests, Freud naturally adopted many of the ideas that were set forth in his adolescent reading. Notably, the metaphysics of the mechanistic world hypothesis made a powerful appeal to him; he remarks in his associations to his dream about Count Thun that for a period in his youth he was "a green youngster, full of materialistic theories" (1900/1953, p. 212). And although he intimates that his contemporary views were less "one-sided," he never attempted to make his metaphysics explicit. For some time, I have been engaged in the fascinating pastime of trying to infer them from his various theoretical positions. Here let me say merely that they are just as much a mixture of incompatible elements as Büchner's. I should add, however, that I have found aspects of both the animistic and the mechanistic world hypotheses in the thought of *everyone* born in the nineteenth century whose work I have examined—including Darwin and Einstein.

Let me go back to the ideal type of pure animism to review the concept of free will in that context. By saying that the root metaphor of animism is the human being, Pepper (1942) meant that anthropomorphic thinking is its central explanatory idea: Every event in nature comes about just as we feel our own behavior does, as the result of an intention or wish. I decided to write this chapter because I wanted to; in a small way it was a creative act. By analogy, therefore, the world itself must have been brought into being by someone who *wanted* to create it and then *decided* to do so. That way of looking at it makes the idea of willing (which is virtually identical with choosing and deciding) as important to the animistic cosmology as the idealized parental figure of God, the original source of the willing that anteceded the Creation. In many creation myths, the deity goes on to endow human creatures with the ability to make conscious choices, which then imposes on them the burden of moral responsibility and guilt. An important accessory concept, that of spirit or soul, is necessary to round out a moderately plausible theory of the universe. Events not being distinguished from actions, every happening requires the postulation of a conscious entity capable of intending and making decisions. The malicious wind that destroys one's crop, the benevolent rain that slakes one's thirst, *and* other human beings—are all thought to have invisible spirits, and a central attribute of such an entity as a soul or spirit is willing.

As crude animism grew into the sophisticated form of orthodox Christian dogma, the soul took on most mental attributes. It was thought to be the vital principle, the source of consciousness and conscience, and the first cause of action. Notice that in pure animism there is no simple physical causation, no abstract physical laws or forces. Water runs downhill because it "seeks its level"—that folk phrase retains the implication that every river has an ondine or water sprite to be *aware* of where the physical substance of the water is and to *want* to flow downhill to its ultimate goal, the sea. In such a world, there is no contradiction in the idea that human behavior comes about because immaterial souls make decisions purely on their own, unaffected by events in the physical world, and direct their fleshly vehicle, the body, to carry out the resulting intentions. Notice, too, that within this view of the world there cannot be any alternative to free will, since there *is* no notion of determinism.

As I have intimated, mechanistic conceptions of cause and effect are just as grounded in our natures as animism, and I believe that much of their staying power comes from their obvious adaptiveness. Any protohuman beings who survived had to find ways of acting effectively on the world—for example, recognizing signs of edible food and signals of danger. In doing so, they had experiences of what White (1963) calls effectance—recognition that it is possible to make interesting and even useful things happen in the world. As tools are natural extensions of hands, so machines directly develop from simple tools. What is so powerful about the machine that makes it the root metaphor for a new conception of the world and how it works? The fact that it is separate from human beings, yet can act and have effects. When during the Middle Ages it became possible for certain machines—clocks—to contain their own source of action, so that once wound up they could continue to move and do useful work for some while without the direct intervention or guidance of a person, they began to have a fructifying impact upon the human imagination. They were now microcosms, intelligible miniatures of the great and mysterious macrocosm. Once the clockwork was invented, mechanical but somewhat lifelike toys and automatons followed, awing the simple and inspiring such great minds as that of Descartes. Here was a vivid metaphor of life and movement, which might by an audacious leap of the imagination enable us to understand the motions of the sun, moon, and stars themselves.

To be sure, it was not by reflecting on a clock that Newton conceived his laws of motion or gravity, but those theories were sophisticated developments of the same type of cause-and-effect thinking that had made the clockwork possible. Though he was far from doing it all himself, Newton at least was responsible for the grand synthesis of mechanism, the second world hypothesis to be, in Pepper's (1942) judgment, generally adequate. (Plato's formism was the first. Animism is emotionally very satisfying, but as an intellectual system it leaves a good deal to be desired: it lacks precision and is full of arbitrariness concealed behind tradition.) Like many a mechanistic scientist after him, Newton was devoutly pious, but he started an intellectual process that led inexorably to the atheism of subsequent, more thorough-going mechanists such as Büchner. The new world view was presented not as a metaphysical system but as science; that helped conceal its basic opposition to the world hypothesis of religion. There was simply no need any more for animistic hypotheses to explain fire, flood, pestilence, eclipse, or any of the other originating problems. Hence, it became possible to be a dualist believing in God, the soul, Heaven, and Hell and still accepting the mechanistic explanation of all observable events. To this day, many of us retain this solution, though it is widely attacked as inconsistent. If you are such a dualist, the fundamentalist accuses you of trying to serve both God and Mammon, of denying the literal truth of his Holy Word and endangering your immortal soul by friendly interaction with secular humanists. The consistent materialist (and there are a few) complains that your hypothesis of a spiritual world is simply redundant, unnecessary intellectual baggage that can only weigh you down.

Notice that in my scenario of the development of the mechanistic world hypothesis, causal—that is, deterministic—thinking plays a central role. It supplied the first source of doubt about free will and the first usable alternative. As soon as one person noticed that another was predictable—that, for example, a potential antagonist could be placated by flattery or bribes—the former had a powerful advantage over any rival who might be a devout and consistent believer that all human behavior stems from the spontaneous and hence unpredictable acts of an immortal soul. Survival is an even more powerful persuader than logic.

It was not difficult, therefore, for mechanistic thinkers to bring forth an explanation of human behavior that explicitly denied the possibility of free will. Indeed, a consistent mechanism has no room for it; if you truly believe that the web of cause and effect is unbroken, that every event has its cause and its consequence, how can an exception be made for *homo sapiens* just because we happen to belong to that species? People may *think* they have free will, just as they think they have immortal souls, but if we study their behavior we can see that it is all explainable by the machine model. As La Mettrie (1748/1966) put it

> The soul is therefore but an empty word, of which no one has any idea, and which an enlightened man should use only to signify the part in us that thinks. Given the least principle of motion, animated bodies will have all that is necessary for moving, feeling, thinking, repenting, or in a word conducting themselves in the physical realm, and in the moral realm which depends upon it [p. 273].

You see now, I hope, why I brought in all this elaborate business about world hypotheses. It is because I believe that the controversy that pits free will against determinism is only a small skirmish in the long war between two great systems of thought, in their attempts to explain the entire universe and everything in it. Because each of these two doctrines has a great many allies, if you aline yourself with one side of this particular fight you find yourself with many partisans. On the side of free will, those partners-in-arms have almost always been churchly and religious types, devout believers in a world hypothesis that is not friendly to scientific psychology—hence, perhaps, an embarrassment.

Surely that seems to have been the way Freud experienced it. For him, the only conceivable alternative to rigorous mechanistic determinism was free will as the intervention of an immaterial soul in a material world where nothing exists except matter and motion (1895/1966, p. 308). Being a firm foe of the supernatural (at least on a conscious level), he had to declare his stout adherence to the determinism that he saw as necessary to science.

And yet, as I have pointed out before, Freud was like Büchner in not pursuing that foolish consistency described by Emerson as the hobgoblin of little minds. It was, after all, for sound empirical reasons that Büchner tried to save a small space of free movement, glimpsed in the interstices of a fabric of natural law that he conceived of as not altogether seamless. Everyone who has thought about the topic must recognize that some of our decisions and actions seem much more constrained than others, that sometimes we feel we have no alternative, whereas on other occasions introspection insistently suggests that there were indeed various possible courses of action and we could easily have chosen another. If one were a truly consistent mechanist, the experience of regret and self-reproach for having made a bad decision would be wholly meaningless, because in such a world view each action is as fully determined as every other. Not even Skinner can manage that degree of detachment from ordinary humanity as he looks back upon his own life (Elms, 1982). This kind of data is, in fact, one of the recurrently embarrassing shortcomings of the mechanistic world hypothesis.

For Freud, however, there was no difference between the mechanistic world hypothesis and science, and he was deeply committed to being not only a scientist but a great one. When he writes with the self-awareness of attempting to create a natural science of psychology, therefore, he most staunchly affirms his faith in determinism and rejects freedom of the will. But when he writes as a keenly observant clinician and an intuitive psychotherapist, he naturally and without any apparent awareness of inconsistency speaks about the need to influence the patient to exert effort against his or her own resistance, to struggle and persevere despite anxiety and the longing for direct gratifications, and to enlarge what Hartmann (1939/1958) was to christen the "conflict-free sphere of the ego." Freud himself put it more simply and directly: "Where It was, there should I become." (I adopt here Brandt's (1961) suggested retranslation of the usual "Where id was, there shall ego be" [Freud, 1933/1964, p. 80].) This *I* of which he spoke is, of course, the observational core of the soul concept, the center of the person to which is attributed awareness, feeling, and intention (Holt, 1975). Freud's dilemma was not very much different from ours. Faced with a choice between either taking the scientific view of the world seriously and accepting the fact that it means conceptualizing all human behavior as lawfully determined or rejecting all that in order to find a place for the data of subjectively experienced freedom, people who want to be scientists and are not deeply committed to a religious outlook will feel strongly constrained to reject free will. (They will be helped to do so, I suggest, by not experiencing in the process itself much sense of freedom to choose!)

Freud's distinctive contribution to the venerable argument was to bring in the concept of unconscious motivation. The testimony of introspection is unreliable, he argued; a person may transparently be acting from an unconscious motive and may protest that he or she made decisions quite consciously, even without any motive at all. As Freud (1901/1960) observed: "But what is thus left free by the one side receives its motivation from the other side, from the unconscious; and in this way determination in the psychical sphere is still carried out without any gap" [p. 254].

Notice that he did not adopt Büchner's solution of preserving a small space of free movement in the cracks between natural laws. With the aid of his hypothesis about unconscious motivation, he was able to find that there are understandable psychological causes for many slips, errors, and other "parapraxes" generally regarded as meaningless. At times, he seemed to be taking the position that there are no accidents or coincidences, all apparent examples being explainable by unconscious and subtle forms of acting out.

Actually, as Gay (1979, p. 45) has helpfully elucidated, Freud's position was more complex: "It was self-evident, to him, that all in life is chance, in one sense, while in another, nothing in life is chance." The former mood is expressed in the final pages of his essay on Leonardo where he wrote: "In fact everything to do with our life is chance, from our origin out of the meeting of spermatozoon and ovum onwards—chance which nevertheless has a share in the law and necessity of nature, and which merely lacks any connection with our wishes and illusions" (Freud, 1910/1957, p. 137). He was saying here that though all events are lawful, from the standpoint of the person they often appear to be random because unpredictable: the strongest and swiftest spermatozoon may win the race to the ovum in a strictly determined way, but from the human standpoint the choice among the many possible combinations of parental genes is as random as a lottery. At the same time, Freud strongly believed that in very many situations where the layman sees a person's behavior as being determined only by such unpredictable external encounters (or, more naively, as not determined at all except "by chance"), a psychoanalyst can discern unconscious motives at work. *The Psychopathology of*

Everyday Life is full of examples, instances in which seemingly random mistakes are shown to be motivated, even including events not of the person's own making: "Many apparently accidental injuries . . . are really instances of self-injury. . . . An impulse to self-punishment . . . takes ingenious advantage of an external situation that chance happens to offer, or lends assistance to that situation until the desired injurious effect is brought about" (1901/ 1960, pp. 178–179). This instance nicely shows how Freud could maintain that there are chance events, and yet their effect is psychologically determined.

A striking feature of Freud's cognitive style, as I have demonstrated elsewhere (Holt, 1965), was his capacity to tolerate contradiction. He was quite capable of maintaining an explicit adherence to a mechanistic outlook, believing it the only way to be a scientist, alongside a primarily implicit faithfulness to a humanistic conception of human beings. As a therapist and as an educator and propagandist for his ideas, he acted consistently as if he believed that people do respond to reason, logic, and factual argument, making decisions rationally and not *only* because of unconscious wishes and defenses. And his insistence on trying to listen to what people told him as attentively as possible and to observe his own behavior with as much detachment as he could muster resulted in his contributing to one of the great changes in human consciousness. The whole Western world has become more psychologically minded, more capable of appreciating the existence of motives, even unconscious motives, as major causes of everyone's behavior. Freud taught us to read meaning where formerly most people saw only chance or chaos and to appreciate the decisive causal role of meanings in behavior, despite the fact that the very concept of meaning itself has no secure ontological status within the mechanistic world hypothesis.

The Advent of Systems Philosophy

In these and in various other ways, Freud burst the narrow confines of the mechanistic straitjacket he attempted to impose upon psychoanalysis in the belief that that type of rigor alone could provide the security of truth. At the same time, Einstein, Bohr, and other modern physicists were even more decisively showing how the metaphysical foundations of physics had to be changed if theory was to attain the beauty of simplicity and inner consistency, and to explain a host of new facts. Similarly, Darwin's revolution in biology generated data for which mechanism had no place because it was too static and atomistic to foster the needed developmental and ecological conceptions.

Space does not permit an adequate account of the interesting world hypothesis of pragmatism, which Pepper (1942) called contextualism and in which relativism of all kinds plays a central role. Though he declared it as adequate as any other and preferred it for many years, even for Pepper this system of thought—which Freud did much to help bring about—played a transitional role. (I have told the story more fully elsewhere; Holt, in press).

In the year before he died, Pepper (1972a, 1972b) wrote two brief papers hailing Laszlo's (1971) systems philosophy as a new, highly promising, and exciting addition to the small number of adequate world hypotheses (of which Pepper, 1942, had listed only four in his book). I feel equally enthusiastic; it is, to say the least, an extraordinarily integrative framework upon which can be built a metaphysics and ethics hospitable not only to all the sciences but the humanities as well.

There is a great deal I would like to add about mechanism, its pervasive and pernicious influence upon mainstream psychology, and its various other inadequacies and evils, but I shall content myself with referring you to Mumford's admirable work, *The Myth of the Machine* (1967, 1970). Likewise, I would enjoy expounding systems philosophy even if this is not exactly the place for it. Let me just give a thumbnail sketch of its major tenets and then move into their implications for our topic.

1. *Ontology.* Systems are the basic reality, systems understood in a structural rather than a substantial sense. Since the most obvious systems known to us—atoms, organisms, the earth, our galaxy, for example—are made up of matter and energy, one may mistakenly believe that this is only a new guise of materialism. But cultures and languages are systems, too, as is mathematics; all are stable, bounded, patterned entities the important properties of which are not exhaustively accounted for by a description of all their parts. Each of these abstract or nonmaterial systems is the proper subject of an ordered inquiry as disciplined as any other science; and, they must be accorded the status of being real. Similarly, the subjective or phenomenological world of someone's mind has all the defining properties of a system and has equal dignity with the coordinate physical system of the accompanying body and the superordinate system of the person within which mind and body are nested. The person in turn is part of larger material systems (for example, an ecosystem) and social systems (such as a family and a nation). It is important to add that this view of reality is not as static as either Plato's formism or mechanism, but is not as Heraclitean as pragmatism, which has no place at all for unchanging structures. Systems follow orderly and characteristic patterns of development, which says that in some respects they are stable whereas in others they constantly change. Finally, systemicity itself is a quantitative attribute; not only do individual systems of any one type differ from one to

another in their nondefining attributes, but some are tightly and coherently integrated although others approach the null state of chaotic or stochastic pattern.

2. *Cosmology*. One can extend the hierarchical systems view outwards, all ecosystems being parts of one grand biosphere, Earth being part of the solar system, which partakes in the Milky Way galaxy, and on to the most inclusive supergalactic systems. Moving inward, the body is a system of such systems as the circulatory and digestive; tissues are systems of cells, whose organelles meet the defining properties of systems themselves. They in turn are made up of molecules, composed of atoms, and on to the smallest subatomic systems that may have been identified yesterday. This hierarchy is unlike any other, in that no value inheres in size, and all levels have equal dignity and importance, including that of the human being. This conception of nature provides us with a home, a niche, and as much value as if each of us were literally a star. (Let me parenthetically remind you that the new world hypothesis adopts and incorporates Einstein's reconceptualization of space and time.)

3. *Epistemology*. Because the systems outlook has some resemblance to such familiar holisms as that of the early Gestalt psychology, the mechanistically minded tend to believe that it exalts synthesis at the expense of analysis. Actually, as a rather direct consequence of the systems view of reality just sketched, it is equally legitimate and equally necessary to move in both directions when studying any given system. One cannot understand it fully without inquiring into the more inclusive system(s) of which it is a part, *and* into the less inclusive systems and nonsystemic parts that make it up. Despite mechanism's disavowal of value in science, there is a strongly implied value in its hierarchical arrangement of the disciplines, the more "fundamental" disciplines being more ultimately important than the less. Stated otherwise, the thematic emphasis of atomism and analytic bias, together with the materialistic ontology, create a steady pressure toward reductionism in mechanistic science. Systems thinking explicitly rejects reductionism as incompatible with its view of reality: If a more inclusive system exists in addition to its component subsystems, then it too is real, and by definition it is more than (hence, not reducible to) the sum of its parts. In other words, its whole-system properties are emergent, and because they exist scientists must devise methods appropriate to their systemic level to study them. Thus, meanings cannot be reduced to configurations of structures, forces, and energies; hence, the clinically observed regularities of psychoanalysis cannot even be satisfactorily translated into the terms of (let alone be explained by) meta-psychology.

4. *Ethics*. Implied in the systems view of the world is the valuing of systems as such, and of higher degrees of systemicity at any given level. Thus, the person is not inherently more or less valuable than the society, but the good person and the good institution alike are more highly integrated with

greater unity in diversity (or organized complexity) than their bad counterparts. Systems ethics follows Köhler (1938) in finding a place for value in the world of fact, through the requiredness that is implied in the very conception of system. It is valid to say that a system *needs* to have certain types of parts in order to exist. If the inner "requirednesses" of two systems (e.g., predator and prey) are in conflict, the ethical question must be resolved by moving to the viewpoint of the larger or more inclusive systems of which both are parts. This formulation is close to the spirit of the ecological ethic urged by Hardin (1968) and the situation ethics of Fletcher (1974). It implies for us a recognition that the survival of all humankind outranks the value of preserving any particular nation or culture, and preserving the total earthly biosphere is our earthly summum bonum. (As the Friends of the Earth put it: Love your mother!) As Freud said, it is Eros that binds all things together; systems philosophy similarly entails an ethics of love over hate and survival over destruction.

Within that systems framework, what is the place of free will? To begin with, systems philosophy is an orderly view of the world; it therefore implies that we can discover and formulate principles of orderliness. A luxuriant profusion of systems exists with common defining properties despite the most striking superficial differences, making it possible to explicate many propositions that apply to living systems from the level of the cell to that of the planetary political system (Miller, 1978). Systems philosophy is thus congenial to Einstein's important methodological discovery, that it is possible to find invariant lawfulness despite the disorder of relativism, by applying sets of mathematical transformations to the disparate formulations. Thus, the Lorenz transformations enabled him to get rid of the esthetically displeasing fact that Maxwell's equations for the electromotive force generated in a conductor took different forms when the conductor moved past a stationary magnet and when the magnet moved and the conductor stood still. He was able to formulate first special and then general relativity on this simple foundation. Elsewhere (Holt, in press), I have attempted to show how much this methodological principle has in common with Piaget's decentering and how widely useful it can be in psychology.

Here, however, I merely want to reiterate my conviction that science must work from the ontological premise that the universe does contain order and the epistemological premise that we human beings can find it if we persevere, learning to look in the right places in appropriate ways. Einstein's principle is, I believe, a more elegant formulation of what Weiss (1969) calls the principle of "determinism, stratified" (p. 28). Interestingly enough, Weiss develops his concept out of a consideration of the problem of free will versus determinism. He objects to a conception of determinism that implies a view of "nature as a micromechanical precision machinery run by strict causality, in which the concession of any degree of freedom of choice to any natural phenomenon would be inadmissible" (p. 28). The flaw, he says, is "in equating science with the doctrine of micro-precise causality" (p. 28). That is, the mechanistic view had to attribute lawfulness in the large to precise determinism on the level of the small; indeed, its reductionistic commitments carried the implication that the ultimate scientific laws must be sought on the most microscopic level. It could not conceive the world of Weiss's biological laboratory where again and again he shows us an amazing degree of random variation in fine detail while larger patterns are faithfully maintained. The view that "well-defined macro-change" is merely a "mosaic of micro-changes . . . is demonstrably untenable in its application to living systems" (p. 28). In a way, you could argue that this is an updated and much more sophisticated version of Büchner's solution. For Weiss, however, there are no arbitrary chinks in a general fabric of scientific laws. Any phenomenon is orderly once you find the appropriate systemic level on which to study it; conversely, even when we have long been familiar with lawful order, it is possible to approach the same phenomenon on an inappropriate systemic level from which vantage point it will appear disorderly, unpredictable, even random. "If one likes," Weiss adds, "one could turn this renunciation of the primacy of microdeterminacy into a positive scientific declaration in favour of the existence of 'free will.' I prefer to give it a more restrained interpretation," he continues (p. 31), but we do not have to be quite so austere.

Much of what Meehl (1978) has described in his score of reasons why it is so hard to make a science out of the softer branches of psychology, like personology, is rather economically summed up by Weiss's principle of stratified determinism. At the level of individual acts by individual persons, one can no more hope to find order and thus predictability than at the level of the Brownian movement of particles in a suspension. Here, however, we have one great advantage over the physicist: we can talk to our erratic individuals. Retrospectively, it may be possible to make a good deal of sense out of their "random walks." From one perspective, a person's behavior may be certifiably random, while it can still be reconstructed as the intelligible result of interactions between uncoordinated systems.

Conclusion

At this point, you may notice, I am abandoning a proposition you may have felt was implied by my previous linguistic usage: that whatever is determined is predictable. Not at all! The randomly zigzagging path of a person's sequential behaviors in response to press generated by all sorts of larger systems in which she or he is embedded is truly unpredictable, for it would take a prophet to know everything in the world that may affect her or his behavior in the next hour. Put into systems terms, the so-called problem of trait consistency vanishes or at best gets restated thus: Being a system of more or less stable subsystems, a person has a characteristic and recognizable pattern that resists deformation; hence, there should be predictable regularities of behavior. But since no individuals exist outside of larger systems, their behavior is also in part a function of those systems, dependent upon regularities or changes in other parts of the suprasystems. It may be useless to look for enough regularity of the person's behavior on which to found even a statistical prediction or empirical generalization if the larger systems are changing in ways we cannot control or predict. In all too many situations it is in principle impossible to find out and measure all of the determinants—the very attempt to measure some would make it impossible to obtain the needed values of others. In that sense, the indeterminacy of molecular events in physics and that of many behavioral acts have a good deal in common.

In a way, it is an unfortunate coincidence that what is freely decided is often unpredictable, for I do not think that predictability has any direct relevance to freedom. An act is freely chosen when the person decides to do it for personal motives and in the pursuit of conscious personal values felt to be closely connected with his or her sense of identity. Thus, I reject Freud's (1901/1960) example of Luther, saying of his own behavior "I can do no other" (p. 253). When he made that defiant statement about his bold action against the ruling hierarchy of the Catholic church, he surely did so with no sense of inner compulsion. His sense of self embraced the new values in the name of which he had nailed up his list of theses; he had behaved in a self-actualizing way. Quite possibly anyone who knew him well while he was mustering his resolve would have been able to predict that he would go through with it. Indeed, choosing a difficult course—one that will entail predictably unpleasant consequences because it is seen as vital to the attainment of one's dearest goals—is a sign of strength of will or of willpower. It would be a strange contradiction if we had to classify any such exercise of willpower as ipso facto not free.

The upshot, for us as practical people, is that we have to recognize severe limits on our ability to predict single human events. It would be supremely important to be able to predict with certainty whether in a particular crisis a given national leader would be able to maintain a resolve not to signal an all-out nuclear holocaust; but that is a good example of the kind of prediction psychologists will never be able to make. Give us a class of related behaviors, escaping from the single event by multiplying occasions, kinds of behavior, or persons, and we can find enough stability.

Such a situation is admittedly discouraging to hopes of building a scientific personology according to available models. True, we have made slow and uncertain progress in the past, with a great deal of floundering around in blind alleys. Nevertheless, I feel that the prospects are a good deal brighter for the future—especially if we first recognize the need to put our metaphysical houses in order, root out the vestiges of animistic and mechanistic world hypotheses in our psychology, and set about consciously choosing or constructing a sounder philosophical foundation for our work.

References

Ackoff, R. L. *Redesigning the future: A systems approach to societal problems.* New York: Wiley, 1974.

Bandura, A., & Perloff, B. Relative efficacy of self-monitored and externally imposed reinforcement systems. *Journal of Personality and Social Psychology,* 1967, *7,* 111–116.

Barker, R. G., & Wright, H. F. *One boy's day.* New York: Harper & Row, 1951.

Brandt, L. W. Some notes on English Freudian terminology. Journal of the American Psychoanalytic Association, 1961, *9,* 331–339.

Brunswik, E. *Perception and the representative design of psychological experiments.* Berkeley, CA: Univ. of California Press, 1956.

Büchner, L. [*Force and matter, or, Principles of the natural order of the universe, with a system of morality based thereon*] (Trans. from 15th German ed. of *Kraft und Stoff.*) London: Asher, 1884 (4th English ed.). (Originally published, 1855.)

Buckle, H. T. *History of civilization in England.* New York: Appleton–Century–Crofts, 1934. (Originally published, 1871.)

Campbell, D. T., & Stanley, J. *Experimental and quasiexperimental designs for research.* Chicago: Rand McNally, 1963.

Chein, I. *The science of behavior and the image of man.* New York: Basic Books, 1972.

Cook, T. D., & Campbell, D.T. *Quasiexperimentation: Design and analysis issues for field settings.* Chicago: Rand McNally, 1979.

de Charms, R. *Personal causation: The rational affective determinants of behavior.* New York: Academic Press, 1968.

Deci, E. L. *The psychology of self-determination.* Lexington, MA: Lexington Books, 1980.

Easterbrook, J. A. *The determinants of free will.* New York: Academic Press, 1978.

Elms, A. C. Skinner's dark year and Walden Two. *American Psychologist,* 1982, *36,* 470–479.

Epstein, S. The stability of behavior: II. Implications for psychological research. *American Psychologist,* 1980, *35,* 790–806.

Feuerbach, L. [*The essence of Christianity.*] (George Eliot, trans.) New York: Harper, 1957. (Originally published 1841.)

Fishbein, M., & Ajzen, I. Attitudes towards objects as predictors of single and multiple behavioral criteria. *Psychological Review,* 1974, *81,* 59–74.

Fletcher, J. F. *Situation ethics: The new morality.* London: SCM Press, 1974. (Originally published, 1966.)

Freud, S. [Project for a scientific psychology.] *Standard Edition* (Vol. 1) (J. Strachey, Ed. and trans.) London: Hogarth, 1966. (Originally written, 1895.)

Freud, S. [The interpretation of dreams.] *Standard Edition* (Vol. 4) (J. Strachey, Ed. and trans.) London: Hogarth, 1953. (Originally published, 1900.)

Freud, S. [The psychopathology of everyday life.] *Standard Edition* (Vol. 6) (J. Strachey, Ed. and trans.) London: Hogarth, 1960. (Originally published, 1901.)

Freud, S. [Leonardo da Vinci and a memory of his childhood.] *Standard Edition* (Vol. 11) (J. Strachey, Ed. and trans.) London: Hogarth, 1957. (Originally published, 1910.)

Freud, S. [New introductory lectures on psychoanalysis.] *Standard Edition* (Vol. 22) (J. Strachey, Ed. and trans.) London: Hogarth, 1964. (Originally published, 1933.)

Galilei, G. [*Dialogue on the great world systems.*] (T. Salusbury, trans., revised, annotated and with an introduction by G. Santillana) Chicago: Univ. of Chicago Press, 1953. (Originally published, 1632.)

Gay, P. Freud and freedom; on a fox in hedgehog's clothing. In A. Ryan (Ed.), *The idea of freedom: Essays in honour of Isaiah Berlin.* New York: Oxford Univ. Press, 1979.

Goldiamond, I. Self-control procedures in personal behavior problems. *Psychological Reports,* 1965, *17,* 851–868.

Hardin, G. The tragedy of the commons. *Science,* 1968, *162,* 1243–1248.

Hartmann, H. [*Ego psychology and the problem of adaptation.*] (D. Rapaport, trans.) New York: International Univ. Press, 1958. (Originally published, 1939.)

Holt, R. R. Freud's cognitive style. *American Imago,* 1965, *22,* 163–179.

Holt, R. R. On freedom, autonomy, and the redirection of psychoanalytic theory: A rejoinder. *International Journal of Psychiatry,* 1967, *3,* 524–536.

Holt, R. R. Freud's mechanistic and humanistic images of man. In R. R. Holt and E. Peterfreund (Eds.), *Psychoanalysis and Contemporary Science* (Vol. 1). New York: Macmillan, 1972.

Holt, R. R. The past and future of ego psychology. *Psychoanalytic Quarterly,* 1975, *44,* 550–576.

Holt, R. R. A historical survey of the clinical-statistical prediction controversy. In R. R. Holt, *Methods in clinical psychology* (Vol. 2). New York: Plenum, 1978.

Holt, R. R. Freud's impact upon modern morality and our world view. In A. L. Caplan and B. Jennings (Eds.), *Darwin, Marx, and Freud: Their influence on moral theory.* New York: Plenum, in press.

Kanfer, F. H., & Goldfoot, D. A. Self-control and tolerance of noxious stimulation. *Psychological Reports,* 1966, *18,* 79–85.

Knoepfmacher, H. Sigmund Freud in high school. *American Imago,* 1979, *36,* 287–300.

Köhler, W. *The place of value in a world of facts.* New York: Liveright, 1938.

La Mettrie, J. O. de. *L'homme machine.* Leiden, 1748. (Trans. by G. C. Bussey & M. W. Calkins as *Man a machine.* Chicago: Open Court Publishing House, 1929). Excerpted in R. J. Heernstein & E. G. Boring (Eds.), *A source book in the history of psychology.* Cambridge, MA: Harvard Univ. Press, 1966.

Laszlo, E. *Introduction to systems philosophy.* New York: Gordon & Breach, 1971.

Meehl, P. E. *Clinical vs. statistical prediction: A theoretical analysis and a review of the evidence.* Minneapolis: Univ. of Minnesota Press, 1954.

Meehl, P. E. Theoretical risks and tabular asterisks: Sir Karl, Sir Ronald, and the slow progress of soft psychology. *Journal of Consulting and Clinical Psychology,* 1978, *46,* 806–834.

Miller, J. G. *Living systems.* New York: McGraw–Hill, 1978.

Mischel, W. *Personality and assessment.* New York: Wiley, 1968.

Mumford, L. *The myth of the machine* (2 vols.). New York: Harcourt, 1967, 1970.

Nolan, J. D. Self-control procedures in modification of smoking behavior. *Journal of Consulting and Clinical Psychology,* 1968, *32,* 92–93.

Pepper, S. C. *World hypotheses: A study in evidence.* Berkeley, CA: Univ. of California Press, 1942.

Pepper, S. C. On "The case for systems philosophy." *Metaphilosophy*, 1972, *3*, 151–153. (a)

Pepper, S. C. Systems philosophy as a world hypothesis. *Philosophy and Phenomenological Research*, 1972, *32*, 548–553. (b)

Popper, K. R. *The poverty of historicism*. Boston: Beacon, 1957.

Popper, K. R. *Conjectures and refutations*. New York: Basic Books, 1962.

Rychlak, J. E. *Discovering free will and personal responsibility*. New York: Oxford Univ. Press, 1979.

Skinner, B. F. *Science and human behavior*. New York: Macmillan, 1953.

Skinner, B. F. *Beyond freedom and dignity*. New York: Knopf, 1971.

Smith, M. B. A psychologist's perspective on public opinion theory. *Public Opinion Quarterly*, 1971, *35*, 36–43.

Strauss, D. F. [*The old faith and the new.*] (M. Blind, trans.) New York: Holt, 1873. (Originally published, 1872.)

Weiss, P. The living system: Determinism stratified. In A. Koestler & W. Smythies (Eds.), *Beyond reductionism*. London: Hutchinson & Co., 1969.

Westcott, M. R. Free will: An exercise in metaphysical truth or psychological consequences. *Canadian Psychological Review (Psychologie Canadienne)*, 1977, *18*, 249–263.

White, R. W. Ego and reality in psychoanalytic theory. *Psychological Issues*, 1963, *3* (Whole No. 11).

Yankelovich, D., & Barrett, W. *Ego and instinct*. New York: Random House, 1970.

6

The Stability of Behavior across Time and Situations*

Seymour Epstein

Introduction

It is always of interest to examine the historical background of ideas. At first glance it may seem that an idea has burst upon one out of nowhere, corresponding to the light bulb or "Aha!" conception of insight. Upon further reflection it invariably becomes apparent that a background of experience and thinking prepared the way for the new thought. The present chapter is concerned with the issues of the consistency of behavior across time and situations and the existence of broad cross-situational response dispositions. What are the experiences that shaped my views on these issues? There is both a long and a short history to the matter. Let us begin with the short history.

Some years ago, I had begun the series of studies on emotions in everyday life, with which I am still engaged. I had subjects record their emotions on special ratings forms each day for 30 days. They selected the strongest positive and negative experience of the day, wrote a narrative description of the event, and rated the degree to which they experienced a number of emotions and response tendencies, the latter corresponding to Murray needs. They also rated the degree to which they expressed the response tendencies in behavior. From the narratives, judges rated the degree to which each of a number of stimulus variables, corresponding to Murray presses, was present. The point

*The writing of this paper and the two new studies reported in it were supported by NSF Research Grant No. BNS 78-12336. The earlier research studies were supported by NIMH Research Grant MH-01293.

of the study was to examine the kinds of emotions people had, the objective situations and the construals that gave rise to them (corresponding, respectively to Murray's alpha and beta presses), and the response tendencies and behavior associated with the various emotions. A second purpose was to compare idiographic and nomothetic procedures. To that end, the data were analyzed in two ways: (a) by obtaining intrasubject correlations for each subject, and (b) by collapsing the data for each subject across the 30 days and obtaining intersubject correlations.

At the time, I was not particularly interested in the issue of stability of personality because it seemed self-evident to me that there could be no such concept as personality without a reasonable degree of stability. Yet, I kept reading articles that seriously questioned whether there was stability in personality. Some went so far as to conclude that it had been established that there was none and that stability existed only in the eye of the beholder. It was evident ot me that there must be some procedural shortcoming that accounted for the failure to demonstrate stability when behavior was measured objectively, but not when ratings of behavior were examined. Yet what could that shortcoming be? Certainly some subtle and profound issue was involved, or else the solution would have been found a long time ago. I had no brilliant thoughts on the matter. But I did happen to have some relevant data on hand from the studies of emotions. How stable would these data be, and how would the stability be affected by the number of events that were averaged?

According to the Spearman–Brown formula, the more items in a test, the greater the reliability of the test. That was true for items in a test, but would it work for items of behavior in real life, where it was less likely that the assumptions required by the formula would be met? Expecting to find some increase in reliability as a result of averaging over occasions, I hoped to break the .30 barrier that was said to exist when correlations were obtained that involved at least one objective measure of behavior. When the results came back from the computer, I could not believe them at first. The correlations of a single item of behavior on one day with the same item of behavior on another day, often in response to a different situation, were in the vicinity of .20–.30, similar to what others had reported. However, when the mean of all of the odd days was correlated with the mean of all of the even days, most of the stability coefficients were over .80, and some were over .90. Could it be that the source of much of the confusion in the great debate was simply that when psychologists conducted studies of stability of behavior, they often examined single instances of behavior, so that the low stability coefficients frequently reflected the noise of measurement rather than the inherent instability of the behavior? This hardly seemed likely to me because, if it were true, it would suggest that the psychological experiment, as normally con-

·ducted, itself had low temporal reliability, or replicability. Rather than come to such an audacious conclusion, I assumed there must be a computer error in my findings. I checked the data carefully and reanalyze them. The results came out the same. When I computed some of the correlations with a desk calculator, the results confirmed the findings from the computer.

I had to conclude that given inherently stable relationships, they would not be detected by the procedures commonly employed by psychologists to investigate stability in personality and that, very likely, the results of many psychological experiments were unreplicable. The findings from the emotions study were as relevant to the issue of cross-situational stability as to temporal stability, as the situations were real-life situations that varied from occasion to occasion. Thus began a series of studies that will be reported here on the effects of aggregation on various kinds of data, ranging from self-ratings of emotions in everyday life to objectively measured behavior in the laboratory. Because one thing leads to another, what began as a casual detour motivated by curiosity about what would happen if available data were aggregated has become a broad area of interest of mine on methodology in personality research. Moreover, it has become evident to me that aggregation has implications that go beyond methodology and include the nature of science and the functioning of the human mind. Reducing error of measurement through redundancy is no small issue.

But what of the long history that provided the context for the short history? In the short history, the influence of Murray was apparent in the selection of variables corresponding to Murray needs and presses and in the choice of a combined idiographic–nomothetic approach in which a group of individuals is studied in depth and breadth. In the long history, the influence of Murray enters in my absorbing interest in the Thematic Apperception Test (TAT). As a Veterans Administration trainee in the clinical psychology program at the University of Wisconsin, I administered a battery of tests that included the TAT. The test fascinated me because it dealt with all of the issues involved in representing a person in interaction with an environment, including the formulation of the underlying psychodynamics that accounted for the surface behavior. Anything that can happen in real life can, and does, happen in stories. Yet, with the TAT one has a limited sample of data, gathered in systematic fashion, with stimuli of known and distinctive properties.

Two important lessons I learned from the TAT were to influence my views on the stability of personality. One was that the stimulus is extremely important and that behavior is highly situationally specific. It would be foolish to interpret stories told about TAT pictures without knowing the pictures about which the stories had been told. A story about a person choking someone is one thing when the eliciting picture is of a choking scene and another when it is told about a picture of two people looking at each other with affection.

Although probably over 90% of the variance in the responses to a set of pictures is determined by the pictures, it is the remaining 10% of the variance that can be worked with. Each story must be interpreted with reference to knowledge about what the stimulus normally elicits. Once one knows this, it is not a problem that choking scenes elicit hostile responses because of the stimulus and not the person. There is enough variation around the development of hostile themes to provide revealing information on individual personalities.

The second lesson I learned is that behavior is so complexly multidetermined that no single response should be given much weight. It is important to find corroboration in the form of threads of consistency or coherence among many responses. Thus, my work with the TAT taught me that although behavior is highly situationally specific, it is also somewhat general across situations; to the extent that they can be uncovered, such generalities provide important information about individual personalities. It also became apparent to me that the generalities themselves varied in degree. Some generalities held up across all stimuli, whereas others were limited to certain classes of stimuli, and this, in itself, varied among individuals. Thus, one individual might exhibit hostile, competitive responses to all stimuli for which such a response was feasible, whereas another might exhibit such responses only in reaction to authority figures.

In summary, from the TAT I learned that behavior to some extent is situationally specific, that to some extent it is cross-situationally general, that there are broad cross-situational dispositions within individuals that identify important components of an individual's personality, and that the breadth of such generalities varies with the nature of the variable and with the individual. But enough of my personal historical background that is the prelude to the issue at hand. It is time to turn to my main endeavor, which includes a theoretical analysis of stability of behavior across time and situations and the presentation of some old and some new empirical findings. Let us begin with a brief review of the historical context in which the issue of stability of personality is embedded.

The Stability of Behavior over Time

Debate on the stability of behavior has resurfaced during the last 80 years. Not long ago, it appeared that the forces of situationism had gained the field: It had repeatedly been demonstrated that when two objective measures of behavior on different occasions are correlated with each other or when either is correlated with a rating of behavior or a score on a personality inventory,

.correlations of less than .30 were usually obtained. Some dubbed correlations in the vicinity of .20–.30 "personality coefficients," and situationists urged their colleagues to accept the dictates of science and abandon their sentimental belief that personality is stable. Further evidence that there is little stability in personality was provided by studies that demonstrated that when proportions of variance in an analysis of variance design were distributed among situations, people, and their interaction, the amount of variance attributable to people was relatively small (e.g., Endler, 1966). In the face of such evidence, the widespread belief that personality is reasonably stable itself became an object of study, and a number of psychologists (e.g., Bem & Allen, 1974; Jones & Nisbett, 1971; Shweder, 1975) demonstrated that people attribute more stability and cross-situational consistency to behavior than is objectively warranted. They concluded that stability lies primarily in the eye of the beholder. The finding that scales in personality inventories have high temporal reliability could be dismissed by noting that it simply demonstrated that people have stable beliefs about their behavior, which is a far cry from demonstrating that the behavior itself is stable. As support for this argument, it was noted that when personality scales are correlated with objective measures of behavior, the familiar personality coefficients reappear.

The above arguments appeared to provide strong support for the conclusion that there is relatively little stability in personality. In response to these arguments, a number of counterarguments were proposed. The argument based on apportionment of variances in analysis of variance designs was countered by noting that the procedure had been used improperly (Epstein, 1977; Golding, 1975; Olweus, 1977) and by the observation that any source of variance can be relatively large or small depending on the procedures for sampling people and situations. Moreover, perfect stability of behavior, as indicated by a stability coefficient of 1.00, is possible when the proportion of variance attributable to persons is small but the situational variance is still higher. Finally, Sarason and his colleagues (Sarason, Smith, & Diener, 1975), after reviewing a large number of studies, concluded that it was a moot point as to which source of variance is greatest because no single source accounted for a great deal of the total variance. As to the argument that stability occurs only in the eye of the beholder, it was noted that one reason why people tend to assume stability in behavior is because behavior often is stable. In any event, demonstrations that stability is assumed to be present when it is not cannot be used as evidence that stability does not occur under other circumstances.

In an elegantly argued treatise on stability of behavior, Block (1977) noted that although it is true that the preponderance of studies failed to provide evidence for stability of personality, science is not a democratic enterprise in which findings of the majority of studies prevail. A great many poor studies do not cancel out a few good ones. He observed that there are several well-conducted studies that provide evidence for long-term stability in personality and that the findings in these studies cannot be explained away by the eye-of-the-beholder phenomenon, by rater bias, or by other artifacts. He acknowledged that although stability in personality had been established in studies that relied on ratings, it had not been demonstrated in studies that employed direct, objective measurement of behavior. Mischel (1975) concurred with Block that an important issue remaining to be resolved was why a reasonable degree of stability in behavior had been demonstrated with ratings, but not with the direct, objective measurement of behavior.

Thus, the one finding for which there seemed to be no adequate response by those who endorsed the concept of stable dispositions across time and situations was the occurrence of personality coefficients (i.e., correlations in the vicinity of .20–.30) when two items of objectively measured behavior were correlated with each other or when either was correlated with another kind of measure, such as a rating or a score on a personality inventory. This problem was shortly to be solved. The key to the solution lay in the observations that the objective measures that had been examined often consisted of no more than single items of behavior and that single items of behavior, like single items in a test, normally have low reliability and a narrow range of generality (Epstein, 1977).

A moment's reflection reveals that a trait refers to a person's average behavior and cannot be adequately assessed by a single instance of behavior. A person who is classified as an extrovert is not expected to be gregarious on all occasions. On any one occasion he or she may not be feeling well, may be preoccupied or may have just had some experience that makes the person feel unfriendly. The fact that an extrovert does not behave in an extroverted manner on all occasions does not make the term useless. It has value to the extent that it increases predictability of behavior beyond chance. If response dispositions, or traits, exist that are somewhat stable over time and situations, they should be manifested in a sample of observations over time and situations but not necessarily in single instances of behavior. Thus, whether one analyzes the failure of objective measures of behavior to produce more than personality coefficients from the viewpoint of psychometrics or from a consideration of the nature of traits, one is led to the same hypothesis: namely, that stable response dispositions can be demonstrated when responses are averaged over adequate samples of behavior but not necessarily when single instances of behavior are observed. To test this hypothesis, a series of studies was conducted (Epstein, 1977, 1979a, 1980b) in which a wide variety of behaviors was averaged over different numbers of observations, and stability was examined as a function of amount of aggregation. The measures included self-ratings, ratings by others, and the direct, objective measurement of discrete items of real-life behavior. The results unequivocally demonstrated that

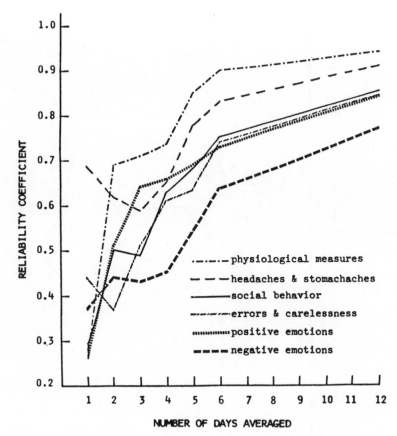

Figure 6.1   Stability coefficients as a function of the number of occasions aggregated. The correlations were obtained by correlating the mean of odd days with the mean of an equal number of even days. The values plotted are the means of the correlations for the variables in a category. Source: Epstein, 1979a.

as the sample of observations increased, the magnitude of the stability coefficients increased to high levels. The results were similar for all the different kinds of data. Moreover, once high stability coefficients were obtained, evidence for validity often emerged in the form of significant relationships with other measures, including standard personality inventories.

For purposes of illustration, some of the findings from three of the studies described above will be discussed. Figure 6.1 presents stability coefficients as a function of the number of occasions aggregated (Epstein, 1979a). It can be seen that as aggregation increases, the stability coefficients increase to values in the vicinity of .80–.90 for the data averaged over 14 occasions. Table 6.1 presents results from a different study on similar variables averaged over 14

TABLE 6.1

Reliability Coefficients for 1-day, 7-day, and 14-day Samples of Daily Feelings and Events and Correlations of Trait Inventories with 14-day Samples of Daily Feelings and Objective Events[a]

Variable recorded daily	Reliability coefficients — No. of days in sample			Trait form of matching scale		Epstein–Fenz anxiety scales			Epstein hostility scales			O–E self-esteem scales	Guilford–Zimmerman scales				Eysenck scales	
	1	7	14	Spec. form	Gen. form	Ins	MT	AA	DH	UH	OH	esteem	Res	Asc	Soc	EmS	Ext	Nrt
Emotions																		
Happy–Sad	.43	.66	.80	—	.44	-.31	-.35	—	-.31	—	—	—	—	—	.36	—	.29	—
Kind–Angry	.55	.78	.88	—	.48	-.43	—	-.29	-.40	—	—	—	—	—	.36	.41	—	-.40
Secure–Threatened	.41	.67	.80	—	.42	-.39	-.39	-.39	-.43	-.35	-.42	—	—	—	—	—	—	-.41
Aroused–Tired	.32	.66	.80	—	.45	—	—	—	—	—	—	—	—	—	—	—	—	—
Spontaneous–Inhibited	.41	.79	.88	—	.40	-.36	—	—	-.31	—	-.30	30	—	.36	.41	—	.45	-.33
Calm–Tense	.34	.83	.91	—	.58	-.42	-.33	-.36	-.37	-.37	-.41	32	—	—	—	.49	—	-.50
External Attn.–Introspective	.22	.55	.71	—	.30	-.47	-.35	—	-.38	—	-.29	—	-.33	—	—	—	—	-.35
Worthy–Unworthy	.56	.79	.88	—	.20	-.42	-.41	-.35	-.46	-.29	-.57	47	—	—	—	.29	—	-.31
Integrated–Disorganized	.52	.84	.91	—	.56	-.49	-.44	-.40	-.32	—	-.47	51	—	.35	.31	.44	—	-.40
Powerful–Helpless	.59	.85	.92	—	.44	-.54	-.47	-.45	-.46	—	-.48	37	-.31	.34	.35	.36	.37	-.43
Peaceful–Agitated	.53	.82	.90	—	.54	-.32	—	-.29	—	-.31	—	—	—	—	—	.34	—	-.36
Attractive–Unattractive	.59	.89	.94	—	.55	—	—	—	-.33	—	-.48	36	—	—	.39	—	—	-.36

	Self-report dimension			Mean corr.														
Optimistic–Pessimistic	.41	.85	.92	—	.66	-.59	-.58	-.46	-.59	-.31	-.59	.55	—	.30	.32	.44	.33	-.53
Alert–Unreactive	.34	.64	.78	—	.59	-.44	-.50	-.29	-.46	—	-.35	.40	—	—	—	—	.33	—
Outgoing–Seclusive	.46	.70	.82	—	.42	-.39	—	-.34	—	—	—	—	—	—	.51	—	.47	—
Mean correlation	.45	.75	.86	—	.47	—	—	—	—	—	—	—	—	—	—	—	—	—
Objective events																		
Heart-rate mean	.70	.88	.94	—	—	—	—	—	.40	—	—	—	—	—	—	—	—	.37
Heart-rate range	.49	.87	.93	—	—	—	—	—	—	.29	—	—	—	—	—	—	.52	—
Calls made	.26	.81	.90	.71	.45	—	—	—	—	—	—	—	—	—	—	—	—	—
Calls received	.45	.91	.95	.72	.61	—	—	—	—	—	—	—	—	—	—	—	—	—
Letters written	.63	.59	.74	.44	.38	—	—	—	—	—	—	—	—	—	—	—	—	—
Letters received	.20	.59	.74	.36	.28	—	—	—	—	—	—	—	—	—	.40	—	—	—
Social contacts	.63	.94	.97	.73	.46	—	—	—	—	—	—	—	-.37	—	—	—	—	—
Hours of sleep	.09	.72	.84	.61	.47	—	—	—	—	—	—	—	—	.31	—	—	—	—
Soundness of sleep	.34	.83	.91	.67	.58	-.38	—	—	—	—	—	—	—	—	—	.30	—	—
Hours of study	.47	.77	.87	.79	.80	—	.57	—	—	—	—	—	—	—	—	—	—	—
Headaches	.39	.75	.86	.44	.51	—	.41	.49	.49	.33	—	—	—	—	—	-.30	—	.41
Stomachaches	.62	.83	.91	.66	.76	.31	.55	.55	.49	.38	—	—	—	—	—	—	—	.33
Mean correlation	.44	.79	.88	.61	.53	—	—	—	—	—	—	—	—	—	—	—	—	—

[a] $N = 45$. For bipolar dimensions, positive scores are in the direction of the first term. For standard inventories, only correlations of at least .29 (significant at .05 level) are reported. Correlations of .38 are significant at the .01 level.

[b] Epstein–Fenz Anxiety Scales: Ins, Insecurity; MT, Muscle Tension; AA, Autonomic Arousal. Epstein hostility scales: DH, Disturbing Hostile Feelings; UH, Undercontrolled Hostility; OH, Overcontrolled Hostility. Guilford–Zimmerman scales: Res, Restraint; Asc, Ascendance; Soc, Sociability; EmS, Emotional Stability. Eysenck scales: Ext, Extroversion; Nrt, Neuroticism.

days correlated with scales on personality inventories (Epstein, 1979a). Examination of the correlations between the standard personality inventories and the data averaged over 14 days indicates a far greater number of significant relationships than would be expected by chance. Many of the relationships exceed the .30 barrier, and none is in an opposite direction from expectancy. All three of the anxiety scales in the Epstein–Fenz Anxiety Inventory (Fenz & Epstein, 1965) correlate significantly in the expected direction with daily ratings of threat and tension. One or more of the anxiety scales correlate significantly negatively with soundness of sleep and significantly positively with stomachaches and headaches. Among the Guilford–Zimmerman scales (1949), the scale of Restraint is significantly negatively ($-.37$), and the scale of Sociability significantly positively (.40), associated with number of social contacts initiated. The scale Emotional Stability is positively associated with daily ratings of integration (.44), kindliness (.41), optimism (.44), and soundness of sleep (.30), and is negatively associated with frequency of headaches ($-.30$). The Eysenck Scale of Extroversion (Eysenck & Eysenck, 1968) is most strongly associated with daily ratings of spontaneity (.45), with outgoing feelings (.47), and with number of social contacts initiated (.52), all of which are elements of extroversion according to Eysenck. There were few significant correlations for a 1-day sample, and among these the correlations were lower and less coherent. For example, the Guilford– Zimmerman Sociability Scale produced only 1 significant correlation for a 1-day sample compared with 9 for the 14-day sample. The 1 significant correlation for a 1-day sample included the variable, Self-rated Attractiveness, which had a relatively high reliability for a 1-day sample (see Table 6.1). Thus, the findings from this study, in common with the other studies in the series, demonstrated that aggregating the data over occasions enhanced validity as well as reliability.

Figure 6.2 presents the results from a study (Epstein, 1977) in which the stability of the personality profiles of individual subjects was examined by correlating the data for each subject across variables for data aggregated to different degrees. The data consisted of ratings of the most pleasant and unpleasant daily experiences over a period of a month. First, correlations were obtained between an individual's profile on Day 1 and Day 2, then for the profile based on the mean of Days 1 and 3 versus the mean of Days 2 and 4, and so on, until an individual's profile based on the mean of all odd days was correlated with the profile based on the mean of all even days. Figure 6.2 presents the mean stability coefficient as a function of different amounts of aggregation. It can be seen in Figure 6.2 that as aggregation over days increases, the stability coefficients for both the pleasant (a) and unpleasant (b) experiences also increase. For a 1-day sample, the mean stability coefficient for an individual profile is not significantly different from zero, whereas for a 14-day sample it is highly significant and of substantial magnitude. An

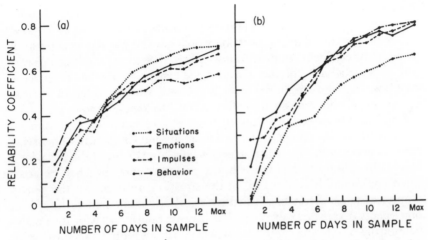

Figure 6.2   Mean intrasubject stability coefficients as a function of the number of occasions aggregated; (a), unpleasant; (b) pleasant. The values plotted are the means of the odd–even correlations for the variables in a category averaged over all subjects. Source: Epstein, 1977. © 1977 by Erlbaum, Hillsdale, NJ.

examination of the range of the stability coefficients for a 14-day sample indicated that although most subjects exhibited a moderately high degree of stability, there were marked individual differences, with some subjects exhibiting very little and others almost perfect stability. It is noteworthy that had only the correlations based on single observations been examined, it would have led to the erroneous conclusion that most people exhibit little stability in their personality profiles.

It may be concluded that objectively measured behavior has been unequivocally demonstrated to be stable over time. Two issues that remain in contention are whether there is stability of behavior across situations and whether there are broad cross-situational response dispositions.

The Consistency of Behavior across Situations

There is ample evidence that behavior is highly sensitive to variations in situational cues. Every experiment that demonstrates a significant effect as the result of the manipulation of a variable provides evidence that behavior is responsive to situational cues. For human behavior to be adaptive and for learning to occur, it is obviously necessary for behavior to be responsive to situational demands. At the same time, in order for human behavior to be adaptive, it is also necessary for there to be some degree of generalization across situations. Without generalization, learning itself would be impossible, for what occurred in one situation would have no bearing on behavior in a slightly different situation. It follows, then, that to some extent behavior must be situationally specific and to some extent it must be stable across situations. It is thus meaningless to argue over whether behavior is situationally specific or cross-situationally general. On logical grounds alone, it is evident that it must be both. Any response to a situation is apt to contain a situationally specific component and a more general component of behavior. In any one situation, the situationally specific component of the behavior is likely to be dominant, and the behavior may therefore appear to be determined completely by the nature of the situation. In order for the general component to be detectable, it is often necessary to compound the specific components. Expressed otherwise, it is because human behavior is so highly situationally specific that aggregation over situations is often necessary before a stable general component can be demonstrated. For the same reason, many experiments are unreplicable because the results are so specific to the experimental environment—which is apt to include incidental sources of influence that the experimenter failed to recognize or considered unimportant. Therefore, it is unlikely they will be reproduced if the study is repeated (see Epstein, 1980b for further discussion of this issue).

Some have argued that although there is impressive evidence for long-term temporal stability of behavior, there is no evidence for cross-situational stability. Such an argument contains an inherent contradiction, for if there is temporal stability, there must be some degree of cross-situational stability, as no situation can ever be reproduced identically. Moreover, a number of studies have reported impressive levels of stability over different stages of an individual's life (e.g., Block, 1971; Olweus, 1977). Surely, no reasonable person would assume that the situations that evoke a particular response from a person at one stage of life are identical with those at another stage. Thus, given long-term stability of behavior, it is not meaningful to question whether there is cross-situational stability of behavior. There obviously must be some. Meaningful questions can be raised about how much cross-situational stability there is for different situations, how best to measure it, including what unit of measurement to use and what factors influence it. In the absence of an adequate system for categorizing and dimensionalizing stimuli and situations, it is, of course, impossible to determine how much generalization there is; what one investigator may consider little generalization, another may consider a great deal.

In order to predict behavior across situations, it would be helpful to have a classification system for situations and a theory that takes into account situations as an aid in determining to what extent different situations are conceptually related to each other. A series of studies by Sroufe and his colleagues

(Arend, Gove, & Sroufe, 1979; Sroufe, 1979; Waters, Wippman, & Sroufe, 1979) provides an excellent illustration of how impressive levels of stability can be demonstrated across time, situations, and modes of response if care is given to measurement procedures and to theoretical considerations that indicate how behavior in certain situations can be expected to be related to behavior in other situations. Among other interesting findings, it was observed that a measure of competence in responding adaptively to the mother at 1½ years of age was significantly associated with measures of ego resiliency and ego control obtained at 4½ years of age.

Because generality of behavior is of critical concern for theoretical reasons as well as for practical problems in the prediction of behavior, it is obvious that an extremely important task confronting personologists is the development of systems for classifying and dimensionalizing situations. To date, far more effort has been expended in classifying and dimensionalizing characteristics of people than of situations. The only personality theory that is an exception in this respect is the theory of Murray (1938), which assigns equal weight to situation variables, person variables, and their interaction.

Recently, there has been renewed interest in classifying and dimensionalizing stimuli, situations, and environments. A number of promising approaches have been proposed by researchers such as Bem and Funder (1978), Frederiksen (1972), Levin (1965), Magnusson (1971), Magnusson and Endler (1977), Magnusson and Ekehammar (1973), Moos (1968, 1969, 1970), and Staub (1980). In a review and analysis of the issues involved in classifying stimuli, situations, and environments, Pervin (1978) concluded that it is too early to uniformly adopt any one system. According to Pervin, what is needed at this stage is creative thinking and research to resolve such basic issues as the following: (1) Should analysis proceed at a molar or a molecular level? (2) Should situations be classified in terms of their objective or perceived characteristics? (3) What is the relationship of situational variables to behavior? Of course, it may well be, and I suspect it is highly likely, that there is no one solution to these questions; the solutions can be expected to vary with the nature of the situations, the responses, and the problem. For certain purposes a subjective approach, and for others an objective approach, will be most useful for classifying stimuli, situations, or environments.

The Existence of Broad, Cross-Situational Response Dispositions

It is important to recognize that a high degree of cross-situational specificity in behavior does not rule out the existence of broad, cross-situational response dispositions. By aggregating behavior over many situations, each of which contributes a small component of general variance, it is possible to obtain a highly reliable and valid measure of a broad response disposition. In fact, in intelligence tests, interitem correlations are typically in the vicinity of .20 to .30, which, ironically, corresponds to the infamous "personality coefficients." A broad dispositional measure, such as a measure of intelligence or extroversion, can, of course, only be expected to predict behavior well at a corresponding level of generality (Fishbein & Ajzen, 1974; Ajzen & Fishbein, 1977; Epstein, 1979a, 1980b). It is thus not surprising that correlations between broad dispositions and specific behaviors are in the order of personality coefficients.

Strangely, some personologists have acknowledged that intelligence is a broad disposition but have doubted that there are other broad dispositions. When objectively measured items of behavior related to personality have been aggregated, the results have been similar to that of intelligence tests. The Hartshorne and May (1928) studies have often been cited as providing evidence that behavior is situationally specific, as it was reported that honesty in any one situation was only weakly associated with honesty in any other situation. What is little known is that when the items in the different situations were aggregated, strong evidence for the existence of a broad personality trait of honesty emerged. The authors concluded:

> Just as one test is an insufficient and unreliable measure in the case of intelligence, so one test of deception is quite incapable of measuring a subject's tendency to deceive. That is, we cannot predict from what a pupil does on one test what he will do on another. If we use ten tests of classroom deception, however, we can safely predict what a subject will do on the average whenever ten similar situations are presented [p. 135].

There is no dearth of other studies that have demonstrated broad response dispositions. Among the variables demonstrated to exhibit broad response dispositions, in addition to intelligence and honesty, are extroversion and emotional stability (Cattell, 1957; Eysenck, 1967; Cheek, 1982); ego resiliency and ego control (Block & Block, 1980; Sroufe, 1979); social competence (Sroufe, 1979; Arend, Gove, & Sroufe, 1979; Waters, Wippman, & Sroufe, 1979); aggression (Olweus, 1973, 1974, 1979); dominance (Moskowitz & Schwarz, 1982); vocational interests (Hogan, DeSoto, & Solano, 1977); and agreeableness and conscientiousness (Cheek, 1982).

In summary, it may be concluded that behavior is situationally specific and organized into broad response dispositions at the same time. The reason that both can occur is that the degree to which behavior is situationally specific is less than complete. Accordingly, by aggregating behavior over many situations, common variance is compounded and situational uniqueness canceled out, thereby revealing broad, cross-situational response dispositions.

Because aggregation is a major tool in test construction, we know a great deal about it in theoretical terms. Yet the principles of test construction have had relatively little influence upon the conduct of laboratory research (Cronbach, 1957). No matter how sound theory is, the problem of relating theory to the empirical world remains. The application of theory requires that certain assumptions in the real world be met, assumptions that are often taken for granted without testing them. Thus, it is not enough to consider abstractly the potential value of aggregation as a general tool in psychological research. It is important to empirically examine the advantages and limitations of aggregation when it is used as a research tool. With this aim in mind, two studies on aggregation were carried out. One was concerned with the effect of aggregation on laboratory data and the other with a comparison of different kinds of aggregation. These studies are reported next.

A Study of Aggregation in the Laboratory

It will be recalled that previous research (Epstein, 1977, 1979a, 1980b) demonstrated that aggregation over occasions produced an impressive rise in temporal reliability for a variety of measures, including self-report data, ratings by judges, and the direct objective measurement of real-life events. Moreover, once high levels of reliability were obtained, evidence for validity followed. The one kind of data remaining to be examined was data gathered under highly controlled laboratory conditions.

In the study reported in this chapter, subjects were tested in the laboratory on 14 successive occasions.[1] Because the entire study is too extensive to present in detail here; only selected aspects are reported.

Nine male and nine female undergraduates, paid for their services, were tested individually twice a week in the laboratory for a total of 14 sessions each. The first 11 sessions were identical and will be the main focus of the present report. In the twelfth through fourteenth sessions different emotions were induced in order to study the effects of emotions on physiological patterns of reactivity, which will not concern us here. However, we will report some analyses of the data from these sessions that have bearing on the issue of cross-situational stability. In an introductory meeting, a battery of personality inventories was administered. The battery included the following tests: the Guilford–Zimmerman Temperament Survey (G–Z) (Guilford &

---

[1]The study was conducted in collaboration with Robert Alexander, a graduate research assistant at the time. Alexander trained and supervised two undergraduates, John Gmeiner and Michael Kaplan, who served as experimenters.

Zimmerman, 1949), the O'Brien–Epstein Self-Esteem Scales (O–E) (O'Brien, 1980), the A-H Anxiety and Hostility Scales (A–H), the Alexander–Epstein Scale of Extroversion (E), and the Mother–Father–Peer Inventory (MFP).

The O–E scales measure 12 components of self-esteem. Among these, only the following were examined in the present study: General Self-Esteem, Likeability, Competence, Body Image, and Internal Consistency. The scale of Internal Consistency is obtained by correlating matched items in the test. Thus, unlike the other scales, it is a measure of actual performance, and not a self-report measure. Results on all scales of the G–Z survey will be presented, except for the scale of Masculinity, which simply reflected sex differences. The MFP inventory is an unpublished test with scales that describe the subjects' reported relationships with mother, father, and peer figures during childhood. One scale measures the degree to which mothers encouraged independence and were not overprotective. Another measures the degree to which mothers were accepting and not rejecting. There are similar scales for relationships with fathers, and there is also a scale of acceptance–rejection by peers. The A–H scales are an unpublished test developed by factor analysis from a wide variety of items on anxiety and hostility. In the present study, three scales of anger and aggression and one scale of anxiety were examined. The E scale of extroversion is an unpublished scale developed by factor analysis of adjective checklists of feelings and of sentence-long statements on characteristics of extroverts and introverts. It is correlated with the Eysenck Personality Inventory (Eysenck & Eysenck, 1968), but contains fewer items of social extroversion and more items concerned with spontaneity and outward versus inward direction of attention. It has been found in preliminary work to correlate more strongly with self-reported emotions than the Eysenck scale.

A laboratory session contained the following 7, 1-minute segments, separated by 10-second intervals: (1) a resting, or baseline, period; (2) the presentation of 3 ½-second blasts of noise (105 db) at 20-second intervals; (3) holding a stylus in a hole while trying not to touch its sides; (4) the same combined with the presentation of the 3 noises; (5) 3 tests of simple reaction time at 20-second intervals; (6) a resting, or baseline, period; and (7) pulling a suspended weight attached to a dynamometer as strongly as possible on 3 trials at 20-second intervals.

At the beginning of each session, individuals rated their current feeling state on a set of bipolar graphic rating scales anchored at one end with three adjectives, such as "happy, cheerful, joyous" and at the other end with three opposite adjectives, such as "unhappy, sad, depressed." In addition, two composite scores were obtained, one consisting of all positive minus all negative emotions, referred to as Positive Affect, and the other of the sum of all emotions without regard to direction of affect, referred to as Emotional

Reactivity. Altogether, 29 emotions and feeling states were rated. The present report will present only the 6 most basic emotions and the two composite scores. After the subjects completed their ratings, systolic and diastolic blood pressure were recorded. Subjects were then connected to a polygraph that continuously monitored their heart rate and electrodermal responses. The following psychophysiological measures were extracted: heart-rate mean, heart-rate range (fastest minus slowest beat), and tonic skin conductance. These were obtained in all periods. The largest skin conductance response in a period was recorded for the periods in which noises were presented and for the period in which the stylus was held. Number of nonspecific skin conductance responses (SCRs) was recorded for each of the two resting periods. To reduce the data further, responses were averaged during the two resting periods, as well as during the periods in which the loud noises were presented and in which the stylus was held. These averages will be designated in the tables by "BL" and "R" in parentheses next to each variable, meaning baseline and reactivity periods, respectively. The period with the dynamometer was not averaged with the other reactivity periods because the motor exertion produced far greater physiological reactivity than during any of the other periods. Behavioral measures consisted of number of stylus hits with and without noise, average reaction time, and average strength of dynamometer pull.

The Effect of Aggregation over Occasions on Reliability Table 6.2 presents temporal reliability coefficients for the first day compared to the second day, the tenth day compared to the eleventh day, the mean of the first 3 odd days compared to the mean of the first 3 even days, the mean of the first 5 even days compared to the mean of the first 5 odd days, and the reliability of the entire 11-day sample estimated from the 5-day sample by the Spearman–Brown formula. In a previous study (Epstein, 1979) with similar data, it had been found that although Spearman–Brown estimates from a single day were often inaccurate, estimates from the mean of a sample of several days were invariably highly accurate. Figure 6.3 presents the mean temporal reliability coefficients in each of the major categories of response variables as a function of increasing aggregation over occasions.

It can be seen in Figure 6.3 that all categories of variables exhibit an increase in reliability as a function of increasing aggregation. The mean reliability coefficient for self-rated emotions for a 1-day sample is .28, consistent with findings by others and corresponding to a so-called personality coefficient. When the data are aggregated over the full sample of 11 days, the mean coefficient rises to .83. The average reliability coefficient for the psychophysiological variables for a 1-day sample is .58 and rises to .94 for an 11-day sample. Although the correlation is highly significant to begin with, it accounts for only 34% of the variance as compared to 88% of the variance for the aggregated data. For the behavioral measures, the average reliability coefficient is sufficiently high (.80) to begin with, so that aggregation can contribute little. Accordingly, the psychomotor variables will not be examined for the effect of aggregation on validity.

Examination of Table 6.2 reveals that there is considerable variation among the variables within a category of the temporal reliability of measures taken on a single occasion. Two of the self-ratings have reliability coefficients

TABLE 6.2

Reliability Coefficients as a Function of Aggregation over Different Days[a]

Variable[b]	Day 1 vs. Day 2	Day 10 vs. Day 11	3 odd vs. 3 even days	5 odd vs. 5 even days	All 11 days (est.)
Self-rated emotions					
Happy–Sad	.40	.52	.54	.73	.86
Kindly–Angry	.32	.79	.58	.77	.88
Secure–Threatened	.52	.59	.68	.75	.87
Aroused–Tired	−.01	.13	.19	.49	.68
Calm–Jittery	.06	.41	.64	.66	.81
Enthused–Apathetic	.39	.41	.49	.75	.87
$\bar{X}$	.28	.48	.52	.69	.83
Positive affect	.38	.57	.41	.77	.88
Emotional reactivity	.52	.77	.88	.94	.97
Physiological measures					
Systolic blood pr.	.66	.44	.85	.85	.93
Diastolic blood pr.	.41	.48	.74	.87	.94
Heart-rate mean (BL)	.67	.69	.88	.92	.96
Heart-rate mean (R)	.76	.62	.88	.90	.95
Heart-rate range (BL)	.50	.41	.89	.91	.96
Heart-rate range (R)	.28	.68	.90	.91	.96
Nonspecific SCRs (BL)	.55	.61	.76	.80	.90
Tonic skin cond. (BL)	.72	.49	.95	.93	.97
SCR magnitude (R)	.63	.58	.86	.84	.92
$\bar{X}$	.58	.56	.85	.88	.94
Behavioral measures					
Stylus hits	.83	.96	.93	.97	.99
Stylus hits with noise	.76	.93	.95	.97	.99
Reaction time	.63	.70	.64	.80	.90
Dynamometer	.98	.97	.99	1.00	1.00
$\bar{X}$	.80	.89	.88	.94	.97

[a]$N = 18$. .47–58, $p < .05$; .59–70, $p < .01$; .71–1.00, $p < .001$.
[b]BL, baseline period; R, reactivity period.

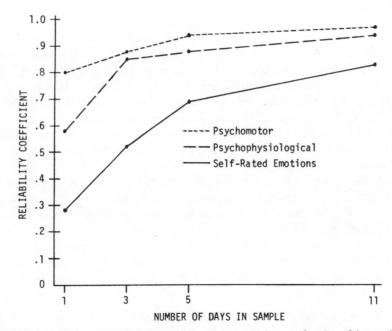

Figure 6.3 Stability coefficients for three kinds of laboratory data as a function of the number of occasions aggregated. The values plotted are the means of the odd–even correlations for the variables in a category.

for a 1-day sample that are close to 0. In both cases, substantial stability coefficients are obtained when the data are aggregated. One psychophysiological variable, heart-rate range, has a nonsignificant reliability coefficient of .28 for a 1-day sample, but with aggregation it increases to .96.

In summary, data derived from a single session produced, on the average, nonsignificant stability coefficients for self-ratings of emotion, modest stability coefficients for psychophysiological variables, and high stability coefficients for psychomotor measures. For the data aggregated over 5 days, all reliability coefficients reached high levels. Estimates of the temporal reliability aggregated over the 11-day sample were very high, often above .90. It may be concluded that the effect of aggregation over occasions on laboratory data is no different from that previously observed for nonlaboratory data. Unlike the results in the previous studies, however, a number of the variables in the present study had relatively high temporal reliability coefficients when observed on a single occasion.

The Effect of Repeated Testing When data are obtained over repeated occasions, the effect of aggregation can be complicated if different sessions produce different effects. To examine the influence of repeated testing, the data were averaged in three-session blocks consisting of Sessions 1–3, 4–6, and 7–9. The means of the blocks were then subjected to an analysis of variance. Significant habituation was found for Aroused–Tired, diastolic blood pressure, magnitude of the skin conductance response, and level of tonic skin conductance. Mean heart rate decreased on Days 4–6 and increased on Days 7–9. Among the psychomotor measures, reaction time and dynamometer performance improved significantly over time, revealing a practice effect. A second set of analyses in which reactions on Day 1 were contrasted with the mean reaction on the remaining days produced the same findings on habituation.

Because of the high reactivity that occurred on Day 1, reliability coefficients for the aggregated data were recomputed with Day 11 substituted for Day 1 in the correlation of the 5 odd days with the 5 even days. The results were unaffected. All relationships among variables were, nevertheless, computed with and without the data of Day 1 included in the aggregation, as it is possible that Day 1 could affect validity independent of its effect on reliability. Again, the results were unchanged. Accordingly, only the results including Day 1 will be presented.

The Effect of Aggregation on the Relationship between Emotions and Personality Inventories Table 6.3 presents the correlations of ratings of daily emotions with scores on personality inventories for all pairs of variables that produced at least one significant correlation with a scale on a personality inventory for the ratings on Day 1, Day 11, or the aggregate of the 11 days. The correlation of 25 personality scales with 8 emotions generates 200 correlations for each of the three conditions in Table 6.3. Out of the total of 600 correlations, 30 can be expected to be significant at the .05 level by chance. As there are 80 significant correlations in Table 6.3, it can be concluded that the results are not likely the result of chance. Moreover, the distribution of the results is not what would be expected by chance; the aggregated data produce almost twice as many significant relationships as the single days. There are 23 significant correlations on Day 1, 20 on Day 11, and 37 for the aggregated data.

By examining the correlations that are significant for the aggregated data but not for Day 1, it can be determined what information is gained through aggregation that would be missed if the investigation had been confined to a single laboratory session, which is the usual procedure. Among the relationships that are brought to light by aggregation, some of the more interesting are as follows.

1. Extroversion (G–Z) is positively associated with daily ratings of happiness, security, arousal, and emotional reactivity.

2. Restraint (G–Z) is negatively associated with ratings of emotional reactivity.

3. Sociability (G–Z) is associated with low ratings of threat and with high ratings of emotional reactivity. The relationship with low threat is of particular interest because it suggests that shy people (shyness is identified in the G–Z manual as the opposite of sociability) view the laboratory situation as an interpersonal threat.

4. Objectivity (G–Z), identified in the manual as "thickskinnedness" as opposed to hypersensitivity, is associated with daily ratings of enthusiasm in the laboratory as opposed to apathy.

5. Cooperativeness (G–Z), which refers to a tendency to establish positive relationships with others as opposed to being critical and rejecting, is positively associated with self-ratings of happiness and arousal and with positive feelings in general.

TABLE 6.3

Correlations of Self-Rated Emotions with Scales on Personality Inventories[a]

Personality variable	Self-rated emotion	Day 1	Day 11	Days 1–11
Body Image (O–E)	Kindly–Angry	.60**	.18	.34
	Secure–Threatened	.49*	.03	.31
	Positive affect	.63**	.28	.42
Extroversion (A–E)	Happy–Sad	.44	.50*	.61**
	Secure–Threatened	.44	.41	.52*
	Aroused–Tired	.20	.57*	.58*
	Positive affect	.66**	.40	.54*
	Emotional reactivity	.41	.59**	.57*
Restraint (G–Z)	Emotional reactivity	−.33	−.51*	−.52*
Boldness (G–Z)	Happy–Sad	.51*	.25	.39
	Aroused–Tired	.21	.54*	.61**
	Calm–Jittery	.47*	−.32	−.10
	Enthused–Apathetic	.37	.54*	.43
	Positive Affect	.49*	.36	.41
	Emotional reactivity	.50*	.35	.45
Sociable (G–Z)	Happy–Sad	.49*	.51*	.57*
	Kindly–Angry	.48*	.33	.36
	Secure–Threatened	.19	.47*	.47*
	Positive affect	.55*	.42	.52*
	Emotional reactivity	.17	.57*	.47*
Stability (G–Z)	Calm–Jittery	.08	.48*	.40
Objectivity (G–Z)	Kindly–Angry	.33	.34	.49*
	Enthused–Apathetic	.44	.07	.51*
Thoughtfulness (G–Z)	Calm–Jittery	.31	−.66**	−.36
Cooperativeness (G–Z)	Happy–Sad	.21	.29	.48*
	Aroused–Tired	.07	.26	.51*
	Positive affect	.14	.32	.47*

(continued)

TABLE 6.3 *Continued*

Personality variable	Self-rated emotion	Day 1	Day 11	Days 1–11
Conflict over Hostility	Happy–Sad	−.53*	.10	−.38
(E)	Kindly–Angry	−.56*	−.29	−.50*
	Secure–Threatened	−.61**	−.09	−.50*
	Calm–Jittery	−.33	−.34	−.65**
	Enthused–Apathetic	−.39	−.21	−.57*
	Positive affect	−.63**	−.30	−.58*
	Emotional reactivity	−.52*	−.30	−.54*
Hostility Avoidance (E)	Aroused–Tired	−.48*	−.04	−.25
Cognitive Anxiety (E)	Kindly–Angry	−.60**	−.35	−.56*
	Secure–Threatened	−.49*	−.13	−.59**
	Aroused–Tired	−.36	−.48*	−.32
	Calm–Jittery	−.18	−.34	−.69**
	Enthused–Apathetic	−.29	−.32	−.54*
	Positive affect	−.48*	−.41	−.58*
	Emotional reactivity	−.52*	−.27	−.54*
Mother Encouraged Independence (MFP)	Enthused–Apathetic	.53*	.11	.29
Mother Acceptance	Happy–Sad	.18	.54*	.44
(MFP)	Enthused–Apathetic	.28	.58*	.43
Father Encouraged Independence (MFP)	Happy–Sad	.14	.57*	.47*
	Secure–Threatened	.13	.47*	.47*
	Emotional reactivity	.21	.53*	.53*
Father Acceptance	Happy–Sad	.09	.61**	.60**
(MFP)	Kindly–Angry	.49*	.51*	.58*
	Secure–Threatened	.21	.44	.63**
	Enthused–Apathetic	.40	.45	.53*
	Positive affect	.37	.52*	.58*
Peer Acceptance (MFP)	Secure–Threatened	.40	.22	.53*

[a]$N = 18$. High scores on the self-rated emotions are in the direction of the first term of the bipolar dimensions.
*$p < .05$.
**$p < .01$.

6. Conflict over Hostility (E) and Cognitive Anxiety (E) are associated with daily ratings of jitteriness and lack of enthusiasm in the laboratory.

7. Father-Encouraged Independence (MFP) is associated with daily ratings of happiness, security, and emotional reactivity.

8. Father Acceptance (MFP) is directly associated with daily ratings of happiness, security, enthusiasm, and general positive affect in the laboratory.

9. Peer Acceptance (MFP) is directly associated with ratings of security in the laboratory.

Thus, overall, when the data are aggregated over occasions a considerable amount of coherent information is obtained that would be lost if the study were conducted in a single session. Aggregation has other advantages as well.

First, the findings are not confined to first-time encounters but are general across sessions. Second, the correlations with the aggregated data have a lower standard error and are therefore more accurate and replicable than correlations established with unaggregated data.

It must be considered that aggregation over occasions can lose information if there are reliable unique effects that occur on particular occasions. As there are fewer significant relationships for the single days than for the aggregated days, the likelihood that any one finding for a single day is a chance result must be taken into account. It is therefore particularly important, in evaluating the results from single days, to seek meaningful and redundant patterns of relationships. It can be seen in Table 6.3 that Body Image (O–E) produces three significant correlations, two of which are significant at the .01 level, with daily ratings of emotions that are not significant for the aggregated data. Given the relatively few correlations that are significant for Day 1 that are not also significant for the aggregated data, an unusually high proportion is associated with Body Image (O–E), an unlikely chance occurrence. A possible interpretation of this finding is that people who are concerned about their physical appearance tend to be threatened by a first-time encounter. This reaction must habituate rapidly, as it is not present when the data are averaged over the 11 sessions. The scale of Boldness (G–Z) is the only other scale that produces more than one correlation that is significant on Day 1 but not on the aggregated data. Boldness is significantly associated on Day 1 with self-ratings of Happy–Sad and Calm–Jittery, neither of which is significant for the aggregated data. The results suggest that for some subjects the first laboratory encounter is a threatening experience and that it is particularly apt to be so for people who are submissive or lacking in "boldness."

In order to establish whether Day 11 has a unique contribution to make, one can examine correlations significant on Day 11 but not on Day 1 or on the aggregated data. There are six correlations significant on Day 11 and not on the other occasions. These six correlations are fairly well scattered among the different inventories and ratings of emotions, with two exceptions. Among all the significant correlations in Table 6.3, there are only two associated with Mother Acceptance (MFP), and both occur on Day 11. Mother Acceptance is significantly associated with self-ratings of Happy–Sad and Enthused–Apathetic on Day 11 only. People who report that their mothers were highly accepting of them when they were children rate themselves in the eleventh session as happier and more enthusiastic in the laboratory than people who report their mothers were less accepting. That is, they report that they maintain their good spirits despite being in a routine, boring situation. Whether it is a chance finding or not will have to await further research. An additional thread of possible consistency is that among the six correlations that are significant only on Day 11, two of them include the self-rating Enthused–Apathetic. Thus, Day 11 may provide a unique opportunity for uncovering relationships between personality characteristics and reactivity to situations that evoke apathy and boredom.

The Effect of Aggregation on the Relationship between Psychophysiological Reactions and Self-Ratings of Emotions Table 6.4 presents the correlations of the ratings of emotions and the psychophysiological reactions on Day 1, Day 11, and the aggregate of Days 1 to 11. Only variables that produced at least one significant correlation among the three conditions are included. The 8 emotions and the 9 psychophysiological variables generate 72 correlations. About 3 or 4 correlations in each column in Table 6.4 can therefore be expected to be significant at the .05 level by chance alone. There are 5 significant correlations on Day 1, 2 on Day 11, and 14 for the aggregated data. Although the number of significant correlations on the single days is about what would be expected by chance, the number on the aggregated days is far greater.

Examination of the significant correlations for the aggregated data indicates the following. Subjects who rated themselves high on "unhappy, sad, and depressed" over the 11 sessions produced large skin conductance re-

TABLE 6.4

Correlations of Psychophysiological Variables with Self-Rated Emotions[a]

Self-rated emotion	Psychophysiological variable[b]	Day 1	Day 11	Days 1–11
Happy–Sad	SCR magnitude (R)	−.39	−.28	−.59**
Kindly–Angry	Tonic skin conductance (BL)	−.26	−.38	−.57*
	SCR magnitude (R)	−.43	−.30	−.47*
Secure–Threatened	Systolic BP	−.49*	−.07	.17
	Heart-rate mean (BL)	−.54*	.19	−.05
	Heart-rate mean (R)	−.50*	.15	.00
	Heart-rate range (BL)	−.33	−.12	−.55*
	Nonspecific SCRs (BL)	−.18	−.29	−.55*
	Tonic skin conductance (BL)	−.24	−.43	−.48*
	SCR magnitude (R)	−.68**	−.19	−.48*
Calm–Jittery	Nonspecific SCRs (BL)	.08	−.16	−.50*
	Tonic skin conductance (BL)	.24	−.43	−.61**
	SCR magnitude (R)	−.31	−.05	−.56*
Enthused–Apathetic	Tonic skin conductance (BL)	−.39	.09	−.53*
	SCR magnitude (R)	−.42	−.17	−.63**
Positive affect	Diastolic BP	−.10	−.50*	−.19
	Tonic skin conductance (BL)	−.24	−.18	−.47*
	SCR magnitude (R)	−.63**	−.23	−.58*
Emotional reactivity	Diastolic BP	.12	−.52*	−.14

[a]$N = 18$.
[b]BL, baseline period; R, reactivity period.
*$p < .05$.
**$p < .01$.

sponses to stimulation. Subjects who rated themselves as "angry, irritated, annoyed" had high levels of tonic skin conductance and produced large skin conductance responses to stimulation. Subjects who rated themselves as "frightened, worried, threatened" exhibited increased heart-rate range, had a high level of tonic skin conductance, and produced large skin conductance responses to stimulation as well as a high number of nonspecific skin conductance responses in the absence of stimulation. Subjects who rated themselves as tense and jittery exhibited high levels of tonic skin conductance, produced large skin conductance responses to stimulation, and had a high rate of nonspecific skin conductance responses. Subjects who reported a high degree of enthusiasm and a low degree of apathy during the sessions exhibited low levels of tonic skin conductance and produced small skin conductance responses to stimulation. Subjects who reported low self-rated positive affect (or high negative affect) based on all emotions combined obtained high levels of tonic skin conductance and produced large skin conductance responses to stimulation.

The electrodermal responses appear to be the most sensitive measures of negative emotional reactivity in general, as electrodermal measures are significantly associated with nearly all the negative emotions in Table 6.4. Nonspecific skin conductance responses appear to be more specifically associated with "jitteriness" and the perception of threat than the other electrodermal measures. Heart-rate range during the resting period is associated with perception of threat and falls slightly short of being significantly related to "jitteriness." Thus, heart-rate range exhibits the same pattern of relationships as nonspecific electrodermal responses, which may follow from the consideration that both indicate sudden changes in reactivity in the absence of stimulation and may be indicative of diffuse anxiety.

Although the number of significant correlations on the single days is no greater than would be expected by chance, four of the five significant correlations on Day 1 involve ratings of Secure–Threatened, which is not likely a chance result. Systolic blood pressure, the two measures of heart-rate mean, and magnitude of the skin conductance response are all significantly positively associated with ratings of perceived threat. Thus, the results suggest that Day 1 provides a particularly good opportunity for examining individual differences in reaction to threat, which is consistent with the observations in the previous section. It is of interest, in this respect, that systolic blood pressure and heart-rate mean are not good indicators of threat for the aggregated data. Unlike magnitude of the skin conductance response, they produce correlations with ratings of threat close to 0.

The Effect of Aggregation on the Relationship of Psychophysiological Reactions to Personality Inventories Table 6.5 presents the correlations of the psycho-

TABLE 6.5

Correlations of Psychophysiological Variables with Scales on Personality Inventories[a]

Personality variable	Psychophysiological variable[b]	Day 1	Day 11	Days 1–11
Gen. Self-Esteem (O–E)	Heart-rate range (BL)	−.51*	−.30	−.33
Competence (O–E)	Heart-rate range (BL)	−.57*	−.53*	−.48*
Body Image (O–E)	Heart-rate mean (BL)	−.44	−.28	−.49*
	SCR magnitude (R)	−.54*	−.36	−.61**
Internal Consistency (O–E)	Diastolic BP	.26	.56*	.46
	Heart-rate Range (BL)	−.56*	−.54*	−.41
Extroversion (A–E)	Diastolic BP	−.11	−.49*	−.56*
	SCR magnitude (R)	−.53*	−.35	−.53*
Energetic (G–Z)	Heart-rate range (R)	−.49*	−.31	−.19
Restraint (G–Z)	Diastolic BP	.20	.48*	.41
Boldness (G–Z)	Diastolic BP	−.10	−.53*	−.52*
Sociable (G–Z)	Diastolic BP	−.11	−.36	−.53*
Friendliness (G–Z)	Heart-rate range (BL)	−.49*	−.42	−.37
	Heart-rate range (R)	−.30	−.53*	−.46
	Nonspecific SCRs (BL)	−.32	−.52*	−.56*
Conflict over Hostility (E)	Heart-rate mean (BL)	.64**	−.01	.45
	Heart-rate mean (R)	.60**	.05	.49*
Proneness to Anger & Aggression (E)	Heart-rate mean (BL)	.74***	−.27	.33
	Heart-rate mean (R)	.69**	−.27	.46
Mother Encouraged Independence (MFP)	Systolic BP	−.09	−.20	−.47*
	SCR magnitude (R)	−.29	−.40	−.51*
Father Acceptance (MFP)	Diastolic BP	.50*	.05	.15
	SCR magnitude (R)	−.50*	−.20	−.55*
Peer Acceptance (MFP)	Heart-rate range (BL)	−.59**	−.55*	−.70**
	Heart-rate range (R)	−.37	−.52*	−.53*

[a]$N = 18$.
[b]BL, baseline period; R, reactivity period.
*$p < .05$.
**$p < .01$.
***$p < .001$.

physiological variables with the scores on the personality inventories. Only variables that produced at least one significant correlation among the three conditions are included. Nine psychophysiological variables combined with 25 personality scales generate 225 correlation coefficients for each of the three conditions. Thus, by chance alone, about 11 correlations can be expected to be significant at the .05 level in each of the conditions. In Table 6.5, it can be seen that on Day 1 there are 14 significant correlations, on Day 11 there are 10, and on the aggregated days there are 14. The data of Table 6.5 thus fail to reveal any significant advantage for the aggregated data over the data of Day 1.

Although the number of significant correlations on Day 1 and on the aggregated data are only slightly greater than would be expected by chance, the observation that almost all the correlations are in the expected direction suggests that something other than chance is operating. Moreover, although the number of correlations could have occurred by chance, the pattern of significant correlations suggests that the results are not random. When the correlations in Table 6.5 are grouped according to common psycho-physiological reactions, some interesting patterns emerge. Heart-rate range in the resting period produces several significant relationships. It is significantly negatively correlated in at least one of the three conditions in Table 6.5 with the inventory scales General Self-Esteem, Competence, Internal Consistency, Friendliness, and Peer Acceptance. People with high heart-rate variability in the absence of external stimulation describe themselves as lower in self-esteem, higher in anxiety, more unfriendly (or resentful), and less accepted by their peers when they were children than people with lower heart-rate variability. They are also more inconsistent in their responses to the personality inventory. This latter observation is consistent with previous findings that heart-rate variability is associated with emotional lability and a tendency to become disorganized (Epstein, 1979a). Both measures of heart-rate mean are significantly directly associated on Day 1 with Conflict over Hostility and Proneness to Anger and Aggression at the .01 level. Diastolic blood pressure for the aggregated data is significantly negatively correlated with the Guilford–Zimmerman scales Extroversion, Boldness, and Sociability. Subjects who had higher diastolic blood pressure than others over the 11 days described themselves in their daily reports as more introverted, submissive, and shy than others. Unlike the findings for Day 1 and the aggregated data, Day 11 produced no significant relationships with either heart-rate mean or magnitude of the skin conductance response. On the other hand, Day 11 produced more significant relationships with diastolic blood pressure than did either the data of Day 1 or the aggregated data. Diastolic blood pressure on Day 11 was significantly positively associated with Internal Consistency and Restraint and significantly negatively associated with Extroversion and Boldness. Thus one obtains a picture of individuals with high levels of diastolic blood pressure on Day 11 as more conscientious, restrained, introverted, and timorous than those with lower blood pressure. The results suggest the tentative hypothesis that diastolic blood pressure may be most useful as a personality measure after reactivity to testing has been well habituated.

The above findings on the relationship of psychophysiological variables and scores on personality inventories indicate that certain coherent findings tend to occur only on Day 1, others only on Day 11, and that the aggregated data reproduced most but not all of the significant relationships on the other days. The aggregated data produced no more significant findings than the data of Day 1. It remains to be seen if the results from the aggregated data will better withstand replication than the findings on the single days, which on theoretical grounds it would seem they might.

The Cross-Situational Stability of Behavior In order to investigate cross-situational consistency of behavior, five divergent situations were selected from the total series of 14 sessions. Included were Day 1, which, as the initial introduction to the laboratory, represented a situation of uncertainty and heightened reactivity; Day 11, which, as the last day in the habituation series, represented a situation that was boring and elicited low levels of reactivity; the "fear day," on which subjects had been threatened with electric shock; the "anger day," on which subjects had been told that they would not receive the money they had been promised; and the "happy day," on which they had been presented in advance with their full pay for the entire experiment plus a $10 bonus and were released from 2 of the 16 sessions that they had agreed to participate in. Clearly, these are phenomenologically highly different situations. Moreover, significant differences in the means of the variables among the different days operationally established that the situations were, in fact, different. Among the differences observed, ratings of emotions distinguished the fear, anger, and happy situations from each other in the expected direction: Physiological reactivity was significantly elevated on Day 1, reduced on Day 11, and elevated again on the days on which emotions were induced, and both stylus performance and reaction time exhibited significant practice effects over days.

Intercorrelations among the five situations with each other yield 10 correlations for each variable. As there are 21 variables, a total of 210 correlations are generated. By chance alone, 10 correlations can be expected to be significant at the .05 level. In the first column of Table 6.6, it can be seen that there are 118 correlations significant at the .05 level (2-tailed test). The findings, therefore, provide evidence that there is widespread cross-situational consistency and stability of behavior across the different situations and occasions. The evidence is even stronger than it appears because no allowance was made for limitations imposed by the temporal unreliability of the variables to the same situations on different occasions. It will be recalled that for many of the variables, 1-day samples of behavior produced modest temporal stability coefficients. Further consideration of Table 6.6 reveals that the degree of cross-situational stability varies markedly among the variables. About half of the 210 correlations are significantly greater than 0. The range of the 10 correlations produced by the interrelationships of the five situations among each other for each variable is relatively large, indicating that behavior across some situations exhibits far greater cross-situational consistency than behavior across other situations. Also, the means of the correlations for the

TABLE 6.6

Cross-Situational Consistency of Behavior: Intercorrelations of the Same Behavior in Five Different Situations[a]

			Mean correlation	
Variable[b]	Number of significant correlations	Range of correlations	Uncorrected for temporal reliability	Corrected for temporal reliability
Self-rated emotions				
Happy–Sad	6	.06–.69	.45	.87***
Kindly–Angry	4	.04–.75	.38	.48*
Secure–Threatened	2	−.13–.59	.31	.53*
Aroused–Tired	1	−.10–.47	.26	1.00***
Calm–Jittery	4	−.48–.59	.21	.51*
Enthused–Apathetic	3	.10–.69	.37	.90***
$\bar{X}$			.33	.72***
Positive affect	8	.40–.84	.60**	1.00***
Emotional reactivity	6	.04–.92	.53*	.69**
Physiological measures				
Systolic BP	8	.31–.72	.55*	1.00***
Diastolic BP	6	.14–.59	.45	.94***
Heart-rate mean (BL)	5	.22–.85	.48*	.70**
Heart-rate mean (R)	5	.25–.84	.54*	.87***
Heart-rate range (BL)	6	.00–.73	.47*	1.00***
Heart-rate range (R)	6	.32–.79	.57*	.84***
Nonspecific SCRs (BL)	6	.24–.66	.50*	.82***
Tonic skin conductance (BL)	9	.44–.95	.70**	1.00***
SCR magnitude (R)	6	.27–.77	.53*	.91***
$\bar{X}$			.53*	.95***
Behavioral measures				
Stylus hits	4	.06–.65	.42	.44
Stylus hits with noise	6	.21–.58	.43	.46
Reaction time	7	.22–.83	.55*	.79***
Dynamometer	10	.82–.96	.92***	.95***
$\bar{X}$			.58*	.65**

[a]$N = 18$.
[b]BL, baseline period; R, reactivity period.
 *$p < .05$.
 **$p < .01$.
 ***$p < .001$.

10 cross-situational correlations for each variable differ greatly among the measures, indicating that some variables are much more cross-situationally stable than other variables. Thus, there is evidence of considerable variation in cross-situational consistency as a function of both situations and modes of measurement in general. Excluding Positive Affect and Emotional Reactivity,

which are themselves aggregates over many items, the self-ratings of emotions (M = .33) are less broadly cross-situational than the psychophysiological measures (M = .53) and the psychomotor measures (M = .58). In fact, none of the means for the cross-situational correlation coefficients for individual emotions is significantly greater than 0. The observation, however, that the mean cross-situational coefficient for each of the two composite emotions is significant, suggests that it may be the low temporal reliability of the unaggregated emotions that prevents them from demonstrating significant broad cross-situational stability. This interpretation is confirmed when cross-situational correlations are corrected for temporal unreliability (see last column in Table 6.6). In order to make the corrections as conservative as possible, the relatively high temporal reliability coefficients for Days 10 versus 11 were chosen as the basis for the corrections for unreliability. The temporal reliability coefficients for Days 10 versus 11 were higher than the average single-day estimate by the Spearman–Brown formula from the correlations of the 5 odd versus the 5 even days.[2] When the mean cross-situational correlations are corrected for temporal reliability, all correlations are significant and many are very substantial. It may be concluded that a major reason for the low mean cross-situational stability coefficients that were obtained for the single items of self-rated emotions was the ceiling imposed by their low temporal reliability.

Having established that there is an impressive degree of average cross-situational stability in response to the different situations in the present study, it is important to keep in mind that the degree of cross-situational stability varies greatly among situations as well as among variables. Some situations are similar and others are not, and some that are similar when judged by performance on one set of measures are not similar when judged by performance on another set of measures, which indicates that situations are often multidimensional in their effects. As an example, let us consider the similarity of Day 1 to the "fear day" and the "happy day." Day 1 produced many significant correlations with the "fear day" and few with the "happy day." The mean correlation for the 6 self-rated emotions on Day 1 and on the "fear day" is .52, compared to .32 for Day 1 and the "happy day." The 9 psychophysiological variables on Day 1 produce a mean cross-situational correlation of .54 with the "fear day" and .37 with the "happy day." The 4 behavioral variables on Day 1 produce a mean cross-situational correlation

---

[2] A few of the estimated correlations in Table 6.6 are 1.00 because with a small N, correlations based on single observations are highly unstable, and, as a result, in a few cases the obtained cross-situational coefficients were actually higher than the coefficients of temporal stability, which can be attributed to sampling error. The instability of the correlations does not bias the overall findings, as it results in no more underestimates than overestimates, but it does mean that any *single* corrected correlation has a relatively high margin of error.

coefficient of .45 with the "fear day" and .34 with the "happy day." All told, 12 variables produce significant cross-situational correlations between Day 1 and the "fear day" and only 5 between Day 1 and the "happy day." That Day 1 is more similar to the situation in which subjects were threatened with receiving electric shocks than to the one in which they received a cash bonus and release from further obligations is understandable when it is considered that most subjects are apprehensive about a new situation in a laboratory in which they know they will be subjected to physiological recording and will be isolated in a sound-dampened room, and are uncertain of what else to expect.

In summary, it may be concluded that the above findings (1) provide evidence for impressive levels of cross-situational consistency of behavior even when behavior in a single situation is compared to behavior in a different single situation on another occasion; (2) indicate that cross-situational stability may be masked by low levels of temporal reliability; (3) indicate that some variables, or modes of measurement, exhibit greater cross-situational stability than others; and (4) indicate that as a result of the degree of differences between situations and variables, even when high levels of temporal reliability are established, some variables and situations will, and others will not, exhibit cross-situational consistency.

Discussion and Conclusions It was found that aggregating data over occasions was no less effective in raising temporal reliability coefficients for laboratory data than previously had been found for nonlaboratory data. Almost all variables in the laboratory study were raised to high levels of temporal reliability as the result of aggregation over occasions, with coefficients often exceeding .90. However, some variables, such as daily ratings of emotions, profited more from aggregation than others because they had lower reliabilities to begin with. For such variables, of course, aggregation is particularly important. It is not surprising, therefore, that many new relationships with other variables emerged when self-ratings of emotions were aggregated over occasions, as reliability is a prerequisite for validity. This occurred both for relationships between self-rated emotions and psychophysiological variables and for relationships between self-rated emotions and scores on personality inventories.

One is left with the puzzle of why aggregation over occasions increased the number of significant relationships of emotions with personality inventories and of psychophysiological variables with emotions, but not of psychophysiological variables with personality inventories. A possibility to consider is that aggregation over occasions is generally more effective for increasing the validity of self-ratings than of psychophysiological variables. To test this possibility, the relationship between self-rated emotions and psychophysiological variables was recomputed, once with only the emotions aggregated and once with only the psychophysiological reactions aggregated. The results indicated that the two kinds of aggregation were equally effective in producing significant relationships, but far less effective than when both kinds of aggregation were conducted simultaneously. The effectiveness of the double aggregation appears to be that it results in a convergence of both measures on the identical sample of situations. There is no such convergence when the physiological measures are correlated with the personality inventories, as the latter provide measures of broad dispositions that are not focused on a specific situation such as a psychophysiological laboratory. Expressed otherwise, although aggregation of the psychophysiological variables over occasions raised reliability, the aggregation did not extend the sample of situations beyond a particular kind of laboratory situation. Assuming this hypothesis is correct, it is still not clear why the psychophysiological variables are more restricted, in this respect, than the self-ratings of emotions, which did exhibit an increase in significant correlations with personality inventories when the data were aggregated over occasions. Possibly aggregation compounds the common method variance that is present in the self-ratings of emotions and is also present in the inventory responses, but is not present in the psychophysiological reactions.

Let us now turn to the implications of the findings of the study for the issue of cross-situational generality versus specificity of behavior. First, consider the exposure of subjects to the identical situation on the first 11 successive occasions. It was found that the "same" situation was changed, in effect, to a different situation simply as a result of the repeated exposure. This was indicated by significant mean changes in self-rated emotions, psychophysiological reactions, and psychomotor performance. At the same time, there was evidence that behavior to some extent is cross-situationally general because aggregating the data over occasions increased temporal reliability, indicating that the different occasions shared some common variance. Additional evidence for cross-situational generality was provided by the observation that in many cases aggregating over occasions increased relationships among different variables. It may be concluded that responses to the same situations on different occasions include both a unique and a general component of variance.

The most impressive evidence by far for cross-situational consistency of behavior was provided by comparisons under conditions in which differences in situations were experimentally manipulated. A considerable degree of cross-situational consistency was found for all categories of variables across a variety of situations that varied from being threatened with electric shocks to being generously rewarded. Not only were the situations phenomenologically very different, but also the differences were operationally verified by significant changes in the very same dependent variables on which cross-situational stability was examined. Despite the changes in means, subjects maintained their rank orders to a significant degree in many of the different situations. The degree to which such cross-situational stability was exhibited varied with situations and variables. For self-ratings of emotions, where temporal reliability was low, the coefficients of cross-situational stability of single items were nonsignificant, in the vicinity of .30, which replicates findings of those who have argued against the existence of cross-situational consistency in behavior. When reliability was increased by aggregating the data over items or when the data were corrected for unreliability, high levels of cross-situational consistency of behavior were widely exhibited. It is obviously important to take into account temporal stability before assessing cross-situational stability as the former is a limiting factor for the latter.

Because behavior is to some extent situationally specific and to some extent cross-situationally general, aggregation over occasions and/or situations has both advantages and disadvantages. Among its advantages, it can produce high levels of temporal reliability. Thus, it is possible to predict with high accuracy the average reaction to one set of stimuli or situations from a knowledge of the average reaction to a different sample of stimuli or situations from the same population. It is also possible to predict from personality inventories or rated behavior to samples of objective behavior, so long as the two measures are sufficiently reliable, and share the same range of generality, and are conceptually related. It is usually not possible to predict a single item of behavior from performance on a single different item of behavior for two reasons: (1) single items of behavior normally have low reliability; and (2) single items of behavior are usually narrow in scope and therefore not likely to have much conceptual overlap with another single item unless it is almost identical. Thus, even if responses to a single stimulus or situation are brought to a high level of reliability through aggregation over occasions, they will not necessarily predict responses to another equally reliable stimulus or situation. Obviously, reliability does not guarantee validity, and situations that on certain dimensions appear even superficially similar may be conceptually different in general or at least with respect to certain dimensions of interest. As indicated in the present findings, some behavior is much more cross-situationally stable than other behavior. Accordingly, no broad generalization can be made about the degree of cross-situational generality in behavior other than that it depends on the reliabilities of the two measures of behavior and their degree of conceptual overlap, which, in turn, is related to the correspondence of the levels of generality at which they are measured.

In addition to increasing temporal reliability and the range of generalization of the findings, aggregation over situations and/or occasions has another advantage: Namely, by reducing error of measurement, it yields correlations that are more representative of the true correlations. As a result the relationships are more replicable, and extrapolations, such as by the Spearman–Brown formula, are more accurate.

Unlike aggregating over items, which may decrease rather than increase reliability unless standard psychometric procedures are used to select the items, aggregating over occasions in very instance in which we have employed it has increased reliability. In this respect, it is noteworthy that in the present study, when items on a single occasion were aggregated into an overall measure of affect, the gain in reliability was less than when the single items were aggregated over a relatively small number of occasions. The major limitation that was observed when data were aggregated over occasions was that aggregation masked order effects. For certain purposes, it is therefore important to examine the contribution of the different occasions before aggregating over all occasions. It is also possible that certain kinds of behavior, such as when responses in a series are reactive to each other, will not exhibit a gain in reliability, let alone validity, when aggregated over occasions.

The Relative Efficacy of Aggregating over Judges, Items, and Occasions

A little-appreciated fact is that, according to the Spearman–Brown formula, it is possible, by sufficient aggregation, to obtain any level of reliability one wishes under many circumstances, so long as one is dealing with behavior that is not completely random. Lest one become too sanguine over the prospect of routinely obtaining very high reliability coefficients, it should be noted that to obtain a high reliability coefficient for a particular variable, it may be necessary to conduct an unreasonably large amount of aggregation. Fortunately, however, there are many variables that can be brought to relatively high levels of reliability with a moderate degree of aggregation (see Epstein, 1979a, 1980b). The Spearman–Brown formula was developed for the purpose of estimating the increase in reliability that occurs when a test is lengthened. So long as the sample of items that is added consists of independent items that are representative of the population of items from which the original sample was drawn and the original estimate of reliability is accurate, predictions from the Spearman–Brown formula should be reasonably accurate.

The Spearman–Brown formula is not only useful in predicting the effect on reliability of length of a test, but it can be applied to the estimation of the effect on reliability of any form of redundancy. The effect on reliability of increasing the number of occasions on which observations are made, the number of judges that rate the behavior, and the number of behavioral responses that are combined into a single score are all predicted by the same formula. Theoretically, the different kinds of aggregation should all result in identical increases in reliability for the same amount of aggregation. The only difference in the effect of different kinds of aggregation should be on validity. Aggregating over judges eliminates the bias of individual judges, aggregating over occasions eliminates the unrepresentativeness of particular occasions, and aggregating over situations or items of behavior eliminates the unique contribution of particular situations or items of behavior. Empirical results do not, however, always conform to theoretical expectations. It is often not possible to meet all the assumptions that are involved. For example, when aggregating over occasions, one occasion may not be equivalent to another because of important order effects, as observed in the previous study. This raises the issue of how much common failures to meet assumptions reduces the increase in reliability and validity that might otherwise be expected as a result of aggregation. Such issues can only be resolved by empirical investigation. Thus, it is important to determine what the actual effects of different kinds of aggregation are both in laboratory and in field studies, in which items of behavior cannot be selected, discarded, and combined as conveniently as in paper-and-pencil tests.

The next study to be presented was undertaken to compare the effects on temporal reliability and validity of aggregating data over judges, items, and occasions. Of course, the results from any one study are not necessarily general. It is likely that with different situations, different items of behavior, and different judges, different results would be obtained. Yet, aggregation is an extremely important experimental technique that has not received the systematic exploration it warrants (see Epstein, 1980b), and one must begin somewhere. Hopefully, the experiment that follows will stimulate others to conduct similar studies until a body of information is accumulated from which it can be determined what the effects of different kinds of aggregation are on temporal reliability, on validity, and on the replicability of findings.

There are two substantive issues of concern in the study reported next. One is concerned with the stability and correlates of individual differences in the perception of an instructor's personality. The other is concerned with the actual stability of the instructor's personality profile. For present purposes, however, the substantive issues are of minor concern. Our major concern will be with the relative influence of different kinds of aggregation on reliability and validity. Based on previous findings and theoretical considerations, it can reasonably be anticipated that aggregation over judges, occasions, and items will all increase temporal reliability coefficients. What is not evident is what their relative contributions will be. Also, it is not clear what effect the different kinds of aggregation will have upon validity, as indicated by the relationships of ratings of the instructor with other variables. In this study it was assumed that there is a relationship between personality and perception of others. It follows, therefore, that to the extent that aggregation of a particular kind enhances validity, it should uncover relationships between perception and personality that were not evident with unaggregated data.

The procedure consisted of having students in a large personality class rate their instructor at each of 13 successive class meetings on 10 personality attributes extracted from the *Jackson Personality Inventory Manual* (1976). It was originally planned to administer the Jackson Personal Preference Schedule at the end of the study, but because it could not be obtained in time, other personality tests were substituted. The Jackson dimensions were selected because they describe Murray needs, or motives, and motives are often considered to be what is most apt to be projected. According to the Freudien model of defensive projection, negative motives that are denied in oneself tend to be attributed to others. To the extent that this is true, there should be a negative relationship between self-ratings and ratings of the instructor on negative motives. According to the concept of assimilative projection, however, people tend to view others in the same way as they view themselves, which suggests a positive relationship between self-ratings and ratings of the instructor for both positive and negative motives.

Each motive was identified by a label, a brief description, and three descriptive adjectives. For example, Aggression was defined as follows: "Enjoys argument; easily annoyed; seeks to get even with people whom he perceives as having harmed him. Descriptive adjectives: Argumentative, Attacking, Antagonistic." The nine other motives were Abasement, Achievement, Affiliation, Defendance, Dominance, Endurance, Impulsivity, Nurturance, and Intellectual Curiosity. Five of the scales identify negative, and five positive attributes, which was confirmed by their intercorrelations and factor analysis. Eight of the scales that received loadings of greater than .30 on a general factor of favorableness were combined into a composite score called Composite Approval. Because a number of subjects missed one or more sessions or turned in forms with missing items or careless errors, a considerable loss of subjects would have occurred if only those who completed all forms without error on all 13 occasions were retained. To maximize sample size, subjects were included if they completed at least 8 forms without error, which resulted in a sample of 71 subjects. For each subject, the data consisted of responses to the first 8 forms filled out without errors or omissions.

Ratings were made in the last 5 minutes of each class meeting. Five-point graphic rating scales were used, with 1 identified as "not at all," 3 as "moderate," and 5 as "very much." Ratings were made for the attributes the instructor exhibited at each class meeting. On the last session, ratings were also made of the instructor's personality "in general," based on an overall impression gained of him over the course of the semester. Volunteers for extra credit completed at home personality inventories consisting of the AHD scales and the MFP scales. The AHD scales (Anxiety–Hostility–Depression) are an expanded version of the A–H scales described in the Section "A Study of Aggregation in the Laboratory." They included three scales of hostility, three scales of anxiety, and scales of Happiness, Sadness, and Happiness minus Sadness. The MFP scales, described in the same section, provide information on reported relationships during childhood with mother, father, and peer figures. Of the 71 subjects who completed the rating sessions satisfactorily, 56 completed the personality inventories.

The Reliability of Individual Differences in Perception of the Instructor There are two ways of aggregating the data on individual differences in the perception of the instructor. The data can be aggregated over occasions and over items. Aggregation cannot be conducted over subjects because this would eliminate the very variable, individual differences, that is the object of investigation. Moreover, such aggregation would not increase the reliability of individual differences in perception, as it would decrease the differences among as well as within the responses of the composite subjects. Aggregation over judges was examined in the second part of the study, which was concerned with the stability of the instructor's personality profile.

Aggregation over items was conducted as follows. A factor analysis was first done to determine whether a group of the items on which the instructor was rated measured a common factor. It was found that there was a highly general factor on which eight of the items received loadings of greater than .30. These eight items were divided, insofar as possible, into matching tests of different lengths based on their factor loadings, means, and standard deviations. More specifically, eight pairs of matching 4-item tests, eight pairs of matching 2-item tests, and eight pairs of 1-item tests were constructed. The eight correlations for a particular test length were averaged to provide the best estimate of the reliability for a particular degree of aggregation over items. It was necessary to obtain the mean of a sample of reliability coefficients, as reliability coefficients derived from data obtained in a few sessions were found to be highly unstable.

Aggregation over items was done separately within each of the levels of aggregation over occasions. First, ratings on Day 1 were correlated with ratings on Day 2; next, ratings averaged over Days 1 and 3 were correlated with ratings averaged over Days 2 and 4; and finally, ratings averaged over Days 1, 3, 5, and 7 were correlated with ratings averaged over Days 2, 4, 6, and 8. This was done separately for 1-item tests, 2-item tests, and 4-item tests.

Figure 6.4 compares the effect of aggregating over items with the effect of

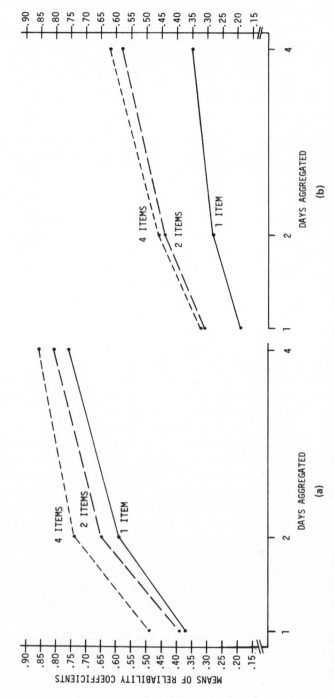

Figure 6.4 Stability coefficients as a function of aggregation over days and items. The values plotted are the means of a sample of correlations. (a), same-item correlations; (b), cross-item correlations.

aggregating over days on temporal reliability coefficients. The reliability co-efficients shown in (a) are for the same items presented on different occasions, which corresponds to test–retest reliability. The correlations indicate how well one can predict performance on one item or set of items from observations of performance on the identical item or set of items on a different occasion. It can be seen that, although the prediction is significantly better than chance (.01 level), performance on one item on a single occasion is not a good predictor of performance on the same item on another occasion ($r = .37$). As responses to the item are aggregated over an increasing number of occasions, predictability increases. The correlation of responses to one item aggregated over 4 days with responses to the same item aggregated over 4 other days is .76. Aggregation of items also increases temporal reliability. A composite of responses to 4 items on one occasion correlates with responses to the same composite of items on another occasion .50, which is a considerable improvement over the correlation of .37 for a single item. When both kinds of aggregation are performed simultaneously, a stability coefficient of .86 is obtained for 4 items aggregated over 4 days. Thus, although relatively little stability in behavior is observed when single items of behavior are examined on single occasions, there is impressive evidence for stability when behavior is aggregated over several items and occasions.

Figure 6.4, (b), presents cross-item stability coefficients. The issue of concern here is with predicting performance on one item or set of items from performance on a different item or set of items on a different occasion. In order to compare the effect of aggregation on test–retest stability (a) with cross-item consistency (b), the procedure for aggregation was conducted in a manner that treated items and occasions in a completely corresponding manner.

The mean cross-item consistency coefficient for a single item on a single occasion is .19 which, unlike the temporal stability coefficient for a single item on a single occasion, is not significantly different from 0. However, when the ratings are aggregated over either days or items, highly significant cross-item consistency coefficients emerge. The correlation of a composite of 4 items aggregated over 4 days with a composite of 4 different items aggregated over 4 different days is .62.

It should be noted that the above findings are highly relevant for the issue of cross-situational consistency in behavior because the identical issues are involved. Given that temporal stability coefficients for a single item of behavior are usually low, often in the vicinity of .30, it follows that cross-item and cross-situational consistency coefficients obtained on different occasions must be yet lower. With this consideration in mind, it is interesting to determine what the cross-item stability coefficients would be if they were corrected for temporal unreliability. If the .19 cross-item consistency coefficient for a single item is adjusted for temporal unreliability, as indicated by the corresponding temporal reliability coefficient of .37, the cross-item consistency coefficient rises to .51. It may be concluded that the reason for the low and statistically nonsignificant cross-situational consistency coefficient for a single item in Figure 6.4 is that it is limited by low temporal reliability. A similar correction of the cross-situational reliability coefficient of .62 obtained for data aggregated over 4 items and 4 days increases the coefficient to .72, indicating a fairly substantial degree of cross-item consistency.

The Temporal Stability of the Instructor's Profile The stability of the instructor's profile was examined by obtaining correlations across the dimensions on which he was rated. When this is done without adjustment, the correlations are spuriously high because certain variables are uniformly given high ratings and others low ratings simply because of judgment of their common incidence in human beings. Accordingly, it was necessary to adjust the profiles by subtracting from them the mean profile for male university professors in general. The personality profile that will be reported reflects the degree to which the instructor is perceived to differ from the average male professor.

The data on the stability of the instructor's profile can be aggregated over raters and occasions, but not, of course, over items, as it is the differences among items that is necessary to establish the personality profile. Odd–even correlations were obtained for Day 1 versus 2, for the mean of Days 1 and 3 versus the mean of Days 2 and 4, and for the mean of Days 1, 3, 5, and 7 versus the mean of Days 2, 4, 6, and 8. Within each level of aggregation over days, three levels of aggregation over judges were obtained. As there is considerable variation among different pairs of judges, a large sample of pairs of judges was obtained, and the mean correlation was taken as the best representation of the true correlation. To make the procedure as similar as possible to that for aggregation over occasions, the 72 subjects were arranged in 9 groups of 8 subjects each, and within each group of 8 subjects coefficients of profile stability were obtained for the ratings of the first student versus the second student, the mean of the first and third students versus the mean of the second and fourth students, and the mean of the first, third, fifth, and seventh students versus the mean of the second, fourth, sixth, and eighth students. The correlations at each level of aggregation were then averaged for the 9 groups of subjects.

Figure 6.5, (a) presents the mean stability coefficients for the instructor's profile as a function of aggregation over occasions and raters for the *same* raters on different occasions. The stability coefficients indicate the degree to which the profile is stable over occasions when ratings are made by the same judges. It can be seen that the mean stability coefficient for single raters on two different days is .49. When the ratings of a single judge are averaged over

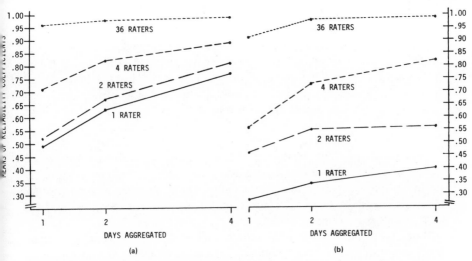

Figure 6.5 Stability coefficients of instructor's profile as a function of aggregation over raters and days. (a), degree of agreement of the same raters on different occasions; (b), degree of agreement between different raters on different occasions.

4 days and compared to the same judge's ratings averaged over 4 other days, the stability coefficient rises to .77. Thus, increasing the number of occasions on which ratings are aggregated, while holding constant the number of raters, produces a considerable increase in the stability of the instructor's perceived personality profile. Likewise, increasing the number of raters, while holding constant the number of occasions aggregated, produces a considerable increase in the stability of the instructor's perceived personality profile. The personality profile attributed to the instructor by four raters on a single day correlates with the profile attributed to the instructor by the same four raters on a different day, .70, which is considerably greater than the .49 obtained for a single rater on a single day. When the data are aggregated over four raters and four occasions, the stability coefficient rises to .89. Thus, the personality profile obtained for the instructor when based on the average of four raters and four occasions is highly similar to the personality profile obtained for the instructor by the same four raters on four other occasions. When the ratings are averaged over 36 raters, extremely high stability coefficients are obtained whether or not the data are aggregated over occasions. Apparently, although the degree of consistency of individual subjects in rating the instructor is only modest, the degree of consistency of a large group of subjects over occasions is very substantial even when only a single rating per subject is obtained, and almost perfect ($r = .99$) when the data are averaged over four ratings per subject.

Figure 6.5(b) presents the stability coefficients of the instructor's profile when the comparison is between *different* judges. These stability coefficients are of particular interest because they reveal the degree to which the instructor's profile is perceived to be stable independent of the rating habits or biases of a particular sample of judges. That is, for high stability coefficients to be obtained, it is necessary for stability to reside in the instructor's perceived profile and not in the memories or biases of a particular sample of judges. It can be seen in (b) that when a sufficient sample of judges is employed, there is a very high degree of agreement among the *different* groups of judges. The average profile attributed to the instructor by 36 judges who observed him on one occasion correlates .91 with the personality profile attributed to him by 36 other judges who observed him on another occasion. The stability coefficient rises to .99 when the data are averaged over four ratings per judge.

When the data for single judges are examined, there is only weak evidence for stability of the instructor's profile. The personality profile attributed to the instructor by a single judge on a single occasion correlates only .28 with the personality profile attributed to the instructor by another judge on another occasion, a figure which is not significantly different from 0. It is noteworthy that stability coefficients rise much more rapidly as a function of an increase in the number of raters than as a function of an increase in the number of occasions on which the ratings are performed. An increase from one to four occasions for a single rater raises the stability coefficient from .28 to .40, whereas an increase from one rater to four raters on a single occasion raises the stability coefficient from .28 to .61. Thus, in order to obtain an accurate estimate of an individual's personality profile, it appears to be particularly important to eliminate the biases of individual raters. This suggests that the personality characteristics of raters may exert a strong influence on how they rate others, a topic to which we turn next.

Aggregation and Validity: The Relationship between the Personality Characteristics of the Judges and Their Perceptions of the Instructor To the extent that aggregation over occasions increases reliability, it should contribute to an increase in validity and enhance whatever relationships exist between the personalities of the judges and their perceptions of the instructor.

To examine the effects of aggregation, results are examined for ratings on Day 1, on Day 8, on the data aggregated over 8 days, and on the general rating made at the end of the observation period. Before presenting the results that are relevant to validity, it will be helpful to examine the reliability coefficients for the entire sample of 72 subjects as a function of amount of aggregation over occasions. This information is presented in Table 6.7. The general rating is not included, as it was obtained only once, at the end of the

TABLE 6.7

Stability Coefficients for Ratings of Instructor

Instructor variable	Day 1 vs. Day 2	Day 7 vs. Day 8	4 odd vs. 4 even days	Days 1–8 (est.)
Abasement	.49	.48	.84	.91
Achievement	.38	.41	.75	.86
Affiliation	.55	.50	.80	.89
Aggression	.28	.44	.73	.84
Defendance	.24	.47	.77	.87
Dominance	.42	.54	.82	.90
Endurance	.44	.41	.75	.86
Impulsivity	.31	.53	.73	.84
Nurturance	.26	.38	.73	.84
Intellectual Curiosity	.51	.30	.75	.86
Mean	.39	.45	.77	.87
Composite approval	.59	.67	.90	.95

$^a N = 72$. .23–.29, $p < .05$; .30–.37, $p < .01$; .38–.95, $p < .001$.

study. It can be seen in Table 6.7 that the reliability coefficients for Day 1 versus Day 2 for single dimensions vary between .24 and .51, that the mean of the reliability coefficients is .39, and that a composite approval score based on all of the items is .59, indicating a considerable improvement in reliability as a result of aggregating over items. The reliability coefficients for Day 7 versus Day 8 are slightly higher than for those on Day 1 versus Day 2, but not uniformly so. The reliability coefficients for the data aggregated over all 8 days are very high for all single dimensions, ranging between .84 and .91, with a mean reliability of .87. The reliability coefficient for the composite scale aggregated over 8 days is .95. On the basis of these findings, it can be anticipated that aggregation should increase the number of significant relationships that are found when ratings of the instructor are correlated with other variables.

Table 6.8 presents the correlations of self-ratings with ratings of the instructor on Days 1 and 8, on an 8-day sample, and for the general ratings made on a single occasion at the end of the observation period. As there are a large number of relationships, the acceptance level for statistical significance was set at the .01 level. Only those relationships are listed in Table 6.8 for which there is at least one significant relationship among the four conditions. The correlation of 11 self-ratings with 11 ratings of the instructor generates 121 correlations for each of the four conditions. Thus, within each condition in Table 6.8, one or two correlations can be expected to be significant at the .01 level by chance. Day 1 produces 15 significant correlations, Day 8 produces 20 significant correlations, the aggregated data 33 significant correlations, and the general rating at the end of the study 38 significant correlations. In all cases, the results are well beyond what would be expected by chance. In evaluating the effect of aggregation, it should be recognized that Day 8 and the general ratings are themselves influenced by aggregation. On Day 8, although subjects were instructed to attempt to make ratings of the instructor independent of their previous impressions, it can be assumed that they can only maintain independence to a limited degree. Evidence in support of this assumption consists of much larger correlations between the aggregated data and the data of Day 8 than between the aggregated data and the data of Day 1. The single general rating, because it is based on the subjects' impressions of the instructor following the entire observation peri-

TABLE 6.8

Correlations of Self-Ratings with Ratings of Instructor on Single and Aggregated Days[a]

Self-rating	Instructor rating	Day 1	Day 8	Days 1–8	Single general rating
Abasement	Abasement	.08	.08	.35**	.41***
	Aggression	.17	.41***	.31**	.28
	Defendance	.22	.17	.23	.47***
	Dominance	.40***	.14	.35**	.36**
	Impulsivity	.03	.25	.41***	.26
	Composite Approval	−.32**	−.28	−.31**	−.37**
Achievement	Impulsivity	.07	.24	.21	.35**
Aggression	Achievement	−.13	−.19	−.20	.37**
	Affiliation	−.32**	−.38***	−.48***	−.35**
	Aggression	.38***	.54***	.55***	.60***
	Defendance	.33**	.25	.45***	.31**
	Dominance	.45***	.14	.37**	.34**
	Endurance	−.09	−.21	−.20	−.35**
	Impulsivity	.27	.61***	.66***	.59***
	Nurturance	−.26	−.32**	−.56***	−.31**
	Intellectual Curiosity	−.15	−.21	−.31**	−.40***
	Composite Approval	−.52***	−.52***	−.61***	−.64***
Defendance	Defendance	.36**	.12	.21	.26
Dominance	Abasement	.09	.04	.31**	.40**
	Aggression	.15	.37**	.29	.34**
	Dominance	.38***	.16	.37**	.28
	Endurance	−.01	−.28	−.04	−.38***
	Impulsivity	.27	.34**	.47***	.32**
	Composite Approval	−.28	−.40***	−.36**	−.45***

(continued)

TABLE 6.8 *Continued*

Self-rating	Instructor rating	Day 1	Day 8	Days 1-8	Single general rating
Impulsivity	Abasement	-.07	.21	.26	.34**
	Affiliation	-.28	-.20	-.34**	-.29
	Aggression	-.35**	.26	.36**	.39***
	Dominance	.22	.17	.36**	.37**
	Impulsivity	.30**	.21	.31**	.44***
	Composite Approval	-.31**	-.30**	-.36**	-.46***
Nurturance	Aggression	-.13	-.39***	-.32**	-.34**
	Defendance	-.17	-.38***	-.38***	-.38***
	Endurance	.13	.23	.36**	.30**
	Composite Approval	.29	.42***	.44***	.34**
Intellectual Curiosity	Defendance	-.13	-.43***	-.25	-.12
	Impulsivity	-.11	-.23	-.23	-.38***
	Intellectual Curiosity	.01	.27	.09	.37**
	Composite Approval	.08	.34**	.17	.28
Self-Composite	Abasement	-.02	-.10	-.37**	-.40***
	Affiliation	.25	.30**	.33**	.15
	Aggression	-.27	-.56***	-.48***	-.53***
	Defendance	-.41***	-.41***	-.49***	-.48***
	Dominance	-.46***	-.26	-.43***	-.38***
	Impulsivity	-.13	-.41***	-.50***	-.40***
	Intellectual curiosity	.11	.18	.27	.34**
	Composite Approval	.45***	.51***	.54***	.57***

[a]N = 72. Only variables that had at least one significant correlation at the .01 level among the 4 conditions are included.

**p < .01.

***p < .001.

od, can be assumed to involve an intuitive averaging. Evidence to support this assumption is that the general ratings correlate much more strongly with the aggregated data than with the ratings on Day 8, although the general ratings and the ratings on Day 8 were made on the same day. It is noteworthy that the general ratings at the end of the observation period do as well in providing evidence for validity as the more laborious procedure of aggregating observations over many occasions. However, the issue is somewhat more complicated than is immediately apparent, and we shall return to it later.

For now, let us consider the least ambiguous comparison for establishing the effect of aggregation, namely the comparison between the findings on Day 1 and the aggregated data. There are no significant correlations on Day 1 that do not also appear for the aggregated data, and there are 18 significant correlations for the aggregated data that do not appear on Day 1. Thus, about two-thirds of the correlations detected at a statistically significant level by the aggregated data would not have been detected had observation been restricted to a single day. As an example of the distortions in interpretation that would have occurred if the data had been obtained from only a single day of observation, let us examine the findings on Abasement. Abasement was defined as "shows a high degree of humility, accepts blame and criticism even when not deserved. Self-blaming; self-disapproving; self-critical." When self-ratings of Abasement were correlated with ratings of the professor on Day 1, only two significant relationships were found: one with Dominance and one with Composite Approval. Because the latter is smaller than the former, it may be assumed to reflect largely its influence. Thus, one would conclude from the findings on Day 1 that the ratings of abasement provide support only for the occurrence of complementary projection—the perception of others in a complementary role to perception of oneself. On the other hand, when the correlations for the aggregated ratings of the instructor are examined, five variables on which the instructor was rated are observed to be significantly correlated with self-rated Abasement: namely, Abasement, Aggression, Dominance, Impulsivity, and Composite Approval. Thus, in addition to providing evidence for complementary projection, the aggregated data provide evidence for assimilative projection, as indicated by a positive correlation between self-rated abasement and ratings of the instructor on abasement. In addition, there is evidence that self-abasement is associated with a broad tendency to view the instructor unfavorably, as indicated by four significant direct relationships with unfavorable attributes on individual items in addition to the negative correlation with the composite favorableness score. Moreover, the ratings of the instructor on Day 1 provide no significant relationships between ratings of the self on any favorable attribute and ratings of the instructor. Thus, if only the data of Day 1 had been available, they would have led to the conclusion that only negative attributes are projected. The aggregated data, on the other hand, reveal that self-ratings of Nurturance are significantly negatively associated with ratings of the instructor on Aggression and Defendance, and significantly positively associated with ratings of the instructor on Endurance and Composite Approval. It may be concluded that, had the ratings of the instructor been restricted to a single day of observation, a limited and distorted picture would have been obtained of the relationship between self-perception and perception of the instructor.

Examination of the Composite Approval Score reveals that aggregation over items compensates somewhat for the low reliabilities that are obtained when data are based on a single day of observations. The correlation of the Self-Composite Approval rating and the Composite Approval rating of the instructor on Day 1 was significant at the .001 level ($r = .45$) and is only modestly increased by aggregation over days ($r = .54$). However, as will be indicated later, the global measure loses the more differentiated information that is provided by the individual dimensions.

Table 6.9 presents the correlations between the ratings of the instructor and the raters' scores on the personality inventories. As in the previous case, only relationships that produced at least one significant correlation at the .01 level among the four conditions in Table 6.9 are included. The 10 scales for rating the instructor plus the single composite score and the 14 scores on the personality inventories generate 154 correlations within each of the four conditions. Thus, about one or two significant correlations at the .01 level

TABLE 6.9

Correlations of Instructor Ratings with Scores on the AHD and MFP Personality Inventory Scales[a]

Scale	Instructor rating	Day 1	Day 8	Days 1–8	Single general rating
AHD					
Conflict over Hos-	Abasement	.37**	.28	.54***	.62***
tility	Impulsivity	.24	.34	.44***	.33
	Composite Approval	−.24	−.31	−.35**	−.34
Prone to Anger &	Abasement	.23	.28	.47***	.54***
Aggression	Impulsivity	.30	.21	.44***	.41**
	Composite Approval	−.33	−.24	−.38**	−.45***
Hostility Avoid-	Intellectual Curiosity	.08	.37**	.15	.18
ance					
Cognitive Anxiety	Defendance	.19	.01	.23	.36**
Autonomic	Abasement	.29	.33	.46***	.47***
Arousal					
Muscle Tension	Abasement	.23	.36**	.49***	.43**
Total Anxiety	Abasement	.31	.28	.50***	.48***
Happiness	Abasement	−.32	−.23	−.37**	−.23
Sadness	Abasement	.21	.09	.38**	.33
Happiness–Sad-	Abasement	−.30	−.18	−.42**	−.31
ness					
MFP					
Mother Acceptance	Abasement	−.14	−.21	−.30	−.39**
Father Acceptance	Endurance	.31	.12	.41**	.16
Peer Acceptance	Abasement	−.19	−.35**	−.42**	−.38**

[a] $N = 52$. Only variables that had at least one significant correlation at the .01 level among the 4 conditions are included.
** $p < .01$.
*** $p < .001$.

can be expected by chance within each condition. In Table 6.9, it can be seen that there is one significant correlation on Day 1, 3 on Day 8, 14 on the aggregated days, and 10 for the general ratings. The results for Day 1 and Day 8, but not for the aggregated data and the general ratings, are within chance expectancy.

Examination of the results for the aggregated data reveals that many of the significant correlations are between inventory scores and ratings of the instructor on Abasement. Why ratings of the instructor on Abasement should produce so many significant relationships is not evident. Although Abasement had the highest reliability coefficient among the individual dimensions for the aggregated data (see Table 6.8), the difference in reliability was not sufficient to account for the results. Mean rating of the instructor on Abasement was relatively low, but the instructor received yet lower ratings on Aggression and Impulsivity. Abasement had a relatively large standard deviation for the aggregated data, revealing marked individual differences in assessing the instructor on that variable, but Dominance had a larger standard deviation, and Nurturance had an equally large standard deviation. None of these considerations, by themselves, can account for the results on Abasement, although a combination of them might.

Examination of the results for the aggregated data reveals that almost all the scales from the AHD scales that are indicative of disturbance, whether in the form of anxiety, hostility, or sadness, are directly associated with rating the instructor unfavorably and are inversely associated with rating him favorably. The results cannot readily be explained away by a general rating style, or halo effect, because a scale of defensiveness produced no significant relationships, and therefore does not appear in the table, and the Composite Approval Score, which measures overall favorableness of the ratings of the instructor, produces smaller correlations than many of the individual dimensions. The degree to which the instructor is rated high on Abasement is particularly strongly associated with the raters' scores on the following personality scales: Conflict over Hostility, Proneness to Anger and Aggression, Autonomic Arousal, Muscle Tension, and Total Anxiety. Of particular interest, two scores on the MFP scale are significantly associated with ratings of the instructor. Father Acceptance is positively associated with rating the instructor high on Endurance, and Peer Acceptance is positively associated with rating the instructor low on Abasement.

The overall results suggest that, in addition to some evidence for assimilative and complementary projection, a major source of individual differences in how people perceive others is that they respond "true to form." That is, if they are hostile people, they view others in a derogatory manner; if they are nurturant people, they view others in a benevolent way. In this respect, perception is no different from other kinds of behavior.

Overall Conclusions The above study was undertaken to examine the effects of aggregation over occasions, items, and judges on reliability and validity. All forms of aggregation increased temporal reliability. Aggregation over occasions raised reliability coefficients to a slightly greater extent than aggregation over items. Although there was no evidence of cross-item consistency when single items were examined on single occasions, there was widespread evidence of cross-item stability when items were aggregated into composite scores or were aggregated over occasions.

There are at least two reasons why single items of behavior exhibit low cross-item and cross-situational consistency. One is that single items of behavior tend to have low temporal reliability. The other is that single items are often narrow in scope, and therefore exhibit a limited degree of conceptual overlap with other single items that are not near-synonyms. Accordingly, in order to demonstrate stable cross-item or cross-situational consistencies, it is usually necessary to increase both temporal reliability and conceptual overlap by appropriate aggregation over items, situations, and occasions. It was observed that when the data were aggregated over occasions and items, high coefficients of cross-item consistency were obtained. If was further demonstrated that the aggregated data provided evidence of broad, cross-item response dispositions indicated by coherent relationships with personality inventories. Not surprisingly, although aggregation over items enhanced certain relationship, it obscured others. This could logically be anticipated from the consideration that behavior is both specific and general, and, as a result, certain relationships can best be detected with broad-band and others with narrow-band techniques.

A finding of considerable interest was that a single general rating made at the end of a period of multiple observations was about as valid as aggregating the individual ratings. This suggests that observers engage in an intuitive aggregation over occasions, which is of considerable practical interest because it takes far less effort to collect a single rating at the end of a period of observation than to obtain ratings throughout the period. However, it should be noted that on the basis of the present findings it is not possible to determine whether a single general rating at the end of the study would have been as effective if repeated ratings had not been made earlier. The repeated ratings provided practice in the use of the scales and helped to focus attention on the variables to be rated. As findings by others have demonstrated, substantial relationships have been demonstrated between objective criteria and ratings of behavior following an adequate observation period (see review in Mischel, 1981). It is thus likely that a period of adequate observation is more important than the actual number of ratings made during that period. In a particularly interesting study (Moskowitz & Schwarz, 1982), the contribution of aggregating over raters and over observation periods was separately assessed. Both produced marked increases in reliability and validity. There was greater correspondence between raters than between occasions, with generalizability coefficients of .67 for 4 observation periods and .91 for 4 raters for the measure of dominance and a comparable difference for the measure of Depeﬧdency. However, validity, as judged by the relationship of the ratings to objective behavioral frequency counts, was increased more by adding observation periods than by adding raters. It is important in this respect to consider that the raters, unlike those in the study on the ratings of the university professor, were given careful descriptions of specific kinds of behavior to judge and had an opportunity to observe the children they rated in a variety of situations. Not surprisingly, depending on the particular conditions in a study, the contribution of aggregating over raters may be more or less than the contribution of aggregating over observation periods. Nevertheless, it is noteworthy that in both studies aggregation made a critical difference in detecting important relationships.

The Virtues and Limitations of Aggregation

Previous studies in the series (Epstein, 1977, 1979a) demonstrated the value of aggregation over situations and occasions for increasing temporal reliability and validity for a variety of data, including self-ratings, ratings by others, the the objective recording of real-life events. The present findings extend the results to laboratory data. Given its widespread effectiveness in increasing reliability and validity, aggregation deserves to be taken more seriously than it has been up to now as a broadly applicable and highly effective research technique.

It is instructive in this respect, to compare the effects of experimental control and aggregation as experimental techniques. In the typical laboratory experiment, an attempt is made to control all incidental sources of variance that can affect the results. Given adequate control of incidental effects, whatever results are found are then assumed to be attributable to the experimental variables that were manipulated. Because of the high degree of control that is exerted on some variables and the manipulation of other variables, experiments are necessarily artificial. As Berkowitz and Donnerstein (1982) have noted in defending the experiment against those who believe that research should be more ecologically representative, the purpose of an experiment is not to reproduce real-life behavior but to establish causal relationships. Although Berkowitz and Donnerstein are correct on that issue, what they and many other experimentalists fail to realize is that the manner in which laboratory experiments are typically conducted makes it highly unlikely that the results obtained provide meaningful levels of generalization that are replicable. The reason for this is that, typically, the events that are studied have little significance to the subjects in the experiment; that is, the experimental effects are low in potency, and the findings are therefore statistically significant only because of the high degree of experimental control that was exerted, which produced a very small error term. As a consequence, trivial results on an absolute basis become highly statistically significant. The difficulty with such an approach is that any incidental effects that were not controlled can determine the outcome of the study. Given the high degree of situational specificity characteristic of human behavior, it is likely that the results of many experiments are determined by nonrandom effects that the experimenter was unable to control or did not believe necessary to control. Included are such variables as the sex and temperament of the experimenter, the period in the semester during which a study at a university was conducted, the exposure to outside influences immediately before a particular session, and perhaps even the weather (see Epstein, 1980b for a more thorough discussion of this issue).

A second weakness with the laboratory experiment as normally conducted is that, in the absence of examining more than one stimulus or situation, it is impossible to establish the generality of the findings. For some strange reason, experimentalists, although they recognize that it is necessary to employ a sample of subjects in order to make generalizations about people fail to realize that the same issue of generalization holds with respect to stimuli. Thus, a critical weakness in most experiments is not that they have failed to obtain ecologically representative samples of stimuli or situations, but that they have failed to sample stimuli or situations at all.

The charge that laboratory experiments, as typically conducted, are often not replicable may seem incredible. After all, how likely is it that such a state of affairs could exist without having been widely detected? I believe it has not been detected because psychologists have been misled by their interpretation of statistical procedures into believing that they can establish the replicability of their findings without having to replicate. After all, if a finding is significant at the .01 level, does it not mean that if the study were replicated 100 times, on no more than one occasion would a finding as great as that obtained occur by chance? The answer is that the probabilities are correct only if the study can be reproduced in all essential features, which it cannot be, as factors that the experimenter considers incidental may not be, or may otherwise not be controllable. It is ironic that physical scientists demand replication before accepting a finding, whereas psychologists, with their less exact science, assume that their use of statistics obviates the need for replication.

Aggregation over stimuli, situations, or occasions, unlike experimental control, increases the ratio of experimental to error variance, not by imposing restrictions on the experimental procedure but by averaging out the effects of incidental relative to experimental variance in the absence of additional restraint. The situation is well illustrated by the measurement of evoked cortical potentials. The reaction of the brain to a single stimulus is undetectable because the noise of measurement is considerably greater than the effect of the stimulus. Rather than attempting to control all the incidental responses, a more efficient procedure is to average the data over many presentations of the same stimulus. The brain's response to the stimulus can then be clearly detected because there has been a sufficient gain in the signal to noise ratio through compounding the stimulus effect and canceling out the noise effect.

Theoretically, all forms of aggregation should contribute equally to reliability but should have different effects on validity. In the second study, it was found that although all forms of aggregation increased temporal reliability, they did not do so equally. Aggregation over raters was particularly important, as there were marked differences among individual raters.

Let us examine the contribution of each of the forms of aggregation. Aggregation over stimuli and situations reduces error variance associated with the uniqueness of particular stimuli and situations and increases the range of generalization of the findings. It therefore permits the detection of broad cross-situational dispositions and allows statements to be made about the generality of the results with respect to the population of stimuli that was sampled. Of course, if two different measures are to be related, it is important that the aggregation be conducted in a manner that makes the measures correspond in level of generality (Epstein, 1979b; Fishbein & Ajzen, 1974).

Aggregation over occasions and over trials within occasions reduces error variance associated with changes over time. As a result, aggregation over occasions should enhance replicability of findings. Unlike aggregation over stimuli or situations, it increases reliability without necessarily increasing the breadth of the concept that is measured, unless, of course, aggregation over occasions also includes an element of aggregation over situations, which is commonly the case when real-life events are sampled. Aggregation over occasions also has the virtue of permitting temporal reliability to be assessed and enhanced. In the two studies that were reported, as well as in earlier studies in the series (Epstein, 1977, 1979a, 1980b), aggregation over occasions was found to be a highly effective technique for raising temporal reliability coefficients to high levels.

Aggregation over judges or raters reduces error variance associated with individual differences among judges and allows generalizations to be made to a population of judges. In the study on ratings of the instructor, aggregating over judges was particularly important, as it was found that the personalities of the judges influenced their ratings. Although there was little agreement among individual judges about the personality of the instructor, there was almost perfect agreement among large groups of judges. In a study by Moskowitz and Schwarz (1982), evidence for broad cross-situational dispositions of dependency and dominance that was not apparent for unaggregated data emerged at statistically significant levels when data were aggregated over raters and observations. Cheek (1982) also reported an increase in validity of four broad personality dispositions as a function of increased aggregation over raters and items.

Aggregation over modes of response reduces error variance associated with different response modes and establishes the range of generalization of the findings for different kinds of responses. In the study on individual differences in ratings of the instructor, aggregation over items was equivalent to aggregation over responses. It was found that aggregation over items in the form of a general score of favorableness enhanced temporal reliability. However, although it produced stronger relationships than the single items with some variables, it produced weaker relationships with others, attesting to the fact that behavior is both general and specific.

Despite the advantages of aggregation under many circumstances, aggregation is not a panacea. It cannot be employed indiscriminately for several important reasons. First, by aggregating over a group of stimuli, situations, or occasions, unique effects associated with specific stimuli, situations, or occasions are lost. It is important to recognize that a response is apt to have both a specific and a general component, and even if it is established that the general component justifies aggregation, unless the specific component is examined, important information for certain purposes may be lost. In the psychophysiological study that was reported, Day 1, although it contributed to the aggregated data, had a unique contribution to make with respect to the measurement of anxiety. Second, there are circumstances in which aggregation is inappropriate because the nature of the phenomenon under consideration, such as startle or surprise, can be properly observed on only a single occasion. Third, aggregation may fail to increase reliability because responding to one stimulus influences responses to the stimuli that follow.

Thus far, aggregation has been considered from the viewpoint of a research tool or psychometric technique for raising experimental, relative to error, variance. The principle of aggregation, however, has important implications that relate to the very nature of validity and to the encoding processes of the human mind. Validity can be defined as the correspondence between a concept and the operations for measuring it. Every concept has a range of generality, meaning that it can be applied to certain stimuli or responses that fall within its range and excludes others that do not (see Kelly, 1955). No single stimulus is sufficient for identifying a concept because every stimulus is multidimensional, and it is not possible with a single item to establish the

range of applicability of a concept. Thus, as noted earlier, it is no less important to sample stimuli than to sample subjects. By establishing what items can
be aggregated in a manner that contributes to reliability and validity, meaningful statements can be made that are not restricted to a particular stimulus of
unknown generality that was fortuitously selected in a particular study. The
range of applicability of a concept determines the range of effective aggregation, and, conversely, the range of effective aggregation establishes the range
of applicability of a concept. It follows from this consideration—plus the
additional consideration that there is always some degree of indeterminacy,
or error of measurement—that the concept of aggregation, or redundancy,
lies at the heart of the scientific endeavor.

Given a considerable degree of indeterminacy in human behavior, it can
reasonably be anticipated that human cognition must necessarily incorporate
the principle of aggregation. Elsewhere (Epstein, 1980a; Epstein & Erskine,
1983), I have presented a theory of personality that assumes that the basic
postulates in an individual's implicit theory of reality are, for the most part,
inductively derived generalizations from significant emotional experiences. It
is through aggregated experience that people construct a preconscious conceptual system that includes a self-theory, a world-theory, and constructs on
the relationships between the two. Once basic postulates are formulated, they
influence a person's emotions and organize and direct the person's behavior.
(See Kelly, 1955, for a similar view.) It follows that a promising procedure
for investigating personality is to examine the repetitive patterns of a person's
emotionally significant reactions and behavior because it is from such patterns that the basic constructs in an individual's implicit theory of reality
(which constitutes the person's personality) can be inferred (Epstein, 1973,
1979b, 1979c, 1980a, 1982).

Although lay people, like psychologists, can usually do no better than
actuarial prediction, in any one situation they are forced to make categorical
decisions in order to act. Thus, even if a person is a reasonably good actuarial
predictor, he or she will often be wrong in particular situations because of a
failure to take into account unique situational factors. It is more efficient for a
person to encode events into constructs which can broadly direct behavior
than to attempt to memorize specific configurations of individual situations.
By its very nature, actuarial prediction is less than perfect, but this is its source
of efficiency. Given the tendency of people to function as aggregators of
experience and actuarial predictors, it is not surprising that psychologists are
able to demonstrate under certain circumstances that people assume greater
cross-situational consistency than is warranted. In short, given a certain degree of indeterminacy of behavior, and the observation that as a result, single
items of behavior are normally undependable sources of information, people

in everyday life, no less than psychologists in the laboratory, may have no choice but to settle for actuarial prediction based on aggregate experience.

The Generality and Specificity of Behavior

The following statements are all true: (1) behavior is situationally specific, (2) behavior is general across situations, and (3) people have broad cross-situational response dispositions. It has too often been assumed that behavior must either be situationally specific or general across situations. As noted previously, the same situation is apt to elicit both a specific and a general component of behavior. In any one situation, the response is usually determined mainly by the situationally specific component of the behavior. In order for the general component to be observed, it is often necessary to cancel out the specific component by aggregating the behavior over many situations. When this is done, high levels of cross-situational consistency and broad response dispositions can often be demonstrated.

The findings on cross-situational consistency for single items of behavior have often been complicated by low reliability. At the very least, reliability over a comparable time interval should be established and used to correct cross-situational consistency coefficients for unreliability. Unless this is done, cross-situational consistency coefficients for behavior observed on different occasions will reflect, to an unknown degree, temporal unreliability, which is often considerable. When cross-situational consistency coefficients are obtained for measures obtained on the same occasion, it is, of course, important that they be corrected for concurrent reliability. The importance of taking into account reliability when assessing cross-situational consistency, should, of course, be self-evident. It bears repeating, however, because it has so frequently been ignored in the past (see, for example, studies reviewed in Mischel, 1968.)

It was found in the second study that although performance on single items failed to predict performance on other single items on a different occasion, performance on a group of items predicted performance on a group of other items on a different occasion reasonably well. This finding is consistent with results on intelligence tests, with the findings in the Hartshorne and May (1928) studies of honesty and with more recent studies of dominance and dependence by Moskowitz and Schwarz (1982), of extroversion, agreeableness, conscientiousness, and emotional stability by Cheek (1982), and of emotions and behavior in everyday life by Epstein (1979a). Thus, there is strong evidence that one can predict reasonably well over time from one group of items or situations to another group of items or situations. This finding provides support for both a meaningful degree of cross-situational consistency and stability in behavior and for the existence of broad response dispositions, or traits. It also has important implications for research in personality because it indicates at least one way to predict behavior with some accuracy; that is, to obtain a sample of behavior in related situations. More important, it provides a means for inferring the constructs with which people organize their experience (Buss & Craik, 1981; Epstein, 1973, 1979b, 1980a, 1982).

Although correlations between single instances of behavior in different situations are often low, even when corrected for unreliability of measurement, this is not always the case. The results depend on the situations and the behavior investigated. Apparently, many kinds of behavior in many kinds of situations are more situationally specific than researchers had originally anticipated, which was so discouraging to some that it produced an overreaction in the form of the belief that there is no cross-situational generality in any behavior. Such a reaction is well illustrated in the following statement by Bem (1972):

> As noted earlier, there was nothing silly about the initial assumption of personologists that everything was glued together until proved otherwise. But since it has now proved otherwise, it seems only fair to give a sporting chance to the counter-assumption that nothing is glued together until proved otherwise. Instead of assuming cross-situation correlations to be +1.00, let us begin by supposing them to be 0.00 until we can explicitly construct them to be otherwise [p. 25].

It is now evident that an important ingredient in the glue that can hold cross-situational correlations together is aggregation. Nevertheless, as noted earlier (Epstein, 1980b) and demonstrated in the first study, some kinds of behavior exhibit high levels of cross-situational generality even in the absence of aggregation. It will be recalled that, when a variety of behaviors was examined in the laboratory under conditions demonstrated to produce significant situational changes, a number of single items of behavior produced high cross-situational stability coefficients, whereas others did not. A moment's reflection reveals that some measures, such as physical strength, habits, and certain physiological reactions, are highly stable across many situations. Other kinds of behavior change readily in different situations. In the first study, some emotions exhibited cross-situational stability coefficients as high as .75 while others were not significantly different from 0. Psychophysiological variables exhibited cross-situational stability coefficients as high as .95 and as low as .14. Behavioral variables exhibited cross-situational stability coefficients as high as .96 and as low as .06. Thus, depending on the variables and the situations, any degree of cross-situational stability of behavior can be demonstrated.

Accordingly, the concern about whether there is or is not cross-situational stability is evidently a pseudo-issue. The real issue that remains to be investigated is the degree of cross-situational generality for different variables, different situations, and different subject populations. Until this is recognized, it can be anticipated that some psychologists will insist that behavior is situationally specific and support their view with evidence, and others will insist that behavior is cross-situationally general and support their view with evidence. Neither group will understand how the other can ignore what to them is a self-evident truth.

In closing, I wish to draw attention to a series of studies that perhaps more than any other illustrates the importance of aggregation as a fundamental technique in personality research. In his classic work, *Explorations in Personality* (1938), Murray described what is very likely the most influential series of studies of personality ever conducted. Subjects were seen over a protracted period of time and their data were aggregated over occasions. They were exposed to different experimental situations and interviewers, and their data were aggregated over situations and response tendencies. Finally, a council of judges discussed the findings on each individual, and the data were aggregated over judges. In effect, what the procedure accomplished was to distill a vast amount of data into a limited number of conclusions purified to a considerable degree in the crucible of aggregation.

Acknowledgments

I wish to acknowledge my indebtedness to Ronald Hambleton and Marian MacDonald for their advice on issues concerning statistics and test construction; to Robert Alexander, who served as a coinvestigator in the first study and analyzed the data in that study; and to John White, who did the data analysis in the second study.

References

Ajzen, I., & Fishbein, M. Attitude–behavior relations: A theoretical analysis and review of empirical research. *Psychological Bulletin*, 1977, *84*, 888–918.

Arend, R., Gove, F. L., & Sroufe, L. A. Continuity of individual adaptation from infancy to kindergarten: A predictive study of ego-resilience and curiosity in preschoolers. *Child Development*, 1979, *50*, 950–959.

Bem, D. J. Constructing cross-situational consistencies in behavior: Some thoughts on Alker's critique of Mischel. *Journal of Personality*, 1972, *40*, 17–26.

Bem, D. J., & Allen, A. On predicting some of the people some of the time: The search for cross-situational consistencies in behavior. *Psychological Review,* 1974, *81,* 506–520.

Bem, D. J., & Funder, D. C. Predicting more of the people more of the time: Assessing the personality of situations. *Psychological Review,* 1978, *85,* 485–501.

Berkowitz, L., & Donnerstein, E. External validity is more than skin deep: Some answers to criticisms of laboratory experiments. *American Psychologist,* 1982, *37,* 245–257.

Block, J. *Lives through time.* Berkeley, CA: Bancroft Books, 1971.

Block, J. Recognizing the coherence of personality. In D. Magnusson & N. S. Endler (Eds.), *Personality at the crossroads: Current issues in interactional psychology.* Hillsdale, NJ: Erlbaum, 1977.

Block, J. H., & Block, J. The role of ego-control and ego-resiliency in the organization of behavior. In W. A. Collins (Ed.), *Minnesota Symposia on Child Psychology* (Vol. 11). Hillsdale, NJ: Erlbaum, 1980.

Buss, D. M., & Craik, K. H. The act frequency analysis of interpersonal disposition: Aloofness, gregariousness, dominance, and submissiveness. *Journal of Personality,* 1981, *49,* 174–192.

Cattell, R. B. *Personality and motivation structure and measurement.* Yonkers-on-Hudson, N.Y.: World Book, 1957.

Cheek, J. M. Aggregation, moderator variables, and the validity of personality tests: A peer-rating study. *Journal of Personality and Social Psychology,* 1982, *43,* 1254–1269.

Cronbach, L. J. The two disciplines of scientific psychology. *American Psychologist,* 1957, *12,* 671–684.

Endler, N. S. Estimating variance components from mean squares for random and mixed effects analysis of variance models. *Perceptual and Motor Skills,* 1966, *22,* 559–570.

Epstein, S. The self-concept revisited, or a theory of a theory. *American Psychologist,* 1973, *28,* 404–416.

Epstein, S. Traits are alive and well. In D. Magnusson & N. S. Endler (Eds.), *Personality at the crossroads: Current issues in interactional psychology.* Hillsdale, NJ: Erlbaum, 1977.

Epstein, S. The stability of behavior: I. On predicting most of the people much of the time. *Journal of Personality and Social Psychology,* 1979, *37,* 1097–1126. (a)

Epstein, S. The ecological study of emotions in humans. In P. Pliner, K. R. Blankenstein, & I. M. Spigel (Eds.), *Advances in the study of communication and affect* (Vol. 5): *Perception of emotions in self and others.* New York: Plenum, 1979. (b)

Epstein, S. Explorations in personality today and tomorrow: A tribute to Henry A. Murray. *American Psychologist,* 1979, *34,* 649–653. (c)

Epstein, S. The self-concept: A review and the proposal of an integrated theory of personality. In E. Staub (Ed.), *Personality: Basic issues and current research.* Englewood Cliffs, NJ: Prentice-Hall, 1980. (a)

Epstein, S. The stability of behavior: II. Implications for psychological research. *American Psychologist,* 1980, *35,* 790–806. (b)

Epstein, S. A research paradigm for the study of personality and emotions. *Nebraska Symposium on Motivation:* 1981. Lincoln: Univ. of Nebraska Press, 1982.

Epstein, S., & Erskine, N. The development of personal theories of reality. In D. Magnussen & V. Allen (Eds.), *Human development: An interactional perspective.* New York: Academic Press, 1983.

Eysenck, H. J. *The biological basis of personality.* Springfield, IL: Charles C. Thomas, 1967.

Eysenck, H. J., & Eysenck, S. B. G. *The manual of the Eysenck Personality Inventory.* San Diego: EDITS/Educational and Industrial Testing Service, 1968.

Fenz, W. D., & Epstein, S. Manifest anxiety: Unifactorial or multifactorial composition? *Perceptual and Motor Skills,* 1965, *20,* 773–780.

Fishbein, M., & Ajzen, I. Attitudes toward objects as predictors of single and multiple behavioral criteria. *Psychological Review,* 1974, *81,* 59–74.
Frederiksen, N. Toward a taxonomy of situations. *American Psychologist,* 1972, *27,* 114–123.
Golding, S. L. Flies in the ointment: Methodological problems in the analysis of the percentage of variance due to persons and situations. *Psychological Bulletin,* 1975, *82,* 278–288.
Guilford, J. P., & Zimmerman, W. S. *The Manual of the Guilford–Zimmerman Temperament Survey.* Beverly Hills, CA: Sheridan Supply Co., 1949.
Hartshorne, H., & May, M. A. *Studies in the nature of character* (Vol. 1). *Studies in deceit.* New York: Macmillan, 1928.
Hogan, R., DeSoto, C. B., & Solano, C. Traits, test, and personality research. *American Psychologist,* 1977, *32,* 255–264.
Jackson, D. N. *Jackson Personality Inventory Manual.* Port Huron, MI: Research Psychologists Press, 1976.
Jones, E. E., & Nisbett, R. E. *The actor and observer: Divergent perceptions and the causes of behavior.* New York: General Learning Press, 1971.
Kelly, G. A. *The psychology of personal constructs* (2 Vols.). New York: Norton, 1955.
Levin, J. Three-mode factor analysis. *Psychological Bulletin,* 1965, *64,* 442–452.
Magnusson, D. An analysis of situational dimensions. *Perceptual and Motor Skills,* 1971, *32,* 851–867.
Magnusson, D., & Ekehammar, B. An analysis of situational dimensions: A replication. *Multivariate Behavioral Research,* 1973, *8,* 331–339.
Magnusson, D., & Endler, S. Interactional psychology: Present status and future prospects. In D. Magnusson & N. S. Endler (Eds.), *Personality at the crossroads: Current issues in interactional psychology.* Hillsdale, NJ: Erlbaum, 1977.
Mischel, W. *Personality and assessment.* New York: Wiley, 1968.
Mischel, W. On the future of personality measurement. Unpublished paper in *The future of personality measurement.* Symposium presented at the meeting of the American Psychological Association, Chicago, August, 1975.
Mischel, W. *Introduction to personality* (3rd ed.). New York: Holt, Rinehart, & Winston, 1981.
Moos, R. H. Situational analysis of a therapeutic community milieu. *Journal of Abnormal Psychology,* 1968, *73,* 49–61.
Moos, R. H. Sources of variance in response to questionnaires and in behavior. *Journal of Abnormal Psychology,* 1969, *74,* 405–412.
Moos, R. H. Differential effects of psychiatric ward setting on patient change. *Journal of Nervous and Mental Disease,* 1970, *5,* 316–321.
Moskowitz, D. S., & Schwarz, J. C. A validity comparison of behavior counts and ratings by knowledgeable informants. *Journal of Personality and Social Psychology,* 1982, *43,* 754–768.
Murray, H. A. *Explorations in personality.* New York: Oxford Univ. Press, 1938.
O'Brien, E. J. *The self-report inventory: Development and validation of a multidimensional measure of the self-concept and sources of self-esteem.* Unpublished doctoral dissertation, Univ. of Massachusetts at Amherst, 1980.
Olweus, D. Personality and aggression. In J. K. Cole & D. D. Jensen (Eds.), *Nebraska Symposium on Motivation 1972.* Lincoln: Univ. of Nebraska Press, 1973. Pp. 261–321.
Olweus, D. Personality factors and aggression: With special reference to violence within the peer group. In J. de Wit & W. W. Hartup (Eds.), *Determinants and origins of aggressive behavior.* The Hague: Mouton Press, 1974.
Olweus, D. "Modern" interactionism in personality psychology and the analysis of variance components approach: A critical examination. In D. Magnusson & N. S. Endler (Eds.), *Personality at the crossroads: Current issues in interactional psychology.* Hillsdale, NJ: Erlbaum, 1977.

Olweus, D. The stability of aggressive reaction pattern in human males: A review. *Psychological Bulletin*, 1979, *86*, 852–875.

Pervin, L. A. Definitions, measurements, and classifications of stimuli, situations, and environments. *Human Ecology*, 1978, *6*, 71–105.

Sarason, I. G., Smith, R. E., & Diener, E. Personality research: Components of variance attributable to the person and the situation. *Journal of Personality and Social Psychology*, 1975, *32*, 199–204.

Shweder, R. A. How relevant is an individual difference theory of personality? *Journal of Personality*, 1975, *43*, 455–484.

Sroufe, A. L. The coherence of individual development. Early care, attachment, and subsequent developmental issues. *American Psychologist*, 1979, *34*, 834–841.

Staub, E. Social and prosocial behavior: Personal and situational influences and their interactions. In E. Staub (Ed.), *Personality: Basic aspects and current research*. Englewood Cliffs, NJ: Prentice-Hall, 1980.

Waters, E., Wippman, J., & Sroufe, L. A. Attachment, positive affect, and competence in the peer group: Two studies in construct validation. *Child Development*, 1979, *50*, 821–829.

7

On the Predictability of Behavior and the Structure of Personality*

Walter Mischel

Introduction

The basic question of this volume, a question of central importance to Henry Murray whom we honor here again, is: How well can personologists now predict behavior? The answer, like the question, is both simple and complex. Put simply, I am confident that we can predict some important human behaviors well, others not very well but enough to make the effort worthwhile, still others not at all. A more complex aspect of the question is: What predictions are worth making, how do they fare, and what do the results tell us about the nature of personality and social behavior? I share Murray's conviction that some personological efforts to predict behavior are as silly as a chemist's attempt to predict what that green chemical on the second shelf of someone else's lab might be doing at 10:30 a.m. a year from next Tuesday. As usual, Murray's example made a significant point. If we ask appropriate questions reasonably, we can hope to get reasonable answers of both theoretical and practical value; if we do not, we can not—as Murray said in the Office of Strategic Services Staff's *Assessment of Men* (1948):

> It is easy to predict precisely the outcome of the meeting of one known chemical with another known chemical in an immaculate test tube. But where is the chemist who can predict what will happen to a known chemical if it meets an unknown

*Preparation of this paper and the research by the author were supported in part by Grant No. MH 36953 from the National Institute of Mental Health and Grant No. HD MH-09814 from the National Institute of Child Health and Human Development.

chemical in an unknown vessel? And even if all the properties of all the chemicals resident in a given laboratory are exactly defined, is there a chemist who can predict every chemical engagement that will take place if Chance, the blind technician, is in charge of the proceedings [p. 8]?

Predicting Behavior

Of course the personologist's task is harder by far than that of the most reasonable and modest chemist. People, unlike chemicals, do not have stable properties that are merely reactive: they spontaneously generate new possibilities and cognitively transform the stimuli that impinge on them in a multiplicity of alternative ways, constructing their lives actively and never in perfectly predictable fashion. Nevertheless, we psychologists can predict all sorts of things. Some of my favorite examples of theoretical and practical interest to personologists include the following handful. Each example illustrates, in my view, a worthwhile route for attempting predictions that have a good chance of being useful for particular purposes. Each example is also intended to illustrate a point about what is and it not reasonably predictable and perhaps even to imply something about human nature.

Predictions from Understanding the Psychological Environment

Psychologists often have tried to relate various indices of the psychological environment—such as a host of child-rearing variables—to the individual's subsequent behavior (e.g., Sears, Maccoby, & Levin, 1957). Usually these studies have predicted behavior from relatively broad and historical aspects of the child-rearing process, using subtle relationship variables like the mother's "warmth" or other interpersonal attitudes as the predictors. The associations between these broad parental child-rearing conditions and the child's later behavior generally have been very low (e.g., Sears, Rau, & Alpert, 1965), understandably reflecting the multiply determined nature of behavior and the limits of predicting specific behaviors from global predictors (Mischel, 1981a). On the other hand, efforts to predict from more specific and theoretically relevant indices of the psychological environment have yielded striking results. For example, Wolf (1966) measured a number of variables in the home that were likely to facilitate intellectual development and academic accomplishments in children. His assessments of environmental opportunities for verbal development included such social learning variables as the quality of language models available to the child, opportunities for enlarging vocabulary, feedback about appropriate language usage, and opportunities for language practice in a variety of situations. Measures of this kind provided an extensive battery for rating the intellectual environment for the child's current development. The results yielded some of the more impressive correlations found in personality research.

The correlation between total ratings for the intellectual environment and tested general intelligence was .69. As Wolf (1966) pointed out, this association provides a substantial increment over the correlations of .20 to .40 usually found between IQ and more global indices of social status. The correlation between Wolf's overall ratings for the environment conducive to academic achievement and actual total achievement-battery test score was .80. This impressive level of association is high enough to permit considerable predictive power. Moreover, Wolf evaluated the effects of combining his measures of the intellectual environment with individual IQ test data. The multiple correlation between IQ and overall rating of the achievement-enhancing environment with the children's total achievement-test battery scores provided an association of .87. Thus the combined measure of environmental achievement supports and IQ test accounted for 76% of the variance in academic achievement scores. This outcome compares favorably to the correlation of .76, accounting for 58% of the variance obtained between IQ alone and academic achievement scores. From my perspective, the importance of this example is not that it illustrates our ability to predict usefully sometimes. More interestingly, it documents the significance of taking serious account of the psychological environment rather than relying exclusively on context-free dispositional inferences.

Predictions from Relevant Past Behavior

Environments, properly analyzed, can enhance prediction. So can data about the person's directly relevant past behavior: "Unless the environmental maintaining conditions change markedly, past behavior tends to be the best predictor of future behavior in similar situations, even when the samples of past behavior are very fragmentary, as in gross indices of previous marital history, occupation, or hospitalization" (Mischel, 1968, p. 292). A vivid example of the value of the past for predicting the future is the fact that an individual's past record of maladjustment and psychiatric hospitalization is a good index of future maladjustment and hospitalization (Lasky et al., 1959). Thus, a correlation of .61 was found between the weight of the patient's file folder and the incidence of rehospitalization. (This study also nicely serves to illustrate that a correlation coefficient is not evidence for a causal relation between variables.)

Predictions from the Person-to-be-Predicted: People as Self-Experts

Often the best predictions in personology are more achievable by the person-to-be-predicted than by the professional personologist. That is, people tend to be the best experts about themselves and the best predictors of their own future actions (Mischel, 1968, 1972). We can see that in many ways, sometimes dramatically. For instance, the simplest self-ratings may supply the best predictions even when compared with costly alternatives. Peterson (1965) pressed the point for simplicity of self-report data to the extreme. He found that two simple and direct self-ratings, one on "adjustment" and one on "introversion–extroversion," each on a 7-point rating scale, may be as useful as time-consuming second-order factor scores calculated from Cattell's 16 P-F test and from cumbersome personality-rating schedules. The mean correlations of the two self-ratings of adjustment and introversion–extroversion respectively with the comparable second-order factors from the 16 P-F were .56 and .66. In addition, the simple self-ratings showed appreciable temporal reliability over a 5-week span and better discriminant validity than data from factor analyses. More recent surveys continue to chronicle the power of self-assessments and self-predictions in diverse contexts (e.g., Mischel, 1981a; Shrauger & Osberg, 1981).

I have long been impressed that our "subjects" are much smarter than many of us thought them to be. So if we don't stop them by asking the wrong questions, and if we provide appropriate structure, they often can tell us much about themselves and what they will—and won't—do. They also can tell us a lot about psychology itself. To pursue the latter, Harriet Nerlove Mischel and I have been asking young children what they know about psychological principles—about how plans can be made and followed most effectively, how long-term work problems can be organized, how delay of gratification can be mastered. We also ask them to tell us about what helps them to learn and (stimulated by Flavell and his colleagues, e.g., Kreutzer, Leonard, & Flavell, 1975) to remember. We are quite impressed by how much even an 8-year-old knows about mental functioning and often wonder how well such young children might perform on a final exam in introductory psychology if the jargon and big words were stripped away. I am not implying that psychologists know little; rather, I believe, people are good psychologists and know a lot. We personologists might be wise to enlist that knowledge in our efforts. At any rate, it is becoming plain that even young children can be accurate predictors, with considerable insight into the principles of psychology that we are seeking to discover (Mischel, 1979; H. N. Mischel & W. Mischel, 1983).

It thus might be wise to allow our "subjects" to slip out of their roles as passive "assessees" or "testees" about whose acts we try to make powerful predictions. Instead, we might enroll them, at least sometimes, as active colleagues who are the best experts on themselves and who are eminently qualified to participate in the development of descriptions and predictions about themselves and about the principles of our field. To be sure, if we want individuals to tell us about themselves directly, we have to ask questions that they can answer. If we ask people to predict how they will behave on a future criterion (e.g., "job success," "adjustment") but do not tell them what specific criterion measures will constitute the assessment, we cannot expect them to make accurate predictions. Likewise, it might be possible to use self-reports and self-predictions more extensively in decision making—for example, to help the person to "self-select" from a number of behavioral alternatives (e.g., different types of therapy, different job assignments). Such applications would require conditions in which people's accurate self-reports and honest choices could not be used against them. We might, for example, expect job candidates to predict correctly which job they will perform best, but only when all the alternatives available to them in their choice are structured as equally desirable. We cannot expect people to give up opportunities unless they perceive appropriate alternatives and options. It is of course obvious that self-predictions and self-reports will always be constrained by the limits of the individual's own awareness. But we too often assume that people are unaware when they are just being asked the wrong questions (e.g., Spielberger & DeNike, 1966). Although a belief in the prevalence of distortions from unconscious defenses such as repression is the foundation of the commitment to an indirect-sign approach in assessment, the experimental evidence for the potency of such mechanisms remains exceedingly tenuous (e.g., Mischel, 1981b).

Predictions from Functional Analyses:
Person—Situation Interactions

Different goals require different foci and measurement strategies, all of which may be legitimate routes for moving toward one's particular objectives. For a more concrete illustration, consider again the old but often forgotten differences between norm-centered and person-centered measurement. Traditionally, most attention in personality measurement has been devoted to comparing differences *between* people on some norm or standard or dimension selected by the assessor. Such a norm-centered approach compares people against each other, usually on a trait or attribute continuum—for example, amount of introversion–extroversion. The results can help with gross screening decisions, permit group comparisons, and answer many research questions. But a norm-centered objective obviously requires a different strategy than one that is person-centered (Mischel, 1968).

A person-centered focus attempts to describe the particular individual in relation to the particular psychological conditions of his or her life. Some especially interesting recent developments in personality measurement have been of this type, arising from clinical work with troubled individuals in the real-life setting in which the behaviors of interest unfold naturally. While there are many methodological variations, the essence of the approach is a functional analysis that investigates in vivo covariations between changes in the individual and changes in the conditions of his or her life. The interest here is not in how people compare with others, but in how they can move closer to their own goals and ideals if they change their behavior in specific ways as they interact with the significant people in their lives (e.g., G. A. Kelly, 1955; Mischel, 1968, 1977). When done well, such person-centered functional analyses can provide not only a helpful service to people who need it; they also simultaneously provide a testing ground for our theoretical notions about the basic rules that underlie behavior.

Predictions from Knowledge of Future Conditions
and from Person Variables

A comprehensive attempt to predict requires attention both to the person and to the psychologically relevant environment. It has already been noted that environmental variables sometimes allow extremely useful predictions. As a case in point, consider again the effort to predict the posthospital adjustment of mental patients. Such investigations have shown that the type, as well as the severity, of psychiatric symptoms displayed depends significantly on environmental conditions, with little consistency in behavior across changing situations (Ellsworth, Foster, Childers, Arthur, & Kroeker, 1968). Accurate predictions of posthospital adjustment require knowledge of the environment in which the ex-patient will be living in the community—such as the availability of jobs and family support—rather than any measured person variables or in-hospital behavior (e.g., Fairweather, 1967; Fairweather, Sanders, Cressler, & Maynard, 1969). Yet we have also seen that the person's past history (e.g., inferred from the weight of the clinical folder) is a useful predictor of future coping.

As another example, when powerful treatments are developed—such as modeling and desensitization therapies for phobias—useful predictions about outcomes can be based on knowledge of the treatment to which the individual is assigned (e.g., Bandura, Blanchard, & Ritter, 1969). But it is also noteworthy that predictions based on specific cognitive social learning person-variables (Mischel, 1973)—such as relevant expectancies—can be superb predictors of treatment success, sometimes even better than knowing the power of the treatment condition itself. Thus, for example, assessment of people's specific self-efficacy expectations allows impressively powerful predictions of their coping responses, reactions to stress, and performance attainments (Bandura, 1982). The nature of person variables and possible candidates that may have both predictive and theoretical value will be considered in later sections. The point to be emphasized here is an obvious one: a comprehensive approach to prediction can afford to ignore neither person variables nor context variables, and for both types of variables the approach must consider the relevant past, present, and future.

Predictions from Understanding Basic Processes

The foregoing examples illustrate that behavior can indeed be predicted usefully for many worthwhile purposes. That is no mean achievement. But prediction itself it not the only goal. It may not even be the most interesting goal for personology. Indeed, Murray and most personologists, myself included, care less about the prediction of behavior than about its analysis to enhance our understanding of basic psychological processes and to clarify the distinctive nature and structure of human personality itself.

To try to understand basic psychological processes of central importance for personality psychology, some of my own efforts have long been concentrated on one seemingly fundamental process: the human ability to defer immediate gratification for the sake of delayed, contingent, but more desired future outcomes. These investigations—like those of so many others studying other basic personological processes—abundantly illustrate that we can not only predict behavior but also clarify the mechanisms that generate it.

To document this optimistic conclusion, it may be worth reviewing at least briefly not only the results of these studies, but also the route that they took. A good deal of research has shown the dramatic role of the person's attention to the rewards in self-imposed delay of gratification. Specifically, initial theorizing (reviewed by Mischel, 1974) suggested that during delay of gratification, attention to the rewards should serve a "time-binding" function and should facilitate the child's ability to wait for them. Empirically, these expectations proved to be exactly wrong: preschool children were able to wait 10 times longer when the rewards in the contingency were not available for

276   Walter Mischel

attention during the delay period than when they were in view (Mischel &
Ebbesen, 1970). In contrast, attention to symbolic representations (pictures)
of the rewards in the contingency ("relevant rewards") made it much easier
for preschool children to delay grafitication (Mischel & Moore, 1973).
Moreover, we found that the effects of the actual rewards physically present
or absent in the situation would be completely overcome and even totally
reversed by changing how the child represented those rewards mentally during the delay period. For example, when preschoolers ideate about the rewards for which they are waiting in consummatory, or "hot," ways—focusing on their taste, for instance—they can hardly delay at all (Mischel & Baker,
1975); but if they focus on the nonconsummatory, or "cool," qualities of the
rewards—on their abstract or nonconsummatory qualities—they can wait for
them easily and even longer than if they distract themselves from the rewards
altogether (Mischel, 1974). Thus hot, reward-oriented ideation decreases
delay by making it more aversively frustrative and arousing. In contrast, delay
is facilitated by ideation about the task contingency and by cool ideation
focusing on the abstract (rather than consummatory) features of the rewards.
In sum, just as greater cognitive availability makes an outcome seem more
likely (Tversky & Kahneman, 1974), so does it seem to make a blocked
(delayed) outcome seem more frustrative (Mischel, 1974). Making the blocked outcome more available, by attending to it or by thinking about it in
consummatory (goal-directed) ways, increases the arousal and makes it more
difficult for the child to delay (Mischel, 1981c). Understanding that process
allows one to make fairly powerful predictions about specific behavior.

The seemingly sharp distinction between the power of the situation and of
the person becomes fuzzy when one approaches both in search of their
psychological properties. Consider the findings that attention focused away
from the rewards in the delay situation (e.g., by covering the rewards or
avoiding them cognitively) potently affects and predicts delay behavior. Do
these results demonstrate the power of situational variables in self-control?
Yes, in the sense that they show how specific changes in the situation and in
what one does in it can make delay either very difficult or very easy. No, in
the sense that these results show how people can and do increase their own
personal ability to control what stimuli do to them by changing how they
think about those stimuli. Once people recognize how their own ideation
makes self-control either hard or easy, the option to delay or not to delay
becomes truly their own; they know how to delay effectively and must merely
choose whether or not they want to, increasingly immune to the physical
situation and able to rearrange it psychologically. Knowledge of situational
variables can become a vital ingredient of each person's power over situations, enhancing the individual's ability to control stimuli purposefully rather
than being controlled by them as the victim of situations. The person's ability
to understand and apply his or her knowledge of how the "situation" (i.e.,

the world) works seems as proper a province of research for the personologist as for the student of metacognition (e.g., Mischel, 1981c).

Attentional focus, assessed as a quality of the person, allows impressive predictions of the individual's actual waiting behavior in the delay situation. For example, we are finding that the child's tendency to attend to the rewards—assessed by measuring what he or she is looking at—allows us to predict the majority of the variance in number of seconds of delay time (Mischel & Peake, 1982). The more the child self-distracts from the frustrativeness of the rewards by avoiding them cognitively during the delay period, the longer the ability to wait for them. Those seconds of waiting time, in turn, appear to be not at all trivial behaviors; they are, instead, remarkably robust indicators of a temporally stable human quality of considerable practical and theoretical significance. We see that result in studies in related directions in which we also are pursuing the personality correlates, the cross-situational consistency, and the temporal stability of delay behavior. The results are providing extensive and intriguing evidence both for the discriminativeness of behavior (across contexts) and for its temporal stability even over many years. Perhaps most impressive, we are finding highly significant continuities, linking the preschooler's delay time while waiting for a couple of marshmallows to his or her cognitive and social competence and school performance a dozen years later (Mischel, 1983). Sometimes even single acts *can* predict meaningful life outcomes! For instance, the number of seconds preschoolers delayed the first time they had a chance to do so in our 1968–1972 studies, regardless of the specific delay situation they encountered, significantly predicted their rated social competence as high school juniors and seniors in 1982 ($r = .34, N = 99, p < .001$).

In sum, here we have a set of data in which a fine-grain analysis of the psychological situation and the relevant basic psychological processes allows excellent specific predictions of specific behavior in a specific, "single act" situation. Yet, most provocatively, these same data lend themselves to demonstrations of the formidable temporal stability, the threads of continuity in lives, that have become increasingly evident even over long periods of time (e.g., Block & Block, 1980).

Searching for the Structure of Behavior

The examples given in the previous section suggest that we often can predict behavior, sometimes quite usefully. Are we then ready to congratulate ourselves and happily adjourn these learned symposia in search of other challenges? Not quite. Because the basic challenge to traditional trait approaches that has provoked so much controversy in recent years does not deny the personologist's ability to predict all sorts of things. Indeed, the controversy concerning the "consistency of behavior" and hence the very nature of personality structure is almost irrelevant to the personologist's ability to predict many aspects of behavior at least sometimes.

What Is Not at Issue?

The critiques of traditional trait approaches in the 1960s (e.g., Mischel, 1968; Peterson, 1968; Vernon, 1964) have too often been read as saying more (as well as less) than they intended. If we can agree about what kind of prediction is *not* at issue, about what is *not* controversial, the route for identifying core issues worthy of constructive resolution may become clearer. So what is *not* at issue? No one questions that psychology journals are full of significant correlations among personality measures. No one suggests that behavior is entirely situation-specific; we do not have to relearn everything in every new situation, we have memories, and our past predisposes our present behavior in critically important and complex ways. Obviously people have characteristics, and overall "average" differences in behavior between individuals can be abstracted on many dimensions and used to discriminate among persons for many purposes. Obviously, knowing how a person behaved before can and does help predict how he or she will behave again. Obviously, the impact of any event depends on the organism that experiences it and, in a sense, just as Bishop Berkeley noted that there are no trees without observers, so also there are no situations without persons to select, categorize, construe, and modify them. No one suggests that a person approaches every new situation with an empty head, nor does anyone question that different individuals differ markedly in how they select and deal with most of the conditions in their lives. On the contrary, there is now abundant evidence that threads of coherence and continuity characterize human development even over long periods of time (Block & Block, 1980; Mischel, 1983b; Mischel & Peake, 1982).

In the previous volume of this lecture series, Jack Block (1981) argued for the existence of some enduring structures of personality, even over long periods of time. I agree with him. In the same volume, McClelland, objecting to what he presented as Walter Mischel's thesis, argued that if we focus on individual lives (Richard Alpert/Ram Dass was his example), we cannot fail to see the existence of continuities. I agree with him also. And Block urged further that rather than ask "Are people consistent over time?" we should be asking "Can we identify the conditions and circumstances related to various kinds of personality change and personality continuity?" (1981, p. 36). Again, I would reach the same conclusion. So I agree with both Block and

McClelland: enduring continuities exist, and observers recognize them. Then what *is* at issue?

Some Core Issues and Background

Several forces seemed to converge in the late 1960s that created something of a "paradigm crisis," an acute questioning of the assumptions, value, and limits of the traditional trait and psychodynamic orientations that for years had served as the core assumptive structure both for personologists and clinicians. The fundamental assumptions underlying these "global dispositional approaches," and the nature of the dissatisfactions with them, have been detailed elsewhere (e.g., Mischel, 1968, 1973, 1981b; Peterson, 1968). While they need no reiteration here, it is worth noting some of their essentials. The dissatisfactions that emerged then included such diverse claims and charges as the limited utility of global dispositional approaches for the planning of specific individual treatment programs, for the design of constructive social change, for the prediction of individual behavior in specific contexts, and for an incisive, theoretically compelling analysis of the basic psychological processes underlying the individual's cognition, affect, and behavior. The criticisms thus ranged from the limitations of global dispositional approaches for specific clinical and practical applications to their tendency to substitute broad labeling or "naming" for deeper, psychological "explaining" and hence their theoretical inadequacy.

Another set of criticisms was aimed at recognizing pervasive, systematic judgmental or "construction" errors in the practice of personology and clinical psychology. These are made readily both by the layperson and the professional due to the operation of "cognitive economics" (or heuristics) through which complex information tends to be reduced and sometimes oversimplified with serious consequences for inference, judgments, and prediction (e.g., Kahneman & Tversky, 1973; Mischel, 1979; Nisbett & Ross, 1980). Of course the discussion of issues in personality by personologists is also not immune to the operation of such cognitive economics. It therefore should not be surprising that many of the original issues in the challenge to global dispositional approaches to personality also have tended to become oversimplified in efforts to recollect and summarize them. Thus, for example, the critique in *Personality and Assessment* (Mischel, 1968) has not infrequently been viewed as a broadside attack on personality itself and even as an effort to replace dispositions and indeed people with situations and environments as the units of study.

My aim in writing *Personality and Assessment* was to defend individuality and the uniqueness of each person against the tendency (prevalent in clinical and diagnostic efforts in the 1960s) to use a few behavioral signs to categorize people enduringly into fixed slots on the assessor's favorite nomothetic trait dimensions. In the 1960s it was not uncommon to assume that these slot positions were sufficiently informative to predict not just "average" levels or "gist" but the person's specific behavior on specific criteria as well as "in general." It was commonplace to attempt extensive decisionmaking about a person's life and future on the basis of a relatively limited sampling of person-ological "signs" or "trait indicators." As a clinically trained psychologist (in the tradition of both George Kelly and Jules Rotter, my mentors at Ohio State in the 1950s), I was especially sensitized to the potential hazards of such attributions, of such categorizations too often made on the basis of scanty evidence. Stimulated by my mentors, my hope was to call attention to the specific reciprocal interactions between person and context and hence to the need to examine those interactions in fine-grain detail when attempting person-centered decisions and predictions. My concern was that clinicians, like other scientists and indeed like the ordinary layperson, try to infer, generalize, and predict too much from too few observations. As has become increasingly recognized, the judgments of clinicians—like everyone else's judgments—are subject to certain systematic biases in information processing that can produce serious distortions and oversimplifications in inferences and predictions (Nisbett & Ross, 1980). Given the fallibility of the human judge, his (or her) hubris seemed especially unjustified.

Deeply impressed by George Kelly's (1955) thinking, I was sensitive to the fact that clients—like other people—don't describe themselves with opera-tional definitions. They invoke motives, traits, and other dispositions as ways of describing and explaining their experiences and themselves. Much of the assessor's task, it seemed to me, should be to help people in the search for such referents for their own personal constructs, instead of forcing the as-sessor's favorite dispositional labels on them. In our role as clinicians, rather than leading clients to repackage their problems in our terms, with our constructs, we need to help them objectify *their* constructs into operational terms, so that they can achieve their own aims through more judicious ar-rangements of the conditions in their lives. We needed, I argued in *Personality and Assessment* (1968), to recognize the idiographic nature of each person while searching for the nomothetic principles, the general rules, that underlie behavior.

But an author's intentions and impact are not necessarily highly correlated. *Personality and Assessment* is often seen as the work of a "situationist" and "peripheralist" (see Chapter 2, this volume). Yet that book ended with this conclusion, which I still believe as much now as I did then:

> Global traits and states are excessively crude, gross units to encompass adequately the extraordinary complexity and subtlety of the discriminations that people con-stantly make. Traditional trait-state conceptions of man have depicted him as vic-

timized by his infantile history, as possessed by unchanging rigid trait attributes, and as driven inexorably by unconscious irrational forces. This conceptualization of man, besides being philosophically unappetizing, is contradicted by massive experimental data. The traditional trait-state conceptualizations of personality, while often paying lip service to man's complexity and to the uniqueness of each person, in fact lead to a grossly oversimplified view that misses both the richness and the uniqueness of individual lives. A more adequate conceptualization must take full account of man's extraordinary adaptiveness and capacities for discrimination, awareness, and self-regulation; it must also recognize that men can and do reconceptualize themselves and change, and that an understanding of how humans can constructively modify their behavior in systematic ways is the core of a truly dynamic personality psychology [p. 301]. © John Wiley & Sons, Inc.

Perhaps the deepest question raised by critiques of the global dispositional approach is the utility of inferring broad dispositions from behavioral signs as *the* basis for trying to explain the phenomena of personality and for making useful statements about an individual's behavior in specific situations (Hunt, 1965; Mischel, 1968, 1973; Peterson, 1968; Vernon, 1964). My reading of the available data in 1968 did *not* imply that useful predictions cannot be generated, nor that different people will not act differently with some consistency in different classes of situations. But in my view the data did then and do now imply that the particular classes of conditions must (1) be taken into account far more carefully than in the past, (2) tend to be much narrower and subtler than traditional trait theories have assumed (especially when one goes beyond recall-based ratings), and (3) require, for purposes of important individual decision-making or for specific predictions, highly individualized assessments of subjective meanings because behavior tends to be idiosyncratically organized within each person on his or her personal dimensions of similarity that do not necessarily match the categories of the trait psychologist (e.g., Mischel, 1968, 1973, 1977). To me the data then and now also suggest that the inferences about global underlying traits and dispositions—especially, indirect inferences—often have less utility for most assessment efforts to predict or therapeutically modify individual behavior than do more economical, alternative analyses based on more direct data such as people's past behavior in similar situations or their direct self-reports and self-statements (Mischel, 1972, 1981a).

My critique of global traits as inadequate causal explanations and the indictment of the utility of indirect trait inferences for many individually oriented assessment and clinical purposes does not imply a rejection of their other possible uses. The layman as well as the trait psychologist pervasively generates and employs broad trait constructs. The question no longer is "Do traits really exist?" The questions are multiple: When are trait constructs invoked? In what data are they rooted? What are their uses and misuses, and for what are they relevant and how? How are trait categories organized?

What is their structure, their syntax, their linkage to behavior? How do the everyday, semantic trait categories used in natural social perception relate to such psychological person variables as encodings and expectancies and goals and plans (Mischel, 1973)? What kinds of person variables seem most promising and viable for a psychology of personality? That is, what are the particular person variables that the psychology of personality requires for its many different purposes? How can these person variables be articulated with the psychological conditions and situations of the person's life? How can they be moderated to reflect adequately their reciprocal interactions with conditions and the discriminativeness of behavior, while simultaneously taking account of the widely shared subjective impression of continuity and consistency in persons? These are exactly the sorts of questions on which our research has been focusing (e.g., Cantor & Mischel, 1979; Cantor, Mischel, & Schwartz, 1982a; Hoffman, Mischel, & Mazze, 1981; Mischel, 1979; Mischel & Peake, 1982; Mischel, 1983b). These efforts have been taking several directions, as indicated next.

Basic "Natural" Trait Categories?

In one direction of our work, recognizing the complexity of the links between traits and behavior, we have become interested in how trait categories are used by the layperson. Here we are trying to understand the nature and function of the categories that people use to classify each other naturally in everyday life (e.g., Cantor & Mischel, 1979; Cantor, Mischel, & Schwartz, 1982a; Hoffman, Mischel, & Mazze, 1981). These natural categories may include an impure mix of trait terms with other everyday "knowledge packages" about types of people found in common speech. These packages are the stereotypes (or the "schemas") we use when we refer to people as "typical absent-minded professors," "jocks," "male chauvinist pigs," "laid back Southern California types," or "crashing-bores-to-be-avoided-at-all-costs." Popular person schemas are also illustrated by Jung's archetypes: the earth mother, the wise old man, the prodigal son.

New interest in everyday natural person categories was created by some important studies of common-object taxonomies conducted by Eleanor Rosch and her colleagues (1976). They asked people to describe the attributes (physical appearance, shape, function, movements) common to the objects included under different category labels (such as furniture or birds) in three-level taxonomies (e.g., furniture, chair, kitchen chair). They found that certain levels of abstraction in these taxonomies maximized such desirable qualities as the richness (number) of attributes commonly associated with most category members. Rosch and her colleagues concluded that the optimal level of abstraction in the three-level object taxonomies was the middle level; at that level broad, inclusive, but still rich and distinctive categories are formed. These categories (called "basic level") are inclusive enough to cover many different kinds of objects within one category, but detailed and vivid enough to allow one to describe in great detail the typical appearance, shape, and function of a typical category member. Categorizing at this middle level of abstraction maximizes both parsimony—a few broad categories are formed—and richness—there are many features common to members of each particular category—making for an ideal system of communication.

We have been trying to extend this general approach to learning about the uses and limits of *person* categories at different levels of abstraction to help clarify the enduring and perplexing problem of selecting the most appropriate units for the study of social behavior (e.g., Cantor & Mischel, 1977, 1979), with commensurate units for the analysis of situations (Cantor, Mischel, & Schwartz, 1982a). As a first step, to construct some representative person taxonomies, we began at the most abstract or "superordinate" level with the major common factors from peer-rating studies of personality (e.g., Norman, 1963). "Emotionally unstable person," for example, was one superordinate category; "extrovert" was another. The middle levels were constructed to have person categories at lower, less inclusive levels of abstraction (such as "phobic" in the unstable person hierarchy or "PR type" and "comic joker" in the extrovert hierarchy). The lowest or subordinate level included such subtypes as "claustrophobic" and "hydrophobic" (in the emotionally unstable hierarchy) or "door-to-door salesman" and "press agent" (in the extrovert hierarchy). After the hierarchical nature of these structures was confirmed, subjects were asked to generate lists of common attributes. The degree of agreement for these person classifications was then assessed to determine the number and type of shared attributes at each level of inclusiveness in each hierarchy.

The results seemed highly encouraging. Specifically, the effort to pursue the analogy between the categorizations of common everyday objects (pants and chairs and cars) and those of people (extroverts and used-car salesmen types)—as well as of psychological situations—so far has yielded considerable convergence. The person types at the middle level in these taxonomies were found to be richer in the sense that they had more shared attributes than those judged to be true of members of the superordinate categories. There also was less overlap between the attribute lists for neighboring categories at this middle level of abstraction than at the more finely tuned and detailed level of subordinate categorizations. The subordinate categories yielded the greatest richness and vivid imageability. But categories at this lower level were not ideal for highlighting the differences between the types of persons in neighboring categories. The middle level in the taxonomies seems to allow one to use just a few basic categories to capture the gist of another person in a rich and vivid way, while still allowing one to contrast that person with other discriminable general types. This middle level may be best when one wants to describe "what X is like in general," distinguish how "X and Y differ from each other," and apply one's knowledge about types of people in general in order to enrich the description of a particular individual. In contrast, to predict what specific molecular behaviors X will perform when observed under particular, well-defined circumstances, the more finely tuned specific, narrow categories of the subordinate level may be more helpful. But to reduce the whole person domain to two or three major categories or dimensions, as in a grand theory of personality (e.g., Jung, 1923; Eysenck, 1967), one may want to use the highest, most inclusive or superordinate level (the level of extroverts, for example). While consistent, coherent descriptions capturing the gist of another's behavior are achieved by moving to more abstract levels of person categorization, more vivid, salient person images require less inclusive slots. The level one chooses surely must depend on the purpose one has. A similar analysis has been completed on a sample of everyday psychological situations (Cantor, Mischel, & Schwartz, 1982b).

The Consistency Paradox

In another direction, we have been exploring the natural organization of behavior, searching for the nature of the consistencies that give rise to the widely shared impressions that a person is, for example, "a typical conscientious student." This work, of course, bears directly on the classic problem of the relative specificity versus consistency of social behavior, and the nature and breadth of the dispositions underlying such behavior, probed in the past by Thorndike (1906), Hartshorne and May (1928), Allport (1937, 1966), Fiske (1961), and many others. The position one takes on these issues deeply influences one's view of personality and the strategies worth pursuing in the search for its nature and implications. Few assumptions are simultaneously more self-evident, yet more intensely argued, than the belief that an individual's behavior is characterized by pervasive cross-situational consistencies in behavior. Reviewers of this debate have repeatedly noted a curious paradox (e.g., Bem & Allen, 1974; Mischel, 1973). On the one hand, compelling intuitive evidence supports the enduring conviction that people are characterized by broad dispositions revealed in extensive cross-situational consistency. On the other hand, the history of research in the area has yielded persistently perplexing results, suggesting much less consistency than our intuitions predict.

There have been two main reactions to this paradox. One reaction has been to question the assumptions of traditional trait theories (as Mischel, 1968 did) and to search for alternative ways of conceptualizing person variables (e.g., Bandura, 1978; Cantor & Mischel, 1979; Mischel, 1973, 1979) and for studying person–situation interactions through more fine-grained analyses (e.g., Magnusson & Endler, 1977; Moos & Fuhr, 1982; Patterson, 1976; Patterson & Moore, 1979; Raush, 1977). Alternatively, others have argued (e.g., Block, 1977; Bowers, 1973; Epstein, 1979; Olweus, 1977) that the problems raised reflect not the inadequacy of traditional conceptualizations of broad traits that yield cross-situationally consistent behaviors but rather the inadequacy of earlier searches for such traits.

Epstein, an excellent exemplar of this method-oriented approach to the consistency issue, has amassed a great deal of data to show the value of enhancing reliability by aggregating measures in the search for better prediction and in the demonstration of personality consistency (Chapter 6, this volume; 1977; 1979). In support of his arguments, he (1979, p. 1098) recently demonstrated that coefficients of temporal stability (e.g., of self-reported emotions and experiences recorded daily and of observer judgments) become much larger when based on averages over many days. Epstein computed split-half reliabilities for samples of behavior varying from 2 to about 28 days. He found that as the number of observations included in the composite increased, the split-half reliability also increased. Recognition of this phenomenon, a fundamental premise of classical reliability theory (Gulliksen, 1950; Lord & Novick, 1968; Thurstone, 1932) is not new to the consistency debate. Most psychologists, far from overlooking reliability, grew up with the recognition that reliability is important and increases with the number of items aggregated. Epstein believes that the "classic debate" can be resolved simply by aggregating our measures to enhance reliability. But the OSS (Office of Strategic Services) project in World War II, the Michigan Veterans Administration project, the Harvard personologists, and the Peace Corps projects—all the large-scale applied assessment projects of the 1940s, 1950s, and 1960s—used aggregated measures, pooled judgments, assessment boards, and multiple-item criteria, but nevertheless yielded overall results that raised basic questions about the usefulness and limitations of the traditional personality assessment enterprise (e.g., Peterson, 1968; Vernon, 1964; Wiggins, 1973).

As Epstein has demonstrated and as earlier work abundantly shows, adequate reliability coefficients can surely be found, especially for similar measurements with similar instruments taken repeatedly over time (Mischel, 1968). But we have to discriminate clearly between demonstrations of impressive temporal stability, on the one hand, and cross-situational generality or consistency in behavior, on the other. By collecting specific observations over a series of days and then computing split-half "stability" coefficients, most of Epstein's data (Tables 1, 2, 3 of Epstein, 1979, for example) are relevant only to the temporal stability of behavior. But temporal stability has never been a central issue in this debate. In my view, and as noted here in previous pages, the crux of the "classic debate" is the cross-situational consistency or discriminativeness of social behavior and the utility of inferring traits for the prediction of an individual's actions in particular contexts, not the temporal stability of behavior within a situation. Epstein does present some data (in Tables 4 and 5 of his 1979 paper) that go beyond the demonstration that aggregation increases reliability coefficients and enhances temporal stability. Those data and the issues they raise are reviewed in detail elsewhere (Mischel & Peake, 1982, 1983).

The Stanford–Carleton Study

Although the search for behavioral consistency has to begin with data aggregated to achieve reliability, it also must go beyond reliability, beyond temporal stability, and beyond scattered self-report and behavior correlations. To investigate cross-situational consistency in behavior we need appropriate and reliable behavior measures sampled across a range of presumably similar situations. Such a search also has to be guided by some conceptualization—even if rudimentary—of how behavior is organized or should be categorized for particular goals (e.g., Cantor & Mischel, 1979; Mischel, 1973, 1979). We have been trying to do just that during the last few years, assessing behavioral consistency among college students at Carleton College in Northfield, Minnesota (see Mischel & Peake, 1982).

The work, begun in collaboration with Neil Lutsky (Peake & Lutsky, 1983), first replicated Bem and Allen's 1974 study, extending greatly the behavioral referents and battery of measures employed. Specifically, 63 Carleton College volunteers participated in extensive self-assessments relevant to their friendliness and conscientiousness. They were assessed by their parents and a close friend and were observed systematically in a large number of situations relevant to the traits of interest. Here only selected features of these data will be used to illustrate empirically the temporal stability and cross-situational consistency that are obtained when reliability and appropriate aggregation are taken into account.

So far analyses have focused on the domain of conscientiousness/ studiousness (henceforth called simply "conscientiousness"), although related work tentatively suggests essentially similar patterns for friendliness (Peake, 1982). The behavioral referents of conscientiousness in this work consisted of 19 different behavior measures. The behavioral assessment of conscientiousness included such measures as: class attendance, study session attendance, assignment neatness, assignment punctuality, reserve reading punctuality for course sessions, room neatness, and personal appearance neatness. Note that the specific behaviors selected as relevant to each trait were supplied by the subjects themselves as part of the pretesting at Carleton College to obtain referents for the trait constructs as perceived by the subjects, in contrast to many studies in which these referents are selected exclusively by the assessors. For each different measure, observations were obtained over from 2 to 12 repeated occasions. Thus, for example, observations of assignment punctuality were obtained on 3 occasions and observations of appointment punctuality on 9 occasions.

First, consider the question of temporal stability. To qualify as a coefficient of temporal stability, the correlation had to consist of two or more observations of the same type of measure. For example, lecture attendance on Day 1 correlated with lecture attendance on Day 6 is a correlation of temporal stability. We computed the percentage of significant coefficients among all the possible coefficients of temporal stability for single occasions (Mischel & Peake, 1982). This analysis showed that nearly half of the temporal stability coefficients (specifically 46%) were statistically significant, even for single occasions before any aggregation to increase reliability. Thus even at the unaggregated, single-occasion level, temporal stability can be demonstrated readily. Given the high level of temporal stability among the single behaviors, it is not surprising either conceptually or empirically that when these were aggregated into composite measures over all occasions, all of the resulting coefficients were significant (with the mean temporal stability coefficient being .66).

A similar analysis was performed for all the correlations relevant to cross-situational consistency (i.e., correlations between the 19 measures). At the level of single behaviors, cross-situational consistency coefficients consist of such correlations as a single observation of appointment punctuality with a single observation of lecture punctuality or with a single observation of classnote neatness (i.e., with any other single observation except another observation of appointment punctuality). Quite typically for findings of this type, although the percentage of significant correlations (11%) exceeded chance, the correlations were highly erratic, with a mean coefficient of .08. The critical question then becomes what gains in cross-situational consistency are obtained when we intercorrelate our more reliable aggregates; that is, when each behavior measure consists of an aggregate of all the occasions on which the behavior was observed over time?

To answer this question we have to examine such correlations as aggregated lecture attendance with aggregated appointment punctuality or aggregated lecture attendance with aggregated appointment attendance. With that goal, 171 cross-situational consistency coefficients were computed by intercorrelating the 19 different aggregated measures of conscientiousness. Of the 171 coefficients, 20% (35 coefficients) reached significance—a number considerably above chance. Some of these coefficients reached substantial levels. These coherences once again testify that individual differences are patterned and organized rather than random. But it is just as clear from the results that behavior is also highly discriminative and that broad cross-situational consistencies remain elusive even with reliable measures. This discriminativeness is further seen in the fact that for the 19 aggregated measures, the mean cross-situational consistency coefficient was only .13.[1]

The results from the Stanford–Carleton project are consistent with past findings and not unique (Mischel, 1983a). Early studies, including the classic investigation by Hartshorne and May (1928) of honesty, by Newcomb (1929) of introversion-extroversion, by Allport and Vernon (1933) of expressive moments, and by Dudycha (1936) of punctuality, routinely employed repeated observations of each behavior to increase the reliability of their measures. Each of these investigators reported substantial reliability coefficients, not as a solution to the consistency problem but as one index of the adequacy (reliability) of their aggregate measures. More importantly, each of these studies obtained cross-situational correlation coefficients around .20 when using the reliably aggregated measures. While Epstein proposes aggregation as a potential cure-all for the consistency problem, it is clear that there is nothing new to this cure; it has been employed routinely for years, and its use only serves to document more clearly the pervasiveness of the phenomena of behavioral discriminativeness.

We do not conclude, however, from the Stanford–Carleton data that there is little coherence among the behaviors studied. Although the overall patterning of correlations was erratic and their values low, on the average (even for our most reliable measures), the results do not suggest that the individual's behaviors are random and unorganized. Some impressive coefficients did emerge, coherent patterns of correlations were evident in some cases, and most of the obtained correlations were positive. Indeed, of the 38 negative correlations, only 2 reach statistical significance, leaving us with far more positive significant correlations and fewer negative significant correlations than we would expect by chance. In sum, the data reflect behavioral discriminativeness, but with a clear positive trend, a coherence or gist among the behaviors sampled, indicating a relatively stable mean level of individual differences.

[1]Of course this is not an absolute ceiling. For example, the coefficient can be increased by application of standard psychometric procedures to include only those "items" of behavior that correlate with the total at specified levels of significance. To illustrate, such a procedure, by eliminating items that do not relate to the total at $p < .01$, one-tailed, can reduce the measures from 19 to 12 but increase the mean cross-situational consistency to .24 (Mischel, 1983a).

Aggregating the Data Appropriately: Avoiding Aggregation of the Issues

It is indeed appropriate to aggregate measures—but only for some purposes. Aggregation of observations over occasions is surely needed for adequate reliability. No one would contend that a person's attendance at today's psychology lecture at 9 a.m. is an adequate index of that person's tendency to attend psychology lectures. By measuring lecture attendance on repeated occasions, a more reliable index of lecture attendance will result. Of course, aggregation does need not stop at aggregation over occasions (Epstein, 1980). The investigator who wants to amass high correlation coefficients could forge ahead and aggregate behavior across different response forms and/or across situations, arriving at the now popular "multiple-act criteria" (Jaccard, 1974; McGowan & Gormly, 1976; Fishbein & Ajzen, 1975; Rushton et al., 1981). Here again, these aggregations will be appropriate and useful for some purposes but not for others (e.g., Mischel, 1983a).

For example, one can combine measures across situations after they have been aggregated over occasions and across response forms within situations. In this way one can treat the specific situations simply as "error" and aggregate across them to form a single composite score and, as the Spearman–Brown formula predicts, convert an average .13 cross-situational consistency coefficient into an internal reliability estimate of .74. Such cross-situational aggregation may be potentially useful for certain purposes in research on individual differences and certainly for gross screening decisions of the sort used in personnel selection, guidance, and counseling. But the more measures are aggregated across situations, the less they bear on the issue of cross-situational consistency because they increasingly cancel out the variance and specificity due to situations, thus bypassing the problem of cross-situational consistency rather than solving it. While achieving reliable measures by sampling over occasions is of self-evident value, further aggregation, across response forms and/or situations, must be dictated by the assessor's goals and by a priori theoretical considerations about psychological similarity (equivalence groupings) and about the level of generality, the units, at which assessment should occur for particular purposes (e.g., Cantor & Mischel, 1979; Mischel, 1977). Although such aggregation is useful for making statements about mean levels of individual differences across a range of contexts, cross-situational aggregation also often has the undesirable effect of canceling out some of the most valuable data about a person. By treating within-person variance, and indeed the context itself, as if it were "error," it misses the point completely for the psychologist who is concerned not with between-person comparisons but with the unique patterning of the individual—a concern that is the core for students of personality and for the creation of the field itself (Allport, 1937). Unfortunately, this concern is too often forgotten and therefore seems to require reiteration (e.g., Lamiell, 1981) years after its original articulation.

In the search for consistency, personologists emphasize their commitment to a focus on individuality (e.g., Carlson, 1971). Such a commitment requires serious recognition of the within-person patterning of attributes and behavior—the crux of the idiographic approach and the uniqueness of the person (e.g., Allport, 1937). But, paradoxically, in this search for consistency, situations have been construed as "error": The within-person patterning tends to be aggregated out and treated as if it undermined the basic phenomena of personality psychology and indeed the existence of reliable individual differences. As a personologist (or clinician), I may be less interested in aggregating a child's total aggressiveness across situations than in noting that she is aggressive with her sister but not with her brother, or is aggressive only when teased in a particular way but never when in the presence of her father. In sum, aggregation may be ideal for canceling out many influences and describing mean level differences between individuals, but such lumping is obtained at the cost of much valuable information—often the most interesting information—about the individual in the particular contexts in which he or she lives. For the clinician as well as for the personologist, aggregation is often the route to weak "on average" generalizations about people in general, while bypassing the uniqueness, specificity—and predictability—of individuality to which a science of personology is ostensibly devoted.

To resolve the consistency debate we must move beyond the search for significant correlations and beyond the recognition of coherence in behavior. We need to understand why the obtained coherences emerge and when and why expected coherences do not. And we need to pursue the oft-neglected path of attempting to understand the discriminativeness that also clearly exists in behavior and demands an interactional perspective that treats situations as sources of meaningful variance rather than as error to be averaged out. For instance, in our research at Carleton College we are searching for consistency at different levels of abstraction-generality in the data, from the most "subordinate" or molecular to increasingly broad, "superordinate," molar levels, guided by a cognitive prototype and hierarchical levels analysis of the sort proposed by Cantor and Mischel (1979). We also are trying to explore the comparative usefulness of measures specifically designed to tap such cognitive social learning person-variables as the individual's relevant competencies, encodings, expectancies, values, and plans (Mischel, 1973, 1979).

We hope that such analyses will help clarify basic processes that underlie both the significant and the nonsignificant coefficients yielded by personality research, the "uneven and erratic patterns" of behavior that characterize person–situation interactions. Aggregation of repeated observations over occasions will help in these analyses by providing a more accurate (reliable) picture of the significant *and* nonsignificant links that characterize the data. The reliability solution, instead of giving a simple panacea for the issues raised regarding the cross-situational consistency of behavior, highlights their complexity. Rather than resolving the consistency debate, the reliability solution underscores the need to find alternative conceptualizations of personality that might facilitate a better assessment and appreciation of both the coherence and the discriminativeness of human behavior, an understanding of the structure of behavior and not just a reiteration of the conviction that such structure exists.

The Structure of Consistency: The Construction of Personality

What are the implications of the data just reviewed for the search for personality? Aggregation over occasions is a necessary step to increase the reliability of measures. Further aggregation, across response forms and especially across situations, will serve to highlight stable mean levels of individual differences by eliminating the variability due to contexts. If traits are defined as such stable mean levels, then their existence is not (and has not been) at issue; at question is not the reality of durable average individual differences, but their breadth across contexts and the best ways of assessing and categorizing them for particular purposes. Sampling behavior extensively in a domain often allows useful predictions of individuals' aggregated mean levels of behavior in that domain. The fact that relevant past behavior is often the best predictor of future behavior is not and was not in doubt. And just as the occurrence of stable mean levels of behavior in a domain does not deny within-person variability across situations, so should the appreciation of such cross-context variability not be mistakenly read to preempt the existence of personal qualities that may have stability over years.

The Problem (and Challenge) of "Similarity"

As Mischel and Peake (1982) have shown, when one increases the reliability of behavior measures within specific situations, rather than assuring impressive increases in the associations between them, one can more clearly see that the discriminativeness of behavior is a valid phenomenon, not just a reflection of poor methodology. It is old wisdom that the prediction of "single acts" is as difficult and generally as unlikely as it is challenging. (That is why it seems so intriguing to be able to predict from a single act like a child's delay time when waiting for a preferred but delayed treat at age 4 to her social competence when entering college!) Usually we must settle for trying to predict from and to an average of repeated observations, to infer a "tendency" that unifies the person over multiple acts and occasions. With that goal, one samples the behavior of interest multiply in the situation, as was done in the Stanford–Carleton project analyses reported. Such sampling of repeated observations within a given setting should not be confused, however, with aggregation across situations in the search for cross-situational consistency. To aggregate cross-situationally is to circumvent the problem rather than to demonstrate its resolution. The risk is that such aggregation may tempt one to aggregate not only the data but also the issues. The hazard is to substitute self-evident psychometrics (that magnify even trivial consistencies by eliminating situational variance) for more complex (and less obvious) psychological analyses of the nature of perceived similarities and appropriate equivalence groupings in the organization of behavior and the construction of personality.

Although I have emphasized the differences obtained empirically in behavioral measures of temporal stability versus cross-situational consistency, this distinction is actually somewhat brittle. Operationally, the search for temporal stability allows one to postpone (momentarily only) the problems of psychological similarity by simply looking for the "same" behaviors (e.g., punctuality at introductory psychology lectures) over multiple occasions in time. The moment the behavior measures are not identical (e.g., lecture punctuality versus appointment punctuality), the problem of psychological similarity surfaces. It seems clear that the distinction between temporal stability and cross-situational consistency is one of degree of psychological similarity among the components. Evidence for higher average coefficients for temporal versus cross-situational consistency suggests that when the situations are as close as possible to identical (i.e., changed only by time), there is impressive average consistency. But when situations become even somewhat dissimilar, the patterns become more complex and uneven, average coefficients become much lower, and consistency can no longer be assumed. The need to search for ways to identify similarity then becomes manifest (see Lord, 1982, and Magnusson & Ekehammar, 1973, for interesting examples). Few problems in psychology seem more basic than that of psychological similarity, (e.g., Tversky, 1977), and its resolution ultimately should have much to say to the study of situational equivalencies and the categorization of behavior. Theory-guided aggregation requires identifying psychological equivalences and the psychological similarity among situations, not just averaging everything that can be summed.

Toward a Theoretical Reconceptualization

To resolve the many issues raised in the long debate about consistency, we need a theoretical reconceptualization of the issues and of personality and situation constructs themselves (e.g., Cantor & Mischel, 1979; Mischel, 1973), not only more clever methods for applying everyday trait terms to people's behavior in particular contexts. Such a reconceptualization, if successful, will unify the analysis of person characteristics with the analysis of cognitive-learning processes, allowing the person and the situation to be analyzed in light of the same psychological principles, not merely described with the same trait terms (e.g., Mischel, 1973). As has been emphasized, that requires a deeper analysis of the nature of person and situation categories (Cantor & Mischel, 1979; Cantor, Mischel, & Schwartz, 1982a) and the nature of psychological similarity (e.g., Tversky, 1977). The search for consistencies without an appropriate theoretical framework can become an ultimately uninteresting hunt for statistically significant coefficients.

It has become traditional for most personality theorists to invoke a few concepts and stretch them to span all the phenomena of human individuality, including the person's cognition, feeling, and action. Most theories of personality have been built on a few body types, on a handful of factors, on simple conditioning and environmental contingencies, on the vicissitudes of one or more favorite motives (sex, aggression, competence, achievement, dissonance, self-realization), or on a humanism that correctly emphasizes the humanity of people but too easily loses sight of its antecedents and the conditions on which that humanity hinges. A striking exception was Murray, whose efforts for breadth were extraordinary. But even Murray could only draw on the psychology available in his time. His work was a noble but necessarily incomplete scaffold for the field, and he was the first to recognize its unfinished structure. His approach to theory building seemed a model of the search for a cumulative science of psychology based on the incremental theoretical insights and empirical discoveries of the field rather than on the biases of theoreticians committed to defending their viewpoints against change. In that vein, we are still searching for a conception of personality that continues to be revised and nourished broadly by the research of the field rather than one committed to favorite assumptions. The massiveness of available research and, of course, its frequent flaws make it possible to read the data of our field in many alternative ways, often with little consensus. In my reading, however, some guidelines for a theoretical reconceptualization do begin to emerge from empirical work on cognition and social behavior, at least in broad outlines.

An adequate reconceptualization needs to contain at least two components. It should provide person variables in the form of psychological constructs that allow an analysis of a person in ways that are closely linked to basic psychological processes. It also should provide a language for the parallel categorization and classification of both persons and situations. Steps toward the first objective were discussed elsewhere (Mischel, 1973, 1981a). Briefly, the cognitive social learning approach to personality shifts the units of study from global traits inferred from behavioral signs to the individual's cognitive activities and behavior patterns, studied in relation to the specific conditions that evoke, maintain, and modify them and which they, in turn, change (Mischel, 1968, 1973, 1977, 1981a).

The focus in such an approach shifts from attempting to compare what different individuals "are like in general" to an assessment of what they *do*—behaviorally and cognitively (externally and in their heads)—in relationship to the psychological conditions in which they do it. The focus shifts from describing situation-free people with broad trait adjectives to analyzing the specific interactions between conditions and the cognitions and behaviors of interest. Specifically, the cognitive social learning person-variables deal first with the individual's abilities to construct (generate) diverse behaviors under appropriate conditions, that is, his or her cognitive and behavioral *competencies*. Next, one must consider individuals' *encoding* and *categorization* strategies—how they group and construe events, including themselves,and how they categorize situations. A comprehensive analysis of the behaviors performed in particular situations requires close attention to the person's specific *expectancies,* including self-efficacy expectations, the person's *goals* and *subjective values,* and his or her *self-regulatory systems and plans.* These five person variables (construction competencies, encoding strategies, expectancies, goals and values, self-regulatory systems) obviously overlap and interact, but the purpose of each is to provide the desired distinctive information about the person. I do, however, want to reiterate that while such person variables as expectancies seem promising candidates, it would be a tempting mistake to transform them into generalized traitlike dispositions by attributing broad cross-situational consistency to them or by removing them from the specific contexts in which they function.

Appropriate cognitive social learning person-variables have the advantage that they directly interface with basic psychological processes. These person variables are not semantic, not adjectives that summarize "average" behaviors on the common semantic dimensions that constitute the thousands of dictionary trait terms basic to approaches like Allport's (e.g., Allport & Odbert,

1936). Instead, person variables are linked to the basic psychological processes that regulate or guide how a person will behave in particular contexts (e.g., Mischel & Staub, 1965). They are not semantic categories like "friendliness" or "conscientiousness." Rather, such variables as competencies, encoding strategies, and expectancies each relate to what persons specifically *do* cognitively and behaviorally in particular contexts, not to what they "are like" in general. It is hoped that they provide a useful structure for studying the syntax of human behavior, not its semantic categorization.

Because such person variables are constructs rooted extensively in earlier empirical and theoretical work, they do not require the personality theorist to start from scratch as if forced to reinvent the world anew. For example, a great deal is known about the nature, genesis, functions, modifiability, generalizability, and maintenance of "expectancies." When we invoke them as person variables, a vast research and theoretical literature (from Wundt and Lewin to Tolman, Rotter, and Bandura) comes to mind. This is the advantage of building on the best available earlier work in our field when seeking a structure for the analysis of persons. A similarly rich network of prior knowledge is available for the other person variables selected in a cognitive social learning approach (e.g., cognitive and behavioral competencies).

In addition to a conception of *person structure* (consisting of person variables), a comprehensive theory of personality also requires a model of how the person variables interact and function as parts of a coherent system. Here one needs a model of *"person operations"* for conceptualizing the "dynamics" among the variables in a cognitive social learning framework. Such a model needs to address in detail how person structures reciprocally interact and are coordinated, modified, and integrated into a coherent, functioning system. Clearly a "self-system," with such properties as intentionality and multiple goals, has an extensive place in such a model. To conceptualize the operations of this system we also do not have to start from scratch. Indeed, a voluminous literature already exists on the self-system (e.g., Bandura, 1982) and on the self-regulatory operations (e.g., Mischel, 1974, 1981c; Mischel & Mischel, 1976) that must be incorporated into such a model. Likewise, the insights available from decades of research into information-processing operations require incorporation, again a formidable task. Although our examples so far focus on the role of cognitions in personality, that emphasis does not exclude recognition and incorporation of the role of affect in the operation of person structure. (For one effort in that direction from a cognitive social learning perspective, see Wright & Mischel, 1983.)

From my perspective, "person operations" encompass how people organize their behavior in meaningful, hierarchical, rule-guided ways in pursuit of their goals and valued outcomes. Even the understanding of simple stories may be guided by a kind of "grammar" that provides a framework of rules for organizing information so that it may be more easily comprehended and remembered. In the same sense, an adequate approach to the understanding of person operations may require the development of a grammar of the individual or the "self." To be useful, such a grammar would help to specify the organization and relations among diverse parts or components of the individual's actions and goals, allowing one to understand his or her long-term projects and transactions with the world in a coherent fashion. Hopefully, in the present and future such a grammar may have a better chance of successful realization than it did in the past. In my view, such an approach may require that we transform the fine-grained formal analyses of the sort modeled by the best psycholinguists and cognitive psychologists (e.g., Anderson & Bower, 1973; Schank & Abelson, 1977) so that they fit the persistently complex, molar, multifaceted lives to which the study of personology is dedicated.

Prototypicality and Person Categories

With the objective of finding a parallel language to describe and classify both persons and situations, our preferred alternative to traditional trait approaches for the categorization of persons (Cantor & Mischel, 1979) and of situations (Cantor, Mischel, & Schwartz, 1982a) has begun to be elaborated. This "prototype" approach to the categorization problem appreciates the reality of individual differences but seeks to reconceptualize the nature of the consistencies they reflect in an interactional framework, guided by cognitive theories of the categorization of everyday objects (e.g., Rosch et al., 1976). The prototype approach recognizes the especially "fuzzy" nature of natural categories and, along the lines first traced by Wittgenstein (1953), searches not for any single set of features shared by all members of a category but rather for a "family resemblance" structure, a pattern of overlapping similarities. The recognition of "fuzzy sets" also suggests that categorization decision will be probabilistic and that members of a category will vary in degree of membership (prototypicality), with many ambiguous borderline cases that produce overlapping, "fuzzy" boundaries between the categories.

To study such "fuzzy sets," one seeks the most relevant, clear exemplars (the prototypical members), and omits less prototypic, borderline instances. The prototype approach to both persons and situations also allows the construction of orderly (but also often "fuzzy") taxonomies containing categories at different levels of abstraction (inclusiveness), from superordinate to middle to subordinate, and predicts different gains and losses at different levels in the hierarchies (Cantor & Mischel, 1979). Knowledge about a particular category is represented by a loose set of features that are correlated, but only imperfectly, with membership in that category. Results so far with this approach seem encouraging and suggest, for example, systematic, widely shared rules for assessing prototypicality in the person domain (Cantor, 1978; Cantor & Mischel, 1979), predictable and orderly person taxonomies, and shared, easily retrievable prototypes for social situations often characterized by the typical person–action combinations expected in them (Cantor, Mischel, & Schwartz, 1982a).

The prototype approach applied to the consistency problem suggests a search for key features and "family resemblance" patterns that identify prototypical exemplars and for an explication of the rules that are used by the everyday perceiver to aggregate disparate responses and distill their essential gist in the judgment of category membership. Such rules, we hypothesize, will draw more heavily on the presence of stable key features central to the prototype than on the observation of high average levels of cross-situational consistency across many or all situations in which the behavior might occur. That is, extensive cross-situational consistency may not be a basic ingredient for either the organization of personal consistency in a domain or for its perception.

The Behavioral Roots of Perceived Consistency

We have been trying to apply the prototype approach more specifically to the analysis of the consistency problem in the Stanford–Carleton data on the structure of conscientiousness (Mischel & Peake, 1982). Consider the following findings from that project. Consistent with findings by Bem and Allen (1974), raters in the Stanford–Carleton project agreed well with each other about people who see themselves as generally consistent with regard to conscientiousness. Like Bem and Allen's raters, these raters also agreed much less well about the attributes of people who view themselves as highly variable. More challenging theoretically is the finding that the Carleton students' perceptions of their own overall consistency or variability on conscientiousness did not appear to be related closely to the observed cross-situational consistency of their behavior. Thus, although interjudge agreement was greater for people who saw themselves overall as consistent in conscientiousness, actual consistency in their cross-situational behavior was not significantly greater for them than it was for those students who saw themselves as variable or for the group as a whole. (The same pattern occurred in the Bem–Allen data, as well as in the Carleton data, as discussed in Mischel & Peake, 1982).

In sum, people who see themselves as consistent on a dimension thus are indeed seen with greater interjudge agreement by others. But—and that is the crucial point—their total behavior is not necessarily more cross-situationally consistent. How can we understand this puzzle? How can we understand the widely shared perception of consistency in a personality disposition if that perception is unrelated to the level of cross-situational consistency in the reliably observed referent behaviors?

Guided by the cognitive prototype view, Mischel and Peake (1982) hypothesized that the impression that a person is consistent with regard to a trait is *not* based mostly on the observation of cross-situational consistency in relevant behaviors. We proposed, instead, that when people try to assess variability (versus consistency) with regard to a category of behavior, they scan the *temporal stability* of a limited number of behaviors that for them are most relevant (prototypic) to that category. That is, we proposed that the impression of consistency is based extensively on the observation of temporal stability in those behaviors that are highly relevant to the prototype, but is independent of the temporal stability of behaviors that are not highly relevant to the prototype. And we further proposed that the impression of high consistency versus variability would be unrelated to overall cross-situational consistency.

Specifically, in the Carleton College data on conscientiousness, we predicted that people who judge themselves overall as consistent across situations (low variable on Bem and Allen's 1974 global self-report measure) will show greater temporal stability but not greater cross-situational consistency than those who view themselves as variable. Temporal stability coefficients were obtained on each of the behavioral measures employed at Carleton, separately for subjects who rated themselves as high (versus low) in variability. Subjects who perceived themselves as highly consistent rather than as more variable across situations had somewhat higher temporal stability across all the behavior measures. The mean temporal stability coefficients were .68 and .55 for those high versus low in self-perceived consistency. There were no appreciable differences in the behavioral cross-situational consistency of those who saw themselves as high ($r = .11$) or low ($r = .14$) in consistency.

The linkage between the global self-perception of consistency and the temporal stability of more (rather than less) prototypic behaviors was of greatest interest for our hypothesis. Ratings of prototypicality were available for 17 of the 19 Carleton behavior measures and allowed us to divide these measures into the "more" and the "less" prototypical (at the median of the total ratings for all items). We assessed the links between the global self-perception of consistency and the behavioral data, divided into more prototypic versus less prototypic behaviors. The pattern of data was exactly as expected. Thus, students who saw themselves as highly consistent in conscientiousness were more temporally stable on these prototypic behaviors than were those who viewed themselves as more variable ($r = .71$ for the low variability self-perceivers; $r = .47$ for the high variability self-perceivers); this difference was highly significant statistically. Moreover, this mean difference was reflected pervasively in the component behaviors. In contrast to the clear and consistent differences in temporal stability of prototypic behaviors, there was no difference between the self-perceived low and high variability groups in the mean temporal stability for the less prototypic behaviors. Finally, as expected, there was no relationship between self-perceived consistency and behavioral cross-situational consistency.

In sum, our data clearly supported the view that the impression of consistency in behavior may be grounded in temporally stable prototypic behaviors rather than in generalized, overall, or average cross-situational consistencies. It thus seems that individuals judge their degree of consistency from the temporal stability of the relevant, more prototypic behaviors, rather than from some cross-situational summation across more dissimilar behaviors and contexts. The fact that the people who perceived themselves as highly variable versus not variable did not differ in temporal stability on the less prototypic behaviors suggests that those less "central" behaviors did not enter into the judgment of consistency. The perception of variability appears to arise from the occurrence of a number of temporally stable, highly prototypic behaviors, regardless of the overall cross-situational consistency of the total behaviors. Perhaps people tend to overgeneralize from the observation of temporal stability in a few prototypic features to an impression of overall consistency. Such an overgeneralization certainly would be congruent with other tendencies to go well beyond observations in social inferences and attributions (e.g., Mischel, 1979; Nisbett, 1980; Nisbett & Ross, 1980; Ross, 1977; Tversky & Kahneman, 1974).[2]

If these results prove to be robust and replicable and apply to other trait domains, they have intriguing implications. They suggest that our intuitions of cross-situational consistency are grounded in data. But, at least under some circumstances, these data may not be highly generalized cross-situational consistencies in behavior. Instead, the intuitions about a person's consistency may arise from the observation of temporal stability in prototypical behaviors. That is hardly an illusory or fictitious construction of consistency. The "error" is only to confuse the temporal stability of key behaviors with pervasive cross-situational consistency and then to overestimate the latter.

[2]While these results seem intriguing, they should not be overinterpreted to imply that observers are incapable of accurate behavior observation and cannot make perceptive assessments of social behavior. Indeed, in other contexts, impressive data are emerging that document the accuracy of observers in judging, for example, children's aggressive, withdrawal, and prosocial behaviors in a variety of situations (Wright, 1983; Wright & Mischel, in preparation).

"Seeing Is Forgetting the Name of the Thing One Sees"

Before firm generalizations can be reached from the results of the Stanford–Carleton study just summarized, we will need thorough replications and extensions to assure the robustness and breadth of the conclusions. Even with these strong reservations in mind, the pattern already obtained seems promising, and I hope will point ultimately to a structural solution for an enduring dilemma in our field. The "consistency paradox" may be paradoxical only because we have been looking for consistency in the wrong place. If our shared perceptions of consistent personality attributes are indeed rooted in the observation of temporally stable behavioral features that are "real" and indeed prototypic for the particular attribute, the paradox may well be on the way to resolution. Instead of seeking high levels of cross-situational consistency, instead of looking for broad "averages," we may need, instead, to identify unique "bundles" or sets of temporally stable prototypic behaviors, key features, that characterize the individual even over long periods of time but not necessarily across many or all possibly relevant situations.

A theory of personality structure does not require everyone to be characterizable by high levels of pervasive cross-situational consistency in behavior. It does require a structure for behavior and a way to discern it. The Stanford–Carleton data suggest to us that the roots of such structure may be in the occurrence of temporally stable but cross-situationally discriminative features that are prototypic for the particular behavior category as perceived by the particular individual. A close analysis of the patterning and organization of such features within individuals should be most interesting, and we plan such an analysis. We expect that the most consistent and prototypic exemplars of a category like conscientiousness or friendliness will be those individuals who stably exhibit a number—but not necessarily many—of its prototypic features, as they themselves define that prototypicality or "centrality." We expect that the particular constellations of features will be idiographically patterned, so that no individuals necessarily share the same configuration, although considerable between-person overlap occurs. Thus the exact pattern that defines conscientiousness may not be identical for any two individuals. But each person who is characterized as consistently conscientious will display some of its features with temporal stability, albeit with a distinctive cross-situational constellation.[3] If so, the route may be open for not only

---

[3] If these hypotheses prove valid, they also would help one understand why the issue of cross-situational consistency is a more serious problem for the nomothetic trait psychologist than for the layperson. To the degree that each individual maintains reasonable temporal stability in his or her distinctive pattern of prototypic behaviors, the impression of pervasive consistency may be preserved. Individuals thus may be perceived as consistent on their particular set of stable behaviors even if those behaviors do not map very well onto the total set of referents selected by the trait researcher to define his or her dimension for all people.

seeing the uniqueness of each personality (which personologists have long appreciated) but also for ultimately understanding its common structure. And in that formidable effort it is worth remembering Paul Valéry's insight: "Seeing is forgetting the name of the thing one sees."

References

Allport, G. W. *Personality: A psychological interpretation.* New York: Holt, 1937.

Allport, G. W. Traits revisited. *American Psychologist,* 1966, *21,* 1–10.

Allport, G. W., & Odbert, H. S. Trait-names: A psycho-lexical study. *Psychological Monographs: General and Applied,* 1936, *47* (1, Whole No. 211).

Allport, G. W., & Vernon, P. E. *Studies in expressive movement.* New York: Macmillan, 1933.

Anderson, J. R., & Bower, G. H. *Human associative memory.* New York: Wiley, 1973.

Bandura, A. Reflections on self-efficacy. In S. Rachman (Ed.), *Advances in behaviour research and therapy* (Vol. 1). Oxford: Pergamon Press, 1978.

Bandura, A. Self-efficacy mechanism in human agency. *American Psychologist,* 1982, *37,* 122–147.

Bandura, A., Blanchard, E. B., & Ritter, B. Relative efficacy of desensitization and modeling approaches for inducing behavioral, affective, and attitudinal changes. *Journal of Personality and Social Psychology,* 1969, *13,* 173–199.

Bem, D. J., & Allen, A. On predicting some of the people some of the time: The search for cross-situational consistencies in behavior. *Psychological Review,* 1974, *81,* 506–520.

Block, J. Advancing the psychology of personality: Paradigmatic shift or improving the quality of research. In D. Magnusson & N. S. Endler (Eds.), *Personality at the crossroads: Current issues in interactional psychology.* Hillsdale, NJ: Erlbaum, 1977.

Block, J. Some enduring and consequential structures of personality. In A. I. Rabin, J. Aronoff, A. M. Barclay, & R. A. Zucker (Eds.), *Further explorations in personality.* New York: Wiley, 1981.

Block, J., & Block, J. The role of ego-control and ego resiliency in the organization of behavior. In W. A. Collins (Ed.), *The Minnesota Symposia on Child Psychology,* (Vol. 13). Hillsdale, NJ: Erlbaum, 1980.

Bowers, K. Situationism in psychology: An analysis and a critique. *Psychological Review,* 1973, *80,* 307–336.

Cantor, N. *Prototypicality and personality judgments.* Unpublished doctoral dissertation, Stanford University, 1978.

Cantor, N., & Mischel, W. Traits as prototypes: Effects on recognition memory. *Journal of Personality and Social Psychology,* 1977, *35,* 38–48.

Cantor, N., & Mischel, W. Prototypes in person perception. In L. Berkowitz (Ed.), *Advances in experimental social psychology* (Vol. 12). New York: Academic Press, 1979.

Cantor, N., Mischel, W., & Schwartz, J. C. Social knowledge: Structure, content, use and abuse. In A. Hastorf and A. Isen (Eds.), *Cognitive social psychology.* New York: Elsevier North-Holland, 1982. (a)

Cantor, N., Mischel, W., & Schwartz, J. C. A prototype analysis of psychological situations. *Cognitive Psychology,* 1982, *14,* 45–77. (b)

Carlson, R. Where is the person in personality research? *Psychological Bulletin,* 1971, *75,* 203–219.

Dudycha, G. J. An objective study of punctuality in relation to personality and achievement. *Archives of Psychology*, 1936, *29*, No. 204, 1–53.

Ellsworth, R. B., Foster, L., Childers, B., Arthur, G., & Kroeker, D. Hospital and community adjustment as perceived by psychiatric patients, their families, and staff. *Journal of Consulting and Clinical Psychology Monograph*, 1968, *32* (5, Pt. 2).

Epstein, S. Traits are alive and well. In D. Magnusson & N. S. Endler (Eds.), *Personality at the crossroads: Current issues in interactional psychology*. Hillsdale, NJ: Erlbaum, 1977.

Epstein, S. The stability of behavior: I. On predicting most of the people much of the time. *Journal of Personality and Social Psychology*, 1979, *37*, 1097–1126.

Epstein, S. The stability of behavior: II. Implications for psychological research. *American Psychologist*, 1980, *35*, 790–806.

Eysenck, H. J. *The biological basis of personality*. Springfield, IL: Charles C Thomas, 1967.

Fairweather, G. W. *Methods in experimental social innovation*. New York: Wiley, 1967.

Fairweather, G. W., Sanders, D. H., Cressler, D. L., & Maynard, H. *Community life for the mentally ill: An alternative to institutional care*. Chicago: Aldine, 1969.

Fishbein, M., & Ajzen, I. *Belief, attitude, intention and behavior: An introduction to theory and research*. Reading, MA: Addison–Wesley Publishing Co., 1975.

Fiske, D. W. The inherent variability of behavior. In D. W. Fiske & S. R. Maddi (Eds.), *Functions of varied experience*. Homewood, IL: Dorsey Press, 1961.

Gulliksen, H. *Theory of mental tests*. New York: Wiley, 1950.

Hartshorne, H., & May, M. A. *Studies in deceit*. New York: Macmillan, 1928.

Hoffman, C., Mischel, W., & Mazze, K. The role of purpose in the organization of information about behavior: Trait-based versus goal-based categories in person cognition. *Journal of Personality and Social Psychology*, 1981, *40*, 211–225.

Horowitz, L. M., Inouye, D., & Siegelman, E. Y. On averaging judges' ratings to increase their correlation with an external criterion. *Journal of Consulting and Clinical Psychology*, 1979, *47*, 453–458. Clinical Psychology, 1979, *47*, 453–458.

Hunt, J. McV. Traditional personality theory in the light of recent evidence. *American Scientist*, 1965, *53*, 80–96.

Jaccard, J. J. Predicting social behavior from personality traits. *Journal of Research in Personality*, 1974, *7*, 358–367.

Jung, C. G. *Psychological types*. London: Routledge & Kegan Paul, 1923.

Kahneman, D., & Tversky, A. On the psychology of prediction. *Psychological Review*, 1973, *80*, 237–251.

Kelly, E. L. Consistency of the adult personality. American Psychologist, 1955, *10*, 659–681.

Kelly, G. A. *The psychology of personal constructs* (Vols. 1 & 2). New York: Norton, 1955.

Kreutzer, M. A., Leonard, C., & Flavell, J. H. An interview study of children's knowledge about memory. *Monographs of the Society for Research in Child Development*, 1975, *40* (1, Serial No. 159).

Lamiell, J. T. Toward an idiothetic psychology of personality. *American Psychologist*, 1981, *36*, 276–289.

Lasky, J. J., Hover, G. L., Smith, P. A., Bostian, D. W., Duffendack, S. C., & Nord, C. L. Posthospital adjustment as predicted by psychiatric patients and by their staff. *Journal of Consulting Psychology*, 1959, *23*, 213–218.

Lord, C. G. Predicting behavioral consistency from an individual's perception of situational similarities. *Journal of Personality and Social Psychology*, 1982, *42*, 1076–1088.

Lord, F. M., & Novick, M. R. *Statistical theories of mental test scores*. Reading, MA: Addison–Wesley, 1968.

Magnusson, D., & Ekehammar, B. An analysis of situational dimensions: A replication. *Multivariate Behavioral Research*, 1973, *8*, 331–339.

Magnusson, D., & Endler, N. S. Interactional psychology: Present status and future prospects. In D. Magnusson & N. S. Endler (Eds.), *Personality at the crossroads: Current issues in interactional psychology*. Hillsdale, NJ: Erlbaum, 1977.

McGowan, J., & Gormly, J. Validation of personality traits: A multi-criteria approach. *Journal of Personality and Social Psychology*, 1976, *34*, 791–795.

Mischel, H. N., & Mischel, W. The development of children's knowledge of self-control strategies. *Child Development*, 1983, *54*, 603–619.

Mischel, W. *Personality and assessment*. New York: Wiley, 1968.

Mischel, W. Direct versus indirect personality assessment: Evidence and implications. *Journal of Consulting and Clinical Psychology*, 1972, *38*, 319–324.

Mischel, W. Toward a cognitive social learning reconceptualization of personality. *Psychological Review*, 1973, *80*, 252–283.

Mischel, W. Processes in delay of gratification. In L. Berkowitz (Ed.), *Advances in experimental social psychology* (Vol. 7). New York: Academic Press, 1974.

Mischel, W. On the future of personality measurement. *American Psychologist*, 1977, *32*, 246–254.

Mischel, W. On the interface of cognition and personality: Beyond the person–situation debate. *American Psychologist*, 1979, *34*, 740–754.

Mischel, W. A cognitive social learning approach to assessment. In T. V. Merluzzi, C. R. Glass, & M. Genest (Eds.), *Cognitive assessment*. New York: Guilford Press, 1981. (a)

Mischel, W. *Introduction to personality* (3rd Edition). New York: Holt, 1981. (b)

Mischel, W. Metacognition and the rules of delay. In J. Flavell & L. Ross (Eds.), *Cognitive social development: Frontiers and possible futures*. New York: Cambridge Univ. Press, 1981. (c)

Mischel, W. Alternatives in the pursuit of the predictability and consistency of persons: Stable data that yield unstable interpretations. *Journal of Personality*, in press. (a)

Mischel, W. *Studies in the discriminativeness of delay of gratification*. Stanford, CA: Stanford Univ. Press, in preparation, 1983. (b)

Mischel, W., & Baker, N. Cognitive transformations of reward objects through instructions. *Journal of Personality and Social Psychology*, 1975, *31*, 254–261.

Mischel, W., & Ebbesen, E. Attention in delay of gratification. *Journal of Personality and Social Psychology*, 1970, *16*, 329–337.

Mischel, W., & Mischel, H. N. A cognitive social learning approach to morality and self-regulation. In T. Lickona (Ed.), *Moral development and behavior: Theory, research, and social issues*. New York: Holt, 1976.

Mischel, W., & Moore, B. Effects of attention to symbolically-presented rewards on self-control. *Journal of Personality and Social Psychology*, 1973, *28*, 172–179.

Mischel, W., & Peake, P. K. ʼBeyond déjà vu in the search for cross-situational consistency. *Psychological Review*, 1982, *89*, 730–755.

Mischel, W., & Peake, P. K. Some facets of consistency: Replies to Epstein, Funder and Bem. *Psychological Review*, 1983, *90*, 394–402.

Mischel, W., & Staub, E. Effects of expectancy on working and waiting for larger rewards. *Journal of Personality and Social Psychology*, 1965, *2*, 625–633.

Moos, R. H., & Fuhr, R. The clinical use of social-ecological concepts: The case of an adolescent girl. *American Journal of Orthopsychiatry*, 1982, *52*, 111–122.

Newcomb, T. M. *The consistency of certain extrovert-introvert behavior patterns in 51 problem boys*. New York: Columbia University, Contributions to Education, No. 382, 1929.

Nisbett, R. E. The trait construct in lay and professional psychology. In L. Festinger (Ed.), *Retrospections on social psychology*. New York: Oxford Univ. Press, 1980.

Nisbett, R. E., & Ross, L. D. *Human inference: Strategies and shortcomings of social judgment*. Englewood Cliffs, NJ: Prentice–Hall, 1980.

Norman, W. T. Toward an adequate taxonomy of personality attributes: Replicated factor structure in peer nomination personality ratings. *Journal of Abnormal and Social Psychology,* 1963, *66,* 574–583.

Office of Strategic Services Staff. *Assessment of men.* New York: Rinehart, 1948.

Olweus, D. A critical analysis of the "modern" interactionist position. In D. Magnusson & N. S. Endler (Eds.), *Personality at the crossroads: Current issues in interactional psychology.* Hillsdale, NJ: Erlbaum, 1977.

Patterson, G. R. The aggressive child: Victim and architect of a coercive system. In L. A. Hamerlynck, L. C. Handy, & E. J. Mash (Eds.), *Behavior modification and families: 1. Theory and research.* New York: Brunner/Mazel, 1976.

Patterson, G. R., & Moore, D. R. Interactive patterns as units. In M. Lamb, S. Suomi, & G. Stephenson (Eds.), *Methodological problems in the study of social interaction.* Madison: Univ. of Wisconsin Press, 1979.

Peake, P. K. *On the relevance and status of various approaches to the consistency debate.* Unpublished manuscript, Stanford University, 1981.

Peake, P. K. Searching for consistency: The Carleton Student Behavior Study (Doctoral dissertation, Stanford University, 1982). *Dissertation Abstracts International, 43,* Section 8 of Part B, p. 2746. (University Microfilms No. AAD 83-01259).

Peake, P. K., & Lutsky, N. S. *Exploring the generality of "predicting some of the people some of the time": The Carleton Student Behavior Study.* Manuscript in preparation, Stanford University, 1983.

Peterson, D. R. Scope and generality of verbally defined personality factors. *Psychological Review,* 1965, *72,* 48–59.

Peterson, D. R. *The clinical study of social behavior.* New York: Appleton, 1968.

Raush, H. L. Paradox levels, and junctures in person-situation systems. In D. Magnusson & N. S. Endler (Eds.), *Personality at the crossroads: Current issues in interactional psychology.* Hillsdale, NJ: Erlbaum, 1977.

Rosch, E., Mervis, C. B., Gray, W. D., Johnson, D. M., & Boyes–Braem, P. Basic objects in natural categories. *Cognitive Psychology,* 1976, *8,* 382–439.

Ross, L. The intuitive psychologist and his shortcomings: Distortions in the attribution process. In L. Berkowitz (Ed.), *Advances in experimental social psychology* (Vol. 10). New York: Academic Press, 1977.

Rushton, J. P., Jackson, D. N., & Paunonen, S. V. Personality: Nomothetic or idiographic? A response to Kenrick and Stringfield. *Psychological Review,* 1981, *88,* 582–589.

Schank, R. C., & Abelson, R. P. *Scripts, plans, goals and understanding.* Hillsdale, NJ: Erlbaum, 1977.

Sears, R. R., Maccoby, E. E., & Levin, H. *Patterns of child rearing.* New York: Harper & Row, 1957.

Sears, R. R., Rau, L., & Alpert, R. *Identification and child rearing.* Stanford, CA: Stanford Univ. Press, 1965.

Shrauger, J. S., & Osberg, T. M. The relative accuracy of self-predictions and judgments by others in psychological assessment. *Psychological Bulletin,* 1981, *90,* 322–351.

Spielberger, C. D., & DeNike, L. D. Descriptive behaviorism versus cognitive theory in verbal operant conditioning. *Psychological Review,* 1966, *73,* 306–326.

Thorndike, E. L. *Principles of teaching.* New York: Seiler, 1906.

Thurstone, L. L. *The reliability and validity of tests.* Ann Arbor, MI: Edwards, 1932.

Tversky, A. Features of similarity. *Psychological Review,* 1977, *84,* 327–352.

Tversky, A., & Kahneman, D. Judgment under uncertainty: Heuristics and biases. *Science,* 1974, *185,* 1124–1131.

Vernon, P. E. *Personality assessment: A critical survey.* New York: Wiley, 1964.

Wiggins, J. S. *Personality and prediction: Principles of personality assessment.* Reading, MA: Addison–Wesley, 1973.

Wittgenstein, L. *Philosophical investigations.* New York: Macmillan, 1953.

Wolf, R. The measurement of environments. In A. Anastasi (Ed.), *Testing problems in perspective.* Washington, DC: American Council on Education, 1966.

Wright, J. C. *The structure and perception of behavioral consistency.* Unpublished doctoral dissertation, Stanford University, 1983.

Wright, J. C., & Mischel, W. The influence of affect on cognitive social learning person variables. *Journal of Personality and Social Psychology,* 1982, *43,* 901–914.

Wright, J. C., & Mischel, W. *Predicting cross-situational consistency: The role of person competencies and situation demands.* Manuscript in preparation, Stanford University, 1983.

Author Index

Numbers in italics refer to the pages on which the complete references are cited.

Subject Index

313